Frederick W. Lander

Brigadier General Frederick Lander, 1861,
from photograph by Mathew Brady
From the author's collection

Frederick W. Lander

The Great Natural American Soldier

GARY L. ECELBARGER

Louisiana State University Press BATON ROUGE MM

Manufactured in the United States of America
First printing
09 08 07 06 05 04 03 02 01 00
5 4 3 2 1

Designer: Barbara Neely Bourgoyne
Typeface: Galliard
Typesetter: Crane Composition, Inc.
Printer and binder: Thomson-Shore, Inc.

Library of Congress Cataloging-in-Publication Data
Ecelbarger, Gary L., 1962–
   Frederick W. Lander : the great natural American soldier / Gary L. Ecelbarger.
         p. cm.
Includes bibliographical references and index.
   ISBN 0-8071-2580-6
   1. Lander, F. W. (Frederick West), 1821–1862. 2. Generals—United States—Biography.
3. United States. Army—Biography. 4. United States—History—Civil War, 1861–1865—
Campaigns. 5. Texas—History—Civil War, 1861–1865—Secret service. 6. United States—
History—Civil War, 1861–1865—Secret service. 7. Explorers—West (U.S.)—Biography.
8. Surveyors—West (U.S.)—Biography. I. Title.
   E467.1.L24 E28 2000b
   973.7'092—dc21

00-009632

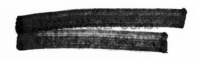

To My Parents

"I have carved my own monument—behold it in my deeds. I have written my own epitaph—go read it in my works!"
—FREDERICK W. LANDER, quoting the Roman poet Horace in response to a correspondent's persistent requests for an interview

Contents

Contents

Illustrations

Illustrations

MAPS

Preface: From a Decade of Significance to a Century of Obscurity

> Lander was brave, noble, true, and ambitious. We write of his public acts,
> but his biographer alone can tell us of his private history. . . . Always at his
> post, ever vigilant, no foe surprised him, and the services he rendered his
> country will make a bright page in its history.
> —A foot soldier in General Lander's Western Division, March 7, 1862

"I do not know any event of my life that in public opinion would be worth noting," wrote Brigadier General Frederick Lander five weeks prior to his untimely death.[1] Apparently, history agreed with his uncharacteristically humble assessment. In the thousands of Civil War books published since the centennial of what William H. Seward coined "the irrepressible conflict," fewer than twenty describe his service in lengths greater than one paragraph. Frederick Lander's self-characterization proved prophetic; based on the sparsity of narratives about him, the events of his life have not been considered consequential enough for a thorough examination of his Civil War career.

Oh, but what a life he lived! Frederick West Lander personified, both in appearance and action, the prototype of the nineteenth-century American hero. His accomplishments proved how shortsighted historiography can be. Not only did he influence the route over which the tracks of the

1. FWL to Messrs. L. Prang & Co., January 24, 1862 [published in the *Boston Journal,* April 2, 1862].

transcontinental railroad were laid, he also directed the career of the man ultimately placed in charge of it—Grenville Dodge. Lander's railroad surveys and wagon road expeditions did not carry the historic magnitude of the Lewis and Clark explorations. However, this should not diminish the fact that he explored dangerous and uncharted regions of the western territories of the United States, authored documents that clearly indicated he was a man with as much foresight as intelligence, and vigorously argued for the rights of the American Indian in a manner that placed him decades ahead of his time. These qualities and achievements indicate the need to understand the inner workings of a fearless and fascinating frontiersman.

In stark contrast to the rugged persona of a western explorer, Lander also demonstrated refined and artistic tendencies. A gifted writer, he published popular short stories based on his experiences. He was a romantic, oftentimes spilling his emotions in poems that were as clever as they were poignant. An equally adept orator, Lander lectured extemporaneously on subjects that varied from the arts to railroads, winning the hearty applause and approval of his listeners. He dabbled in politics, presenting memorable (if not controversial) speeches at conventions. Whenever he had something to say or write, Lander could always find the most far-reaching medium to air his views. Both an egotist and a master of self-promotion, he kept his name in the newspapers in a way that won him more admirers than detractors. By the spring of 1861, Frederick W. Lander's name ranked among the most recognized in America.

Brevet Lieutenant General Winfield Scott, the highest-ranking officer at the initiation of the Civil War, dubbed Lander the "Great Natural American Soldier."[2] This sobriquet, though not as catchy as "Old Grizzly" (the appellation Lander earned on the frontier), was an outstanding tribute, for Lander awed and inspired those around him on the battlefield. Imbued with the loyalty and patriotism he felt for his country, he proffered his services without pay or rank, earning a rapid and unprecedented promotion based upon what he did rather than who he was. General Lander led by example and continued to grab headlines, but he did not

2. "Agate" (Whitelaw Reid) to the editor, February 6, 1862, *Cincinnati Daily Gazette,* February 11, 1862. A somewhat altered sobriquet was offered by H. S. Wells of the Eighty-fourth Pennsylvania, who, while describing a camp scene to his hometown readers, reported, "It is the HQ of General Lander, of whom it is said General Scott loves to call 'the great National Soldier'" ("A Volunteer" to the editor, February 18, 1862, *Muncy [Pa.] Luminary,* March 4, 1862).

live long enough to reap the fruits of his labor. His death was marked by three funerals, attended by 40,000 people, including President Abraham Lincoln and his cabinet, Supreme Court justices, senators and representatives, and the top Union army officials.

Immediately and for years afterwards, Lander's name rolled off the lips of admirers who praised his accomplishments and lamented on the potential lost with his early death. "He was our beau ideal, a brave man, daring, of fine presence, in fact, all soldier," worshiped one of his foot soldiers one week after he died. Two decades later an acquaintance ruminated, "Of all the gallant figures of the great conflict, there was none more chivalric and romantic than General Lander. . . . None gave more brilliant early promise of distinguished service to the country."[3]

How is it that a man who climbed to such a state of importance while he lived, particularly in the eight years between 1854–1862, fell into an abyss of obscurity? Lander died before the four-year Civil War had completed its first year. After the smoke of battle cleared in 1865, the small engagements that he had influenced lost their impact when compared with the monstrosities of later encounters. Lander died before the battles of Shiloh, Antietam, Gettysburg, Chickamauga, and the Wilderness—gargantuan conflicts that greatly overshadowed the western Virginia engagements of 1861–1862. His life ended three weeks before the first battle of Stonewall Jackson's 1862 Shenandoah Campaign, and although his men won that first battle, defeating Jackson for the only time in his military career, Lander could not be awarded posthumous recognition.

Lander was erratic, impetuous, and impatient—character traits that usually hinder the effectiveness of a field commander. Although several who served under him were quick to take note of these limitations, others gauged him favorably with more renowned leaders who shared similar tendencies. One admirer steadfastly maintained that when Lander died, "the Union Army had lost its Stonewall Jackson."[4] Others who served under him felt that Lander's leadership against Stonewall in the Valley would

3. Daniel Daggett to his family, March 10, 1862, in George H. Daggett, "Those Whom You Left Behind You," *Glimpses of the Nation's Struggle: Papers Read before the Minnesota Commandery of the Military Order of the Loyal Legion of the United States, 1897–1902*, vol. 5 (St. Paul, Minn., 1903), 337; "Obsequies of General Kelley," newspaper clipping, ca. 1891, LP 10.

4. Luke Emerson Bicknell, "The Sharpshooters," 1883 (Microfilm copy in Massachusetts Historical Society, Boston), 20–1.

have made a difference during the spring of 1862. "Had Lander lived to lead us for the subsequent three months," wrote an Ohio officer in 1886, "the history of that campaign would, in my judgment, read very differently. His legitimate successor, in all that goes to make up the great military leader, seems not to have appeared in that Valley at the head of our troops until more than two and a half years after Lander's death."[5] Regardless of the soldier's opinion, Lander died much too early to allow favorable comparison of his potential with the concrete successes of Thomas J. Jackson, Phil Sheridan, or other victorious generals.

Frederick Lander's performance in early war clashes impressed other participants; however, no Civil War monuments have been erected to commemorate his daring exploits. At Philippi, a college sprawls over the site where Lander's Ride commenced; at Rich Mountain, Lander's Rock still protrudes from the slope of the ridge where the climactic battle of the war's first campaign was waged, but few historians of that engagement understand its significance. The Virginia side of Edwards Ferry—the spot where Lander received the wound that eventually killed him—lies on private property, while a massive housing development encroaches the site and obliterates its significance. Lander's headquarters at Hancock is a parking lot today. No markers exist in the town to explain how he hindered Stonewall Jackson's winter campaign plans. Bloomery Gap sits in pristine anonymity; few who pass through the area understand what happened there on Valentine's Day, 1862. At the sleepy town of Paw Paw—where a division commander encamped 11,000 troops for one month and died unexpectedly in his headquarters—even the most historically minded citizens have never heard of Frederick Lander, let alone can tell you where he died.

Even his final resting place accentuates his obscurity. Lander rests in an unkempt cemetery in a tomb simply inscribed with his mother's maiden name. His surname appears nowhere in the burying ground. The "great natural American soldier" essentially lies in an unmarked grave.

Lander's explorations in the West have garnered him more lasting mementos. A city in Wyoming, a county in Nevada, and a few natural features are named in his honor. However, even the accomplishments that earned those laurels have lost their impact. The late-nineteenth-century

5. John S. Cooper, "The Shenandoah Valley in Eighteen Hundred and Sixty-Two," *Military Order of the Loyal Legion of the United States, Illinois Commandery: Military Essays and Recollections,* 4 (1907): 42.

West, a frontier marked by gunfights and brutal Indian clashes, outmuscled and overshadowed the prewar feats achieved during railroad and wagon road explorations. It is difficult for those who bask in the familiarity and comforts of a widely populated United States today to appreciate the hardships suffered by frontier explorers like Lander, including trekking for months in uncharted rugged landscapes without contact to a civilized society. "I have ridden 48 hours on a mule without rest—fought the Indians, the Mormons, and the grizzlies, gone for three days without food, walked thousands of miles afoot over alkali plains," Lander once told a reporter.[6] Although his claim was embroidered, he had good reason to be proud, for it still required the same degree of undaunted courage to explore the West in the 1850s as Lewis and Clark had demonstrated half a century earlier.

Lander's life achievements piqued the interest of several friends and historians in the 130 years that followed his death. Attempts to recount his story date back to the 1800s. One month after his death, William D. Northend, Lander's longtime friend, wrote Mrs. Lander about securing information from her husband's associates to prepare a "proper biography" of him. "If you can think of no better person, I will undertake it," offered Northend. "I think a book made of his life on the Plains and during the war principally would be very interesting and gratifying to his friends."[7] But Northend's responsibilities in an escalating war diverted his attention from the project. Major Dwight Bannister, a former member of the general's staff, also kept up a friendly correspondence with Lander's widow, partly in an effort to write her late husband's memoirs. "It will be a most interesting book," Bannister explained to Mrs. Lander.[8] Apparently she concurred and sent both men several items from her husband's collection. Neither Northend nor Bannister ever wrote his book.

Lander's accomplishments prior to the Civil War have received scholarly attention in the twentieth century. A few articles about his western activities were published in historical journals, including an analysis of his role in railroad expansion written by Paul Glad and a similar treatment of his wagon road work authored by E. Douglas Branch. In the 1980s, Benjamin A. Riley, then a graduate student at Marshall University, au-

6. "Life on Board the John L. Stephens," November 27, 1859, newspaper clipping, LP 10.
7. Northend to Mrs. Lander, April 2, 1862, LP 11.
8. Bannister to Mrs. Lander, May 30, 1862, LP 11.

thored two monographs covering Lander's role in prewar events. Most recently, Alan Fraser Houston and Jourdan Moore Houston teamed together on a monograph of Lander's relationship with and influence on three western landscape artists.

Two books about Lander and his 1850s achievements were awarded limited publication. Jermy Wight, a Bedford, Wyoming, resident with uncanny expertise about the history and geography of the mountain states, extracted and analyzed four years of microfilmed wagon road expedition reports and correspondences to write *Frederick W. Lander and the Lander Trail* in 1993. His book sketched Lander's life with a detailed focus on the history of his three-year work on the wagon road that bears his name. Also in 1993, the University of Nevada's Desert Research Institute in Reno published a biographical sketch of Lander, an effort made possible by an endowment given to the institute by the general's last surviving niece, who died in 1966. Professor emeritus Joy Leland, then the acting executive director of the Desert Research Institute's Social Science Center, oversaw the project and was aided by two research assistants, Mavis Shahrani and Alice Baldrica.

Their work began in 1979 and carried on for ten years before unforeseen circumstances forced a change. Although the project was initiated as a fully documented biography, Dr. Leland's retirement and the departure of the assistants, combined with the expenditure of the funds for other endowment purposes, resulted in a decision to turn the decade-long collection of Lander material into a chronological compendium of facts about the general. Realizing that factors beyond her control had limited the scope of the project, Dr. Leland explained that "it seemed clear that our compilation of widely scattered materials concerning Lander, even without the context and analysis which only an historian could supply, would be useful to scholars and of interest to general readers of western U.S. history."[9] The result, *Frederick West Lander: A Biographical Sketch,* was a ground-breaking documentation of Lander's activities, particularly his railroad surveys, wagon road expeditions, and relationship with Native Americans during the 1850s. The book's more cursory treatment of Lander's Civil War activities—certainly understandable given the impediments to the project and the institute's desire to document western his-

9. Joy Leland, ed., *Frederick West Lander: A Biographical Sketch (1822–1862)* (Reno, Nev., 1993), v [hereinafter cited as *Lander*].

tory—still exceeded any other compilation published in the Civil War literature. Considering Lander's ubiquity and impact during 1861–1862, a thorough treatment of his role in the first year of the war is long overdue.

The purpose of this biography is to chronicle and analyze Frederick W. Lander's life using a trove of unpublished primary sources, much of which flowed from the general's own hand. Attention is paid to narrate his role in United States history without overstating his accomplishments or deifying his character. Although nearly every documented aspect of Lander's life is covered, this book emphasizes his Civil War activities to fill a void that has impeded the interpretation of three campaigns that transpired in the war's first year.

Implicit to the appreciation of one of American history's intriguing personalities is placing his achievements in the context of the era in which he lived. If the reader finishes the book asking himself, "I wonder what would have happened had he lived longer?" then the author has accomplished his objective.

Acknowledgments

The story of one man's life requires the efforts of many to depict that life accurately and comprehensively. Instrumental to the understanding of this subject are the previous works written by "Landerphiles": Mavis Shahrani, Dr. Joy Leland, Jermy Wight, Alan Fraser Houston, Jourdan Houston, and Benjamin Riley. All have provided the framework for this project by researching and documenting aspects of Lander's pre–Civil War career. They have been generous in offering their advise and expertise while helping me add to the foundation they have built over the past fifteen years.

Other experts on campaigns in which Lander participated have also contributed to the biography. This includes R. Hunter Lesser, the guru of McClellan's 1861 western Virginia campaign, who educated me about the summer of '61 and guided me to the summit of Rich Mountain. Thanks are also extended to Kim Holien for his Ball's Bluff expertise, and Dan Jenkins for his impeccable knowledge of Stonewall Jackson's 1862 winter campaign. David Hobbs has aided me tremendously with his research into the Andrew Sharpshooters. Robert Poirer provided me with insight into the history of Norwich University, the VMI of the North. Drs. Depak Soni and Thomas LoRusso were instrumental in diagnosing the most likely cause of Lander's denouement. Bryce Suderow knows every nook and cranny at the National Archives and has been helpful in acquiring some Lander material from there. A special thanks to Dr. Joseph Harsh of George Mason University for providing me with his findings from his expansive research collection, including several Lander dispatches written to George McClellan in 1861. Thanks also to Allan Tischler for locating a rare sketch of the general.

The staffs at the archival depositories housing Lander material throughout the country have been patient and generous in guiding me through their collections, whether in person, by phone, by letter, or by email. The length of the bibliography they helped to produce limits acknowledging them all individually, but a few warrant recognition for going above and beyond their normal duties. This includes Julie Bressor, the archivist at the Kreitzberg Library at Norwich University, Carolyn Autry, who handles the special collections at the Indiana Historical Society, Patricia White, archival specialist at Stanford University Libraries, and Dee Anna Grimsrud, reference archivist at State Historical Society of Wisconsin.

It has been a blessing to form friendships with individuals who have been especially kind to share material from their own research projects or from their ancestors. This includes Ted Browne, an afficionado of the First Ohio Light Artillery, Battery H, and a descendant of its captain. David Richards of Gettysburg, Pennsylvania, offered letters from the Eighty-fourth Pennsylvania, and Scott Clohan of Chicago provided his ancestor's letters from the First West Virginia. John Hennessey directed me to Virginia and Amos Pearsall of Des Moines, Iowa, who possess an original Lander letter written to Dwight Bannister (Virginia's grandfather). Harriett Condon, an extremely thoughtful friend, donated a rare print of Lander she found during her travels. The late Marilyn Clark-Snyder deserves special mention for donating her ancestor's letters. Her genealogy work on this project provided the understanding of the Lander-Derby-West ancestry.

I am indebted to my friends, including professional and amateur Civil War historians as well as laypersons, who donated their time to read and critique portions of the manuscript during various stages of its development. Rod Gainer, Dr. Joseph Harsh, David Hobbs, John Howell, Kim Holien, Dan Jenkins, Rick Katos, Tom Kissinger, Hunter Lesser, Jamie Lupton, Lt. Col. (USA, Retired) John P. McAnaw, J. Michael Miller, Scott Patchan, and Rick Wolfe have all been instrumental in fine tuning the biography. I am especially indebted to Karen Fojt for line editing the manuscript for me.

My gratitude is extended to those professionals who are skilled in converting my manuscript into a published work. This includes two members of the LSU Press editorial department: Sylvia Frank, acquisitions editor, for her support of my original proposal and her efforts to gain acceptance from the Press Committee for its publication; and Gerry Anders, LSU Press editor, for overseeing the manuscript through the steps necessary for its release. A sincere "thank you" to Elizabeth Simon, who copyedited the biography, ironed out the style and grammar wrinkles, and carefully reviewed the text for clarity and consistency. Cartographer Steve Stanley of Stafford, Va., also lent his expertise to the project by converting my rare but often unreadable contemporary maps into clear, computerized adaptations to allow the reader to follow Lander's footsteps.

Finally and most importantly, I thank my wife, Carolyn, for her tireless patience and her countless sacrifices made over the past four years to afford me the time to dedicate to this book. I am thankful that she provided the opportunity to research and document the life of Lander, and I am forever grateful for sharing my life with her.

Abbreviations

ALP	Abraham Lincoln Papers, Manuscript Division, Library of Congress
BP	Nathaniel Banks Papers, Manuscript Division, Library of Congress (container number: folder number)
CL	Thomas Clark Letters, Possession of Author
CP	Salmon P. Chase Papers, Manuscript Division, Library of Congress
EC	William Ellis Collection, Kreitzberg Library, Norwich University, Northfield, Vt.
FWL	Frederick W. Lander
GBM	George Brinton McClellan
HA	Henry Anisansel Court-Martial File, Case File 11-693, RG 153, National Archives
HR 56	U.S. Congress. House. *Executive Document No. 56: Reports, explorations, and surveys to ascertain the most practicable and economical route from the Mississippi River to the Pacific Ocean, 1853–55.* 1860. 36th Cong., 1st sess. [Serial Set Number 955]
HR 64	U.S. Congress. House. *Executive Document No. 64: Maps and reports of the Fort Kearney, South Pass, and Honey Lake Wagon Road, by F. W. Lander.* 1861. 36th Cong., 2nd sess. [Serial Set Number 1100]
HR 70	U.S. Congress. House. *Executive Document No. 70: Practicality of Railroads through South Pass.* Transmitted February 13, 1858

	by F. W. Lander to Secretary of the Interior J. Thompson. 35th Cong., 1st sess. [Serial Set Number 955]
IHS	Indiana Historical Society, Indianapolis
JCCW	U.S. Congress. *Report of the Joint Committee on the Conduct of the War.* In three parts. Washington, D.C., 1863.
LC	Library of Congress. Washington, D.C.
LCR	Lander Collection, Special Collections Department, University of Nevada, Reno, Library, Reno, Nev.
LFP	Lander Family Papers, Stanford University Libraries, Palo Alto, Calif.
LP	Frederick West Lander Papers, Manuscript Division, Library of Congress (volume number: document number)
MP	George Brinton McClellan Sr. Papers, Manuscript Division, Library of Congress (reel number: document number)
NA	National Archives, Washington, D.C.
NWR	National Weather Records, Asheville, N.C.
OHS	Ohio Historical Society, Columbus
OR	U.S. War Department. *The War of the Rebellion: A Compilation of the Official Records of the Union and Confederate Armies.* 128 vols. Washington, D.C., 1881–1902. Unless specified, all references are to Series I.
PDV	Pierce-Dahlgren-Vinton Family Papers, Yale University Library, New Haven, Conn.
SD 29	U.S. Congress. Senate. Executive Document No. 29: *Report of the Secretary of War communicating copies of all reports of the engineers and other persons, employed to make explorations and surveys to ascertain the most practicable and economical route for a railroad from the Mississippi River to the Pacific Ocean, that have been received at the Department.* 1855. 33rd Cong., 1st sess. [Serial Set Number 695]
SD 36	U.S. Congress. Senate. Executive Document No. 36: *Report and Map of the Central Division of the Fort Kearney, South Pass, and Honey Lake Wagon Road.* 1859. 35th Cong., 2nd sess. [Serial Set Number 984]
SD 78(1)	U.S. Congress. Senate. Executive Document No. 78: *Report of explorations and surveys to ascertain the most practicable and economical route for a railroad from the Mississippi River to the Pacific Ocean, made under the direction of the Secretary of War*

in 1853–1854. 1855. Volume 1, 33rd Cong., 2nd sess. [Serial Set Number 758]

SD 78(2)   U.S. Congress. Senate. Executive Document No. 78: *Synopsis of a report of the reconnaissance of a railroad route from Puget Sound via South Pass to the Mississippi River, by F. W. Lander, Civil Engineer, transmitted to the Secretary of War, November 23, 1854.* 1855. Volume 2, 33rd Cong., 2nd sess. [Serial Set Number 759]

SP   William Henry Seward Papers, Manuscript Division, Library of Congress

WR   Records of the Secretary of the Interior relating to Wagon Roads, 1857–1860, M95, 8 reels, National Archives (reel number: page number)

Frederick W. Lander

Prologue: "The Finest Specimen of the Class"

As Brigadier General Frederick W. Lander returned to his headquarters astride his white horse, his striking figure complemented the mountainous landscape that outlined his division's camp. His presence had always impressed, for he appeared every inch the leader of men. "I selected him as the *American-esque* man of whom to make a sketch as the finest specimen of the class," observed renowned poet Nathaniel P. Willis, who had limned the general after a chance meeting on the streets of Washington, D.C., a few months earlier. "There was not an angle in his whole movement. With no signs of the martinet, no military stiffness or restraint, he was wonderfully alert and agile, wiry and fearless, as well as careless and graceful. He had the proper 'pathfinder' look like a hunter trained on the prairie. And his horse seemed pleased to be a part of him."[1]

The general entered the telegraph room to receive and return dispatches. The day had been a most satisfying one for him. True, he won no laurels in battle—he merely reviewed his troops. But the military ceremony with his men held that afternoon had been replete with pomp and patriotism, and it filled his chest with pride. He knew his speeches to his regiments had been inspiring, for his westerners teemed with confidence and were begging for a fight. After personally watching them one week before march forty-three miles and rout an unsuspecting enemy force—all within twenty-eight hours—Lander maintained that he led troops that

1. N. P. Willis, "General F. W. Lander," *Williams County (Ohio) Leader,* April 3, 1862.

were a cut above Major General George McClellan's soldiers lying in their camps surrounding the Union capital.

The general had always been a tremendous physical specimen. Noted sculptor Thomas Dow Jones concurred with the sentiments of Nathaniel P. Willis. He described Lander only a few years earlier in glowing terms, raving about his unique prowess. "When I saw him last," Jones wrote, "he had not an ounce of spare flesh on him—all bone and muscle."[2] Jones had not seen the general in three years. Lander still carried tremendous power in his six-foot-two-inch frame, but the bone had begun to dominate the muscle. The winter campaign had been severe. Lander was not well, but only he seemed to know it. He had attempted to resign only eight days earlier, but General McClellan and Secretary of War Edwin Stanton had talked him out of it.

He stayed in command, more as a resolve to complete unfinished business than to assuage his superiors. "I have done little yet," he complained to a friend one week earlier. "I am broken down in health, yet for an advance, could ride forty miles tomorrow. . . . I would have done much here if the means had been given."[3] Only one man could prevent him from attaining his long-sought glory. Unfortunately, that man was General George McClellan, his superior. McClellan had restrained him for two months and Lander resented it. He took to mocking McClellan in prose and complained openly about his restrained style—"Caution, caution, caution. Never a blow"[4]—all to no avail. McClellan wielded tremendous influence and power in Washington. Lander realized this and had suffered for it. He had pleaded with Secretary Stanton to intervene by ordering him to advance his men somewhere—anywhere. He warned Stanton that "I am never so sick as when I cannot move."[5] His complaints apparently had fallen on deaf ears.

Lander did not battle this particular day, but he nevertheless remained in good spirits. The time had passed 9:00 P.M.; the thermometer had barely budged from the afternoon high of forty-five degrees. This was the sixth consecutive day of a warming trend that converted the roads from frozen paths into abominable thoroughfares of mud. But the general was ready to test the roads this very night, for he had received an unconfirmed

2. "Who Colonel Lander Is," newspaper clipping, LP 10.
3. FWL to Preston Blair, February 16, 1862, LP 3:6566–7.
4. Ibid.
5. *OR*, 51(1):533.

report from his adjutant. The Confederate force he had opposed all winter appeared to be marching northward from Winchester again, inviting Lander to attack them. That the enemy division was led by Major General Thomas J. Jackson electrified him. He had faced "Stonewall" down seven weeks before, he had jeopardized the southerner's entire campaign, and his daring leadership had threatened Jackson's position merely one week before. Now it was time to destroy him. Lander immediately wired McClellan his plan:

Maj. Gen. McClellan—
Jackson's whole force is reported as advancing on Bath from Winchester. If he is ass enough to do this I shall move on his rear via Bloomery Furnace and beat him to death. Recent thaws have placed the roads in bad condition but I have sent out cavalry reconnaissance and rest assured that you will hear a good account of this army. I shall move on the first intimation that he is north of my line. I do not know what he has south of him but under the circumstances regard it as my duty to risk a battle with my whole force. I have called in my detached parties and if he has made the military mistake stated you will hear of a very short battle within forty-eight hours. My only weak point is my artillery which I cannot move through the mud with facility. I am using ten horses to the gun and shall do the best I can. I have any number of beef cattle on which to subsist my men—baggage is cut down to the minimum—forage for artillery and cavalry horses being the bulk of my trains. Passed the men in review today and addressed them. We are in the best possible condition for a fight.[6]

The general had accomplished much in the past decade of an adventurous life, more than most could ever dream of achieving, but he needed this victory to offset the disappointment that prevailed within him. He knew that time was against him, and he was ready to act immediately. Few who knew him doubted his ability to win. One of his friends easily identified the attribute that best suited Frederick W. Lander as a leader of men: "He is no chicken, I assure you."[7]

6. FWL to GBM, February 22, 1862, MP 47:85969.
7. "Who Colonel Lander Is," newspaper clipping, LP 10.

1

"Old Grizzly"

Thou record of the young earth's overthrow,
    When mountain strove with mountain, and the ocean
Dashed his wild billows o'er the nations. Lo!
    Thy face reveals that dark hour's deep emotion
When the green hill tops knelt in their devotion,
    Endowing thee with being; tempest-hurled
Through plains and forests heaving with commotion,
    Thy torrents hissed, and flaming billows curled
Around the broken dregs and chaos of a world.
                    —F. W. Lander

Nearly half a century after Meriwether Lewis and William Clark traversed the western region of North America from the Mississippi River to the Pacific Ocean, Washington Territory governor Isaac Stevens launched his own expedition to survey a route for the future construction of the first transcontinental railroad. Reaching St. Paul, Minnesota, by steamer on the evening of May 27, 1853, Stevens entered Camp Pierce west of the Mississippi River early the next morning. There he found his expedition crew and 172 mules ready to trek westward. Satisfied at the condition and organization of his team, Stevens set his men out on Tuesday, May 31.

Two civil engineers accompanied the expedition, rugged men who assisted in breaking the riding mules during the last week of May. Each engineer set out with a small party on the rainy Tuesday morning to explore the railroad route. Stevens learned immediately that one of his engineers, Frederick Lander, not only possessed the unique skills of his profession, but also demonstrated an unrelenting determination to carry out his work. The engineer proved this through an accident that morning while straddling an unbroken mule. The animal bucked Lander and hurled him several feet in the air. Crashing to the ground on his shoulder, Lander stood up to find his entire arm knocked out of joint. Survey team members ran to his aid; it took three men's concentrated strength to pull out Lander's heavily muscled shoulder and lock it back into the joint.

Witnessing the painful scene, Stevens expected the accident to hamper his expedition. He was astonished to see the undaunted engineer ignore his injury and immediately set out at the head of his party. Proudly describing the incident in a report to the Senate three days later, Stevens said, "I refer to these facts, to show the spirit of my command, and the promise thus given that all the difficulties must disappear before the hardihood and the resolution thus exhibited."[1]

Although his career would forever be associated with the western frontier, Frederick W. Lander descended from a New England seafaring family. So prominent was his heritage that his middle name was mysteriously changed from William to West long after he died—not because of Lander's love for the frontier, but as a tribute to his mother and her ancestry.

The West family called northeastern Massachusetts home for several generations. The first Wests in America migrated to Salem, a beachhead fifteen miles northeast of Boston. Three generations of Wests were living in Salem during the summer of 1692 and likely witnessed the infamous trials and subsequent executions of nineteen citizens suspected of witchery. During the American Revolution, Nathaniel West, Frederick Lander's maternal grandfather, gained a lasting name for the family as a master mariner. Captain West commanded the privateer *Black Prince*. He married Elizabeth Derby in the spring of 1783, officially joining two families of wealth and prominence in eastern Massachusetts.[2]

Like the Wests, the Derbys also had been Salem residents since the sev-

1. SD 29, pp. 7, 10, 23–4, 27.
2. Sidney Perley, *The History of Salem, Massachusetts* (Salem, Mass., 1926), 304–6; James G. Wilson and John Fiske, eds., *Appleton's Cyclopaedia of American Biography*, vol. 6 (New

enteenth century. Elizabeth's grandfather, Richard Derby, was an outspoken and influential merchant who gained a reputation for his defiance of Parliament and the Salem establishment. He earned a place in family lore for resisting Lieutenant Colonel Alexander Leslie and his 200 British troops when they marched to Salem to seize cannons two months before the "shot heard 'round the world" was fired at Lexington. The elderly Derby refused Leslie's demand for the cannons in true patriotic tones: "Find them if you can! Take them if you can! They will never be surrendered!" Richard Derby's fleet of sailing vessels delivered the first news of the patriots' successful fighting to England. The ships were also first to bring back the news of the Treaty of Paris, the 1783 agreement to officially end the Revolutionary War. Richard Derby died in November of that year.[3]

Richard Derby's son, Elias Haskett Derby, stood out as the wealthiest and most prominent member of Frederick Lander's ancestry. He turned Derby Wharf, which was the longest wharf in town and had been built by his father, into the focal point for Salem's prominence in the eighteenth century. The younger Derby aided the colonists during the Revolution by making improvements in shipbuilding, loaning ships and supplies to the government, providing coal for the allied French fleet, and successfully engaging in privateering against British commerce. After the Revolution Elias Haskett Derby not only prevented Salem from languishing in a postwar depression, but his boldness and vision as a leading shipping merchant also revitalized and enriched the town to make it the sixth largest city in America. He opened trade with India and other countries and contributed money, supplies, and advice to help President John Adams establish a national navy for the new country.[4]

Elizabeth's marriage to Captain West displeased her father, but Elias

---

York, 1899), 441; Secretary of the Commonwealth, *Massachusetts Soldiers and Sailors of the Revolutionary War* (Boston, 1902), 898–9; Essex Institute, *Vital Records of Salem, Massachusetts,* vol. 4 (Salem, Mass., 1924), 455.

3. National Park Service, *Salem: Maritime Salem in the Age of Sail,* Official National Park Handbook, no. 126 (Washington, D.C., 1987), 28–9; Wilson and Fiske, *Appleton's Cyclopaedia,* vol. 2 (1898), 146; John A. Garraty and Mark C. Carnes, eds., *American National Biography,* vol. 6 (New York, 1999), 468–9.

4. National Park Service, *Salem,* 41–7; Wilson and Fiske, *Appleton's Cyclopaedia,* vol. 2 (1898), 146–7; Garraty and Carnes, *American National Biography,* vol. 6 (New York, 1999), 465–7.

Haskett Derby eventually warmed to his son-in-law enough to name him one of the heirs to his vast estate. Derby died in 1799, leaving more than $1 million in money and property—believed to be the largest fortune in the country at the time—to divide among his children.

The fourth child of Captain West and Elizabeth, Eliza, was fifteen years old in 1806 when her mother startled the West family and the town of Salem by suing Nathaniel West for divorce. Elizabeth Derby West claimed adultery in her suit and—according to a diarist in Salem—divulged in open court "all the sweepings of the Brothels of Boston, and all the vile wretches of Salem, Marblehead, Cape Ann, etc." Elizabeth's brother, Elias Haskett Derby II, openly supported her in an attempt to recover some of his father's money from Nathaniel West. At one point, Derby and West took their dispute from the courts and onto Derby Wharf, where the brothers-in-law engaged in a fist fight. The court eventually granted the divorce. As part of the settlement, Elizabeth Derby West moved her six children to Oak Hill, a large estate in South Danvers, Massachusetts.[5]

On October 19, 1813, Eliza West celebrated her twenty-third birthday by marrying Edward Lander. Lander descended from four generations of English-Americans, all from Salem. The son of Peter Lander, a Revolutionary War mariner who commanded a schooner (owned by Elias Haskett Derby), Edward Lander thrived as a merchant and helped form the Salem Light Infantry in 1805. One year after his wedding, he earned a lieutenancy with his company when it was incorporated into Colonel Joseph White's First Massachusetts Militia regiment during the waning days of the War of 1812. Lieutenant Lander's service amounted to eight days spread over two years. During this time he moved his new bride into a three-story brick house in Barton Square in Salem, where he sired two sons and two daughters over the next five years. On December 17, 1821, Edward Lander heard the newborn cries of his third son. The Landers named the baby Frederick William Lander.[6]

Born in a country that had yet to celebrate its fiftieth birthday, "Fred" was constantly reminded about the efforts of his ancestors to create and

5. Mavis Shahrani, "The Lander Family," in *Frederick West Lander: A Biographical Sketch (1822–1862)*, ed. Joy Leland (Reno, Nev., 1993), 3; National Park Service, *Salem*, 59.

6. Essex Institute, *Vital Records of Salem*, vol. 1, 505 and vol. 3, 584; Secretary of the Commonwealth, *Massachusetts Soldiers and Sailors*, 463–4; Edward Lander Sr. to Edward Lander Jr., October 4, 1855, LCR; Edward Lander, service record, NA.

preserve America. The seven Lander children (two more sisters were born after Fred) grew up with both Revolutionary War grandfathers nearby. Peter Lander was in his eighties during the 1820s and remained close to his Barton Square grandchildren, himself living in a handsome Essex Street home where he still conducted business as president of a marine insurance company. Captain Nathaniel West, who remarried after the ugly divorce, also remained close to his children and grandchildren. His first wife and Frederick's grandmother, Elizabeth Derby West, died in 1814, four months after Fred's parents married. Her property was divided among her three daughters. Shortly after Fred turned eleven, the Landers moved to Oak Hill, the elegant South Danvers estate, which had more room to raise the children.[7]

Fred spent most of his childhood and early teenage years at Oak Hill. He excelled in sports and was a leader among his playmates, benefitting from his towering size and his booming confidence. He was celebrated as an adept wrestler, boxer, equestrian, and marksman. Lander also exhibited a spirit of fairness and kindness. One day the boy surprised his mother when he came home barefoot. When she questioned him as to the whereabouts of his shoes, Fred revealed that he had given them to a boy who had none.[8] The act of charity was an isolated one; later in life, Fred would reward only those he felt had earned it.

Fred Lander excelled in the classroom with a dominance that rivaled his prowess on the playground. Edward and Eliza Lander saw to it that their children attended the best private schools in the area. Fred attended Franklin and Phillips Academy in Andover. The instructor primarily responsible for influencing young Lander's life was a master of trigonometry and land surveying at Phillips Academy named Frederick A. Barton. His teachings opened Fred's eyes to the intricacies of civil engineering, a field offering much potential in the first half of the nineteenth century. Fred attended the academy during a new movement to improve education

7. Edward Lander Jr. to David Lander, 1882, quoted in David Lander, *History of the Lander Family of Virginia and Kentucky* (Chicago, 1926), 7–8; William C. Endicott to Louisa Lander (with reply), December 5, 1922, Endicott Family Papers, Essex Institute, Salem, Mass.

8. John G. Shea, *The American Nation: Illustrated in the Lives of Her Fallen Brave and Living Heroes* (New York, 1862), 299; "Obsequies of General Kelley," newspaper clipping, 1891, LP 10.

in the New England schools. The days of the three "Rs" (reading, writing, and arithmetic) had given way to a new effort to expose the students to a variety of topics. Rather than being pushed through the routine of rote memorization, Lander and his classmates benefitted from a new teaching philosophy that stressed mathematics, geography, grammar, history, philosophy, chemistry, and political economy. The students also were granted time to ask questions and suggest doubts. A local writer visited Phillips Academy during the period and was impressed with the transformation. The new methods, he wrote, "are pursued . . . in every exercise, which give employment to the whole intellect, and not to certain favored faculties merely, while the rest are suffered to lie neglected."[9]

Lander graduated from Phillips Academy in 1837 and immediately stepped into Governor Dummer Academy, a private school established in Byfield, Massachusetts. Founded in 1763 under the will of Massachusetts Bay Colony lieutenant governor William Dummer, the school boasted John Hancock, Paul Revere, and John Quincy Adams as former students. A sixteen year old at Dummer, Lander struck up a friendship there with Byfield native William D. Northend, a boy one year younger than Fred. The two shared many interests, chiefly hunting and trapping. Northend soon acknowledged that his pal was a cut above the average sportsman.[10] Although their career paths would diverge from Byfield, the two would remain close friends for the next twenty-five years.

Dummer Academy specialized in training future lawyers, particularly those who would extend their careers at Harvard University. Edward "Ned" Lander, Fred's oldest brother, went from Dummer to Harvard, from which he was graduated two years before Fred entered Dummer Academy. Northend also chose a career in law and attended Bowdoin College in Maine. But Fred Lander's interests lay in civil engineering and railroads. In 1838, shortly after he graduated from Dummer Academy,

9. Edward Lander, "A Sketch of General Frederick W. Lander," *Historical Collections of the Essex Institute* 40 (1904): 313; "Col. Fred. W. Lander, The Pacific Railroad Explorer and Engineer," *Frank Leslie's Illustrated Newspaper,* April 6, 1861; Claude M. Fuess, *An Old New England School: A History of Phillips Academy, Andover* (Boston, 1917), 210–1. The Phillips Academy archives list Frederick W. Lander as a member of the class of 1836. Barton was a faculty member from 1832–1838.

10. Frederick West Lander biographical note, LP; Charles S. Ingham to William Ellis, September 20, 1909, EC; Northend to Jean Lander, March 4, 1862, LP 11; "William Dummer Northend," William Dummer Northend Papers, Emory University, Atlanta, Ga.

the seventeen year old landed his first job working on the Eastern Railroad.[11]

Growing up in Massachusetts offered advantages for civil engineers wishing to map railroad routes. The state hosted the first lines of the steam locomotive movement in the United States. Before Lander had walked into his first classroom, the Bay State Colony had taken the lead in the mass industrialization that was sweeping the northeast. The first railroad line in America ran for two miles at Quincy in 1826; twelve years later a full system of railroads was established in New England with Boston positioned as the world's first "junction city." During the 1830s, the hub saw seven lines run from its depot. Lander took advantage of his proximity to Boston and gained employment on one of the spokes. The Eastern Railroad stretched sixty-five miles from Boston northeast along the Atlantic coast through New Hampshire and into Maine. Lander's efforts on the Eastern Railroad landed him a job on the Maine Railroad, where the Eastern line terminated. By 1841 Fred found himself in charge of the line that ran between Saco and Portland, two towns on the eastern Maine shore. He was still a teenager.[12]

Three years of railroad work bought Lander valuable experience, but he felt there was more to learn in his trade. Late in 1841, he enrolled in Norwich University, the nation's first private military college, in Norwich, Vermont. The brainchild of former West Point Superintendent Captain Alden Partridge, Norwich sat across the Connecticut River from Dartmouth College. Although chartered as a university in 1834, the twenty-two-year-old school was essentially a military academy with the students making up its corps of cadets. The Ivy Leaguers attending Dartmouth had no respect for the Norwich cadets, jeering "brass buttons" at them from the New Hampshire side of the river. In retaliation, the Norwich cadets derided the Ivy Leaguers as "ladies." On more than one occasion, fist fights erupted following the insults.

Alden Partridge planted the spirit of individual initiative within his

11. "Governor Dummer Academy," in Education and Career Center (Byfield, Mass.: Governor Dummer Academy, ca. 1997 [January 1, 1998]); available from http://www.petersons.com/; Northend Papers, Emory University; Edward Lander Biographical Sketch, LFP; Ingham to Ellis, EC; Shahrani, "Lander Family," 6.

12. James E. Vance Jr., *The North American Railroad: Its Origin, Evolution, and Geography* (Baltimore, 1995), 18–21, 44–60; Edward Lander to William Ellis, January 31, 1899, EC.

cadets by training them to rise above obstacles. Lander would carry the risk-taking spirit into future endeavors, but he did not care much for the school's motto: "I Will Try." Partridge adopted the phrase from the Battle of Chippewa, where New Hampshire Colonel James Miller pledged the words when asked to assault a battery. Lander would reprimand at least one subordinate who used the indefinite response twenty years later during the American Civil War.[13]

More than 1,200 cadets had trained at Norwich by the time Lander enrolled; however, rival private institutions, such as the Virginia Military Institute, pulled many southern cadets out of Norwich. Still others who graduated from Norwich extended their military training through appointments to West Point. Lander chose to remain at Norwich. He considered his engineering studies to be the paramount reason for attending; a military education was not his primary objective. Displaying a penchant for secrecy, Lander never told his brothers and sisters about his advanced education. In 1841 they thought their brother was still working on railroads. Although frequently in contact with his siblings over the next twenty years, Fred never revealed to them that he had donned the dark blue uniform of a Norwich cadet.[14]

In 1842 Lander left Norwich before completing the necessary course work for graduation. His brother Charles had started an ice company at Wenham Lake near Beverly, Massachusetts. He offered Fred a position to supervise the construction of a group of ice storage houses at the northeastern edge of the lake, as well as to build a spur track to connect them to the Eastern Railroad that Fred knew so well from his previous employment. Fred found an old abandoned church and moved it onto the lake to use as the main building to store ice.

Three years later the Lander brothers took on an apprentice to help them with their ice business. Fourteen-year-old Grenville Dodge, a Danvers native, had been working for their mother at Oak Hill preparing vegetables, milk, and butter to sell at markets in Salem and Danvers. Eliza

13. Robert G. Poirer, *By the Blood of Our Alumni: Norwich University Citizen-Soldiers in the Army of the Potomac* (Mechanicsburg, Pa., 1999), 1–12, 306–7. The fact that Lander's influential mentor had been an alumnus of Norwich may have played a role in his decision to attend. Frederick A. Barton was a member of the class of 1825.

14. William Ellis, ed., *Norwich University, 1819–1911: Her History, Her Graduates, Her Roll of Honor,* vol. 2 (Montpelier, Vt., 1911), 337; Edward Lander to William Ellis, January 31, 1899, William Ellis to Louisa Lander, May 17, 1910, both EC.

Lander filled the boy's head with tales of her Revolutionary family. Hearing her stories and seeing 1812 veterans gave the lad a desire to be a soldier. But the young Dodge met Fred during one of Lander's visits to his mother at Oak Hill. Lander took an immediate liking to the slightly built, intelligent, and ambitious lad. He escorted the boy to Boston for a fish dinner during which he talked about engineering and railroads. Dodge absorbed Lander's stories and was intrigued with Lander's work. Lander offered Dodge a job to help him with the spur track to the icehouse. Grenville Dodge eventually followed in his mentor's footsteps and enrolled at Norwich University. Like Lander, Cadet Dodge resolved to become an engineer. Lander would affect his career choice again after Dodge graduated.[15]

Lander became a railroad contractor in the mid-1840s. Four years later he rose to the position of consulting engineer for other railroad contractors and companies.[16] It was in this capacity that he was hired as chief engineer for the Franklin and Kennebec Railroad Company. The fledgling organization, established in 1846 by an act of the Maine legislature, immediately set their sights on constructing a railroad that ran from the state capital at Augusta to Farmington. Fred had become prominent in the state for his work on the Saco-Portland line several years earlier; therefore, the young engineer was chosen to explore the new route.

Lander surveyed the thirty-seven miles between the proposed depot at Augusta to a point 500 feet east of the courthouse in Farmington. Lander's report to the railroad company, submitted shortly after the end of the survey, consisted of eight pages of scientific language mixed with pensive opinion and criticism. Clearly and concisely, he noted changes in soil consistency, grades, and potential hazards caused by the waterways that traversed the route. He annotated the costs and suggested the option of reducing expenses by selecting English iron over American ore. Lander closed his report with formal optimism, a trademark of his work, by claiming that the railroad route he surveyed "is most worthy the serious attention not only of the Capitalist, but of the Farmer, the Mechanic, and the

15. Shahrani, "Lander Family," 6; J. R. Perkins, *Trails, Rails, and War: The Life of General G. M. Dodge* (New York, 1981), 5–6; Stanley P. Hirshson, *Grenville M. Dodge: Soldier, Politician, Railroad Pioneer* (Bloomington, Ind., 1967), 6.

16. "Address of Colonel F. W. Lander, on an Inter-oceanic Railroad," September 22, 1859, *San Francisco Daily Alta California*, October 1, 1859.

Tradesman" and that it was "an undertaking commenced to open the riches" of the "surrounding country."[17]

Lander's use of the term "country" referred to a small section of Maine; the United States soon realized riches of its own. The Treaty of Guadeloupe Hidalgo, ratified in February of 1848, ended the Mexican War and ceded California along with other Mexican territory to the United States. One month earlier prospectors had discovered gold nuggets in the new territory. Over the next three years, a flood of emigrants rushed to the Pacific coast. Towns and villages sprang up throughout California.

These events fueled the ongoing debate over the construction of a transcontinental railroad to link the Atlantic coast with the Pacific coast. An anonymous writer for an Ann Arbor, Michigan, newspaper had sparked discussion of this ultimate railroad in 1832. Twelve years later, New York merchant Asa Whitney had proposed purchasing a sixty-mile wide swath of land from Lake Michigan to the Pacific Coast, which he would sell to pay for track construction. He was responding to the recent treaty signed between the United States and China that encouraged commercial interest in the Orient. But Whitney's proposal was limited at the time by the land available to the country.

By 1850 the fruits of the Mexican War, in combination with the settlement of ownership of the Oregon region, opened the West and expanded the possible routes for the railroad. By that time, however, the United States found itself in a quandary over the best route for line construction. Sectional politics exerted strong influence as the differences between the North and South created a rivalry over the designated route. Southerners feared that a central or northern route would widen the gap already existing in industry, commerce, and population between the two segments of the country. Northerners were concerned that a southern route would expand slavery in the trans-Mississippi territory. Local interests also muddied the waters as politicians and businessmen realized that a railroad running through their regions could produce instant wealth there.

The federal government took on the issue because it was expected to subsidize the railroad's construction. Congress established the Pacific Railroad Survey to employ the Corps of Topographical Engineers, already

---

17. F. W. Lander, *Report of the Examinations and Surveys for a Railroad Route, for the Franklin and Kennebec Railroad Co.* (Farmington, Maine, n.d.), 3–8.

mapping unknown territory in the West, to perform a scientific study of the most logical route for a transcontinental railroad. The grand survey was placed under the auspices of Jefferson Davis, Franklin Pierce's secretary of war. The selection of Davis, a Mississippian, rankled northerners, who believed his bias would favor a southern route, but Congress appropriated $150,000 to fund the study of four routes: two southern routes (at the thirty-second and thirty-fifth parallels), and two northern routes (at the forty-first parallel and between the forty-seventh and forty-ninth parallel). When it was all over, the total cost exceeded twice the allotted appropriations.[18]

Davis appeared unconcerned about the assumption of bias. He decided not to conduct a survey of the forty-first parallel, relying on a previously submitted report of the exploration of a wagon road that could be used by the army. For the northernmost survey, at the forty-seventh to forty-ninth parallel, Davis formed a single exploring team. He shunned a member of the Corps of Topographical Engineers to lead this party, choosing instead the newly appointed governor of the Washington Territory, Isaac Stevens.[19]

Stevens seemed to be an appropriate choice for this route. After he graduated first in his West Point class of 1839, the five-foot-one-inch Stevens spent the next seven years in the Corps of Engineers constructing and repairing fortifications in the Northeast United States. He served in the Mexican War and was breveted twice for gallantry, after he was severely wounded during the assault on Mexico City. He resigned his lieutenant's commission early in 1853 to become governor of the same territory where a considerable portion of Davis's northernmost survey was expected to be conducted.[20]

Stevens, four years Lander's senior, also was a Phillips Academy graduate. Hailing from the same region of Massachusetts as the Lander family (his boyhood home was Andover), Stevens was familiar with Lander's engineering skills. This, in combination with Ned Lander's new role as a judge in Washington Territory, may have helped secure Fred's appointment as civil engineer for the railroad. Working as chief engineer for the Boston Land Company early in 1853, Fred Lander instantly changed ca-

18. Vance, *North American Railroad,* 148, 151–68.

19. Ibid., 151. Captain Howard Stansbury's wagon road report, published in 1853, was submitted for the forty-first parallel survey.

20. Ezra Warner, *Generals in Blue: Lives of the Union Commanders* (1964; reprint, Baton Rouge, 1992), 475.

reers when he was offered the opportunity of a lifetime. By April he was exploring the Mississippi River region to ascertain the departure point for the main train of the reconnaissance party prior to Stevens's arrival on May 29.[21] Impressed by Lander's skills, Stevens must also have been pleased at the engineer's determination to disallow a separated shoulder from slowing his mission. He quickly found that with his strong physique and high threshold for pain, Lander was well suited to the rugged landscape of the West.

Lander felt entirely at home on the frontier, a fact that did not go unnoticed by Stevens. "I am exceedingly pleased with your progress," wrote the governor to his subordinate early in June. Confident in Lander's ability to work independently, Stevens dispatched him often with a small crew (including an expert regional guide and buffalo hunter) as they advanced westward through Minnesota. On June 12, Lander took four men to explore the south bend of the Sheyenne River. Two weeks later he and several axe men were cutting timber to bridge the Wild Rice River. After completing this project, Lander and four men rode eighty miles farther to explore the western branch of the Sheyenne. This journey took them beyond the contingent states and into territorial regions of the country.

Lander completed the mission in twenty-eight hours, meeting with his first "harrowing" experience since injuring his shoulder. While riding south to Dead Colt Hillock, Lander noticed suspicious movement in the tall prairie grass ahead. Leveling his spy glass, Lander saw a black-and-white object poking through the grass as it moved steadily, defying their approach. Convinced that this was a hostile Indian spying on the party, Lander left no room for chance. He ordered his band to charge; this they did with revolvers blazing. When Lander galloped up to his strike he found that what he thought was an Indian was merely a skunk that had erected its tail through the grass a few minutes earlier and now lay riddled with bullets. Demonstrating a willingness to laugh at himself to enhance camaraderie, Lander returned to Stevens's camp that night and recounted his adventure, much to the amusement of all.[22]

Undaunted, Lander took his party on another mission, beginning on

21. "Address of Colonel F. W. Lander, on an Inter-oceanic Railroad," September 22, 1859, *San Francisco Daily Alta California,* October 1, 1859; SD 78(1), p. 77.

22. Stevens to FWL, June 9, 1853, PDV; HR 56, pp. 61–2. Lander's mission at this stage was conducted in North Dakota, known in 1853 as "unorganized territory."

the fourth of July. He and his crew, whom he had begun calling his "men of iron," celebrated their country's seventy-seventh birthday by continuing to explore uncharted territory within its northern boundary. It did not take long for the party to consume the fifteen pounds of flour they had brought, and they were forced to live exclusively on game meats. Riding into the evening hours of July 8, Lander caught sight of a lone bison bull grazing on the prairie. It was likely the first buffalo he had ever seen, and this time the sight was unmistakable. Lander and three men spurred their mounts toward the bull. It outdistanced the horses of all the hunters except for the mare carrying Lander. Lander closed the gap with the buffalo, but suddenly the animal turned and charged him. He quickly drew his revolver and fired. The pistol failed to stop the buffalo, which snorted defiantly and charged him again. Bullets eventually won over brawn. The "men of iron" rode up to find Lander standing next to the dead bull, the first buffalo kill experienced in Stevens's expedition.[23] This time Lander needed not mock himself when he relayed his adventure to his comrades.

Lander's adventurous spirit had won over the men in his party; however, this was accomplished at the expense of his animals. He returned with great difficulty to Stevens's camp on July 12 due to the jaded condition of his horses. Stevens was forced to dispatch two men to meet them four miles out to aid the return. Lander and his worn-out animals reached camp by sundown. Lander's following trips usually resulted in similar outcomes, earning him the dubious reputation of being "an inveterate horse-killer."[24]

One month later Stevens's party entered Nebraska Territory, averaging fifteen miles per day. Lander's side reconnaissances were even more impressive; in the next two months, he covered more than 1,000 miles of territory, much of it uncharted. After resting near Fort Union at the confluence of the Missouri and Yellowstone Rivers for a few days, Stevens sent Lander northward with a small crew to find the source of the Souris River. The mission carried Lander's party into Canada and into a region well outside the intended boundaries of the survey. Lander and his men encountered several bands of Indians, most of whom were hostile to their

23. HR 56, pp. 61–2.
24. Hazard Stevens, *The Life of Isaac Ingalls Stevens,* vol. 1 (Boston, 1900), 330–1.

presence. Lander and his men tactfully avoided clashing with the Indians and quickly crossed back to the territories of the United States.[25]

Lander returned to Fort Union only to be sent on another peripheral reconnaissance as Stevens's main party continued westward. During the final days of August, Lander diverted northward from the main party with survey artist John M. Stanley to obtain a good vantage point to sketch the country in the direction of the Rocky Mountains. The two ran into trouble on the mission; they lost the trail due to bad advice from an incompetent guide, ran short on rations, and suffered from devastating winds that swept across the countryside. Still, they managed to rejoin Stevens at Fort Benton, near Great Falls in western Nebraska Territory, with the Rocky Mountains stretching across the horizon.[26]

Lander had read about them, talked incessantly about them, and had pictured them in his thoughts. Exploring the Rockies had epitomized his desires as an engineering student in New England. Fifteen years and 2,500 miles later, Lander faced his goal, and the sight of the Rockies did not disappoint him. Stevens quickly gave Lander the opportunity to explore the Rockies when he sent him with a small party to thoroughly reconnoiter Marias Pass and the country up to the Hudson Bay Kutenai Post in Canada.[27]

Lander led his team northward sixty-five miles to conduct his newest mission, but on September 11 Stevens sent word to abandon the exploration. Four factors led to his decision. An officer talked Stevens out of the practicality of this pass because of the heavy forest growth around it. The season was also growing late for surveying, and Stevens had to look for shortcuts in time and money (having determined that the $40,000 allotment for the survey would be entirely exhausted in a month).

The final deciding factor was Frederick Lander. "There was not that harmony in Mr. Lander's party which I deemed indispensable to making the examination which I had intrusted to him," explained the governor. Lander's and Stevens's relationship had begun to disintegrate between

25. Kent D. Richards, *Isaac I. Stevens: Young Man in a Hurry* (1979; reprint, Pullman, Wash., 1993), 124–5.

26. Joy Leland, "The Northern Pacific Railroad Explorations," in *Frederick West Lander: A Biographical Sketch (1822–1862),* ed. Joy Leland (Reno, Nev., 1993), 29. Today, the region between Forts Benton and Union lies entirely within the state of Montana.

27. Stevens to Davis, September 8, 1853, SD 29, pp. 33–4.

Forts Benton and Union. Stevens had become well aware of Lander's desire to free himself from authority and of his resentment of army officers. Shortly after Lander returned from the aborted mission to Fort Benton, their differences came to a head as he and the governor engaged in a bitter argument. The discussion became so heated that Stevens ended it by threatening Lander that he would "shoot him down like a dog" if he disobeyed his orders. Lander yielded by professing his readiness to obey instructions.[28]

Lander's newest instructions were to "get in side-work, and make the necessary estimates" of the region surrounding and including Lewis and Clark Pass (the break in the Rockies that Meriwether Lewis discovered on the return trip from the Pacific in 1806). At the same time, Stevens and the main party were to pass over the continental divide through Cardottes Pass, twelve miles south of Lewis and Clark Pass. All parties were to rendezvous at Fort Owen, a trading post situated in the Bitterroot Valley thirty miles south of that river's junction with the Clark Fork and Blackfoot Rivers.[29]

Exploring the foothills of the Rockies, Lander and a seven-man crew ran a line southward from the Marias River past the Teton River and the Sun River, to the Dearborn River. Five days into the reconnaissance, Lander caught sight of a moving object far off on a prairie near a lake between the Teton and the Sun. Believing the animal to be a buffalo, Lander convinced three crew members, including a Blackfoot Indian guide, to join him for the evening hunt. But once he gained ground on the beast, Lander realized he had made a grievous error. He found himself matched against the symbol of the Rockies and the western frontier—a grizzly bear.

The bear was monstrous, and it immediately charged Lander. Armed merely with a revolver, Lander turned in his saddle and emptied his six-shooter into the bear while the other crew members kept a wary distance. Lewis and Clark had trouble with grizzlies years earlier; it required several

28. The Fort Benton story was relayed by Isaac Stevens's son, Hazard, who was neither a participant in nor a witness to the events, but likely was told the story by his father afterward, perhaps while the younger Stevens served as a member of his father's staff during the Civil War. Hazard Stevens characterized Lander as a "bold, energetic, high-strung man" who "could ill brook any authority," an accurate depiction of a man he likely never met (see Stevens, *Life of Isaac Ingalls Stevens,* vol. 1, 369–72).

29. SD 29, pp. 55, 73; Richards, *Isaac I. Stevens,* 124–5. The headwaters of the Clark Fork River are often referred to as the Hell Gate River in period reports.

shots from their Kentucky rifles to drop the threatening bears. Lander must have appreciated their plight when he found that his shots did little to slow his adversary. As the bear lumbered toward Lander, he rode back to his cowering crew and urged them to join him. Hearing their refusal, Lander grabbed a second revolver and rode back to the bear. Reining within twenty feet of it, Lander drew his gun, but the behemoth was nearly on him as he fired. His crew watched in awe as the grizzly reeled from the shot and Lander poured several more rounds into it. Lander fired his twelfth and final shot into the head of the animal. It reared on its hind legs, stood for a moment pawing the air frantically, and then fell back—dead.

The crew ambled toward Lander's kill and counted eleven bullet holes in it; any nine of which they determined would have killed any other animal except a grizzly. Estimating the beast to weigh 1,200 pounds, the men cut it up and packed the meat onto a mule. On the return to their lakeside camp, the Blackfoot guide admitted that his people never attempted to stir trouble with grizzlies during the summer months, when the bears are most active. He was so impressed with what he had witnessed that evening that he spread news of Lander's exploit to the other Indian guides. The Blackfoot guides christened Lander "Kaya," a name that translated to "Bear of the Mountains." The non-Indian crew members Anglicized Kaya to a more euphonious nom de guerre that Lander would carry for the rest of his life: "Old Grizzly."[30]

In the third week of September and immediately after his grizzly bear encounter, Lander's party crossed the continental divide to survey Lewis and Clark Pass, known as the easiest break in the mountains in that part of the country. Using his barometer and compass, Lander entered the historic pass and followed the course of the Blackfoot, then crossed river valleys to what he thought was the Bitterroot, but was actually the Clark Fork River. As he explored the region Lander did not share the governor's enthusiasm for the prospective route. Lander forecast excessive costs for bridging the rivers the prospective line would have to cross in several places as it wound through the mountains. He also took note of the steep

30. [Edward J. Allen], "A Grizzly Bear-Hunt," *Knickerbocker* (June, 1854), 642–4; "The New Fighting Hero—Graphic Historical Sketch of Col. Lander—'Old Grizzly,'" *San Francisco Daily Evening Bulletin*, May 15, 1860; "Col. Fred. W. Lander, The Pacific Railroad Explorer and Engineer," *Frank Leslie's Illustrated Newspaper*, April 6, 1861; HR 56, p. 122.

grade and predicted extra costs to cut through rock. His reservations about the route initiated thoughts of exploring a route not covered by the government's survey act.

Lander realized while within the Rockies that he was not advancing on the Bitterroot. Rather than retrace his steps, he led his troops from the river valley over a number of divides and streams and onto an old Indian trail. He followed the path to Fort Owens, arriving there on September 27, two days before Stevens's party. His feat was extraordinary, but it did not impress Stevens, who had given Lander the best animals at Fort Benton and now complained that the teams were "exceedingly jaded."[31]

Once the party passed through the Rockies, Stevens directed his men to connect with another party of explorers heading eastward from Puget Sound across the Cascades. The largest team of surveyors was active on this northern route, which became the most thoroughly explored in 1853. Twenty-five-year-old Captain George Brinton McClellan, an Ohioan, West Point graduate, and Mexican War veteran, led the eastbound party. On October 28, Stevens's team linked with McClellan's party near Spokane in Washington Territory. Thus far, Stevens was buoyed by how his men had kept to their schedules without trouble from Indian tribes. He also praised McClellan and his crew for being well organized and efficient. But McClellan had shunned two of his duties: he had failed to construct a wagon road from Walla Walla to Steilacoom and he had not examined any of the passes in the Cascade Range.

Stevens never criticized McClellan for the omissions, but the latter one was most damaging to Stevens, for the legitimacy of his entire survey rested on his ability to convince the skeptics in Washington that the rail line could pass with ease through any of the mountain ranges in the Northwest. He was satisfied with his Rocky Mountain explorations, but the unfamiliarity with the Cascades presented a problem. The same day he united his parties at Camp Washington, Stevens urged McClellan to explore Naches Pass in the Cascades. McClellan refused, citing his suspicion of deep snows in the range. McClellan further reasoned that his animals were unfit for snowbound travel and he lacked the necessary equipment for mountain exploration. Realizing his impasse with the stubborn cap-

31. HR 56, pp. 275–6; Stevens, *Life of Isaac Ingalls Stevens,* 381; Richards, *Isaac I. Stevens,* 125.

tain, Stevens insisted that the passes be examined. He turned the job over to Frederick Lander. Then the governor rode on to the Dalles.[32]

Noting that snow covered the Cascades in the first week of November, Lander viewed his instructions with trepidation. His orders came from Stevens, but McClellan acted as commander of the survey party in the governor's absence. On November 8 an Indian guide informed Lander that emigrant wagons had been abandoned in the pass and all the animals were lost in the heavy snows. Lander wrote McClellan the news and asked him what to do. "Should your opinion justify me risking the animals and endeavoring to cross the mountains, it is my desire to do it," explained Lander in his missive. But McClellan was not comfortable in making the decision since Lander's information fortified his belief that too much snow made the mission dangerous. He was also miffed that Governor Stevens undermined his credibility by giving the job to Lander. "I have done my last service under civilians and politicians," he jotted in his journal on November 9; then he fired back a caustic reply to Lander's dilemma. Repeating what he had told Stevens earlier about the risky nature of the directive, McClellan refused to issue any instructions to aid Lander since Stevens's order to Lander "has been given in direct opposition to my own judgment." Hampered by the lack of leadership on the issue, Lander felt he had no other option but to defer to McClellan's opinion. He abandoned the exploration and circled around the Cascades via the Columbia River.[33]

Lander's final survey explored the route to Puget Sound by the Columbia and Cowitz Rivers. He completed the work and submitted a technical report of the survey on January 5, 1854, earning a commendation from Stevens for his performance. But Lander's unfortunate interlude with McClellan blemished the latter portion of the survey. Although a second warning was sent to McClellan on November 10 about the heavy snows in the mountain passes, the information was erroneous—no emigrant trains had been lost in the Cascades because the mild Puget Sound climate kept the passes open until December.

Stevens was very charitable in not censuring Lander for his failure to

32. SD 29, pp. 37–8, 80–1; Richards, *Isaac I. Stevens,* 133–6, 409 (n. 42).

33. FWL to GBM, November 8, 1853, with reply on November 9, 1853, PDV; Steven W. Sears, *George B. McClellan: The Young Napoleon* (New York, 1988), 39; W. Turrentine Jackson, *Wagon Roads West: A Study of Federal Road Surveys and Construction in the Trans-Mississippi West, 1846–1869* (Lincoln, Nebr., 1964), 92–3.

follow his instructions, but he could not hide the fact that he was disappointed. "In a new country it is very difficult to get the truth from the information given," Stevens reported after months of reflection, "and it has been found our most vexatious experiment on the whole march. But it would have proved, in my judgment, an entirely practicable undertaking, and would have made our information more complete."[34]

Lander also was disappointed. He faced up to the controversy by admitting to Stevens "an error in judgement." But when the governor wrote Lander to inform him that he would not censure his conduct in failing to explore the Cascades, Lander scribbled a defensive response. "[T]he man who decides to the best of his knowledge upon a line of duty which makes him the object of criticism, perhaps of obloquy, to many parties whose good opinion he might wish to preserve," explained Lander in closing, "is as much entitled to praise as he who, against the dictates of his better judgement, plunges blindly into a mountain pass for the purpose of seeking a questionable eclat."[35]

Stevens wrote to Secretary Davis in December, claiming to have located two routes and insisting that the climate within the northern route—the greatest concern for all personnel involved with the surveys—posed no threat to the construction of the line, nor would it impede passage of the trains. Still, Lander could not bring himself to endorse the governor's route. His greatest objection was not the climate, but the expense required to construct and maintain it. He expressed his concerns to other party members, including Dr. George Suckley, an eccentric surgeon-naturalist who had been attached to Stevens's surveying party. Citing Lander's opinions, Suckley wrote, "A road might be built over the tops of the Himalayeh mountains—but no reasonable man would undertake it. I think the same of the Northern route. Tunnels of two miles in length are not our only obstacles; gullies, steep grades and deep cuts are bad enough, but the almost innumerable heavy and strong high bridges required, and the large number of short and sudden curves, frequently of less than 1,000 feet radius, are very serious obstacles." On February 15, 1854, Lander submitted his official expedition report to Stevens. He conceded that all of his objections disappeared once the Columbia River was

---

34. Excerpt of Stevens's report quoted in Leland, "Northern Pacific Railroad Explorations," 42.
35. FWL to Stevens, January 9, 1854, PDV.

reached, acknowledging that a line constructed here would be done under favorable circumstances.[36]

While in Washington Territory during the winter of 1853–1854, Lander spent considerable time visiting his brother Ned, now a territorial judge in Olympia living near the mouth of Puget Sound. The Lander brothers exchanged letters with their father and sisters, who had returned from Danvers to Salem after Fred's mother, Eliza West Lander, died in 1849. Edward Lander Sr. was still adjusting to life as a widower. He cherished the company of his daughters and the infrequent correspondence with his sons, including Charles, who had moved to California during the gold rush. The elder Lander took pains to keep his boys informed about local and national interests, and expressed relief that Fred had traversed the Indian country safely, writing, "I flatter myself you have escaped being scalped." Sister Liz informed Fred, "We toasted you on Thanksgiving day," in a December 3 letter. Martha, Fred's youngest sister (he called her "little fool"), admitted that she felt heartsick with thoughts of him suffering during his travels.[37]

Frederick Lander proved to be a magnetic figure with an uncanny ability to charm those who crossed his path. The territory's only newspaper sang Lander's praises by describing him as harboring "great ability as a scientific engineer" with "energy and force of character necessary to carry on a work of this kind." Judge Lander wielded clout in the region and introduced Fred to the area's key residents. One of Ned's friends was Edward J. Allen, a twenty-four-year-old Pittsburgh transplant who had organized a road-working party and spent the previous summer and fall clearing a path through the formidable Cascades to entice Oregon Trail emigrants into Washington. One winter night at his Olympia homestead, Allen listened intently as one of Stevens's crew members who had witnessed Lander's grizzly bear kill related the amazing story. Allen recorded the interview and sent the story to a nationally circulating magazine. Lander appreciated Allen's efforts to publicize his exploits as well as his assistance in

36. William Goetzmann, *Exploration and Empire* (New York, 1966), 285; William Goetzmann, *Army Exploration in the American West, 1803–1863* (New Haven, Conn., 1959), 282; Leland, "Northern Pacific Railroad Explorations," 45.

37. Essex Institute, *Vital Records of Salem*, vol. 5 (1925), 387; Edward Lander Sr. to FWL, October 19, 1853, LFP; Louisa "Nannie" Lander to FWL, December 3, 1853, LFP; Martha and Liz Lander to FWL, January 19, 1854, LCR; Edward Lander Sr. to Edward Jr. and Frederick Lander, February 4, 1854, LCR.

making connections with other laborers. The two maintained a close friendship for the rest of Lander's life.[38]

During his sojourn in Washington Territory, Lander gained enough popularity, met enough influential people, and borrowed enough money from his brother to propose an independent expedition. He was convinced that a route from Puget Sound through the easiest break in the Rockies at South Pass and following the Platte River Valley was the most viable route for a transcontinental railroad. This central route lay between the thirty-fifth and forty-fifth parallels and offered all the advantages of the route he explored for Governor Stevens without the latter's inherent obstacles. Three weeks after submitting his official report to Governor Stevens, Lander sought approval to conduct the independent survey with the legislative assembly of Washington Territory. Lander stressed that he needed to conduct the mission immediately, before Secretary Davis and Congress made a decision based on the 1853 expeditions. Considering Lander's proposal "a matter of the highest importance to the interests of this Territory," the assembly, in defiance to their governor and his route, endorsed Lander's alternative in a series of resolutions passed on March 8.[39]

Lander understood the importance of building a coalition. He wrote McClellan in San Francisco to obtain an endorsement from a prominent Californian, and he procured a letter of introduction to Senator Sam Houston, whom he intended to convince once he reached Washington, D.C. He also corresponded with Brigham Young, territorial governor of Utah, explaining to the Mormon leader how a transcontinental railroad along the northern border of Utah Territory would benefit his people. Lander asked Young for his political support.

Over the next ten days, Lander put together a team to explore the route. Having such a limited time to collect a crew restricted Lander to five participants, a far cry from the scores who had worked for Stevens. He also obtained first-class saddle horses and mules and packed them with

38. *The National Cyclopaedia of American Biography,* vol. 30 (New York, 1943), 540–2; "E. Jay A." [Edward J. Allen] to the editor, March 4, 1862, *Pittsburgh Daily Evening Chronicle,* March 6, 1862; [Edward J. Allen], "A Grizzly Bear-Hunt," 642–4. Allen, who characteristically signed his submissions "E. J. A.," dated his piece, "Allen's Claim, near Olympia (W. T.,) January, 1854."

39. Joint Resolution of the Legislative Assembly of the Territory of Washington Relating to F. W. Lander, Esq., March 8, 1854, PDV.

subsistence. Lander and his team set off from Olympia on March 18, 1854.[40]

Lander's proposed route closely followed the exploration conducted by Robert Stuart forty years earlier. Lander's team reached the swift waters of the Columbia River and followed it to the eastern region of Washington Territory. They diverted southward from the river valley to explore passes in the Blue Mountains and picked up the Snake River as it serpentined southeastward.

Their troubles began early. The team slogged through ground soaked by heavy seasonal rains. Storms pummeled Lander and his men as they attempted to explore the snow-choked passes of the Blue Mountain range. Mountain fever forced two members to quit the team and knocked Lander off his feet for ten days. The remaining four (including Lander) regained their health and arrived at the opposite side of the Blue Mountains, where the Malheur River wound around their eastern foothills. Lander safely forded the river only to see all of his clothing swept away in its swift waters. By the time they reached the valley of the Snake River, the men realized they had entered Indian country and would have to seek the hospitality of the natives.

A fortnight was lost due to a serious injury to an unidentified member of the party. When they resumed exploration of the Snake River Valley, the quartet followed its winding course southeastward. During May they crossed from the Snake River Valley to the northward-flowing Bear River, apparently by following the Portneuf River to Soda Springs. Following the Bear River upstream, Lander and his men probably took the Sublette Trail to cross the mountain country, where they reached the flat desert dominated by the Green River.[41]

Supplies dwindled, which forced the men to rely on their hunting and fishing skills. Late that spring the men plodded across the continental divide to find themselves in a broad and easy break in the Rocky Mountains.

40. FWL to GBM, March 8, 1854, PDV; J. Patton Anderson to Sam Houston, March 23, 1854, LP 1:6046; Leland, "Northern Pacific Railroad Explorations," 46; SD 78(2), 27–8.

41. Robert M. Utley, *A Life Wild and Perilous: Mountain Men and the Paths to the Pacific* (New York, 1997), 31–4; SD 78(2), 27–8; newspaper clipping, Lander Scrapbook, LP 9 (hereinafter cited as Scrapbook); "From General Lander's Division," February 19, 1862, newspaper clipping, LP 10. The newspaper clipping in Lander's Scrapbook appears to be an excerpt of an interview that Lander gave describing the journey.

Within this twenty-mile-wide corridor, the waters divided between the Sandy River tributaries, which flowed westward to the Green River, and Muddy Creek, which flowed eastward until it met the Sweetwater. The quartet was elated; they had reached South Pass.

But the odyssey was barely half over. Those survey members who had gone with Lander on Stevens's expedition one year earlier longed for the benefits of a large team with a vast supply train. Undaunted, Lander left his worn-out horses and tired party members near South Pass while he took one of his experienced team members with him. They found a native to guide them on a long reconnaissance of the Great Divide Basin, a red desert encircled by the Continental Divide. Lander and his companions explored the passes of the upper rim of the basin, exposed to violent storms of snow and sleet, while avoiding hostile Indians. Although Lander had to cut short his explorations to reach Washington, D.C., before Congress adjourned, the excursion still inspired him.

Leaving the Rockies, Lander was accompanied only by John R. Moffet, two others having quit the expedition. Moffet, a Virginian who had conducted meteorological observations for Stevens's expedition, did the same for Lander but had not fared well in the mountain country. The two now had to cross the sparse plain between the Missouri River and the Rockies, a 700-mile stretch of unforgiving terrain. Although they must have passed westward bound emigrants, the two starved and slept little as they traversed the country of the Platte River, eating thistle roots and mule meat. In one three-day stretch, they ate nothing. Even so, Lander remained focused on his mission, carefully noting the soil, the grade of land, and the water supply.[42]

A hot June eventually gave way to a sweltering July as Lander and Moffet struggled eastward along the Platte. On July 9 the two thin and ill travelers stumbled toward the Elkhorn River in Nebraska Territory, only twenty-five miles west of the Missouri River. A solitary log cabin came into view, then Lander noted a farmer. Riding up to the man, Lander could not believe his eyes. The frontier farmer was Grenville Dodge—the same Grenville Dodge whom he had tutored in engineering back in Massachusetts! Dodge, who had since married and moved to Nebraska

42. Utley, *Life Wild and Perilous,* 33; newspaper clipping, Scrapbook; SD 78(2), 44–5; "Col. Fred. W. Lander, The Pacific Railroad Explorer and Engineer," *Frank Leslie's Illustrated Newspaper,* April 6, 1861; "Life on Board the John L. Stephens," November 27, 1859, newspaper clipping, LP 10.

shortly after graduating from Norwich University, was equally astonished to recognize Lander, the man who had influenced his career path. Dodge welcomed the two into his modest prairie home, fed them, and made them comfortable. Later on, Lander and Dodge sat out on the river bank, watching the fireflies. The two engineers talked railroads that night. "Dodge," Lander said, "the Pacific Railroad is bound to be built through this valley and if it doesn't run through your claim, I'll be badly mistaken." Dodge agreed, rhetorically asking Lander where else a line could feasibly run from the Missouri this far north. Then Lander informed Dodge that he doubted Secretary Davis would support the central route since his bias would direct him to select a southern one. "I'm going to oppose his views as soon as I get to Washington," he declared.[43]

He had conducted his expedition in haste and it had almost cost him his life. Yet Lander remained dedicated to the central route, for his survey showed that the South Pass route offered many advantages over the northern route. The next task was to convince everyone else. Before heading to Washington, the invigorated Lander crossed the Missouri River into Iowa and rode to Council Bluffs to address interested citizens about the importance of their location for a transcontinental railroad.

A shorthand reporter for the local paper recorded Lander's speech that night. "I have but little to say to you this evening to rouse your enthusiasm," downplayed Lander to his audience. "Public attention in Washington and Oregon Territories is excited and much interest manifested in the probable location of the Pacific Railroad by Congress. The trade of the gold region, [and] the growing wealth and important commercial interest of San Francisco having already fixed its terminus. I cannot think there are ten men in Oregon who believe that the line adopted for the great natural thoroughfare will be that surveyed during the last season under the direction of Governor Stevens."

Having publicly expressed his opposition to a route he had helped survey, Lander took pains to differentiate some of the advantages of Stevens's route over the other official surveys conducted in 1853, including passing through a rich timber country. "Beyond this advantage the northern line does not compare as a railroad route with that I have recently examined," continued Lander. "I believe the route up the Platte River valley to be peculiar favorable for cheap construction." Lander continued to laud the

43. Perkins, *Trails, Rails, and War*, 29–30.

benefits of a line that would bring great wealth to their region. He praised the even grade, the favorable soil, and an abundant water supply offered by the Platte River. He compared this route with the other four surveys, and closed his speech by reminding the Council Bluffs crowd that public activism was necessary for success. "I might say something here of the important position [and] the future prospects of your city," lectured Lander, "but I do not appear before you to flatter your creative fancies by any expression of opinion upon questions of a local character." Reminding his audience that he was not favoring Council Bluffs specifically but was completely satisfied with the character of the land within twenty miles of the town, Lander closed, "[T]he interest the people of any community take in a great subject of this kind may have its effect upon their future and aid in securing its advantages and [I] suggest to everyone present the importance of an energetic movement in regard to a matter of such transcendent importance."[44]

Lander easily won the favor of a friendly audience. Heading east back into the states, he stopped in Chicago on July 20 to address interested parties about the importance of the Windy City as a hub to his route. He then stopped in Pittsburgh to see Edward J. Allen's father. Before Congress adjourned at the end of the month, Lander reached Washington. He convinced Representative James McDougal of California to seek passage of a resolution that Secretary Davis furnish Congress with Lander's report in addition to the official 1853 surveys. Lander's visit corresponded with Stevens's submission of a draft of his northern route report. Lander was informed that Stevens had downplayed his role in the exploration of the northern route. Lander was so infuriated that he considered challenging the governor to a duel. Cooler heads prevailed and Stevens assured Lander that he would correct the record to Fred's satisfaction.

After a brief trip to Boston, Lander relaxed in Salem to write his official report of the survey. "I am now at home working on my notes," Lander informed Ned on August 19. It was his first communication to his brother in five months (since he left Olympia). He recounted his troubles with Stevens in Washington, but did not go into details about his own survey, the one for which Ned had loaned more than $3,000. With the arduous mission still fresh in his thoughts, Fred painfully admitted, "I came very near dying on the plains but now I am doing well." The same could not

44. "South Pass Pacific Railroad." *Council Bluffs (Iowa) Bugle*, July 1854.

be said for his meteorologist. Fred had pulled out a short newspaper clipping relating to Mr. Moffet and scribbled underneath it, "Dead From Exposure." Feeling somewhat responsible for Moffet's death, Lander reportedly contributed a portion of his earnings to Moffet's widow in Virginia.[45]

Lander's independent survey had elevated him to the role of a celebrity in Salem. His exploits during Stevens's expedition—particularly the grizzly bear encounter—became public knowledge when Allen's story about it appeared in the June issue of the widely read New York magazine *The Knickerbocker.*[46] It was pleasing to Fred to be treated "politely" (his characterization) in Salem near the end of a tumultuous year, but he was determined that Congress adopt his route.[47]

Late in November, Lander completed his report and returned to Washington. Knowing that Secretary Davis would not support a survey that would challenge the southern explorations, Lander printed his report as a pamphlet and published it before year's end. The government report created a mild sensation in Washington; the Senate had 10,000 copies printed. The privately printed version also sold well; it differed from the government report in that it included a letter Lander wrote to Stevens challenging him on the northern route. Both versions detailed the benefits of the central route, which Lander believed was as important as the Ohio River was to the eastern side of the continent.[48]

The most noteworthy aspect of Lander's railroad reports—including the ones submitted in 1854 and for six years afterward—were his heady and thought-provoking observations. They conflicted with public opinion, yet stood out as keen insights. Lander warned against overexpansion and offered unique ideas about the construction and financing of a transcontinental railroad, wherever it was to be built. Rather than construct a first-class railroad that would become obsolete before it was com-

45. FWL to Ned Lander, August 19, 1854, LCR; newspaper clipping, Scrapbook; SD 78(2), p. 44; "Col. Fred. W. Lander, The Pacific Railroad Explorer and Engineer," *Frank Leslie's Illustrated Newspaper,* April 6, 1861.

46. Edward Lander Sr. to Edward Jr., April 4, 1854, LCR; [Edward J. Allen], "A Grizzly Bear-Hunt," 642–4; W. D. Northend to Jean Lander, April 2, 1862, LP 11.

47. FWL to Ned Lander, August 19, 1854, LCR.

48. Edward Lander Sr. to Edward Jr., March 20, 1855, LFP; E. Lander, "Sketch," 314; Frederick W. Lander, *Remarks on the Construction of a First Class Double Track Railway to the Pacific* (Washington, D.C., 1854), 13.

pleted, Lander preferred a less expensive preliminary road of T-rails spiked to cottonwood cross ties. He argued that a completely wooden line could be run through rough terrain in the mountains since this material would last twenty years. Lander also disliked the idea of a single "grand trunk" line. He proposed a branching route from the central location to San Francisco and to Washington Territory. He argued that the primary objective was connecting the Pacific Ocean with the states; improving communication was secondary.

As for financing the project, Lander railed against land grant proposals that would appropriate land that otherwise would be available for settlers. He met with Asa Whitney, the father of the transcontinental movement, who openly favored the land grant system, to try to sway his opinion. Lander believed the federal government could easily afford to finance $5,000 per mile of railroad and grant builders sections of land only within town sites, leaving the vast country between towns open to the rights of western settlers. The actual cost to build the road would be six times more per mile than his proposal, but Lander maintained that the influx of settlers brought on by the construction would populate the region sufficiently to pay for itself.[49]

Lander left Washington in 1855 and went to New York, where he considered opening a permanent office. But in October a new survey project sent him to Indiana, where a 400-mile railroad to Canada guaranteed lasting employment with a considerable daily salary of fifteen dollars. He started the job in Logansport and instantly was called on to speak at the courthouse about the national significance of the transcontinental railroad. By this time correspondents were addressing him as "Colonel" Lander. The honorific bore no official military significance.[50]

Lander now realized that it would take years to settle the issue as to where the route would run. Jefferson Davis submitted all the requisite surveys, including Lander's independent route, in 1855. As expected, he disregarded Stevens's northern route and Lander's central route in favor of the southern route across the thirty-second parallel. Davis's recommen-

49. FWL to James B. MacDougal, October 2, 1856, LP 1:6070–1; Paul W. Glad, "Frederick West Lander and the Pacific Railroad Movement," *Nebraska History* 35 (September 1954), 185–8.

50. Edward Lander Sr. to Edward Jr., October 4, 1855, LCR; FWL to Messrs. P. Pollard, William Chase, and others, October 9, 1855, *Logansport (Ind.) Pharos*, October 1855.

dation was considered partisan and political; therefore, the Pacific Railroad Survey produced no resolution until those political differences were resolved. Still, the Pacific Railroad Survey was by far the most extensive geographical investigation of the American West that had been made up to that time.[51] Frederick Lander's involvement in two of the five routes had converted this privileged and privately educated New England engineer into a figure whose name was synonymous with the romance and excitement of western frontier exploration.

This is how Grenville Dodge viewed Frederick Lander, his boyhood idol. Five years after Lander had trudged onto his Nebraska Territory farm, Dodge chatted for two hours with a politician on the front porch of the Pacific Hotel in Council Bluffs, Iowa. Remembering the conversation with Lander that July night on the banks of the Elkhorn River, Dodge recounted Lander's insistence on the superiority of the central route over all others. The politician listened intently and assured Dodge that nothing was more important to him than the transcontinental railroad. After meeting with Dodge, the politician repeated to several Council Bluffs citizens the same argument that Lander had espoused since the summer of 1854: the rail route to the Pacific should pass through the Platte River Valley.[52]

The politician hailed from Illinois. His name was Abraham Lincoln.

51. Vance, *North American Railroad,* 168.
52. Hirshson, *Grenville M. Dodge,* 31.

2

"Super-Americo-Contracting Virtue"

Speaking in thoughts whose radiance can reveal
    A dim and outworn majesty of form;
Mocking the ardor of the poet's zeal
    And artist's pencil in a fiercer storm
    Of things inanimate that can conform
To mortal breasts till thus grown strangely near—
    Pierced by the lightning of its power to warm,
When dazzled not by glory we can hear
The angel tones that woo to startle not the ear.
                    —F. W. Lander

Frederick Lander returned to Washington, D.C., early in 1857, and in the days before the official spring season he made his presence known. The fledgling Washington Art Association celebrated its inception by sponsoring a series of March lectures delivered at the hall adjoining the gallery on H Street. Rufus Dawes and the Honorable George Taylor delivered the first two lectures. Lander's turn came on Saturday, March 20.

This was the golden age of the lyceum movement, when orators entertained and enlightened their audiences with hours-long speeches. When Fred Lander stepped up to the podium that Saturday evening, the audience knew him as the civil engineer who had explored the West in two railroad surveys, as the frontiersman who participated in buffalo hunts, as the celebrity who dropped a grizzly bear with a revolver. So little was known about Lander as a lyceum speaker that the association felt it necessary to advertise Lander's lecturing ability and appreciation of the arts in newspaper articles printed during the previous week. One ad went out of its way to promise the would-be attendees that they would hear his oration "with profit and with deep gratification."[1]

Lander rendered the trumped-up preview unnecessary that night, for his audience absorbed the captivating speech delivered by their multi-talented lecturer. He titled his talk, "Aptitude of the American Mind for the Cultivation of the Fine Arts." Lander defined the American mind as a composite that blended characteristics from all the nations of the earth. He asserted that the United States had manifested the possession of more pith and energy of purpose than any one of the nations from which it derived its existence. America was still too young a nation and too little cultivated, Lander opined, to appreciate the high offices of art, which in turn had denied the American character of heart, soul, and inspiration that the gift of art and poetry offered. He declared that American passions were linked to patriotic sentiments; therefore, the encouragement of art could only be secured by productions illustrative of the nation's history. From this arousal should spring the greatest poets, painters, and sculptors the world had ever known. He closed his speech by reciting one of his poems, stanzas that embodied all of his views presented in the lecture.[2]

It was a stirring, thought-provoking presentation, and the audience reacted with a hearty ovation. The Washington Art Association was so impressed that they thanked Lander in a series of resolutions, including a formal request for a copy of his address (Lander complied by sending a rough draft with his apology that he did not have time to produce an elaboration of his notes). The content of the speech was memorable, but the style in which it was delivered caught the attention of the critics and reporters. The *Washington Evening Star* noted in its review that Lander captured the undivided attention of his audience with "the excellence of his enunciation, and to the power possessed by him, in an eminent degree of fixing the attention by that indescribable magnetism which is known to be the attribute of all natural orators."[3]

1. "An Attractive Lecture," newspaper clipping, Scrapbook.
2. *Washington (D.C.) National Intelligencer,* March 23, 1857.
3. Horatio Stone to FWL, April 29, 1857, LP 1:6073; FWL to Washington Art Association, March 8, 1858, LP 1:6075–6; "Washington Art Association Lecture," *Wash-*

Lander solidified his ties with the visual arts by becoming one of the Washington Art Association's charter members, but he also demonstrated a literary flair several weeks after his memorable lecture. Lander published a short story titled "The Trail, the Trace, and the Wagon-Road" in the May issue of *Putnam's Monthly* magazine, a Salem-based and nationally circulated periodical dedicated to literature, science, and art. He submitted the fourteen-page piece anonymously, describing the story of a New Englander named Gardiner, his tempestuous southern partner named Wilson, and an Indian named Kaya who teamed together on a western exploration that included a buffalo hunt and an encounter with hostile natives. Lander ostensibly based his story on the latter half of his 1854 survey, when he conducted a side reconnaissance with Hector McArthur and an Indian guide (given the same name in this story that was bestowed on Lander for his grizzly bear exploit). Although Edward J. Allen exaggerated when he pronounced his friend's story "worthy of [James Fenimore] Cooper," Lander's versatility could not be overlooked. Exactly how much of the story was based on fact versus his fertile imagination will never be known.[4]

Lander spent much of the spring of 1857 in Washington as a consultant for issues dealing with the western territories he had explored three years earlier. Early in March he discussed the characteristics of the frontier with Major Henry H. Sibley, who needed to understand the area to move troops through the territories. One month later he detailed the topography around South Pass for Albert H. Campbell, the general superintendent of all the Pacific Wagon Roads. Campbell, in turn, was subordinate to Jacob Thompson, the secretary of the interior in the new administration of President James Buchanan. Thompson, a Mississippi native, inherited a $300,000 program initially passed under the auspices of the U.S. War Department at the end of the Pierce administration. The money was allotted to explore and construct several wagon roads, including one from

ington (D.C.) Evening Star, March 23, 1857. For Lander's close link with the Washington Art Association, see Alan Fraser Houston and Jourdan Moore Houston, "The 1859 Lander Expedition Revisited: 'Worthy Relics' Tell New Tales of a Wind River Wagon Road," *Montana: The Magazine of Western History* 49 (summer 1999): 50–70.

4. [Frederick Lander], "The Trail, the Trace, and the Wagon-Road; Being Sketches of Wild Life West of the Missouri," *Putnam's Monthly* 9 (May 1857): 449–63; Leland, "Northern Pacific Railroad Explorations," 50; E. J. Allen to the editor, March 4, 1862, *Pittsburgh Daily Evening Chronicle*, March 6, 1862.

Fort Kearny in Nebraska Territory through South Pass and extending to Honey Lake on the eastern boundary of California.[5]

Although emigrants to the Pacific Coast had trod a familiar path for decades through the Platte Valley through South Pass to Fort Hall (and branched off either to Oregon or California from there), the federal government felt compelled to sponsor the first national road in the West to ensure a safer and less hazardous path to the Pacific. Chief among emigrants' complaints were hostile Indians, parched desert country immediately west of South Pass, poor trails, and slow mail delivery to the Pacific Coast. Secretary Thompson oversaw the construction of four roads, the most prominent being the Fort Kearney, South Pass, and Honey Lake Wagon Road. This road, a shorter route than the trails currently in use, would be constructed in three segments: from Fort Kearny to Independence Rock; from Independence Rock to City of Rocks; then from City of Rocks to Honey Lake.[6]

Lander was not the only expert consulted about its construction. Thompson sought the opinions of several others, including William M. F. Magraw, a Virginia native since removed to Philadelphia who had gained experience in western geography from a mail contract that he had held until 1856. Magraw carried political backing from Democratic legislatures. A close friend of President Buchanan, he also had a brother who was courting Buchanan's niece, Harriet Lane. This improved Magraw's chances when he applied for the superintendency of the central route wagon road. Thompson granted Magraw the appointment for the first two road divisions in April.[7]

Lander was an obvious choice for chief engineer of the wagon road survey and construction, except for the fact that he harbored a malignant mistrust of Magraw, the man expected to be his superior. Magraw had be-

5. A. A. Humphreys to Henry Sibley, March 6, 1857, LP 1:7474–5; FWL to Albert H. Campbell, April 7, 1857, WR; Mavis Shahrani, "Wagon Roads—1857 Season," in *Frederick West Lander: A Biographical Sketch (1822–1862),* ed. Joy Leland (Reno, Nev., 1993), 63.

6. Jackson, *Wagon Roads West,* 191–2. Fort Kearny is often incorrectly spelled as "Kearney" in most official and unofficial wagon road documents. All references to the wagon road, hereinafter, will retain the misspelling. The name "City of Rocks" is now shortened to "City Rocks."

7. Ibid.; Shahrani, "Wagon Roads—1857 Season," 64, 69–70. For a detailed account of the career of Magraw, see William P. Mackinnon, "The Buchanan Spoils System and the Utah Expedition: Careers of W. M. F. Magraw and John M. Hockaday," *Utah Historical Quarterly* (1963): 127–50.

come notorious for incompetence (this is why he had lost the mail contract one year earlier), and his vile temper and his disdain for the Mormons invited danger once the survey crew approached the Great Salt Lake region. When Thompson offered Lander the appointment on April 22, Lander apparently objected to his instructions to serve entirely under Magraw and subsequently tendered a letter of resignation. Thompson quickly rectified the matter; he called Lander into his office and smoothed over his concerns in a long discussion held during the last week of the month. Promised a little independence on the expedition, Lander changed his mind and accepted the appointment on April 27.[8]

Money also influenced his decision. Although the efforts of James McDougal in Congress had granted Lander $5,000 to compensate his 1854 independent survey, its dispersal was held up in legislation and Lander never saw a penny of it (he incorrectly predicted, "I am pretty sure to live until paid by Congress"). He had financed the expedition with the help of family members (Ned lent him $3,252, then wrote it off in his will). The chief engineer position for the wagon road carried a $2,500 annual salary; this money was guaranteed. Magazine articles and art lectures could not compete with such a salary.[9]

Thompson's expedition instructions, issued on May 1, also placated his chief engineer, for Lander was given a separate command to examine the area west of South Pass to City of Rocks thoroughly while Magraw and another crew focused on the region east of South Pass. Only when improvements were completed on this end of the trail was Magraw to extend his crew on the west side of the pass and meet Lander's crew at City of Rocks. Then the combined parties were instructed to go over the third section of the road, a segment delegated to a different team of engineers.[10]

Lander reached the Mississippi River two weeks after receiving his instructions. Sickened with bronchitis, he lay bedridden in the Planter House

8. Thompson to FWL, April 22, 1857, WR 1:1; FWL to H. K. Nichols, September 23, 1857, Letterbook, 1857–1858, LP 9 [hereinafter cited as "Letterbook"]: 75. Great Salt Lake was shortened to "Salt Lake" in 1869.

9. E. Douglas Branch, "Frederick West Lander, Road-Builder," *Mississippi Valley Historical Review* 16 (September 1929): 175; FWL to "Ned" Lander, August 19, 1854, LCR; Edward Lander Jr., Last Will and Testament, February 28, 1854, LCR; Thompson to FWL, April 22, 1857, WR1:1.

10. Jackson, *Wagon Roads West,* 192.

Hotel in St. Louis immediately after arriving there. He was still sick when he dragged himself on board a steamer bound for Independence, up the Missouri River. Lander wrote Brigham Young on June 1, reminding the Mormon leader of his earlier communication of 1854. "I now take pleasure in again calling your attention to the fact of a second exploration I am about to undertake," wrote Lander, diplomatically asking for any aid the Mormon population could offer. The entire team idled in Independence for two more weeks, giving members time to test the instruments and break in the mules. Feeling better on the ninth, Lander held a dinner party for his engineers and approximately thirty locals, who assembled under a tent where the food was spread out in camp fashion. But the evening of levity did little to assuage Lander's impatience. "Mr. Lander is anxious for his party to get off," noted one of the team members two days later.[11]

Finally, on June 15, Magraw ordered Lander's departure. Lander set off with twelve men, including five engineers, in the direction of South Pass. They took rations of flour, sugar, bacon, biscuits, coffee, and other supplies to sustain them for sixty days. Although Magraw's incompetence prevented supplies from being procured at Fort Leavenworth, Lander and his men still managed to cover nearly forty miles per day by mule. One month after leaving Independence, Lander's party entered South Pass, where they rested for a day to replenish their supplies and reorganize.[12]

Exactly three years earlier, Lander had passed through the Rockies from the West, regretting at the time that he did not have time to explore the mountains on the west side more thoroughly. His 1857 mission was to do just that, and Lander divided his party into three surveying groups. He took a small crew and explored a potential route to Soda Springs that would shorten the distance normally used on the Oregon Trail. He reached Soda Springs without incident, met a mountaineer who had worked on Stevens's expedition, and convinced him to join the survey team. Together they returned to South Pass, then headed northward to explore mountain passes. He took along a Lemhi Northern Shoshone chief named

11. Henry Nichols journal, May–June 1857, William Robertson Coe Collection, Yale University Library, New Haven, Conn., 5–10; Melchior Long journal, June 4–9, 1857, in WR 7; FWL to Brigham Young, June 1, 1857, quoted in Shahrani, "Wagon Roads—1857 Season," 72–3.

12. Long journal, June 15, 1857, WR; FWL to Magraw, June 17, June 21, and October 7, 1857, Letterbook, 22–3, 29–30, 82.

Tentoi as a guide. Lander returned to South Pass for a third time on August 18 where he rendezvoused with the other two parties.[13]

The party Lander had handpicked at the beginning of the expedition was performing to his perfectionist standards. His engineers included a mix of easterners (John Mullowney and Calvin Crocker, the latter a troubled man who would commit suicide before year's end), a westerner (John H. Ingle), and two foreign-born men (William W. Wagner and Edward Gotzkow). The other seven nonengineers on the crew hailed from the East, including Alexander Mitchell, a Canadian, and Benjamin Ficklin, a Virginia native. An eleven-year-old tag-along named William Kelly drove the measuring wagon used to log mileage for the engineers. Lander had selected Ficklin and Mullowney to head the other two teams, and they performed their functions to the letter of their instructions.[14]

Lander issued new orders to his engineers, divided the men into parties again, and headed back toward Soda Springs to explore more passes in the Wahsatch Range. The parties met at Soda Springs, Lander's base for more side reconnaissances while staying clear of the formidable Blackfoot tribe. On a solo trip, Lander—riding "a broken down mule"—inadvertently wandered into an Eastern Shoshone camp. The natives fed him, gave him a fresh horse, and supplied a guide to accompany Lander back to his party. Realizing that the season was nearing its close, Lander, along with Ficklin and Mitchell, rode back toward South Pass.[15]

Lander was proud of what he had accomplished in ninety-one days in the field. His crew had covered 3,000 miles of terrain and discovered and explored sixteen passes in the northern Wahsatch Range. In doing so he became the first explorer to define the topography of those mountains west of South Pass. After exploring scores of routes and cutoffs, Lander felt that two practicable continuous routes for the wagon road existed be-

13. FWL to Magraw, October 7, 1857, Letterbook, 83–4, 107; Shahrani, "Wagon Roads—1857 Season," 80–1. Tentoi is often spelled "Tendoy." The Idaho town named after him today adopts the latter spelling.

14. Jermy Benton Wight, *Frederick W. Lander and the Lander Trail* (Bedford, Wyoming, 1993), 25; FWL to Ficklin, July 16, 1857, Letterbook, 57–9; FWL to Mullowney, July 16, 1857, Letterbook, 60–2.

15. Shahrani, "Wagon Roads—1857 Season," 82; FWL to Magraw, October 7, 1857, Letterbook, 107–8. The Wahsatch Range (not to be confused with Utah's Wasatch mountains) was a nineteenth-century name used to describe a composite of the Wyoming, Salt River, and Bear River ranges.

tween South Pass and City of Rocks. One was a dry and sandy route void of vegetation. Although it would fail as an emigrant trail, he believed it useful as a mail route because it shortened the original trail by several days of travel. The most practical emigrant route, Lander maintained, ran north of the potential mail road and was fed adequately by the main waters and tributaries of the Green and Sandy Rivers. It also boasted good timber land and grass for emigrant travel. Lack of ferry tolls created an additional advantage for ox-team migration.[16]

Lander quickly discovered that his success was offset by his superior's failures. On September 16 a messenger found Lander and his two comrades west of South Pass and handed him a letter. Dated September 3, the letter was signed by nine members of Magraw's party, including seven engineers, a physician, and a disbursing agent. They informed Lander that they had quit the survey due to Magraw's erratic behavior. Among their grievances was Magraw's chronic intoxication, which slowed the party up by several weeks and forfeited any chance to reach California before the end of the season. Apparently, Magraw also had used government wagons to transport personal supplies—mainly 6,300 pounds of liquor that he intended to sell at Fort Laramie for personal profit.

The engineers' disgust with Magraw had peaked early in September when the superintendent informed them that he intended to go into winter quarters rather than continue the expedition. Magraw managed to turn his laborers against the engineers, and the workers threatened the professional men. Feeling they had no options available, and running low on subsistence, the nine complainants resolved to leave the party. Furthermore, the authors of the letter urged Lander to take over the expedition in place of the incompetent Magraw.

Lander's quandary deepened when he reached South Pass. He found Magraw and learned that the malcontents had indeed left the team and had dispersed to either Great Salt Lake City or the Missouri frontier. The whole affair confirmed Lander's mistrust of Magraw, but he refused to take over the expedition. Magraw had to remain in charge, Lander reasoned, because the public property had been assigned to his care and Lander intended to follow to the letter his instructions set forth by the Department of the Interior. Those instructions placed him in a subordi-

16. Jackson, *Wagon Roads West*, 195–6; FWL to Magraw, October 7, 1857, Letterbook, 98–103.

nate role to Magraw, and Lander would not violate the concept of official etiquette.[17]

Lander's ire, though inwardly directed at Magraw's incompetence, was outwardly expressed toward those party members who quit the expedition before the work was complete. "I cannot follow the line of conduct you have prescribed for me," he told one of the malcontents. "Were any small ambition or insane folly of mine to cause me to accept the office of Superintendent at your hands, I have given no bonds, and my drafts upon the Department would not be honored," he said. Despite the hardships incurred by the wrath of Magraw, Lander saw no excuse for the engineers' behavior. "In my own estimation," he explained, "discipline is the first, last, and intermediate step towards efficiency of progress, and the success of explorations in the wild interior; and the etiquette of those official forms by which the discipline is attained, should be observed to the letter."[18]

Another ailment knocked Lander off his feet on September 22, but he received quality treatment from the physician of the Tenth U.S. Infantry. Colonel Edward B. Alexander led the unit toward Utah Territory to comply with President Buchanan's order to subdue Brigham Young and his Latter-day Saints, whom the president accused of—among other things— "frenzied fanaticism." Colonel Alexander was awaiting the arrival of his superior, Colonel Albert Sydney Johnston. Lander warned Alexander to stay out of Utah Territory as the Mormons appeared extremely volatile. Less than two weeks earlier, Indians and Mormon militiamen had massacred 120 emigrants at Mountain Meadows.

Alexander ignored Lander's advice and continued to goad Brigham Young by exchanging angry letters with him. Young retaliated against the U.S. Army's direct threat by sending out "Mormon Raiders" to destroy supply trains and stampede horses. Benjamin Ficklin, conducting a reconnaissance in the region, bore witness to Young's wrath. On October 6 he returned to camp and informed Lander that he had counted seventy-two burned supply wagons at the Green and Sandy Rivers. Colonel Alexander, noting the loss of the wagons and 1,400 head of cat-

17. Branch, "Road Builder," 180–1. For a detailed and chronological explanation of Magraw's activities that led to the trouble, see Leland, *Lander*, 82–95.

18. FWL to Henry Nichols, September 21, 1857, Letterbook, 67–79; FWL to the editor, n.d., newspaper clipping, Scrapbook.

tle, pulled his men into winter quarters 115 miles northeast of Great Salt Lake City.[19]

Lander demonstrated tremendous growth as a leader and a subordinate compared to his oft-contentious episodes in the Northern Pacific Railroad Survey four years earlier. By balancing his critique between the engineers and Magraw, Lander's diplomacy eventually reaped a reward. Leaving Magraw and his dispersed party to winter in the Rockies, Lander returned to Washington, D.C., during the closing weeks of 1857 and laid out the facts before Secretary Thompson. Lander urged Thompson to hear both sides of the case before he rendered his decision on Magraw. Unswayed by his desire to hold Magraw's position, Lander produced counterevidence to support Magraw, including several favorable letters written by expedition men. He also contacted one of Magraw's brothers to ask him to support his beleaguered sibling and offered to assist any way he could.

Thompson did not need to dwell over the evidence long to see that Magraw's erratic and reckless conduct was indefensible by a superintendent. Magraw made the final decision easier for Thompson by abandoning the expedition to camp with the U.S. Army. Thompson saw this as a violation of the dual compensation rule. Considering Magraw's action as a voluntary resignation, Thompson turned to Lander to take charge of the road work he had mapped out on the frontier.

Lander at first declined the offer, citing the fact that no representatives of Magraw had endorsed him as a suitable replacement. Delegates from the Oregon and Nebraska Territories quickly stepped up to voice their approval of Lander; therefore, he reversed his earlier decision, and on January 27, 1858, Lander officially became superintendent of the Fort Kearney, South Pass, and Honey Lake Wagon Road. Two months later, Magraw learned of his "voluntary resignation" and immediately indicated that he would not shrink quietly away from the position he felt he still deserved. "I think Mr. Thompson has acted a bit hastily, how wisely future

19. Otis G. Hammond, ed., *The Utah Expedition, 1857–1858: Letters of Jesse A. Gove, 10th Inf., U.S.A., of Concord, N.H., to Mrs. Gove, and Special Correspondence of the* New York Herald (Concord, N.H., 1928), 66–8; Shahrani, "Wagon Roads—1857 Season," 96; Kenneth M. Stampp, *America in 1857: A Nation on the Brink* (New York, 1990), 202–7; B. F. Ficklin to Magraw, October 7, 1857 (in Magraw to Jacob Thompson, October 9, 1857), WR 5:5.

developments will determine," Magraw wrote to President Buchanan, "At all events, I am content to bide my time and wait the results."[20]

The results were turned in now by Superintendent Lander. Determined to demonstrate to the Buchanan administration that he was up to the task, Lander spent the first four months in the capital preparing for the season's work. His first order of business was to submit a report on the practicality of a railroad through South Pass to link with the Pacific. This he turned in on February 13, highlighting the benefit of the central route again (this time with more exploration experience west of South Pass) and continuing to strengthen his case for a temporary light wooden line over a heavy gauge rail. Turning his attention to the upcoming wagon road season, Lander submitted to Secretary Thompson an ambitious blueprint of what he planned to accomplish. Knowing that an arduous season was in store for his crew, Lander urged Thompson to employ only rugged frontiersmen: "Men are required for this kind of service who will eat dried mule." Secretary Thompson adopted Lander's plan and granted him unprecedented authority and responsibility. Lander's virtuous performance over the previous season also swayed Thompson to award him a maximum annual salary of $4,000.[21]

Superintendent Lander left Washington for St. Louis in mid-April to initiate a season of progress. Reaching the Mississippi River, Lander learned the Mormon conflict had essentially ceased. After a brief sojourn in Independence to resupply the train, the expedition headed westward on April 29, 1858. The party encountered the ragged and hungry men who had survived a winter in the mountains, including some former members of Magraw's crew. Lander hired some of these experienced workers and continued westward. On June 14 Lander and his men bivouacked at South Pass again. Lander intended to find Magraw, who was still believed to be with the U.S. Army near their winter camp in Utah, but learned that the soldiers had since moved toward Great Salt Lake. Lander abandoned the idea of pursuing Magraw and accepted the fact that he must buy new equipment, as the army had detained much of Magraw's supplies from the previous season.[22]

20. Jackson, *Wagon Roads West*, 200–1.

21. FWL to Thompson, February 13, 1858, HR 70; FWL to Thompson, February 13, 1858, WR 4:5; Thompson to FWL, March 25, 1857, WR 1:3.

22. FWL to Jacob Thompson, January 20, 1859, SD 36, pp. 47–8. Lander titled his report, including an emigrant guide, "Narrative of Progress of Expedition."

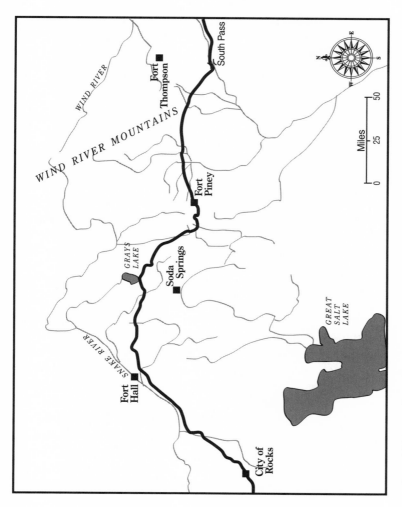

Central Division of Fort Kearney, South Pass, and Honey Lake Wagon Road, 1857–1858
Adapted from Senate Document 36, Serial Set 984, LC

Accompanied by skilled lumberjacks and bridge builders from Maine, Lander set off into the rugged region west of South Pass on June 18 and began blazing a narrow trail through the Wahsatch Range. He had prepared a train with gifts for Indians encountered along the way, but when Lander first bumped into the Eastern Shoshone near the Green River basin, he realized the gift train rolled well to the rear. Lander parted with one of his horses, giving it to the antelope-hunting tribe as a peace offering. In return, the natives promised to avoid hostilities against the surveyors and road builders.[23]

Not all ran smoothly with the expedition. Lander allowed himself to engage in a quarrel with his chief engineer, John Lambert, after he failed to locate the route Lander blazed during the 1857 season. Lander bluntly informed Lambert that he suffered from "ineptitude to practical details" and refused to place him as the ranking officer of the expedition to head the party during Lander's absences. His subordinates had become painfully aware that Lander refused to tolerate excuses and incompetence within his team. Near the end of July, Lander fired Lambert. He disbanded Lambert's party by sending some of the members home and retaining most to continue under his own leadership.[24]

Lander's mission could be successful only through the skills and labor of his employees and with the approval of those who inhabited the areas that the government road was to traverse. To gain the latter, Lander's skills in diplomacy were tested time and again, particularly with the Mormons, Bannocks, and Shoshones. Lander soon learned that to be effective, he needed to engage in closer relations with the tribes to assure that emigrants on the trail were allowed a safe passage. That diplomacy, initiated this season, must be carried on the following year. He sympathized with the Indians, claiming that to characterize them as "treacherous" was unfair to a people who killed emigrants only as a form of retaliation. At the same time, however, Lander's sympathies were reversed regarding the Indians' treatment of prisoners, which he considered barbaric. By seeming to condone some acts and condemn others, Lander essentially was admitting he had much to learn about the nature of Indians.[25]

The season had come to a close, and Lander had to alter his original

23. SD 36, pp. 47–50, 68–72.
24. FWL to Lambert, July 7, 1858, WR 5:3; FWL to Lambert July 27, 1857, WR 5:5.
25. SD 36, p. 71.

plans to winter in the mountains. The Crows and Shoshones had been warring this season, so Lander thought it necessary to return his crew to the states. Deeming his road complete except for minor repairs, Lander issued orders to protect it during the winter. He detached Charles Miller, a reliable and experienced mountaineer, to stay at Gilbert's Station at South Pass to record weather conditions and promote the new road to passing emigrant trains.[26]

Lander also sent an assistant with a Shoshone interpreter and two others to Great Salt Lake City for the winter. With them returned Mormon workers whom Lander had hired early in the summer. Grateful for the participation and production of the Mormons, Lander wrote Brigham Young to inform him that he was returning to the states and would use strong influence to win favor for the Latter-day Saints.

Despite the astounding success that season, Lander entertained thoughts of giving it all up. His mood swung sharply when he learned that Magraw had been complaining about how Lander had supplanted him. Knowing that Magraw had close ties with President Buchanan, Lander felt threatened. He aired his frustrations in his letter to Brigham Young, posturing that if he heard himself criticized when he reached Washington, he would resign. Appreciative Iowans had given him land in Nebraska Territory four years earlier, across the Missouri River from Council Bluffs, and now Lander entertained thoughts of settling there and entering politics as a delegate from the territory. Nationally popular and a gifted lyceum speaker with strong opinions, Lander and politics seemed a perfect fit. Asking for his support, Lander intimated to Young, "[R]est assured that the constitutional claims of every white man on American soil shall be dear to me ever and advocated with heart and voice."[27] Lander headed eastward and was back in Washington by December to meet with Secretary Thompson.

Thompson could not help but be pleased with what the superintendent had accomplished with a work ethic antithetical to Magraw's corrupted and slothlike habits. The 350-mile cutoff from the Oregon Trail eliminated many of the obstacles to the emigrant in that rugged country. Lander reported that his expedition moved 62,000 cubic yards of earth

26. Jackson, *Wagon Roads West,* 209.

27. FWL to Brigham Young, September 23, 185[8], in Mavis Shahrani, "Wagon Roads— 1858 Season," in *Frederick West Lander: A Biographical Sketch (1822–1862),* ed. Joy Leland (Reno, Nev., 1993), 116–17; FWL to "Ned," August 19, 1854, LCR.

and rock as well as eleven miles of willow forest and twenty-three miles of heavy pine timber. Lander's workers erected two blockhouses, two corrals, and built seven bridges over impeding waterways. More important for Thompson was the speed and efficiency with which Lander had worked that season. He had planned for his specialist to complete the work in eighteen months; Lander happily informed him that the work was done in eight.

Completing the work in less than half the time allotted saved tremendous amounts of money. Appropriated $75,000 to do the job, Lander used only $40,260. Newspapers were quick to report the unprecedented accomplishments. "It is, indeed, reassuring to know there is one government officer who is too honest to spend all the money he can," reported the *St. Joseph Journal,* "and his name should be emblazoned in gold and put up in the Halls of Congress as an example to all generations." The *St. Louis Herald* appeared equally impressed. "We still think there is some mistake about it," admitted the staff at the paper, calling it "an evidence of super-Americo-contracting virtue, which it will be hard to convince us exists anywhere in the world discovered by Columbus."[28]

The positive press buoyed Lander's ever-increasing confidence and refocused his interest away from Nebraska and back onto the wagon road. Letters of support came from friends and family, telling Lander that his exploits had been found worthy of print in newspapers published on far away continents. Josiah Pierce, a brother-in-law serving as a U.S. State Department representative in Russia, wrote Lander from St. Petersburg in January, informing Fred that his youngest sister was pregnant and doing well. "Martha and I have traced your wanderings on the map with the aid of the frequent notices the newspapers gave of them," wrote Pierce. "We have imagined how you looked, eating salt trout among the mountains, smoking the calumet with your questionable friends the Nez Perces, or fraternizing with the Mormons, hoping you did not make the Latter Day Saints believe you practiced their principles regarding the fair sex." Pierce continued to feed his brother-in-law's ego by stating "we have the greatest confidence that you were meeting all obstacles, and driving on your undertakings in a way to do yourself much honor and to do our Uncle Sam much good."[29]

28. SD 36, p. 52; "A Miracle," *St. Joseph (Mo.) Journal,* n.d., Scrapbook; *St. Louis Herald,* n.d., Scrapbook.
29. Pierce to FWL, January 10, 1859, LP 1:6078–9. Official correspondence dominates

Lander spent the next few weeks in Washington writing his report of the 1858 expedition. He turned in the piece on January 20, including a map drawn by his cartographer and an emigrant guide that noted all conditions and distances for those travelers taking the cutoff. The guide exemplified Lander's meticulous dedication to his work and his desire to inform the emigrant about every aspect of his trail. For example, Lander believed that the five-mile stretch of road from Little Sandy Creek to Big Hole was "a good laying up place. A large valley; abundance of grass and pine timber." He included eighty-three other descriptions in the five-page guide.[30]

Inevitably, Lander and Magraw met in the capital. During the first week of March, they exchanged heated words. Lander challenged him, but Magraw chose not to engage his feisty replacement. A couple of days later, on the night of March 4, Lander walked into Willard's Hotel, one of the most popular social spots for the more prominent members of Washington society. He went there to relax and socialize. He had learned earlier that day that Charles Miller, one of his most reliable expedition members, was murdered after an argument and scuffle with another man at a South Pass mail station.[31] Seeing Magraw again that night at Willard's exacerbated Lander's ill mood.

Lander and Magraw approached each other for the second time in three days. This time Magraw appeared more prepared to settle the long-standing dispute. When Lander again hurled some epithets at him, Magraw drew a slung shot, equipped with an eight-inch flexible handle on one end and connected to a leaden shot on the other. With all his might, Magraw struck Lander three blows across the top of his head. Lander reeled as blood poured from his torn scalp. He rallied in seconds, grabbed Magraw before he could muster another swing, and pitched him several feet onto the hotel lobby's tessellated floor.

Enraged, Lander jumped on Magraw and pummeled him. Witnesses agreed that Lander would have killed him at that moment had not several waiters intervened and pulled him off. Lander was furious that he was not allowed to finish the fight. "Cowards!" he yelled at the waiters in a voice that resonated throughout the corridors, "Is this a way you treat a man? I

the Lander collection at the Library of Congress. Lander apparently saved very few personal letters from family members. He cherished his brother-in-law's letter enough to retain it.

30. SD 36, pp. 48–62.

31. FWL to Thompson, March 4, 1859, WR.

am a Massachusetts man, and unarmed. I have challenged the scoundrel, and he refused to fight me, and now he assails me with a slung shot!" After ranting a few more minutes, Lander was conveyed from the scene, and friends escorted Magraw in the other direction. "I was knocked to my knees and lost about a quart of blood," Lander acknowledged to a friend nearly three weeks later, "but [I] got to the man after a while and cleaned him out."[32]

Compounding his troubles with Magraw was wavering support in Congress over funding for Lander's cutoff—the Fort Kearney, South Pass, and Honey Lake Wagon Road. Some legislators tried to divert some of the funds to other projects, mainly mail routes. Lander refused to allow the talk to continue without defending his two years of toil. Offering to carry on repairs for the upcoming season, including work on the third section of the road from City of Rocks to the California border, Lander proposed to Secretary Thompson to work with the same crew he used the previous season. Those men had wintered near Troy, Kansas, and supposedly had replenished the stock needed to complete the work.

Thompson sent instructions on March 25, 1859, for Lander's third season of road work. Lander was ordered to return to South Pass to make improvements on the section of road he constructed between South Pass and City of Rocks. He then was to proceed to the Honey Lake Valley in western California to conduct a continuous survey over the entire road. Additionally, Lander was to act as an Indian agent on the trail to provide presents to those Indians who might otherwise impede his progress. Lander set off with those crew members who returned with him to Washington and by late April found himself on the Mississippi again, this time at St. Joseph, Missouri.[33]

Lander stayed in St. Joseph for two weeks to refit and reorganize his crews. Knowing the trails westward were already jammed with prospectors hoping to become rich at Pikes Peak, Lander sent out a small light party in advance to work their way toward the Humboldt River Valley to explore the area and ensure a safe passage for the main party. A few nights before he headed out with the main party, Lander was the special guest at a din-

32. "Perley" to the editor, March 5, 1859, *Boston Journal,* March 1859; FWL to John F. Potter, March 22, 1859, John Fox Potter Papers, State Historical Society of Wisconsin, Madison.

33. FWL to Thompson, March 16, 1859, WR 5:1; Thompson to FWL, March 25, 1859, WR 1:1.

ner held by prominent members of the town. Several toasts were offered in this night of merriment and Lander gratified his sponsors with two speeches, both well received. On May 11 the main party headed westward.[34]

The 1859 expedition sported a new look compared to Lander's two previous years of road work. Lander's fondness for the arts spilled over in his expedition work. Perhaps missing the visual documentation that John M. Stanley and Gustavus Sohon had provided Isaac Stevens six years earlier, Lander lobbied for specialists to capture the images of the West on canvas to use as a promotional tool for his wagon road work. He had full support from his superiors in the matter since Jacob Thompson, Albert H. Campbell, and Secretary of War John B. Floyd had all been connected with the Washington Art Association.[35]

What Lander would later call a "full corps of artists" was probably just a few men, including Albert Bierstadt, Francis Seth Frost, and Henry Hitchings. Bierstadt, the most talented of the artists, was a twenty-nine-year-old German immigrant who grew up near New Bedford, Massachusetts. He had honed his skills by painting European landscapes in the 1850s and had matured as an artist to produce great works about the western frontier. Several artists had sketched or painted the West in the four decades before Bierstadt first stepped onto the frontier, but Bierstadt's trip carried greater impact. In 1859 curiosity about America's frontier had reached a fever pitch, due in great part to artists and explorers who had written extensively about it—including Frederick Lander.

Personally, Bierstadt's interest focused on the Rockies, the only American hope to match the grandeur of the Swiss Alps and other European mountain chains. Landscape artists and writers had been greatly disappointed in the small rounded hills east of the Mississippi. They yearned for something they could call majestic. Bierstadt saw the Rockies for the first time during Lander's 1859 expedition, and—like Lander—was awed by their dramatic beauty. Gratified that the granite peaks matched the Alps, Bierstadt happily wrote home,"[W]hen we look up and measure the mighty perpendicular cliffs that rise hundreds of feet aloft, all capped with snow, we then realize that we are among a different class of mountains."

34. W. H. Wagner, "Rough notes of travel taken in field of advance party," 1859, in WR 7; "Complimentary Dinner to Colonel Lander," *St. Joseph (Mo.) Gazette*, May 11, 1859.
    35. Houston and Houston, "1859 Lander Expedition," 57.

Lander's expedition sparked the decades-long career of one of the greatest artists ever to paint the West.

Bierstadt sketched several landscapes, drawings that he converted into grand western scenes when he returned to his Massachusetts and New York studios. Of equal importance, he carried along cumbersome equipment to capture scenes with the relatively new technology of photography. Bierstadt took dozens of photographs during the first few months of Lander's expedition, including scenes in Kansas, Missouri, and Nebraska. He generally shunned grand landscapes and limited his photographs to men and equipment. He photographed wagons crossing at fords, encampments, emigrants, and Indians. A few of his sketches were converted to woodcuts and published in *Harper's Weekly* that summer, giving the public a visual image of Lander's work for the first time. To continue promoting his work, Lander also allowed a Utah Territory congressional representative to travel with his artists.[36]

While Lander set up within his familiar surroundings at South Pass, his leading expedition party, under William Wagner, came within seven miles of City of Rocks, the termination point of the middle section of the trail. There, near his camp on the Raft River, Wagner met Pocatello, the formidable Northern Shoshone chief. The previous September, Pocatello and his men had disrupted mail service and attacked emigrant trains heading to California from Great Salt Lake. Lander had spoken with the chief in an attempt to stop the raids, promising in return to write a favorable report to Congress and then to distribute gifts the following season. Pocatello—whom Lander dubbed the "White Plume"—kept his word and Lander determined to keep his. Per Lander's instructions, Wagner dispersed gifts of blankets, cloth, handkerchiefs, knives, paints, and other goods to Pocatello and the Western Shoshones. Pocatello did not dispute the passage of Wagner's party, allowing him to ride to City of Rocks and start his surveys of the western segment of the trail.[37]

In addition to mastering negotiations with the Sioux, Bannocks,

36. Ibid.; HR 64, p. 5; Nancy Anderson and Linda S. Ferber, *Albert Bierstadt: Art and Enterprise* (New York, 1990), 69–75, 143–5; Mavis Shahrani, "Wagon Roads—1859 Season," in *Frederick West Lander: A Biographical Sketch (1822–1862)*, ed. Joy Leland (Reno, Nev., 1993), 123.

37. Brigham D. Madsen, *Chief Pocatello: The "White Plume"* (Salt Lake City, Utah, 1986), ix, 43–4; Wagner, "Rough notes," WR 7.

Cheyenne, and the various bands of Shoshones along his trail, Lander also engaged in an all-out effort to promote the new road while at South Pass. After Charles Miller's murder, no one was available to direct emigrants onto Lander's road. Traders on the old routes took advantage of the void to divert traffic onto the inferior roads to assure their own profits. Lander's arrival put an end to that. He replaced Miller with Major Edmund Yates, a South Carolinian who was instructed to direct the thousands of emigrants reaching South Pass onto the new trail and to provide them with any information necessary to promote it. Handicapped because his emigrant guide had not yet been printed, Lander placed a premium on promoting his cutoff. He selected "volunteers" from his expedition to write out 1,000 copies of his meticulous guide to distribute until the printed version arrived. Leaving Yates at the pass, Lander headed westward as June turned to July. The extra attention paid off. Yates estimated that 13,000 emigrants took Lander's route to the West in the summer and fall of 1859.[38]

The 1859 season was marred by drenching spring rains, which swelled the rivers and impeded the road work. Lander hired local laborers to re-grade the road on higher ground to avoid washouts. Before he knew it, Lander's labor crew exceeded 150 men. These were additional unforeseen expenses to add to the costs to reequip his crews in Kansas. Allotted only $25,000 from depleted government coffers this season, including money earmarked for Indian gifts, Lander would not be returning unspent money in the autumn.[39]

On the last day of August Lander's eight-wagon train, after working its way down the Humboldt River west of City of Rocks, linked up with Wagner's advance party at Tufts Meadows. "Great rejoicing" was how Wagner described the event. Another successful season could be reported back in the states. All of Lander's objectives were met. Additionally, Wagner's summertime surveys had found a way to avoid the great obstacle created by the Goose Creek Mountains. Lander realized that an alternate route, with an estimated cost of $10,000, could bypass the range. On September 11 Lander and his party crossed into California. Wagner tallied the distance from St. Joseph, Missouri (the point of departure four months

38. HR 64, p. 3; Edmund L. Yates to FWL, January 20, 1860, LP 1:6102–3.
39. HR 64, p. 3; Jacob Thompson to FWL, March 25, 1859, WR 1:1.

earlier). Lander and his men covered 1,754 miles—the entire extent of the government road.[40]

Deeming the season's work nearly complete, Lander's workers searched out a camp for the winter. The superintendent had strengthened a special bond with his men, some of whom had shared hardships with him for three years running. Lander expected much, tolerated little, and the men proved to be equal to his demands. These men ate mule meat, endured day-long rides without rest, conducted scientific surveys, and engaged in arduous labor. Although their days were marked with pain and sweat, the nights were time to unwind. Some played as hard as they worked. Others relaxed at campfires, serenaded by the tunes played by a fiddler. This winter season, like the last, was to be a most satisfying one.

While his men set up a camp on Neale's ranch near Honey Lake on the eastern border of California, Lander rode to San Francisco, where he arrived on September 22.[41] There he met his brother Ned, whom he had not seen for more than five years. Both Lander brothers were in San Francisco for the same purpose—the Pacific Railroad Convention. The convention had begun two days earlier; its mission was to adopt measures that would push forward the construction of the transcontinental railroad to benefit the people of California, Oregon, and Washington Territory. Ned Lander attended the convention as a Washington Territory representative. Fred arrived in town and was asked to address the convention that night.

His public presentations over the past three years had been confined to speeches made before the Washington Art Association. Lander loved the arts, but the topic of railroads seemed to arouse his passions unlike any other. Lander's speech immediately made clear that his dedication to the construction of a transcontinental railroad over the central route had not been diminished by three years of U.S. Wagon Road employment. Lander's "indescribable magnetism" took hold of the convention that night as it never had before.

"It is perhaps proper for me to state that I shall speak, not without authority but with some little egotism, my views on the subject of the construction of a railroad across the American continent," began Lander in

40. Wagner, August 30, September 13, 1859, "Rough notes," WR 7.
41. Ibid.; Shahrani, "Wagon Roads—1859 Season," 138.

his unique staccato style. He went on to remind his listeners of his twenty-year interest and dedication to the project. He knew what strings to pull to produce the most enthusiastic responses from his audience. "I covet inquiry into this question," he continued minutes later, "because the subject is so vast in its nature; it has cost me so much money, so much time, so much energy, and so much faith, that, standing here, as I do, tonight before a Convention of the Pacific Coast, which I have just reached, I ignore all thoughts of self, whatsoever."

Thunderous applause followed the remark, and ovations were repeated several times during the course of the speech. Lander milked the moment continuously. He recounted his past experience on surveys; he provided a spirited defense of the central route, then reminded his audience that the railroad was necessary for improved communication between the coasts and for the defense of the country. He was well aware how divisive the issue of slavery in the territories had been throughout the decade. "I don't think the nigger question should come into California, and I can't understand why it does . . . California has nothing to do with it." He also put aside his own favorable opinion of the Mormons, knowing California residents felt much apprehension about them. "You may say they are polygamists and break the law," he continued, but then asked, "What law? There is nothing in the constitution and laws forbidding it. As long as the population there consists of seven-eighths Mormons and one-eighth Gentiles, they have the control of the legislature and can pass such enactments as they please." With this set-up, Lander proposed that the Pacific railroad would solve the issue by transporting enough non-Mormons into Utah to change the composition of the legislature to issue new and more favorable laws.[42]

His speech was delivered to a friendly and supportive audience, and it was received with little question or criticism. But Lander realized that it would require a tremendous effort to pass the railroad bill through Congress—a process that could take several years. He had more pressing issues to deal with in the meantime. Captain James H. Simpson of the U.S. Army challenged Lander's three-year effort on the federal cutoff, claiming that his own surveys had found a route that was 300 miles

42. "Address of Colonel F. W. Lander, on an Inter-oceanic Railroad," September 22, 1859, *San Francisco Daily Alta California*, October 1, 1859.

shorter than Lander's road. Simpson submitted his findings to the *Daily Alta California,* a San Francisco newspaper that published the letter one week after Lander's convention remarks.[43]

Lander needed to return to Washington to defend his work, but he remained in California for two more months to sell off his expended mules and some of his leftover goods. Ned had an accident while in California that incapacitated him for several weeks. Lander assisted him at his brother Charles's home in San Francisco. Fred saw Charles's three children for the first time, including an infant boy that Charles had named after his increasingly famous brother. The Lander brothers could have no idea that the fall of 1859 marked their last reunion.[44]

Frederick Lander had traversed the West seven times in seven years, establishing himself as one of the most experienced and recognized frontiersmen of the country. Not one to shy from public attention, Lander nevertheless felt a little embarrassed as a large contingent of friends escorted the superintendent and members of his party to the San Francisco wharf on Monday morning, November 21. Lander boarded the *John L. Stephens,* a steamer filled to capacity with 500 passengers, including the highest-ranking officer in the U.S. Army: Brevet Lieutenant General Winfield Scott. As the steamer began to head out at noon, Lander's boisterous party members urged all around to join them in three cheers "for Fred Lander of the Overland Wagon Road!" Lander quickly corrected the injustice. "Boys," he declared as he stepped forward, "you forget yourselves. There is only one man here to be cheered—it is the old soldier of America, perhaps bidding you farewell for the last time. I demand three times three for General Scott!" All on board complied with Lander's request.[45] General Scott must have appreciated Lander's reverence.

The trip to the Panama isthmus would take two weeks, providing Lander a perfect opportunity to establish a relationship with General Scott, the hero of two American wars. But the *John L. Stephens* ran into rough water almost immediately after pulling away from its dock. As the Pacific waters tossed the steamer without mercy, a reporter on the excur-

43. Captain J. H. Simpson to editor, September, 1859, *San Francisco Daily Alta California,* September 27, 1859.

44. Edward Lander Jr., to FWL, December 19, 1859, LP 1:6088–90; Shahrani, "Wagon Roads—1859 Season," 140–1. Lander's nephew and namesake died in 1860.

45. "Col. Fred. W. Lander, the Pacific Railroad Explorer and Engineer," *Frank Leslie's Illustrated Newspaper,* April 6, 1861.

sion noted with bemusement that although Lander was "possessed of the form of a Hercules, he was no match for old Neptune." Almost immediately Lander lay on his back, groaning with seasickness. Between episodes of vomiting, he managed to confess that despite all the hardships he suffered on the plains and in the mountains, this was the most miserable he ever felt.[46]

Thus, the descendent of famous seamen exhibited to all that he had broken completely away from family tradition.

46. "Life on Board the John L. Stephens," November 27, 1859, newspaper clipping, LP.

3

"You've Got Pluck"

Fair Girl
> With all that Fame accords,
> Wilt thou not claim a gentler part?
>> A name that rests with hallowed words
> Traced on the tablets of the heart?

Thou should not scorn it—portals wide,
> For sympathies thou spirits know
Who climb ambition's mountain side,
> And gaze upon their kind below
>>>> —F. W. Lander

In the six years that spanned 1854–1859, Frederick Lander's railroad and wagon road expeditions, captivating speeches, and notorious fist fights attracted newspaper coverage throughout the country. In 1860, his became a household name from events that were both astounding and notorious. "Old Grizzly" initiated the new decade with a roar that resonated throughout Washington, and in the same style he had demonstrated in his previous three sojourns in the capital.

The year began very well for Lander, for he was quickly able to defuse the controversy over his cutoff. Captain James Simpson, who claimed to have discovered a shorter route for emigrants the previous autumn, received a letter from Lander on February 2. In it Lander reminded the captain about a separate letter written by former Kit Carson guide Tim Goodale, who admitted that both Lander's and Simpson's routes had merit, but Lander's was superior for driving stock, as was common for emigrant travel. Using this opinion from an experienced and knowledgeable explorer, Lander asked Simpson, "Are you ready to advocate [your route] as suitable for the ox-team emigration?" Simpson wrote a letter one week later, admitting that his road was better used as a mail route than an emigrant road.[1]

Lander included both letters in a report of the Fort Kearney, South Pass, and Honey Lake Wagon Road that he submitted on March 1. Proud of his accomplishments and three years of work on the road, Lander was further supported by the emigrants' resounding satisfaction with the route. Of the 13,000 emigrants who chose Lander's cutoff in 1859, 9,000 signed a paper to endorse their approval of it.[2] Lander now saw only one obstacle to complete support of his accomplishments. That obstacle was William M. F. Magraw.

Throughout the 1859 season, while Lander was negotiating with Indians and improving the road, he learned that Magraw had made a great effort to denigrate him in front of anyone who would listen. This occurred in Missouri, near Great Salt Lake City, and even along Lander's road. Major Yates, whom Lander had placed at South Pass to promote the trail throughout the year, encountered Magraw at the end of 1859 and heard the former superintendent boast that he had whipped Lander in the Willard's Hotel fight the previous March. When Yates arrived in Washington early in 1860, he passed the information on to Lander.[3]

Fuming and out of control, Lander learned on March 6 that Magraw was back in Washington. Lander addressed a note to him, demanding a retraction and an apology for the assertions leveled at him. Magraw refused to read the note, provoking Lander to attempt vindication by other means. Learning that Magraw was staying at the Kirkwood House, a hotel on the corner of Twelfth Street and Pennsylvania Avenue, Lander and Yates arrived there late in the afternoon of March 7.

1. FWL to Simpson, February 2, 1860, in HR 64; Simpson to the editor, February 8, 1860, *Constitution*, February 11, 1860, newspaper clipping, LP 10.

2. FWL to Jacob Thompson, March 1, 1860, in HR 64; Shahrani, "Wagon Roads—1859 Season," 142.

3. FWL to unknown addressee, n.d, LP 1:7511; newspaper clippings, LP 10; Edmund L. Yates to FWL, January 26, 1860, LP 1:6102–3.

Magraw was stepping out of a carriage in front of the Kirkwood House and approaching the steps with some friends when Lander intercepted him. Pointing to Yates, Lander yelled to Magraw, "I demand from you an explanation of your remarks to this gentleman." Magraw stepped back on the steps and muttered something as he put his hand against his pocket. Lander was uncontrollable. "Speak up, and speak loud, Sir!" he seethed as he struck Magraw on his chest and pushed him backward. Magraw entered the hotel with Lander following close behind.

Lander would not allow Magraw any room to maneuver within the hotel entrance. He grabbed Magraw around the shoulder and yanked him, shouting for all to hear, "Turn around now, sir, and face me, and answer me!" Mr. Kirkwood, the proprietor of the hotel, refused to allow any scene to be created within his establishment and quickly interposed himself between the two to prevent a fistfight. Motioning to the women watching from the floor above them, Kirkwood asked Lander not to create a disturbance. Lander desisted and allowed Magraw to back up. But as Magraw distanced himself by ten steps, he reached into his pocket and for the second time in consecutive years, he pulled out a weapon. This time he drew a revolver. Pointing the gun directly at Lander, Magraw warned him, "Approach me again, sir, and you are a dead man."

"Old Grizzly" snapped with rage at Magraw's method of retaliation. He leaped forward and roared, "I am unarmed, you scoundrel, but no matter." Kirkwood stepped into his path. Lander composed himself for a moment, but could not let the matter drop. He beckoned Magraw to step outside where he would take him on in the avenue, weapon notwithstanding. Magraw said and did nothing, prompting Lander to taunt him as a liar, thief, blackguard, and scoundrel. None of Lander's epithets took effect. Lander then dared anyone in the crowd of Magraw's entourage to meet his challenge. Getting no response, Lander made sure everyone knew a summary of the events: "You have refused my challenge . . . you have struck me with a billy and were whipped by me for it, and you have lied to the contrary; and now you scoundrel, you have refused a scratch fight; you with a loaded pistol and I unarmed." Lander pointedly told Magraw that this would be their last confrontation. Before he left, Lander apologized to Mr. Kirkwood, begged his leave of the ladies, and exited the building.[4]

4. Newspaper clippings, LP 10. The incident was recorded in three newspaper accounts

Another controversy reared up at the same time Lander was settling his differences with Magraw. Secretary Thompson informed him that the California delegation in Congress was trying to replace him as superintendent with one of their own constituents. Lander ignored the politicians and set out to prepare for another season of work on the third section of the wagon road. He answered Congress's questions about his railroad survey in the last week of March, then he sent his cousin, William West, by steamer to California on April 5 to prepare for the arrival of Lander and the rest of his party not already encamped near Honey Lake. Shortly afterward, the California delegation brazenly asked Lander to help them secure the appointment of their selection, claiming that an experienced engineer like Lander was not needed this season. Thompson disagreed and felt Lander's expertise was indeed imperative. He overrode the desires of select congressmen and assured Lander that he would head westward in a matter of a few weeks.[5]

But Lander's confrontation with Congress had not ended. On April 5, Illinois Republican Owen Lovejoy stood to address a House of Representatives so politically charged and sectionally divided that members carried weapons into the chambers and supporters did likewise in the galleries. Years of compromise between North and South were wearing thin. A recent example of how divided the country had become had occurred the previous October when John Brown attempted to spark a slave insurrection at Harpers Ferry. The zealot was captured and subsequently hanged, northern abolitionists hailing him as a martyr and southern secessionists labeling him a villain. Moderate voices seemed to weaken with each passing month. By April, those voices were nearly inaudible.

The theme of Lovejoy's speech, the evils of slavery, fanned the flames already burning within the House. As Lovejoy gesticulated about the wickedness of slavery, he entered the point of no return when he advanced toward the Democratic benches and expressed the opinion that the doc-

---

kept by Lander. One was written by Major Yates, the only known eyewitness who recorded the event.

5. "The Pacific Railroad," *New York Times,* March 28, 1860; Shahrani, "Wagon Roads—1859 Season," 148; FWL to Thompson, April 9, 1860 LP 1:6111–12; FWL to Joseph Lane, March, 1860, LP 1:6106; Lansing Front to FWL, April 5, 1860, LP 1:6108–9; FWL to Thompson, April 11, 1860, LP 1:6113–14; FWL to Senators and Representatives of the State of California, April 12, 1860, newspaper clipping, LP 10.

trine of slavery existed "no place in the universe outside the five points of hell and the Democratic party."

Virginia Democrat Roger Pryor had heard enough. Offended by Lovejoy's rants, Pryor rose from his seat and berated him for his "treasonable and insulting language." Wisconsin Republican John F. Potter jumped to Lovejoy's aid, declaring that the Democrats had been guilty of the same language during a recent House struggle to select a speaker. Within minutes, several members of the House were on their feet in the central floor. Mississippi Democrat William Barksdale shouted toward Lovejoy, "Order that black-hearted scoundrel and nigger-stealing thief to take his seat and this side of the House will do it." Order was quickly restored, but Pryor could not get the incident out of his head, particularly when he read Potter's corrected version of his words in the *Congressional Globe* six days later. He challenged Potter to a duel and set the ground in Virginia (dueling was illegal in Washington).

Potter quickly accepted Pryor's challenge and, knowing that the Virginian was an expert marksman, chose Bowie knives as the dueling weapons. Word of the duel spread through the capital; Lander quickly learned of it. Lander had struck up a friendship with Potter from previous stays in the capital. Although a Democrat by family tradition, Lander did not see the situation as political. He wrote Potter on the night of the eleventh, "However we may differ in politics I believe in the right of any American citizen to speak his mind without being annoyed by any ruffian of any party," thus offering his service to the Republican. Potter gratefully accepted, and Lander acted as his go-between to deliver late night messages to Pryor's people. Additionally, Lander prepared a chronology of the affair with a compilation of notes he gave to Potter.

The duel never occurred. Pryor objected to Potter's selection of Bowie knives and sent his principle to declare them as a "vulgar, barbarous, and inhuman mode of settling difficulties." Lander quickly offered to take Potter's place (without consulting the Wisconsin congressman), upping the ante by not restricting location or weapons. Pryor's second, T. P. Chrisman, refused Lander's challenge and the affair ended with no duel.

The press refused to let the matter go away. Newspapers quickly published the written exchanges between the principles. Smaller papers throughout the country scooped up the original accounts in the New York and Washington dailies. Potter received much positive press throughout the exchange. Admiring friends reportedly presented him with a Bowie knife with the phrase "Always ready for a Pryor engagement" inscribed on the blade. Not surprisingly, the northern press derided Pryor as a coward.[6]

The greatest beneficiary of the nonevent was Frederick W. Lander. He was mistakenly credited with choosing the Bowie knives. By not correcting the error, Lander basked in the attention created by the trumped-up affair. By the third week of April, a large readership learned how this brazen explorer had offered to sacrifice himself as a second to protect the principle of free speech. Editors found Lander fascinating and published his biography under such titles as "Who Col. Lander Is" and "The New Fighting Hero." Acquaintances of Lander stepped up to laud his exploits. One friend indicated that Lander "has far more Presidential material in him than a dozen Frémonts," referring to noted explorer John C. Frémont, the Republican Party's first presidential candidate, who had lost to Buchanan in 1856.[7]

Lander never shied from publicity but was pleasantly surprised at the groundswell of attention he received in the matter. While in New York a few days after the event, Lander heard a midnight serenade performed by admirers and a band that had gathered outside the Metropolitan Hotel where he was staying. He appeared on the balcony and addressed the well-wishers with mock surprise, asking why the throng had called him forth in such a charming way. "Because you've got pluck," came the reply from a voice in the crowd, followed by throaty cheers of affirmation.[8]

Lander's stay in New York was brief. He had received his instructions from Secretary Thompson on April 16 to work on the third section of the Fort Kearney, South Pass, and Honey Lake Wagon Road. Lander's attention was to be focused on the section of road west of City of Rocks where

6. Bruce Catton, *The Coming Fury* (New York, 1961), 22–3; FWL to Potter, March 22, 1859, April 11, 12, 13, 14, 1860, John Fox Potter Collection, State Historical Society of Wisconsin, Madison; Ben A. Riley, "The Pryor-Potter Affair: Nineteenth Century Civilian Conflict as Precursor to Civil War," *Journal of West Virginia Historical Association* 8 (1984): 30–9; L. A. Gobright, *Recollections of Men and Things at Washington, During the Third of a Century,* Rev. ed. (Philadelphia, 1869), 193–6; "The Potter-Pryor Quarrel," newspaper clipping, PDV; "Pryor Shows the White Feather" and "Mr. Potter and the Code," newspaper clippings, both LP 10.

7. "Who Col. Lander Is," newspaper clipping, LP 10; "The New Fighting Hero—Graphic Historical Sketch of Col. Lander—'Old Grizzly,'" *San Francisco Daily Evening Bulletin,* May 15, 1860.

8. Newspaper clipping, PDV; "Serenade to Col. F. W. Lander," *New York Herald,* April 20, 1860.

he was to do light grading, remove obstacles, and—most important—construct water reservoirs in the dry and arid Nevada country. Thompson obtained $40,000 to provide his superintendent for the season's work. Lander, with members of his crew in tow, boarded the *North Star* on Friday, April 20. Disembarking under a canopy of coconut trees at the eastern end of the Panama isthmus, Lander and the rest of the California-bound passengers reboarded the steamer, *Golden Age,* on the Pacific side of the isthmus and headed toward San Francisco on April 29.[9]

The trip from Panama to San Francisco took two weeks (by this time, Lander was able to stomach the voyage). Of the 826 passengers traveling with Lander on the *Golden Age,* none captured his interests more than a British native who celebrated her thirty-first birthday on the steamer. Lander shared her birthday with her; before the year closed he had determined to share the rest of his life with her.

Her name was Jean Margaret Davenport, a name that was at least as recognizable in early 1860 as that of her beau. Born in Wolverhampton in Staffordshire, England, Jean made her first appearance in the Richmond Theatre at the age of seven. Her father, a former lawyer who ran the theater, allowed her to perform in Ireland and Scotland in addition to her native England. It did not take long for the gifted child to earn the sobriquet "The Little Dramatic Prodigy." In 1838 she traveled to the United States and performed there for four years before returning to Europe to act in Holland and Germany. She also studied music. While she was still a teenager, Jean Davenport's name graced the broadsides for "The Countess" and "The Hunchback." In 1849 she emigrated to the United States with her mother to resume her acting career in the country she had come to love during her earlier visit.

Theatergoers in the United States, including Fred Lander, were instantly captivated by Jean Davenport. Lander had made her a subject of his poetry as early as 1850, ostensibly after seeing her perform in Boston. Jean lived with her mother in a house in Lynn, Massachusetts, in the early 1850s. It probably was there that Lander, whose family lived nearby, met her at social events when he stayed with relatives and friends between western explorations. In 1855, Miss Davenport relocated to California with her mother (her father died in 1851); from there she took two

9. Thompson to FWL, April 16, 1860, WR, 268–70; newspaper clippings, PDV and LP 10; "Arrival of the 'Golden Age,'" *San Francisco Weekly Herald,* May 17, 1860.

cruises to England and continued to perform on the stage to appreciative audiences and favorable reviews.

Fred Lander, though always attracted to the young actress, spent more time in Washington social circles between western trips in the mid- and late 1850s than in Davenport's company. In fact, rumors spoke of his engagement to Josephine Chesney, another beautiful young actress. But Lander's four-week cruise with Jean Davenport in the spring of 1860 confirmed a relationship anchored by strong roots. In 1857 the couple became engaged.[10] Neither gave a wedding date to family or friends.

By the time the *Golden Age* docked at San Francisco on May 13, Lander had learned that his work on the western segment of the road would be more arduous than he had anticipated. Shortly before Lander left Washington, he had received a letter from a western rancher complaining that the Northern Paiute (referred to as Pah-Utah or Pah-Ute in period correspondences) had stirred up a conflict by stealing goods and killing three settlers. He claimed that Winnemucca, the chief, had received the settlers and heard their grievances. The settlers requested that Winnemucca release the murderers to the white men, but the chief refused and went on to demand that the settlers pay him $16,000 to prevent further plunder in the Humboldt River Valley. The situation boiled over on May 7 when Paiutes and Bannocks killed several white inhabitants at a Carson River stop called Williams Station. The incident initiated the Pyramid Lake War; four detachments of volunteers set off to sack Paiute villages under their motto: "An Indian for breakfast and a pony to ride." The volunteers marched into a trap near Pyramid Lake on May 12. The Paiutes, with a loss of only three wounded, killed 46 of the 105 whites. The fiasco touched off a panic that reached the Pacific Coast at the same time as Lander's arrival there.[11]

California newspaper correspondents sought out Lander's opinion on

10. T. S. Pugh, *Biographical Sketch of Mrs. F. W. Lander, Formerly Miss Jean M. Davenport, Tragedienne, with Criticisms of the Press on Her Rendition of Elizabeth, Queen of England* (Philadelphia, 1867), 3–4; Wilson and Fiske, *Appleton's Cyclopaedia,* vol. 3, 604; Garraty and Carnes, *American National Biography,* vol. 13, 103; Biographical Note of Jean Margaret (Davenport) Lander, LP; Kate Sperry journal, March 7, 1862, Handley Library Archives Room, Winchester, Va.; newspaper clippings, LP 10.

11. Alice Baldrica, "Lander and the Settlement of the Pyramid Lake War," in *Frederick West Lander: A Biographical Sketch (1822–1862),* ed. Joy Leland (Reno, Nev., 1993), 161; Myron Angel, ed., *History of Nevada* (Oakland, Calif., 1881), 151–8.

the uprising, knowing that the conflict was bound to affect his road work. Lander downplayed the activity by claiming that he believed there were fewer Indians than reported, but he also did not want to travel to the hostile area unprepared. Lander officially requested side arms for his men plus forty rifles from the temporary commander of the California militia, but his petition was denied on the grounds that he was not a military officer. Refusing to embark on his mission unarmed, Lander purchased the weapons using wagon road funds. He altered his plans for the upcoming season, knowing that it would be difficult to contract out the road work in hostile territory. Instead, Lander requested from Secretary Thompson $10,000 to pay for a handpicked crew and to arm them. "The line of duty you have prescribed for me leads the expedition into the most dangerous part of the Indian territory," he warned Thompson. After a mere eleven days of preparation, Lander left Sacramento on May 24 with a crew of forty, eight covered wagons, fifty-seven mules, and twenty-seven Spanish horses.[12]

Anticipating a trip that would start out averaging twenty to thirty miles per day, the expedition party crawled at eight miles per day. The emigrant road they had heard so much about was little more than a blazed trail. Once they ascended the Sierra Nevada range, heavy snow held them up at the summit for several days. Short on hay and grain, Lander sent his horses and mules forward under the charge of James Snyder to the next valley while he and the rest of his crew shoveled a path through the snow for the wagons.

Emigrant trains passed them on their journey to the coast. Lander's men heard their tales about the Paiutes. Estimates of their numbers ran as high as 3,000 warriors. One member of the party took heart in the estimate of his boss. "Superintendent Lander thinks . . . that not over six hundred can be concentrated and sustain themselves for a week at any one point," he informed a California newspaper on June 2.[13] The correspondent failed to highlight the point that if Lander was accurate, the Indians still outnumbered the expedition crew by more than ten to one.

On June 4, Lander and his men moved eastward from the crest of the Sierra Nevada and entered Honey Lake Valley eight days later. He was

12. FWL to Thompson, May 18, 1860, WR 4; Baldrica, "Settlement of the Pyramid Lake War," 166–7.
13. "Oro" to the editor, June 2, 1860, *Sacramento Daily Union,* June 8, 1860.

greeted there by his cousin, Charles West. The editor of the *Territorial Enterprise* also met Lander, a key subject for his Virginia City newspaper. Always seeking publicity, Lander allowed a few journalists to accompany his expedition. E. D. Knight was one of the reporters who had been with the party since mid-May; he authored frequent dispatches, which found their way into several California newspapers. Knight took careful note of the region's panic. "The residents of the valley are delighted to see the Colonel, and are anxious that he should use his men and arms in protecting them from the Indians," he wrote to the *Sacramento Daily Bee,* "What his plan of operations will be I am unable to say, as he has not disclosed them to us yet."[14]

Lander needed to devise a plan immediately. On the night of June 12, news entered camp that a party of eleven prospectors had been driven from Smokey Canyon by 300 natives, losing all their wagons and provisions. The region from which they had been driven stood directly in the path of Lander's prospective road work. As the men somberly listened near the campfire that night, Lander spelled out what he intended all of them to do:

> Gentlemen, you know that we are under orders from the Department to execute this work. I have always entertained the belief that we should meet the Indians in force on our march, after their having been driven north by the troops. They are now before us. I might feel justified in turning back, as Mr. Noble turned back year before last in Minnesota, and as Captain Mullen, an old explorer, [did] in Washington Territory, both of whom were Superintendents of overland roads. . . . We shall simply obey orders and go on. I rely on you who have been with me before, and the twenty men armed with Sharp's rifles to do the fighting. I have every confidence that you will stay with me to the last. If we are not strong enough to win, we are at least enough to do as every American gentleman should do—stay upon the ground.[15]

Lander had prepared to settle the Paiute conflict before he left California. He procured an interpreter to arrange a meeting with Chief Winnemucca. The arrival in Sacramento of Major Frederick Dodge, an Indian agent sent with special instructions from the Department of the Interior, changed those plans. Lander was also disappointed in his attempt to acquire locals

14. Knight to the editor, June 13, 1860, *Sacramento Daily Bee,* June 20, 1860.
15. "Oro" to the editor, June 13, 1860, *Sacramento Daily Union,* June 23, 1860.

to add to his numbers and balance the strength of the Paiutes. He discussed the situation with Isaac Roop, territorial governor of Nevada, on the morning of June 13, but learned in two days that no citizen was volunteering to join his crew. His expressman, who was to bring back valuable information from Carson City, disappeared. Adding to the difficulties was Lander's health; he had been suffering from severe chills and vomiting episodes. Believing that the coming expedition would "bring me up," Lander wrote Ned on Sunday night, June 17, to announce that he would be going after Winnemucca's Paiutes. "We travel with packs, single blankets, and a saddle, dried beef for rations—in my old style of '54," Fred explained. "I go because it is necessary to clean out the Indians before I can move a wagon train down the road. . . . We shall take to the mountains and approach in their own style."[16]

Lander's mission took an unexpected turn the following day. While finalizing preparations at camp on Monday afternoon, word reached the men that the Paiutes had murdered a cattle owner named Horace Adams, whose farm was located twenty miles below Lander's camp. In less than half an hour, Lander armed twenty men and led them to the site to ascertain the Indians' route. Riding all night, the men returned to camp, packed their horses, then set out with thirty-seven men from Lander's party and twenty-five stalwarts from Captain William M. Weatherlow's Honey Lake Rangers. The force of sixty-two, armed with Sharps and Colt revolvers, headed northward to Willow Creek.

The party discovered moccasin tracks while crossing a sandy desert and followed their direction westward. On the morning of June 23, Lander spied an Indian waiting in ambush and suggested to Captain Weatherlow that they flank the high ground to cut off the Paiutes. Captain Weatherlow concurred and left orders to climb a rocky hillside, then he rode ahead with a scout into the canyon where the Indian had fled. Weatherlow's second in command mistook the orders as a direct push into the canyon and led the men forward. Lander was unable to correct the error with the lieutenant and dutifully followed, but once the men entered the rocky walls of the canyon, towering hundreds of feet above them, Lander shouted, "Remember, gentlemen! I do not bear the responsibility."[17]

16. Isaac Roop to FWL, June 13, 1860, LP 1:6137–8; FWL to Isaac Roop, June 14, 1860, LP 1:6139–40; FWL to Ned Lander, June 16, 1860, newspaper clipping, LP 10.
17. E. D. Knight to the editor, July 2, 1860, *San Francisco Daily Alta California*, July 17, 1860; "Oro" to the editor, June 23, 1860, newspaper clipping, LP 10.

Captain Weatherlow returned to the men only to discover that the mistake his lieutenant made could not be rectified. The party marched through the canyon with Lander riding in front, accompanied by James A. Snyder, Captain Weatherlow, and a ranger named Alexander Painter. Near the mouth of the canyon a party of Indians, concealed behind the rocky canyon walls, fired at the head of the column. The bullets whizzed by Lander, but Painter was struck in the chest. As the Paiutes blazed away at them, Lander barked orders for his men to spread out and return fire. He directed several men to charge the eastern wall, then wheeled his horse toward the western wall of the canyon—where the gunfire originated—and headed toward the Indians' flank with ten men. In a matter of minutes they dislodged the natives, who retreated toward the mountains. Lander moved his party out of the canyon and onto a vast plain, where he and his men encamped. Painter, the only casualty of the day, died during the night.

Early the following morning the Paiutes reappeared on the rocky hill over which they had fled the previous day. Lander tried to decoy them; he occupied a smaller hill jutting from the main eminence the Indians occupied and sent a flanking party of ten men to ride around the opposite side of the hill. Lander, with fifteen men, coaxed twenty-five Paiutes down the hillside, where they engaged in a brisk skirmish fire. The Indians discovered Lander's plan before he could cut them off, and they fled. Lander and his men watched them ride to join the rest of the marauders in the distance. It appeared to the naked eye that the Paiutes numbered nearly 300.

Lander felt that the opportunity was ripe to settle the conflict peacefully. Leaving his rifle in plain view propped against a cedar tree, Lander grabbed a flag and rode out toward the foot of the mountain in an effort to precipitate a meeting with their chief. Instead of coming forward to negotiate peacefully with him, several armed Paiutes crept cautiously toward the unarmed Lander. Lander's men put an end to the stalking, and the Indians, under fire again, fled into an inaccessible canyon. At dusk, one of the warriors—believed to be involved in the murder of rancher Adams—was flushed out into the open. After a spirited chase by two of Lander's men, the native was gunned down, then dragged back to the camp to the cheers of the white party and the angry yells of the Indians who had witnessed the incident from a distant hill.[18]

18. E. D. Knight to the editor, July 2, 1860, *San Francisco Daily Alta California*, July

The two-week mission ended on June 30 when Lander and his party returned to Honey Lake. Although they had neither destroyed the Indians nor settled affairs peacefully with them, Lander maintained that the Indians' spirit was broken by what occurred in the canyon country and felt it was safe enough to reembark on the road work. After a festive Independence Day celebration, the crew set out on July 5.[19]

By the end of the month Lander and his men had split up into smaller parties to cover a wider area around the 450 miles of road. They bridged one waterway and improved four watering stops by lining the bottom of the spring with rocks to prevent it from drying up, and by sinking wells and holding tanks where necessary. At Hot Springs in the Black Rock Desert, the crew diverted the water into a cooling reservoir. Lander advertised the improvement by erecting a signpost at the crossroads east of the spring.

Just to the east of the crossroads was Rabbit Hole Springs—a sight of extreme frustration for the emigrant. Three separate springs poured water into one pond, but the water was almost instantly reabsorbed into the desert, preventing travelers and their animals from drinking there. Consequently, grass disappeared by summertime while carcasses and skeletons ominously littered the perimeter, forcing emigrants to trek another forty miles to find a decent water supply. Lander and his men spent three weeks at the springs, working into August to capture the water in a huge cement reservoir. While this work was carried out, another crew improved Antelope Springs, the watering hole closest to the Humboldt River.[20]

While working in the sweltering heat at Rabbit Hole Springs, Lander received promising news about settling the Paiute conflict. His assistant commissary agent, George H. Butler, captured five Northern Paiute near the Humboldt River. Knowing that Lander wanted an interview with Winnemucca, Butler interrogated the captives and learned that they were well informed about the wagon road expedition and also wished to make peace with the whites. Butler released two of them after he was promised that they would return with their immediate leader, a Paiute named

---

17, 1860; "Oro" to the editor, June 23, 1860, newspaper clipping, LP 10; James A Snyder to the editor, July 2, 1860, newspaper clipping, LP 10.

19. FWL to the editor, July 7, 1860, newspaper clipping, LP 10.

20. Baldrica, "Settlement of the Pyramid Lake War," 174–6; E. D. Knight to the editor, July 31, 1860, *San Francisco Daily Alta California*, August 3, 1860; Robert Amesbury, *Nobles' Emigrant Trail* (Susansville, Calif., 1967), 14–19.

Naanah. The news pleased Lander. His patience had worn thin, and he felt confident that discussing the situation with Naanah would lead to an interview with Winnemucca. He predicted that if no settlement was reached soon, the emigrants would be in constant and grave danger.

Lander met Naanah on the Humboldt on August 12. Together, they proposed a truce: The Paiutes would end hostilities for the year, and Lander would persuade the U.S. government to pay them for lands that the whites had taken from them. Unfortunately, Naanah's jurisdiction was limited to his band, which numbered fewer than thirty Paiutes. Lander realized that an effective truce could only be accomplished by negotiating with Winnemucca, the leader of all the Northern Paiutes. Naanah agreed and sent messengers to find Winnemucca at his camp near Pyramid Lake. Naanah was true to his word. Lander and Winnemucca would meet on August 21 at Deep Hole Springs, fifty miles west of Honey Lake.[21]

On his return to Deep Hole Springs from the Humboldt, Lander witnessed the effectiveness of his labors. Passing Rabbit Hole Springs, he discovered that the masonry tank that his crew built was working to perfection. Eighty thousand gallons of water swirled in the tank, six feet deep. New grass sprouted from previously barren ground, and waterfowl floated in the reservoir. Pleased at the accomplishment, Lander later reported the Rabbit Hole Springs project to be "one of the most peculiar results I have ever had the opportunity of recording during the conduct of many explorations and works in the wild interior."[22]

On the appointed date, both parties arrived early to the meeting site, but Winnemucca insisted on waiting until sunset to speak with Lander. While they waited, Lander and his men took note of the chief and the band he led. "In appearance he is all that romance could desire," marveled one of Lander's crew, "deep-chested, strong-limbed, with a watchful, earnest expression of countenance, indicative of graver thought and study common to the aboriginal race."[23] The war chief went by two names. Often referred to as Winnemucca, he was in fact the second leader to carry that name. An older "Winnemucca" resided in the Smoke Creek Desert and led as the shaman of all the Northern Paiute. The shared names be-

21. Baldrica, "Settlement of the Pyramid Lake War," 177, 179.

22. FWL to Jacob Thompson, October 31, 1860, LP 1:6150.

23. "Voltigeur" to the editor, September 4, 1860, *San Francisco Daily Alta California*, September 10, 1860.

tween the older and younger Winnemucca bred confusion, forcing some to use their less common names of Poito for the elder Winnemucca, and Numaga for the younger chief.

The Paiutes ate a meal prepared by Lander's men, and—as the sun dipped beneath the western horizon—Lander and Numaga sat side by side at the far end of a tent with Lander's men on the right and Numaga's men on the left. Interpreters took their places in the center. All watched in silence as Lander and Numaga lit their pipes and smoked without speaking a word. Lander initiated the talks by stating that he had come only as a listener who could make no promises. He then asked the chief to list his grievances in a straightforward manner for Lander to relay to the "Great Father" in Washington.

Numaga told Lander that he was pleased to hear no promises from him because no previous promises by the whites had ever been kept. The chief acknowledged that he could not prevent some of the roaming bands of Paiutes from killing the settlers at Williams Station in May, but pointedly noted that the "Great Father" in Washington also lacked the power to keep whites from massacring Indians at a California reserve. Lander then pointed out that many eastern tribes farmed their lands and asked Numaga if the Paiutes would be interested in farming and herding cattle. Numaga remained defensive; he replied that the Paiutes wished to learn how to farm their lands but this was another promise that was broken by the white man. The chief then rattled off a litany of grievances to demonstrate to Lander that his men had no choice but to retaliate against the white man's offenses.

Lander tried to carry the discussion away from the past and into the future. In an attempt to extend the promise made by Naanah, Lander requested that Numaga restrain his men from all acts of hostility against the whites for one year. In the meantime, Lander would relay Numaga's concerns to the "Great Father" in Washington and would work to produce a treaty that would guarantee the Northern Paiutes not only the possession of the lands they currently held, but also those lands seized from them through western expansion. Numaga acquiesced to the proposal and promised to bring Poito (the elder Winnemucca) to meet with Indian agent Frederick Dodge to produce a more lasting truce.[24]

24. Several versions, some apocryphal, describe the negotiations between Lander and Numaga. For a detailed discussion of what took place, as well as a picture of young

Barely an hour had passed when Lander and Numaga bid each other good night after negotiating their tentative agreement. The chief and his followers spent the night in Lander's camp. The next morning the whites and Indians parted ways. Lander and his crew covered the fifty miles back to Honey Lake in two days and quickly spread the word that a peace was reached. Public meetings were arranged, producing resolutions to maintain the peace that Lander had worked out with Numaga. Copies of these pledges were read in newspapers throughout Nevada Territory and California. In the meantime, Lander bid adieu to the prominent settlers of the area, then presented Captain Weatherlow with a fine Sharps rifle in a respectful ceremony. On September 5, Lander and his crew crossed the Sierra Nevada into California.[25] The next day he rode into the town of Oroville.

Nearly one year earlier, Lander had strode into California and had barely had time to shake the dust out of his clothes before he addressed the public with an inspiring speech about the transcontinental railroad. History repeated itself eleven months later. A special convention was held at Oroville on the evening of September 6, just hours after Lander entered the town. The Democratic Party in California had split into factions in several cities to select delegates to serve in the electoral college after the national presidential election in November. But in 1860 the states were far from united; North and South had drifted so far apart that few believed that they could ever share similar ideals. The North was by and large more supportive of the new Republican Party. Their candidate was Abraham Lincoln, an Illinois lawyer who had made a name for himself in his campaign for the senate in 1858 (a hard-fought race he eventually lost to Stephen A. Douglas).

Unlike the Republicans, the Democratic Party was severely divided, as were their constituents. In April of 1860 the national Democratic convention had met in South Carolina but splintered into quarreling factions over the same issue that was dividing the country—the institution of slavery. After a proslavery platform was rejected in Charleston, South Carolina, delegates from eight southern states departed and the convention adjourned without selecting a candidate. The party reconvened in Baltimore in June, but delegates from four states—including California—walked out

Winnemucca, see Alice Baldrica's well-researched monograph "Settlement of the Pyramid Lake War," in Leland, *Lander,* 155 (n), 178, 180–2.

25. Petition to FWL, August 29, 1860, LP 1:6142; "Voltigeur" to the editor, September 4, 1860, *San Francisco Daily Alta California,* September 10, 1860.

when some of the original southern state dissenters were denied readmission. The remaining state delegates selected Stephen Douglas as the Democratic nominee. The southern defectors eventually selected Vice President John C. Breckinridge as their candidate, one who supported their platform that called for the protection of the right to own slaves. John Bell, a moderate southern Democrat, was nominated by a group composed mostly of former Whigs. The three Democrats competing for votes in the same election seemingly assured Republican Abraham Lincoln of the presidency, a result that seemed likely to provoke secession by southern state representatives.[26]

California's miniconventions in September also resulted from the divisiveness in the Democratic Party. Frederick Lander, although priding himself on being a staunch Democrat, nevertheless was disheartened by the party's fractionation. He was faced with a dilemma in 1860: which candidate would he support? He owed his employment to the Buchanan administration, where Breckinridge was second in command. But Lander was an ardent Unionist, and most Breckinridge Democrats appeared to be southern secessionists. Still, Lander's support remained in Breckinridge's direction because of the platform under which he was nominated. This platform included ideals that resonated within Lander; it specifically stated the plan to construct a railroad from the Mississippi to the Pacific Coast.[27] Although the platform supported slavery, Lander believed Breckinridge to be a Unionist like himself and considered this paramount over "the peculiar institution" of slave labor.

Because California delegates selected Breckinridge at the national level, most of the California towns held Breckinridge conventions in September, although Douglas was still guaranteed votes by the party. Lander's presence in Oroville on September 6 coincided with a meeting of Breckinridge supporters there. Enjoying tremendous popularity in California, Lander was courted by the Breckinridge faithful—consisting mostly of enthusiastic young men—to address their organization. He spoke extemporaneously that night, just as he had done at the railroad convention, and his presentation once again captivated his audience. "His speech was characterized by profound thought, soundness of views, strong argument, and felicity of expression," reported a newspaper correspondent. "For a man

26. James M. McPherson, *Battle Cry of Freedom* (New York, 1988), 213–30.
27. Catton, *Coming Fury,* 77.

to make so good a speech as he did on the spur of the moment and without any preparation whatever, evinces an order of talent which we had not previously supposed the Colonel to possess."[28]

Following Frémont's path, Lander had become an attractive political figure in his own right. Handsome, strong, and fearless, an adept negotiator with what was considered to be hostile Paiutes, and an intelligent and gifted orator, Lander embodied most of the attributes necessary for a successful political life. The Breckinridge Club recognized this, and they asked Lander to be Butte County's representative in the Breckinridge State Convention. Lander at first declined, citing his lack of knowledge on local candidates for the office of electors. Still, Lander made his way to Sacramento where the state Breckinridge convention was held on September 11. The correspondence between Lander and the Oroville club was entered into the official minutes. He learned of a motion made by a San Francisco delegate for Lander to have a seat at the convention, but he also found out that he was a political figure surrounded by controversy.

Some delegates spoke up against Lander because they could neither forget nor forgive Lander's notorious support of northern Republican John Potter against the Virginia Democrat Roger Pryor the previous April. "I am at a loss to know why this convention should compliment Colonel Lander," complained J. C. Manter, a delegate from Tuolomne. "Some of the actions of Colonel Lander should not meet with the approval of this convention, and I do not think that we should be called upon to approve them." Despite the dissent, Lander won admission to the convention by an overwhelming vote.[29]

Lander's foray into the Breckinridge convention exposed his paradoxical nature. His temper exploded on hearing of Manter's dissent. As a result, Lander impetuously challenged the delegate to a duel. Lander's modus operandi to settle a dispute took diverging paths. He grew famous for his ability to peacefully negotiate with Numaga, and he grew infamous for attempting to settle disputes with Senator Pryor and William M. F. Magraw with bloodshed. In this instance, Manter was spared; Lander reconsidered before he sent the official letter of challenge.[30]

28. Newspaper clippings, LP 10.
29. FWL to members of the Breckinridge Club, September 11, 1860, Scrapbook; *Sacramento Daily Union*, September 12, 1860; *Sacramento Daily News*, September 12, 1860.
30. FWL to [J. C. Manter], n.d., LP 1:6127–8; "Duels," newspaper clipping, LP 10.

Lander's politics also betrayed an internal conflict. Aligning himself with Breckinridge publicized his support of slavery. Lander did not mince words when he stated his reasons in a letter published in the *Marysville Daily National Democrat* on September 29:

> I said, that the dicta of the Republican party, in an endeavor to confine slavery to the old States of the Union, was a terrible aggression upon the North. As an idea, it was the erection of the bulwark against the grand column of free labor yearly reinforced by 100,000 white men from Europe. These working men were passing down into the border slave states, renovating the worn out farms of Virginia, Maryland, and Delaware, and occupying the undeveloped lands of Missouri. They were penetrating every portion of the public domain adapted by climate and soil to the necessities of white labor. I said that the Republican leaders, with no adequate comprehension of the laws of nature and progress, were engaged in the idle task of endeavoring to prevent slavery from seeking its inevitable outlet into those lands and climates not adapted to the pursuits of Northern industry. I said that the opening of the markets of Japan and China was to create a demand for cotton fabrics unparalleled in the histories of modern commerce. I maintained that the cotton lands of Tehauntepec and the Gulf were peculiarly the heritage of the South, and hence that the expansion of this Republic was a foregone conclusion. . . . I said it was especially the duty of California, whose ports would in the future largely share in this expansion of Pacific commerce, to sustain the Breckinridge platform.[31]

Lander's beliefs were not shared by many who hailed from Massachusetts. But this was his doctrine, one that illustrated his separation from the majority in the Bay State, where the wealthy and highly educated sectors preached abolitionism. Lander had linked himself to the Pacific Coast, as had his two older brothers before him. With each passing year Lander distanced himself from his New England roots, claiming that "my long absence from Massachusetts has practically disenfranchised me."[32] He maintained ties with family members in the Northeast, but he knew that a future political career would not thrive in his birth state.

Lander dabbled in politics, but he did not commit himself to it in the autumn of 1860. He did, however, make two decisions to steer his future course. Considering himself a Californian, Lander decided that when he finished his superintendency for the Department of the Interior, he would

31. FWL to the editor, n.d., *Marysville (Calif.) Daily National Democrat,* September 29, 1860.
32. FWL to members of the Breckinridge Club, September 11, 1860, Scrapbook.

move to San Francisco. No longer was he considering settling in Massachusetts or even on his Nebraska Territory property. He believed his future would be in the Golden State, and he intended to make California his home. He quietly purchased 200 acres in Honey Lake Valley, east of Susansville and directly on the wagon road he had committed himself to improve. Paying ten dollars per acre, he planned to convert the property into a ranch once he was settled in a home that he had earlier purchased in San Francisco. Eventually he would stock his ranch with fine blood horses and move there.[33]

His second decision was that he would not spend his future alone. On October 13, two months shy of his thirty-ninth birthday, Frederick W. Lander married Jean Margaret Davenport in San Francisco. The city's *Daily Times* cleverly reported the event under the title "The Union of Mars and Thespis." The wedding culminated a twelve-year relationship and a three-year engagement. Immediately after the ceremony, bride and groom rode out to the San Jose Valley to spend their honeymoon at Crystal Spring. The new Mrs. Lander shared her husband's love for California. She announced that she would retire from the stage and settle in San Francisco with him. Her wealth rendered the decision less difficult—Jean's personal fortune in 1860 was estimated between $75,000 and $100,000.[34]

Returning to San Francisco near the end of October, Frederick Lander wrote two reports: one on the Pyramid Lake War to submit to the commissioner of Indian affairs, and the other a synopsis of the wagon road fieldwork for Secretary Thompson. Early in November, Lander kissed his wife good-bye and headed to the wharf. He would spend the holiday season in Massachusetts and then head to Washington to complete his superintendency work for the U.S. Department of the Interior. Jean would eventually join him in the East to make her arrangements; then together the newlyweds would traverse the country—the ninth time for Fred in eight years—to San Francisco.[35]

He was buoyed by the blessings of his wife, as well as the supportive

33. Newspaper clippings, Scrapbook; Baldrica, "Settlement of the Pyramid Lake War," 184.

34. "The Union of Mars and Thespis," *San Francisco Daily Times,* October 15, 1860; newspaper clipping, Scrapbook.

35. FWL to Jacob Thompson, October 31, 1860, LP 1:6145–5; Baldrica, "Settlement of the Pyramid Lake War," 186.

letters from friends. "Much luck to you my friend," wrote one well-wisher shortly after Lander's wedding, hinting to "Old Grizzly" that he wanted "young Grizzly [to] be abundant." He continued, "You have performed well your arduous part. Exploration has been your passion, and various valuable discoveries have rewarded your efforts."[36]

Lander stepped aboard the crowded steamer *Sonora*. As the ship pulled away from the wharf and steamed toward the isthmus, Lander discussed national issues on deck with other men of prominence, including Senators Edward D. Baker (Oregon), Judah P. Benjamin (Louisiana), William M. Gwin (California), and Reverdy Johnson (Maryland).[37] During their four-week voyage, the passengers learned the result of a single national example of democracy, one that would produce an extraordinary event to test whether that democracy would survive. Little did Lander realize that in a matter of months he would be pitted not only against some of the men aboard the steamer, but also against men with whom he had worked throughout the previous eight years. Lander's strongest-held values were about to strengthen, his deepest passions would intensify, and his future would steer toward an unfamiliar and wholly unexpected course.

On November 6 Abraham Lincoln won the presidential election of 1860. Six weeks later, South Carolina seceded from the United States of America.

36. Letter to FWL, n.d., LP 1:6156.
37. Newspaper clipping, LP 10; Anne Vandenhoff, *Edward Dickinson Baker: Western Gentleman, Frontier Lawyer, American Statesman* (Auburn, Calif., 1979), 68.

4

"Colonel Lander Is a Valuable Man to Us"

Why droop the eagle's wings?
Has Freedom's heart no fire—
Strike nerveless things,
The sounding strings,
And tune her sacred lyre.

Our stars still gleam on high,
Our country's flag unfurled;
Flung out to fly, against the sky,
Still one, the startled world
　　　　　　　—F. W. Lander

Frederick Lander walked the streets of Washington in the early days of 1861 as a much more widely recognized figure than he had been nearly one year earlier. Much had transpired in Lander's life throughout 1860 to draw the newspapers' attention. Physical confrontations with William Magraw and the publicized willingness to slash Congressman Pryor with a Bowie knife highlighted his most recent sojourn in Washington. Those violent incidents were certainly controversial, but they had done much to enhance "Colonel" Lander's reputation. No longer was word of his West Coast accomplishments confined to California. Lander's role in the settlement of the Pyramid Lake War caught the eyes of influential personnel in the East, owing in some degree to the reputation he had garnered by the time he left Washington the previous April. And although the new Mrs. Lander would not join her husband until the spring season, Lander's marriage to the famous actress boosted his financial worth as well as his reputation in the hierarchy of Washington's social circles.

Lander had taken a vehement pro-Union stance during the fall presidential campaign, but by casting his lot with John Breckinridge and the Democratic Party, he had thrown his future into uncertainty. In January of 1861 President Buchanan's Democratic administration still occupied the White House, but all of Washington was in transition. The new Republican Party was geared to take over a capital and a nation with an uncertain future. South Carolina had seceded on December 20 after a unanimous vote by the state legislature in Charleston. In doing so they successfully carried out their threat made after Abraham Lincoln's election. The Palmetto State's bold move initiated a domino effect on other southern states. Six more states officially seceded from the United States of America over the next ten weeks. The headline in the *Charleston Mercury* spoke volumes with four words: "The Union Is Dissolved!"[1]

While the nation was growing more chaotic, Lander established himself a little stability in the capital by renting a house in the 400 block of E Street. His first order of business was to complete a document that included additional estimates for the Fort Kearney, South Pass, and Honey Lake Wagon Road for the House of Representatives. The meat of Lander's official report stressed future expenditures needed to make his cutoff from the Oregon Trail safe for travelers. He focused on the necessity to construct a bridge over the Green River to eliminate the emigrants' chief criticism of his route. He also reiterated the need to continue negotiations with Chief Numaga and the Northern Paiutes, offering to visit them himself. He went on to insist that he could convince the Indian leaders to accompany him to Washington to negotiate a treaty.[2]

Lander penned the document on January 5, addressing it to Secretary of the Interior Jacob Thompson. On the same day, the merchant ship *Star of the West* set sail from New York carrying a cargo of 250 Federal

---

1. Bruce Catton, *The American Heritage Picture History of the Civil War* (New York, 1982), 50–1.

2. FWL to William Northend, December 4, 1861, Northend Papers, Emory University; FWL to Jacob Thompson, January 5, 1861, HR 64. Lander's letter to Northend is headed with his address: "456 E Street, Washington." The location was within the same block as—and likely next door to—Salmon P. Chase, the secretary of the treasury.

troops. Its destination was Fort Sumter in Charleston Harbor, a Federal fortress existing in seceded territory of South Carolina. Major Robert Anderson defended Sumter with eighty-four troops and paltry supplies. The decision to send aid to the fort continued to divide President Buchanan's cabinet, already in chaos with dissention and resignation. Secretary Thompson, a Mississippi resident (and Frederick Lander's boss), resigned on January 8 in protest over the decision to reinforce Sumter. Before he left Washington, however, Thompson notified South Carolina of the pending relief expedition. The *Star of the West* never reached its destination; the alerted Carolinians fired on it when it entered Charleston Harbor and forced it to turn around and head north again.[3]

The *Charleston Mercury* hailed the event as "the opening ball of the Revolution." Lander, witnessing Buchanan's cabinet disintegrate, realized that he no longer could serve the administration, particularly when a new political party he opposed would take over in a matter of weeks. Lander's document eventually reached the desk of Moses Kelley, the interim secretary of the interior. It turned out to be Lander's last official act as a government engineer. On February 1, 1861, he resigned his position as superintendent of the wagon road, effective on inauguration day, March 4.[4]

Too impatient to remain jobless, Lander called on General Winfield Scott three days after he sent in his resignation to let him know that he was available for any duty that Scott might assign him. The venerable General Scott, looking every minute of his seventy-five years, had recently moved from New York to Washington and found himself as the center of military affairs within the capital. Scott had been breveted lieutenant general, a rank previously bestowed only on George Washington. Although highly revered for his service in the young United States Army through two wars in half a century, General Scott's best days were well behind him. Previously trim at six feet four inches, the gout-ridden general now weighed 300 pounds. Too feeble to ride a horse, Scott had been relegated to the post of glorified adviser, an effective position for him to use his mind rather than his body. The same day Lander called on him, Scott had held

3. Stewart Sifakis, *Who Was Who in the Civil War* (New York, 1988), 651–2; William C. Davis and the Editors of Time-Life Books, *Brother Against Brother: The War Begins* (Alexandria, Va., 1983), 123–6.

4. Davis et al., *Brother Against Brother*, 127; FWL to Moses Kelley, February 1, 186[1], LP 1:6103.

a council with the leading army officers to discuss military operations in Washington and Federal forts in southern states.

Winfield Scott thought highly of Frederick Lander, whom he had met fourteen months earlier. "Old Fuss and Feathers" complimented Lander for quelling the Paiute uprising at the California border. On hearing the frontiersman's proposition to do anything for the preservation of the Union, Scott thanked him for his frank patriotism and told him that he hoped there would be no necessity for calling on anyone.[5]

But Lander knew better. The signs had been apparent for years and never stronger than now. He was reminded by a young friend of a prediction he had made three years earlier: "We are fast drifting toward a revolution on this soil—then we men of soul rather than [senses] . . . will be required and must be ready. I am a leader when and where other men falter and are faint."[6]

Lander had been prepared for this revolution for three years. He had demonstrated with the Paiutes his personal bravery and negotiation skills. He had earlier intended to dissolve his East Coast responsibilities and relocate to the Pacific, but Lander's chief loyalty was to the preservation of the Union. It superseded his unusual position on slavery. Unfortunately, even if the situation came to a head, politics could keep Lander stagnant. Although openly supportive, General Scott was an old-line Whig (he had lost a presidential campaign to Franklin Pierce eight years before). Therefore, the dinosaur's clout could be diminished with the placement of Lincoln's Republican administration. By publicly supporting Breckinridge and his controversial platform in California, Lander risked anonymity in Washington.

In an ironic twist, a staunch abolitionist Republican named William Henry Seward discarded political differences and pulled Lander from the brink of obscurity. The sixty-year-old New York senator had been designated a shoo-in as Republican nominee for president, but Abraham Lincoln upset those plans in the Chicago Republican convention. Seward returned to Washington to complete his senatorial duties knowing he was to take a seat as secretary of state in March; he had earned the seat for throwing his support to Lincoln after losing the presidential nomination

5. "Conference of Military Chiefs," February 4, 1861, newspaper clipping, LP 10; Margaret Leech, *Reveille in Washington*, 2d ed. (New York, 1991), 1–5.
6. A. J. Chamberlain to FWL, February 6, 1861, LP 1:6161–2.

to Lincoln in August. It was widely held that although Seward did not carry the title of president, his position and experience meant that he would essentially be working as such. A savvy negotiator and politician, Seward realized that to idle until the inauguration would be disastrous for northern interests. He considered it "necessary to assume a sort of dictatorship for defence" in an effort to secure vital interests of the United States of America.[7]

One of those vital interests was to keep undeclared states on the Union side of the conflict. Seward deemed it paramount to keep informed about states below the Mason-Dixon line that had yet to vote on secession. Although many of those southern states had openly declared their disunion feelings, Maryland and Virginia remained undecided.

To Seward, keeping Virginia in the Union was a priority, chief among many reasons being its proximity to the capital. The state's future was uncertain. The Virginia General Assembly met in Richmond in January and passed a series of legislation that appeared hostile to Washington, issuing $2 million in treasury notes, authorizing the sale of bonds for militia companies, and sending a commission to England to purchase weapons. The legislature called for a state convention to determine Virginia's future course; however, the members of the General Assembly would not attend, as they would stay in session. Therefore, special elections were held throughout Virginia on February 4 to select 152 delegates who would meet in Richmond nine days later.[8]

Seward employed a network of special agents to attend other state conventions and to report back to him on the mood of its delegates. The same must be done in Virginia. Seward realized that the agent sent to Richmond must be acceptable to the delegates meeting there, a nonabolitionist whose presence would not threaten the convention. The agent should be a well-known personality who represented the political bent of the majority of the delegates—Breckinridge Democrats. Those necessary qualifications directed Seward to choose Frederick Lander for the role. Seward had become acquainted with him in the 1850s during Lander's work on the wagon roads. Although their political differences appeared extreme, both men shared strong Union sentiments.

7. Frederic Bancroft, *The Life of William H. Seward*, vol. 2 (New York, 1900), 11.
8. Clayton R. Newell, *Lee vs. McClellan: The First Campaign* (Washington, D.C., 1996), 4–5.

The Virginia delegates met in Richmond on February 13 and Lander reported back to Seward about their mood and decisions. None of the convention members appeared to hold a grudge against Lander regarding his support of Republican Potter against Virginia Representative Pryor ten months earlier. The first days in Richmond seemed to be the most promising in terms of a compromise. Simultaneously in Washington, a peace conference with twenty-one states was taking place. The delegates in Richmond, listening to various proposals, bided their time in anticipation of results transpiring elsewhere.[9]

Lander attended the first ten days of the Richmond convention. He reported back to Seward at midnight on Friday, February 22, with an eight-page letter filled with information, opinion, and advice. Indicating that the conservative Whig element predominated among the delegates, Lander informed Seward that many wished to hear the president-elect's inaugural address on March 4 before they voted for any reaction. Lincoln's upcoming speech, Lander stressed, would direct what would happen in Virginia. Agent Lander turned presidential adviser by notifying Seward of the essential elements that must be included in the inaugural address and his subsequent actions thereafter. "It is absolutely necessary for [Lincoln] to pursue an extreme reactionary yet statesman-like course," Lander insisted, believing a hands-off approach to secession was the best policy to pursue to keep the border states within the Union. "Leave the seceding states to the extremity of their own folly during the first part of his administration," he continued. "Should he further recommend no action against the claims of the South as to the territories, I believe that secession should be disarmed."

Reminding Seward that Lincoln had fallen 900,000 votes short of achieving a majority in the November election (he won the four-candidate race with forty percent of the national vote) and that no slave state cast an electoral vote for him, Lander insisted that Lincoln must not be tyrannical toward the southern populace and should keep quiet about his intentions until he was officially inaugurated. Lander closed his communication with a heady observation: "It appears to me that the madness which creates revolutions refines itself in this city to comprehend realities. Men say that

9. David M. Potter, *Lincoln and His Party in the Secession Crisis* (New Haven, Conn., 1942), 300–2; Richard Orr Curry, *A House Divided: A Study of Statehood Politics and the Copperhead Movement in West Virginia* (Pittsburgh, Pa., 1964), 30; Catton, *Coming Fury*, 239–40, 246.

it is in vain to declaim that the incoming president intends no wrong to southern institutions while the strength of his assertions on the construction of doubtful clauses of the Constitution are hardly dry on the manuscript which reports them."[10]

Lander arrived back in Washington on Sunday morning. President-elect Lincoln had arrived in the city the previous day. It is unlikely that Seward relayed much, if any, of Lander's acrid opinions to the new head of the Union; however, Lander made it a point to be heard again on his return. He informed Seward that the coercion resolution that was to be adopted by the delegates was postponed from Saturday to Tuesday. He admitted that a few young men "talked fight" at the convention, but Seward was assured that Virginia did not appear to support secession and was still taking a wait-and-see approach to the matter. Lander continued to advise that Lincoln could shape public opinion by the words he chose for his inaugural speech.[11]

On March 4, fifty-two-year-old Abraham Lincoln was inaugurated as the sixteenth president of the United States of America. Knowing that he was taking over a divided nation, Lincoln expressed his hope that the country could stay united and avert a civil war that appeared to many to be inevitable. "We are not enemies, but friends. We must not be enemies," closed Lincoln in his stirring inaugural address. "The mystic chords of memory, stretching from every battlefield, and patriot grave, to every living heart and hearthstone, all over this broad land, will yet swell the chorus of the Union, when again touched, as surely they will be, by the better angels of our nature."[12]

Lincoln's plea for the preservation of the Union came the same day that Texas governor Sam Houston proclaimed that his state had seceded from the United States of America. Texas's legislature had adopted an ordinance of secession by a state convention vote of delegates on February 1, the seventh state to do so. Sam Houston, the Lone Star State's original hero, opposed the decision and still harbored ambitions to reestablish Texas as a separate republic. Those hopes were dashed when a popular referendum was held in Texas—the only seceding state to undergo the formality—on February 23. By a vote of three to one, the people favored se-

10. FWL to Seward, February 22, 1861, SP.
11. FWL to Seward, February 24, 1861, SP.
12. Don E. Fehrenbacher, comp., *Abraham Lincoln: Speeches and Writings, 1859–1865,* vol. 2 (New York, 1989), 224.

cession. On March 5, the convention officially placed Texas among the Confederate States of America.[13]

The recent events in Texas caught the attention of Abraham Lincoln and William Seward. Both incorrectly believed that pro-Union sentiment dominated within the state, and hoped it could still be held in the Union. Early in the second week of March, Lincoln instructed Secretary Seward to bring Frederick Lander to the White House, ostensibly to discuss the Texas crisis. This was to be the first meeting between Lander and the president, an association that would continue more informally in the future. Lincoln had heard much about Lander from Seward and earlier from Grenville Dodge, who relayed Lander's views on the transcontinental railroad when Lincoln had visited Council Bluffs, Iowa, in 1859.

The midday appointment for Sunday, March 10, came and went without Lander's appearance. Seward informed Lincoln that he would bring Lander to him later that evening. But any plans that Lincoln and Seward had designed for Lander's skills would have to wait. Lander fell dangerously ill; by March 11 he was confined to his bed. Newspapers reported him contracting diphtheria, a malady that killed one out of every three of its victims.[14]

Although Lander's illness incapacitated him, it did not threaten his life. His thoughts remained clear; they aimed westward when he wrote the acting commissioner on Indian affairs to resolve the Paiute conflict, revealing his plans in the same letter to head to California again. Newspapers speculated on a political career for the popular extrovert. Given his role in quelling the Northern Paiute conflict the previous summer, the *New York Herald* reported that Lander was "favorably spoken of" as territorial governor of Nevada to replace Isaac Roop. He also had been reportedly urged by Republicans to bid for the same office in New Mexico. Lander, however, never sought the positions and no offers were tendered to him. He did lobby for his friend Captain Weatherlow for the office of Indian agent to the Northern Paiutes, to replace Frederick Dodge. The support carried no clout; the position was awarded to Warren Wasson.[15]

13. Catton, *Coming Fury*, 235–6.

14. Seward to Lincoln, March 10, 1861, ALP 18:7959; FWL to Charles E. Mix, March 11, 1861, LP 1:6167; *Boston Evening Transcript*, March 14, 1861. For a brief discussion of the intrigue posed by the planned March 10 meeting, see Appendix 2.

15. FWL to Charles E. Mix, March 11, 1861, LP 1:6167; "Col. Lander Again," *New York Herald*, March 20, 1861; "The Governorship of Nevada," *New York Herald*, March

Lander's frustration over his weakened body was offset by the appearance of his wife, who, with her mother, had entered the capital in the second week of March. In addition, Lander's sister, Louisa, also paid a visit. An accomplished sculptress, Louisa came to Washington with the reported intention of making a bust of her brother, but Lander's illness likely dissuaded her from the endeavor.[16]

While his agent recuperated, Secretary Seward tried to stay abreast of Governor Houston's situation in Texas. But nearly nonexistent telegraphy in the Lone Star State rendered this difficult, if not impossible. Seward would be delayed to learn about the delegates's vote to unite Texas with the Confederacy, a vote that ran contrary to Houston's desire to return Texas to the status of an independent republic rather than affiliate it with the seceding states. To make matters worse for Houston, the convention usurped his authority and summoned him to take an oath of allegiance to the Confederacy. Houston refused, and on March 16 he was no longer the acting governor of the state.

In mid-March Seward, with Lincoln's endorsement, called on Lander with a proposition. Seward briefed his agent about the military situation in Texas. Brigadier General David E. Twiggs, the septuagenarian federal commander at San Antonio, had ingloriously surrendered more than $1 million worth of army property to secessionists one month earlier. The only U.S. military support existing within Texas' borders belonged to Colonel Carlos A. Waite of the First U.S. Infantry, who had replaced Twigg at San Antonio with fewer than 1,000 men and essentially nothing to command.

Apparently unaware that Houston had been ousted as governor, Seward instructed Lander to proceed to Texas to deliver a letter to Hou-

---

21, 1861; Newspaper clippings, Scrapbook; Captain William Weatherlow to FWL, January 26, 1861, LP 1:6158–9.

16. *Washington Evening Star,* March 14, 1861; Charlotte Streifer Rubinstein, *American Women Artists: From Early Indian Times to the Present* (New York, 1982), 86–7; John Idol and Sterling Eisiminer, "Hawthorne Sits for a Bust by Maria Louisa Lander," *Essex Institute Historical Collections* 114 (October 1978): 207–12. Louisa Lander had spent the previous two years in Italy. Among her accomplishments overseas was a statuette depicting the first American-born child in the Lost Colony, Virginia Dare, as an adult. (Frederick Lander crafted a poem in tribute to the creation.) She also had persuaded Nathaniel Hawthorne, a fellow Salem native, to sit for several sessions in her Italian studio while she formed his image from clay. But a nebulous scandal tarnished her reputation in Europe, so she returned to America to resurrect her career.

ston at Austin. The confidential letter informed Houston that Colonel Waite, by General Scott's instructions, would be ordered to pull back and entrench at Indianola on the Gulf Coast. The Lincoln administration desired to keep U.S. troops there to provide Houston with a military force to keep Texas in the Union. Given $500 to fund the expedition, Lander signed for the money on March 19 and immediately set out for the Southwest.[17]

Houston had been acquainted with Lander from his work on the railroad surveys. Late in 1854, Lander had met then-senator Houston in Washington while the former was soliciting support for his independent expedition. Seven years later Lander found Houston again, this time in Austin, and delivered Seward's message. Knowing Houston's antisecession sentiments, Lander and the Lincoln administration expected him to welcome the aid. But Houston's loyalty to the state he created superseded his loyalty to the country. Adhering to the wishes of the majority of Texas citizens, Houston refused the offer and vehemently objected to the United States reinforcing within the state's borders.

Both Houston and Lander drafted letters on March 29 to be delivered to Colonel Waite, who was stationed seventy miles south of them at San Antonio, informing him of Houston's desire to remove all troops from Texas "at the earliest day practicable." Lander was determined not to create a public catastrophe. Advising Waite to delay carrying out General Scott's instructions to entrench on the Gulf Coast, Lander added, "I could only take this peculiar liberty under the absolute change of circumstances, which renders nugatory the action at Washington, and requires my immediate return there."[18]

Lander realized that it would take more than a week for him to personally inform Seward of the unexpected turn of events at Texas. Although

17. Catton, *Coming Fury,* 229–30, 233; FWL to William H. Seward, March 19, 1861, Houghton Library, Harvard University, Cambridge, Mass.; *OR* 1:598–9; E[rasmus] D. Keyes, *Fifty Years' Observation of Men and Events, Civil and Military* (New York, 1884), 419–20.

18. J. Patton Anderson to Sam Houston, March 23, 1854, LP 1:6046; *OR,* I:550–2, 598–9. Even though General Scott's messenger departed Washington for San Antonio before Lander left for Austin, Lander reached his destination in three fewer days. Lander's concerns about Colonel Waite's haste were nullified because Waite did not obtain Scott's March 19 instructions until April 1—one full day after he had learned of Houston's objections.

Seward preferred a showdown between North and South on the Texas gulf, he had envisioned Houston to be on the Union side. Lander knew it was imperative to inform him that this was impossible.

To this point, all messages of the mission had been carried by couriers. No telegraph existed in Austin; all wired messages from Texas had to travel from Galveston to New Orleans, where they subsequently were transmitted onward. Somehow Lander was able to get a message through. He wired: "You must take your large mules off this farm forthwith"—a cryptic message to Seward to inform him that the United States troops must be removed from Texas.[19] Uncertain if or when the message would carry through, Lander headed east and returned to Washington.

Lander rode into the capital on April 9 and returned $400 of unspent funds for the mission. Upon his return, Lander learned that the press had made him famous and infamous at approximately the same time. The April 6 edition of the popular weekly periodical *Frank Leslie's Illustrated Newspaper* ran a full-page biographical feature about him. Lander had turned down two attempts by the paper to interview him, but a young attorney friend named Fred Aiken stepped in to give *Leslie's Illustrated* a sometimes accurate and sometimes fanciful story of Lander's life through 1860. The *New York Herald* was not nearly so kind to him. Lander was surprised that, despite his best precautionary efforts, the Texas mission and its results were published in the *Herald* on Thursday, April 11. Without revealing Lander's name, the paper summarized his report to Colonel Waite, then went on to editorialize about how the politics of the "distinguished democrat" ran antithetical to the philosophy of Lincoln's Republican administration. The paper claimed that the disappointed president immediately sent another messenger to Houston, a claim that never was substantiated.[20]

19. "Agate" to the editor, February 12, 1862 [published in the *Cincinnati Daily Gazette*, February 17, 1862]. Ten months after the fact, Lander revealed to "Agate" (Whitelaw Reid) the story of telegraphing the coded message to Washington. He did not explain how he got the message off, but he likely sent a courier to Galveston, rather than riding there himself. Galveston had roundabout telegraphy with New Orleans in 1861, but this mode was neither quick nor reliable. Two hundred miles separate Austin from Galveston; no rail line connected the two cities. Lander's message could not have reasonably carried on to Washington until the end of the first week of April at the earliest, perhaps weeks longer if the message was delayed in arriving at New Orleans. See Westwood, "President Lincoln's Overture to Sam Houston," 128 n. 6.

20. W. J. Hunter to FWL, April 9, 1861, LP 1:6169; "Col. Fred. W. Lander, the Pacific

Whenever claims of political differences were noted, Lander fumed at the insinuation that such differences affected his patriotism. The same morning that the *New York Herald* and its accusations reached the public, Lander wrote to Secretary Seward detailing the funds that he felt should be paid to various scouts around the city. Lander stressed the importance of hiring fifty experienced frontiersmen to serve as mounted spies along the rail lines in Virginia and Maryland. "I have no intention of becoming a govt. spy," wrote Lander in closing, "and only desire to meet the secession movement and secret organizations by counter action."[21] One day later, on Friday, April 12, South Carolina troops bombarded Fort Sumter into submission, forcing Major Anderson to surrender the garrison. Although cautious skeptics in Washington questioned the reliability of the report, all doubt was eliminated on Monday when the president called for a 75,000-man three-month militia.[22] Civil war had begun.

Washington was in imminent peril, surrounded by hostile country on nearly every border. The convention in Richmond was destined to vote Virginia out of the Union. A respected United States officer, Colonel Robert E. Lee, declined the offer to command the Federal army, resigned his commission, and sided with his home state of Virginia and the Confederacy. The Federal arsenal at Harpers Ferry lay vulnerable to a southern capture. Wary of the heated secessionist element, Washington's citizens freely distributed ammunition in the streets. Guards manned Chain Bridge and Long Bridge, the two spans that linked the Confederacy's Virginia with the Union's capital. Still, no Unionist in Washington felt safe. Rumors spread throughout the city that Washington was about to be invaded by Virginians.[23]

Jean Davenport Lander had good reason to believe the rumors, for she bore witness to a plot to disrupt the United States government. Late that Thursday, April 18, Jean Lander came across an acquaintance—a long-haired, swaggering Virginian—who had entered town looking for a sad-

---

Railroad Explorer and Engineer," *Frank Leslie's Illustrated Newspaper,* April 6, 1861; "Refusal of General Houston to Cooperate with the Administration," *New York Herald,* April 11, 1861. For a detailed description of the evidence that refutes the *New York Herald* claim, see Benjamin A. Riley's monograph "Frederick W. Lander: Secret Agent for the Lincoln Administration," Marshall University, Huntington, W.Va.

21. FWL to Seward, April 11, 1861, SP.

22. Leech, *Reveille in Washington,* 54–5.

23. Ibid., 57–8; John G. Nicolay, *The Outbreak of Rebellion* (New York, 1881), 98.

dle. He confided to Mrs. Lander that he and six others "would do a thing within forty-eight hours that would ring through the world." The talkative Virginian revealed that one of the six included in the plot was a Richmond-based daredevil guerilla named "Ficklin." This was the same Benjamin Ficklin who had worked so adeptly with her husband during the 1857 wagon road season.

Fearing that the men planned to capture or assassinate the president, Mrs. Lander sped to the White House to call on Abraham Lincoln, accompanied by Ann Stephens (her friend). John Hay, one of the president's secretaries, intercepted the two women at the White House. Hay was taken aback by Mrs. Lander's presence; he had been smitten by Jean Davenport ever since he had seen her on stage. Jean told Hay of the threat by the Virginian, and then left when he promised that he would tell the president. Hay relayed her story to a grinning Lincoln, who was still awake in his bed. The next morning, Hay either took the story seriously or merely wanted an excuse to see a favorite actress again. He rode to Lander's house, met Jean and Louisa there, and had Mrs. Lander relate the story to him again. "I like Jean M. more and more," confessed Hay in his diary entry for the day.[24]

Frederick Lander was not at home when Hay paid a morning visit to his wife. Despite Lander's week-old claim that he did not wish to serve as a government spy, Secretary Seward convinced him once again to aid the Lincoln administration, which had become concerned about the capital's vulnerability to Virginia-based hostilities. During the evening of April 18, Lincoln and his cabinet received verification that Virginia had indeed seceded. Responding to rumors of Confederate battery placements on the numerous promontories on the Virginia side of the Potomac River, Seward instructed Lander to conduct another special mission on behalf of the U.S. government. Late that night, Lander saddled his horse and crossed the Potomac at Long Bridge. He rode along the river front, taking note of any suspicious activities that could threaten the defenseless capital. Finding nothing out of the ordinary, he returned to Washington during the early morning hours of April 19. Later that day the U.S. government seized four steamboats at Aquia

24. William R. Thayer, *The Life of John Hay,* vol. 1 (Boston, 1915), 93–5; John Hay diary, April 18, 19, 1861, in Michael Burlingame and John R. Turner Ettlinger, eds., *Inside Lincoln's White House: The Complete Civil War Diary of John Hay* (Carbondale, Ill., 1997), 1–2.

Creek to use as transport vessels and to deprive Virginia of key material for a flotilla on the Potomac.[25]

Seward reimbursed Lander for his midnight mission, but no sooner did Lander sign for the money on April 20 than he learned of another event that threatened the nation's security. The Lincoln administration considered the greatest threat to the safety of the capital to be not the Confederate state of Virginia, but the state of Maryland, which hugged Washington's northern and western boundary with no river protection. Although Maryland governor Thomas Hicks declared himself a Unionist, he admitted great difficulty in preventing a moblike atmosphere from developing in secession-laden pockets along the eastern side of the state. The most threatening town was Baltimore, an unfortunate location for hostilities for Lincoln because the only rail line to the North from Washington ran through it. The first troops to answer Lincoln's call—460 volunteer Pennsylvanians and a company of regulars from Minnesota— entered Washington on April 18 after a hostile mob stoned and harassed them in Baltimore. The situation came to a head the next day when the Sixth Massachusetts Infantry was attacked by a mob and retaliated, killing twelve civilians and suffering four dead and thirty-one wounded within its own ranks.[26]

Although most of the Bay Staters reached the capital unharmed, Washington became more isolated after Governor Hicks tried to control the mob furor by burning the railroad bridges and destroying communication links to prevent any other northern troops from instigating a riot. As Washington's citizens streamed from the threatened capital, General Scott decided to bypass Baltimore and bring troops in from Annapolis, where another rail line—the Elk Ridge Railroad—ran westward for twelve miles before linking with the northward-running Baltimore and Ohio line at Annapolis Junction. All of these routes ran well south of Baltimore. On Sunday, April 21, Lincoln and his cabinet learned that three regiments of infantry had landed at Annapolis, under the overall command of Brigadier

25. Leech, *Reveille in Washington,* 60–1; Shea, *American Nation,* 302; Newspaper clipping, Obituary Scrapbook, LP 9; Mary Wills, *The Confederate Blockade of Washington, D.C., 1861–1862* (Parsons, W.Va., 1975), 15–17.

26. Receipt to FWL, April 20, 1861, SP; Benjamin F. Cooling, *Symbol Sword and Shield: Defending Washington During the Civil War,* 2d ed. (Shippensburg, Pa., 1991), 22–6; William C. Davis and the Editors of Time-Life Books, *First Blood: Fort Sumter to Bull Run* (Alexandria, Va., 1983), 23–4.

General Benjamin Butler. The problem for the would-be saviors of Washington was that the rail line to Annapolis Junction was a wreck, and the only road to Washington from Annapolis was believed to be patrolled by armed secessionists. General Scott had sent several messengers to Annapolis with dispatches for the troops there, but none of them reached their destination. The tension produced by the losses of Harpers Ferry and the navy yard at Norfolk, combined with the inability of volunteer militia to march into the capital, wore heavily on the new president. "I don't believe there is any North," he was heard to complain.[27]

It was under these conditions that Secretary Seward called on one of his most reliable agents. Briefed about the critical situation in Annapolis, Seward handed Lander a dispatch written by General Scott to be given to Colonel Erasmus D. Keyes, his aide at Fort McHenry. Lander set out with three companions on a mission to reach the troops there and ascertain the best way for them to reach Washington. They left under cover of darkness late on Monday, April 22, cautiously advancing along the Bladensburg Pike. The rumors of armed secessionists blocking the roads turned out to be accurate. In the early morning hours of April 23, Lander and his companions found themselves surrounded. His companions surrendered, but Lander refused to capitulate. Galloping away from the southern sympathizers, Lander somehow escaped capture but had advanced farther into hostile country without any support. Nevertheless, his frontier experience guided him eastward and late in the morning Lander trotted into Annapolis.

The Union infantry waiting in Annapolis included the Seventh New York and Eighth Massachusetts. "The day was halcyon," remembered a member of the Seventh, "the grass was green and soft; the apple trees were just in blossom: it was a day to be remembered." Lander's arrival made the day more memorable for the New Yorkers because of the news he brought. Colonel Marshall Lefforts and two of his captains interviewed Lander, who told them his story of temporarily being taken prisoner by "a large party of secessionists" and warned them that the roads were infested with armed troopers. Lander pointed out that Lefforts's regiment would meet heavy resistance if it attempted to take the roads, and that Lefforts could expect to lose large numbers of his command. Nevertheless, Lander urged Lefforts to conduct the forward movement "at any cost," stressing

27. Leech, *Reveille in Washington,* 60, 63–5.

that Washington needed the troops immediately. Lander informed the colonel that his sick and wounded would have to be left where they fell because there was no means available to convey them to safety. "Such were the statements and opinions of Colonel Lander," remembered Captain Emmons Clark who was present at the interview, "and they were certainly calculated to awaken considerable apprehensions as to the result of the pending movement."[28]

Late in the day, Captain Morris S. Miller, assistant quartermaster of the U.S. Army, entered Annapolis with orders for the troops to take the railroad to Washington, repairing the tracks as they advanced. This route, endorsed by General Butler, ran contrary to Lander's concept of fighting through road blocks to reach Washington.[29]

Early the next morning Lander rode northward along the bank of the Chesapeake to Fort McHenry, where Colonel Keyes had been supplying the troops. Lander handed Keyes General Scott's dispatch to him, then Keyes gave Lander several dispatches to take back to the capital. Lander rode back to Annapolis with one of Keyes's messengers and written orders for Colonel Lefforts to get Lander back to Washington as soon as possible because "he carries messages of the highest importance for the government." To assure that he reached Washington without being harassed by the secessionists, Lander received a written letter of safe conduct from Governor Hicks.[30] Lander returned to the capital without incident late that night.

On April 25 General Butler delivered his Annapolis regiments to Washington. The New York and Massachusetts soldiers paraded down Pennsylvania Avenue, much to the delight of President Lincoln and the citizens who still remained in town. Knowing that the Annapolis route would be vital until the situation in Baltimore was resolved, Lander felt it

28. Newspaper clipping, Scrapbook; William J. Roehrenbeck, *The Regiment that Saved the Capital* (New York, 1961), 102–3; Colonel Emmons Clark, *History of the Seventh Regiment of New York, 1806–1889,* vol. 1 (New York, 1890), 489–90.

29. *OR,* I:591; Roehrenbeck, *Regiment that Saved the Capital,* 103–4.

30. FWL to unknown addressee, April 24, 1861, LP 1:6173; Keyes to Lefforts, April 24, 1861, LP 1:6176; FWL to Thomas Hicks, April 24, 1861, LP 1:6181–2; Thomas Hicks to FWL, April 24, 1861, LP 1:6178–9. Scott's dispatch to Colonel Keyes informed him that because Keyes had gone on his mission without Scott's consent, "I think it [necessary] to terminate our official connection without further correspondence or irritation." (Keyes, *Fifty Years' Observation,* 404.)

necessary to offer his opinions of the best means to keep that line open. He wrote to Seward that night, advising the secretary to supply Captain Miller (who remained at Annapolis) with appropriate funds to compensate and placate the area's citizens for lost property and detailing the equipment needed to repair the rail line. "Too much care cannot be taken on the telegraph line at the junction," continued Lander. "It should be disconnected from the Baltimore wire and should be repaired between Annapolis and the junction." To initiate the repairs without attracting the attention of Baltimore, Lander proposed that U.S. troops demonstrate north of Baltimore, but be careful not to fight or drive the secessionists too far southward on the Annapolis line of communication. Then Lander repeated his desire to serve the Union more directly than as a special agent. "Put the funds and arms of right class in my hands and I will raise the men and horses for scouts to protect the line to Annapolis," proposed Lander. "This force should be Maryland Union men with a preponderance of Northerners."[31]

However, during the final week of April, Lander again ruminated on how he could best serve his country. The Maryland threat had quickly disappeared. The Annapolis-Washington railroad route could shuttle 15,000 soldiers per day with or without chaos in Baltimore. General Butler had taken charge of the rails in Maryland and in so doing, crowded Lander out of any opportunities there. Lander now looked westward, beyond the Blue Ridge. Although Virginia had taken itself out of the Union (a pending May 23 popular vote was considered a mere formality), the western counties had begun to stir attention. A series of resolutions calling for a Wheeling convention on May 13 to decide their future course received widespread newspaper coverage late in the month. The Union force created to cover that area—including the vital Baltimore and Ohio (B & O) Railroad that passed through it—was named the Department of the Ohio. Governor William Dennison of Ohio appointed George B. McClellan— the same McClellan who had worked with Lander on Stevens's expedition eight years earlier—as major general of volunteers to take command of the department. McClellan quickly formed a staff and organized his forces from his headquarters in Cincinnati.

Hot-blooded and impatient, Lander kept track of the developments in the northwestern Virginia sector and deemed this theater as a prime op-

31. Davis et al., *First Blood*, 29; FWL to Seward, n.d., LP 3:6463–4.

portunity for him to see action in the war. As April turned to May, Lander updated his proposal to the secretary of state. Allow him to raise a regiment of loyal Virginia troops, Lander advocated, and he would use them as a semiguerrilla force to conduct special operations along the B & O in northwestern Virginia. Sold on the proposal, Seward wrote Abraham Lincoln on May 2, "Colonel Lander's project of raising a Virginia Regiment seems to me to be one worthy of all aid and encouragement, and he is the very man for that undertaking. Can you accord him an opportunity to lay the matter before you?" Lincoln concurred but felt strongly that his top military advisers needed to endorse it. Lincoln turned Seward's letter over and scrawled on the back, "Colonel Lander is a valuable man to us. Will Genl. Scott see him a few minutes, and consider the feasibility of his plan?"[32]

Seward did not know that Lander had already set his brainchild in motion prior to receiving permission to do so. He corresponded in cipher to Edward J. Allen, his Washington Territory friend now stationed in eastern Virginia, to help him organize the force. He solicited Allen to round up some of his experienced wagon road comrades to officer the special force yet to be assembled. But as he was in the early stages of organizing his unit, Lander was disappointed to learn that his idea would not be supported by Simon Cameron, Lincoln's secretary of war. Apparently, Cameron did not nullify the proposal, but he tabled it and let the plan die. Lander was convinced that the lack of enthusiasm for his idea stemmed from the influence of newspapers that earlier had questioned his loyalty. He believed that despite his life-threatening exhibitions of patriotism over the previous three months, politicians in Washington were still suspicious of him and therefore were responsible for killing his idea.[33]

32. Davis et al., *First Blood,* 29; Sears, *McClellan,* 69; Newell, *Lee vs. McClellan,* 63–4; Seward to Lincoln, May 2, 1861, Abraham Lincoln Collection, Illinois State Historical Society, Springfield; Lincoln to Scott, May 4, 1861, in *The Collected Works of Abraham Lincoln,* vol. 4, ed. Roy P. Basler (New Brunswick, N.J., 1953), 355.

33. "E. Jay A" [Edward J. Allen] to the editor, March 4, 1862, *Pittsburgh Daily Evening Chronicle,* March 6, 1862; FWL to F[rederick] M. Seward, May 18, 1861, SP; FWL to Adjutant General Schouler, June 17, 1861, Massachusetts Historical Society, Boston. Although no direct evidence links Secretary Cameron with blocking Lander in his desire to lead a regiment, Lander's letter to Frederick Seward, along with the inflammatory remarks he made about Cameron months later, suggest a deep-seated animosity against Cameron. Considering Lincoln's and William Seward's endorsement of Lander's proposal and General Scott's personal fondness for him, Cameron was the most plausible obstacle to Lander getting a regiment.

Regardless of the reasons behind the inaction, Lander was afforded no time to lobby for his proposal. Secretary Seward sent him to New York in response to a plea from the Metropolitan Police there to infiltrate "a nest of secessionists" and gain information from them. Lander employed his friend Fred Aiken as an agent under his supervision. The two completed the assignment, but at the same time Lander kept his attention focused on the northwestern Virginia theater. He spoke in front of the Union Committee on the movement of the delegates at the Wheeling convention to separate the pro-Union counties of Virginia from the secessionist Tidewater region. He also met with Governor John A. Andrew of Massachusetts and spoke briefly with him about sending arms to McClellan's army. Lander hoped the interview would someday lead him to command Massachusetts troops to quell the rebellion.[34]

Most important, Lander corresponded with McClellan while he worked in New York. McClellan had asked for staff appointments and had rapidly filled all his commissioned posts. Lander's options in a young war were either to continue as Seward's agent, a position that reimbursed him but guaranteed only limited action, or to act as an unpaid volunteer aide at the front. Lander informed Seward's son, Frederick, of his decision from New York on May 18: "As the Secretary of War was entirely indisposed to aid me to serve the country in a more honorable field of service than that which detained me in Washington and prevented me from availing myself of opportunities here now closed to me, I am on my way to Major General McClellan who is at least a soldier and being an old comrade of mine may appreciate better my past experience of transportation."[35]

The announcement teemed with the bitterness borne of the months-long frustration Lander felt toward those who had not heartily supported him. His decision carried risk, for if McClellan failed in western Virginia, Lander was destined to wallow in obscurity in a remote and desolate theater of operation. But for the first time since the commencement of the war, Lander saw the opportunity to fight, and he seized the opportunity.

One week later Lander's train rolled into its Cincinnati depot. He met General McClellan at his headquarters and received his instructions. On

34. FWL to F. M. Seward, May 18, 1861, SP; Newspaper clippings, LP 10; Central Department of New York Metropolitan Police to Gov. [Thomas] Hicks, May 1, 1861, LP 1:6183; FWL to Adjutant General Schouler, June 17, 1861, Massachusetts Historical Society, Boston.

35. FWL to Frederick Seward, May 18, 1861, SP.

May 26 Lander entrained again, this time accompanied by Captain W. G. Fuller, who was to construct the first military telegraph lines in the history of warfare. The train headed eastward through southern Ohio, carrying Lander to the front for the first time in the American Civil War. It was also removing him from an arena controlled by politicians, who he believed could easily ruin the desires of patriots without any willingness to actively participate in the war they had initiated. "Lawyers and Diplomats make excellent paper warriors," Lander had opined one week earlier, questioning the bravery of such men by adding, "I have yet to learn their capacity to meet a desperate and decided enemy on the battle field."[36]

As the train screeched to a halt at its Marietta depot, Lander looked across the Ohio River toward the Confederate state of Virginia. Pleased at the thought that he would soon exhibit his skills on the battlefield, no one could fault "Old Grizzly" if a rare smile broke across his normally stern countenance. As far as Lander was concerned, his gamble had already paid off.

36. Ibid.; W. G. Fuller, "The Corps of Telegraphers Under General Anson Stager During the War of the Rebellion," in *Sketches of War History, 1861–1865: Papers Read Before the Ohio Commandery of the Military Order of the Loyal Legion of the United States,* vol. 2 (Cincinnati, 1888): 392–6.

5

"That Must Be a Remarkable Man"

Salt tears we well have shed
    Tears that the false may feign
We weep the dead that nobly bled
    On freedom's southern plain.

O'er all this broadened land
    From our far western wave
Prepared to stand and hand to hand
    Keep what our fathers gave.
                    —F. W. Lander

As his steamer pulled away from the Marietta dock on the morning of May 28 and cut across the Ohio River, Frederick Lander studied what lay on the opposite shore. The sight of the western Virginia mountains struck a familiar chord. The hills lacked the towering brilliance of the Rockies, but Lander knew how to operate in this country.

What pleased him most was the field command. Although he was hired as a volunteer aide, General McClellan remained in Cincinnati and allowed his subordinates to control operations in western Virginia. McClellan planned to unite two bodies of troops from his Department of the Ohio at Grafton, where the B & O Railroad and the Northwestern Virginia railroad converged. He sent Lander across the river to initiate the movement of the Fourteenth Ohio from Parkersburg, 100 miles east to

Grafton. Concurrently, the First (Union) Virginia, under the command of Colonel Benjamin Franklin Kelley, had begun to advance along the B & O from its Wheeling terminus. Three regiments accompanied Kelley's First Virginia: the Second Virginia, Fifteenth Ohio, and the Sixteenth Ohio. The movements were designed to remove all threat from the rail lines.[1]

Lander disembarked on the Virginia shore and entered Parkersburg to cheers from the Unionists. The former frontiersman had become a celebrity in western Virginia for his publicized challenge of Tidewater Representative Roger Pryor two years earlier. Lander found Colonel James B. Steedman, whose Fourteenth Ohio Volunteers had entered town the previous day and encamped on the heights to the east. Steedman, like Lander, was an imposing figure. The forty-four-year-old giant had participated in the Mexican War as a member of the Texas army, then returned to Ohio. In 1849 he took part in the California gold rush, but returned to Ohio again where he took over ownership of the *Toledo Times.* Lander knew a little about Steedman's past and asked him if he had not crossed the Plains. "Yes sir," Steedman replied, "in charge of an emigrant train and my lieutenant colonel is . . . from California." "So I heard," Lander retorted, pleased by the confirmation. "Thank God for it. We shall move then, not crawl."[2]

Before he could move, Lander needed to ensure that his base of operations was organized. He found Parkersburg in disorder. Low on supplies, arms, and ammunition, and threatened by the presence of southern sympathizers, Lander stressed to Steedman the importance of ignoring the handicaps and proceeding toward Grafton.

A Confederate force of 700 infantry and cavalry occupied Grafton. Commanded by Colonel George A. Porterfield, the six Virginia infantry companies took over the town on May 25. The southerners were sent there to prevent meetings of Union sympathizers but lacked arms, ammunition, and men to conduct successful operations. Porterfield, a Virginia Military Institute graduate and Mexican War veteran, was displeased with the composition of his rank and file. "This force is not only deficient in

1. GBM to FWL, May 27, 1861, LP 2:6187–8; GBM to Thomas Morris, May 28, 1861, MP 46:558–9; Benjamin F. Kelley, "Military History of Brig. Genl. B. F. Kelley, U.S.V.," March 2, 1864, U.S. Army Generals' Reports of Civil War Service, Papers of the Adjutant General's Office, RG 94, M1098, NA.

2. John A. Chase, *History of the Fourteenth Ohio Regiment, O. V.V. I.* (Toledo, Ohio, 1881), 6; LP 2:6190.

drill, but ignorant, both officers and men, of the most ordinary duties of the soldier," he complained to the Confederate War Department. Despite his troop handicap, Porterfield still carried off some defensive measures by sending out guerrilla parties from Grafton to destroy bridges from both railroads.[3]

As Steedman and the Fourteenth Ohio set out toward Clarksburg on May 29, Lander took steps to secure and reinforce Parkersburg. He arrested a suspected secessionist and oversaw reinforcements coming into Parkersburg. First came the Eighteenth Ohio, a regiment lacking uniforms and short on ammunition and muskets. Colonel James Barnett of the First Ohio Light Artillery arrived next with eighty-four men and two cannons. The presence of an organized Union force put an end to Lander's concern about harassment from southern sympathizers.[4]

Lander relied heavily on the citizens in and around Parkersburg. To feed the men he ordered three tons of hardtack to be sent to the town. In the meantime, bakers in Parkersburg and across the river in Marietta worked overtime making bread. Notwithstanding the efforts of patriots, Lander was disappointed in what he considered "slight interest" manifested by Parkersburg's residents to the defense of their town. He found it to be a chore but quickly succeeded in swearing in 350 townsmen as the Parkersburg Home Guards and supplied them with flintlocks. Although he payed close attention to the goings on in town, Lander did not neglect the Ohio River behind him, making sure that any vessel floating past him carried only Union men and matériel.[5]

Lander's final reinforcements arrived late on May 31 in the form of the Sixth Indiana Infantry, commanded by Colonel Thomas T. Crittenden. The regiment had been mustered into service less than one week earlier. Lander stationed select companies of Hoosiers on Jackson's Hill, an eminence that commanded the town. He sent a stream of dispatches to Mc-

---

3. *OR*, 2:70; Festus P. Summers, *The Baltimore and Ohio Railroad in the Civil War* (1939; reprint, Gettysburg, Pa., 1993), 72.

4. FWL to GBM, June 8, 1861, MP 46:364–5; FWL to GBM, May 28, 1862, LP 2:6191–2. Lander's June 8 letter embodies his official report of the Philippi campaign, a report that was not published in the *Compilation of Official Records of the Union and Confederate Armies*.

5. FWL to GBM, June 8, 1861, MP 46:365–6; FWL to GBM, May 30, 1861 LP 2:6216; FWL to GBM, May 31, 1861, Department of Ohio Headquarters, Telegrams Received Book, vol. 178, RG 393, NA.

Clellan during this time detailing his rearguard action. At the same time, McClellan kept Lander apprised of Kelley's advance on Grafton from Wheeling by using Stager's telegraph network. Lander learned on May 30 that Kelley had taken Grafton without firing a gun—Porterfield had evacuated the town two days earlier. With bemusement he informed McClellan that the southerners were evacuating the entire region, "going in every direction and in no order." While Kelley's force occupied Grafton, they awaited Steedman's arrival.

Steedman crawled along the Northwestern Railroad, following to the letter McClellan's advice to "use great caution." He stopped the train at each of the numerous railroad tunnels to carefully inspect them for potential ambushes. He was also hampered by downed railroad bridges that he needed to reconstruct before moving on. Early on June 1, Colonel Steedman wired Lander from Clarksburg, a town twenty miles west of Grafton and eighty miles east of Parkersburg. The message informed Lander that the Fourteenth Ohio was susceptible to an attack from a southern force only eleven miles away. A few hours later the telegraph line was mysteriously cut, and the 11:00 A.M. train to Parkersburg had not arrived by 2:30 P.M.[6]

Growing concerned, Lander ordered Crittenden to advance seven companies of the Sixth Indiana up the railroad to reinforce Steedman. To his surprise, Crittenden refused, citing the danger of a railroad collision. Lander offered to move in front of the Hoosiers with a single engine. With dusk arriving and likely miffed at the notion that an unranked aide-de-camp dared to issue orders to a colonel, Crittenden refused again. "My participation demands, at my hands, the right to ascertain the state of advance," a very flustered Lander wired to his superior. "Since being superceded by Col. Crittenden," Lander continued, "[I] must not be held responsible for the success of this endeavor."[7]

Lander had had enough. Gathering fourteen men from the Fourteenth Ohio (they had been left at Parkersburg while the rest of the regiment headed eastward), Lander hired a driver and a foreman to man the single

6. FWL to GBM, June 8, 1861, MP 46:366–8; FWL to GBM, May 30, 1862, Department of Ohio Headquarters, Telegrams Received Book; Andrew Grayson, *History of the Sixth Indiana Regiment in the Three Months' Campaign in Western Virginia* (Madison, Ind., ca.1875), 20–1; C. C. Briant, *History of the Sixth Regiment Indiana Volunteer Infantry* (Indianapolis, 1891), 61.

7. FWL to GBM, June 8, 1861, MP 46:366–8; FWL to GBM, June 1, 1861, Department of Ohio Headquarters, Telegrams Received Book.

engine. He rode the engine up the railroad, passing through every tunnel without stopping. Lander met up with Steedman just beyond Clarksburg early on June 2 and found his Buckeyes safe.

Realizing there was no need for undue caution, Lander sent orders back to the Sixth Indiana to join Steedman. "Come on, in God's name, and endeavor to execute the orders of the Major General!" he implored Crittenden. Lander then proceeded eastward, taking his express engine past the town of Webster and riding on to Grafton. From there, he sent word back to Steedman to push on to Webster with his available force and "prepare for moving." Concurrently, Lander ordered the Sixth Indiana to reinforce them before nightfall.[8]

A mounting Federal force controlled Grafton by the time Lander arrived on Sunday morning, June 2. Overall command of the regiments that arrived from the Wheeling expedition belonged to Thomas A. Morris, a militia general. Morris, a former West Pointer who had begun the war in charge of the Indiana Brigade, assumed command by McClellan's order when he arrived at Grafton on June 1.[9] Knowing that Porterfield had withdrawn his command to Philippi, a Tygart's Valley River town fifteen miles south of Grafton, Morris had originally planned to attack Porterfield on June 1, but he suspended the operation after he became convinced that spies had alerted the Confederates to the pending operation. Shortly after Lander reached Grafton on June 2, Morris called him into council at his Grafton Hotel headquarters with Colonel Kelley and the militia general's staff.

Studying a map prepared by a captain of the Sixth Indiana, the three officers concocted a surprise attack involving two independent columns advancing on Philippi simultaneously. Kelley prepared to take twenty-one companies of infantry from his own First Virginia, Colonel Robert H. Milroy's Ninth Indiana, and Colonel James Irvine's Sixteenth Ohio, put them on B & O boxcars, and head east from Grafton five miles to Thornton. The short train ride was designed to deceive potential whistle-blowers in and near Grafton that Union troops were leaving the theater of operations. Kelley's 1,500 soldiers were then to disembark at the Thornton station and march southward to Philippi on a seldom-used road that

8. FWL to Crittenden, in dispatch to GBM, June 2, 1861, Department of Ohio Headquarters, Telegrams Received Book; FWL to Steedman, June 2, 1861, LP 2:6294.
9. GBM to T. A. Morris, May 28, 1861, MP 46:358–9.

skirted the river on the east. Kelley planned to cut off Porterfield's retreat from Philippi by intercepting the pike on a crossroad south of the town.

The second column was to converge on Philippi by direct route from Webster. To assure the element of surprise, this force would advance during the night to initiate an attack before dawn on June 3. This column, consisting of nineteen infantry companies and two cannons, equaled Kelley's in size. Colonel Ebenezer Dumont, who had detrained his regiment at Grafton the night before, was pegged to lead eight companies of his Hoosiers, five companies of Colonel Steedman's Fourteenth Ohio, and six companies of Colonel Crittenden's Sixth Indiana.[10]

Lander sat impatiently in the council to ascertain his role in the synchronized expedition. Although his capacity was as an unpaid aide and his colonel's rank was merely an honorific, General Morris showed tremendous faith in the frontiersman when he instructed Lander to move with Dumont's troops. Morris quickly issued Special Orders Number One: "Colonel F. W. Lander is authorized if he deems it proper to assume command of the Expedition against the Rebels near Philippi."[11]

The meeting broke up at 8:30 A.M. Before he united with his command, Colonel Kelley approached Lander to finalize the plans. The tall, goatee-sporting Kelley was a compelling presence whose formidable appearance masked a life scarred by personal tragedy. He had lost both his father and his first wife while still a teenager; his second wife had died in an insane asylum in 1850. A New Hampshire native, Kelley had lived in Virginia for most of his fifty-four years. He helped to raise the First (Union) Virginia Regiment to fight in the war, a unit in which one of his sons also was an officer. Before Kelley left Grafton with his regiment to participate in their first battle of the war, he handed Lander a note requesting him to attack precisely at 4:00 A.M. on June 3. Shortly after Kelley took his leave, Lander wired a telegram to the plodding Colonel Steedman to "move to Webster as fast as you can."[12]

Kelley immediately organized his command, entrained at Grafton at

---

10. *OR*, 2:66–7; FWL to GBM, June 8, 1861, MP 46:368–9; G. W. H. Kemper, "The Seventh Regiment," in *War Papers Read Before the Indiana Commandery, Military Order of the Loyal Legion of the United States* (Indianapolis, 1898), 122.

11. Thomas A. Morris, Special Orders Number One, June 2, 1861, LP 2:6302.

12. John B. Frothingham, *Sketch of the Life of Brig. Gen. B. F. Kelley* (Boston, 1862), 1–6, 20; FWL to GBM, June 8, 1861, MP 46:369; FWL to Steedman, June 2, 1861, LP 2:6300.

10:00 A.M., and headed eastward to the Thornton station. There they disembarked and marched down the simple dirt road, covering the first miles of the twenty-two mile expedition. The heat was uncomfortable, but the road itself did not appear to hinder the soldiers. At 4:00 P.M., Kelley rested his men in a meadow where the foot soldiers stacked arms and enjoyed a meal of hotcakes, butter, and ham prepared by the Unionists in the area. Exactly twelve hours separated them from their destination at Philippi.[13]

Lander left Morris's headquarters with instructions in hand and boarded a car to Webster where he met Colonel Steedman, Crittenden, and their respective commands. Lander spent the day preparing the Hoosiers and Buckeyes. At 9:00 P.M. Colonel Dumont and the Seventh Indiana rolled into Webster, greeted by a continuous, drenching rain. The officers spent the next two hours providing the men with two days' rations and aligning them for their twelve-mile march to Philippi. At 11:00 P.M. Dumont set his force in motion, the Seventh Indiana in front, followed by a section of Colonel James Barnett's First Ohio Light Artillery, the Fourteenth Ohio, and the Sixth Indiana marching behind them. Despite the orders allowing him full discretion to take over the expedition, Lander never took command away from Colonel Dumont, choosing instead to serve as his guide and aide.[14]

Draping storm clouds blocked out the moon and star light. As the column wound through darkened woods, the soldiers in front frequently stumbled off the road. Ignoring the risk of detection, Dumont allowed a lantern to illuminate the van.[15] The murky march was nothing new to Lander, but the night was forever branded into the memories of the three-month volunteers. "Every one of those with us will remember that dreadful nights' march," recounted a Hoosier bringing up the rear, "A cold rain was pouring down unceasingly the entire trip. It was muddy and slippery, and dark was no name for it. It seemed as if a black wall rose a few feet ahead of us all the way, and it was the muddiest and most slippery road in the country at that period of time. We could not tell each other apart, only by our voices."[16]

13. Benjamin F. Kelley, "Military History of Brig. Genl. B. F. Kelley, U.S.V.," March 2, 1864, U.S. Army Generals' Reports of Civil War Service; Member of the First (Union) Virginia to the editor, n.d., *Wheeling (Va.) Daily Intelligencer,* June 8, 1861.

14. FWL to GBM, June 8, 1861, MP 46:369; Colonel Ebenezer Dumont, Official Report, June 4, 1861, *New York Herald,* June 16, 1861.

15. FWL to GBM, June 8, 1861, MP 46:369.

16. Grayson, *History of the Sixth Indiana,* 22.

The weather slowed down the pacing of Dumont's march as the Beverly-Fairmont Pike turned to quicksand from the kneadings of 1,500 foot soldiers. Lander agonized as 3:00 A.M. passed with Dumont's column still five miles short of its destination. Dumont quickened the pace and the men covered four more miles within the next hour. By this time Lander knew that he was late. Putting spurs to his gray charger, Lander galloped forward with the two cannons of Barnett's First Ohio battery while the infantry pulled to the side of the road to rest. A skirmish detachment remained busy; they surrounded the Thomas Humphreys house near the crest of Talbott's Hill. Mr. Humphreys was not at home; neither was his oldest son, Newton, who was down at Philippi serving as a private in the Upshur Grays. The only two inhabitants of the house were Thomas Humphreys's pro-southern wife and her twelve-year-old son, Oliver, who were awakened by the approaching Federals. Mrs. Humphreys told Oliver to ride to Philippi and warn Porterfield of the invasion. She then pulled a pistol and fired two shots at the Union soldiers. Her aim was poor and the bullets whizzed harmlessly by, but her action had helped Oliver escape from the two Federal privates who tried to detain him. He mounted a horse and sped toward Porterfield's camp.[17]

In the meantime Lander—unaware that the boy had escaped—rode to the crest of Talbott's Hill, which commanded the sleepy town of Philippi. Lander ordered the guns rolled forward. The time passed 4:30 A.M. Realizing he had exceeded his rendezvous time and believing that Kelley had already positioned himself behind the Confederates, Lander watched as Porterfield's men bustled below him to evacuate their camps (either Oliver Humphreys had delivered the news or the Confederates had heard Mrs. Humphreys's pistol shots). Porterfield, whose pickets took it on themselves to take shelter in camp during the night despite a warning of the assault the day before, ordered his 700 soldiers to head toward Beverly. Hundreds of muskets and other accoutrements were left

---

17. FWL to GBM, June 8, 1861, MP 46:370–1; "From Grafton. Particulars of the Fight at Phillippi," *Wheeling (Va.) Daily Intelligencer,* June 6, 1861. The town of Philippi (pronounced FIL'-li-pee) is often misspelled as "Phillipi" or "Phillippi" in soldiers' accounts and newspaper reports. A fanciful account claims that Mrs. Humphreys shot directly at Lander (see newspaper clippings, LP 10), but Lander does not mention this in his detailed report to McClellan about the campaign.

behind. Unknown to Lander, Kelley had been misdirected by his guide and had yet to reach his position. The sound strategic plan had fallen apart.[18]

With cannon barrels pointing at the town and the covered bridge that spanned the Tygart's Valley River, Lander ordered Barnett's gunners to fire. At 5:00 A.M. the first rounds fired during a land action in the American Civil War arched toward Porterfield's camp. The effect on unsuspecting troops was predictable. "Out they swarmed, like bees from a molested hive," wrote an Ohio artillerist. "This way and that the chivalry flew, and yet scarcely knew which way to run." Within minutes Dumont rode up to Lander, asking what road to take to attack the Confederates. Lander fed Dumont the appropriate directions and then, in the approaching light of dawn, he discerned the leading element of Kelley's column making its way toward Philippi. Dumont's Seventh Indiana was conducting the requisite winding march toward the covered bridge; they could not complete their mission in time. Overcome by the importance of the moment, Lander decided that he must ride forward to bring on Kelley's men if there was any chance to capture Porterfield. Heading in the same direction as Dumont guaranteed a slow road to failure, so Lander—without contemplating the consequences—spurred his horse over the edge of Talbott's Hill and rode furiously toward the bridge.

It took merely seconds to complete what everyone associated with the attack at Philippi would simply call "Lander's Ride," but his impetuosity and horsemanship created an event savored by the participants for decades to come. The southern face of Talbott's Hill descended on a steep grade and was covered with heavy underbrush. Lander ignored the foreboding terrain and forced his horse to charge at breakneck speed. One of the soldiers witnessing the exploit called it "the most hazardous ride ever seen by man." The Seventh Indiana caught a glimpse of Lander as they wound down the circuitous road toward town. Thirty-five years later, a Hoosier declared, "I presume this ride of Colonel Lander has never been surpassed." A company of the Sixth Indiana watched it from the artillery position on the crest of Talbott's Hill. Ordered to follow in Lander's path, the Hoosier soldiers found they had to sit down and slide to the bottom. Incredulous that Lander was able to cover the same ground on horseback,

18. FWL to GBM, June 8, 1861, MP 46:371–2; *OR*, 2:73–4;

a member of the company afterward considered Lander's Ride "one of the most daring exploits of the war."[19]

Lander bolted to the covered bridge, galloped across it, and spurred his horse down the pike. He reached the van of Kelley's column and reined his charger in front the leading companies to direct them toward the fleeing southerners. Kelley watched as some of his front-line infantry apparently mistook Lander for the enemy. As he admonished his soldiers not to open fire on Lander, a shot rang out from behind one of the Confederate wagons and knocked Kelley from his saddle. Lander was closest to the Confederate, an assistant quartermaster named William Sims, and he immediately cornered him near a fence and jumped on him. Within seconds, Kelley's vanguard companies, believing Sims had mortally wounded their beloved colonel, approached Lander and his captive with an intent to kill the southerner. Lander refused to give up the southerner to draconian measures. Maintaining that Sims had surrendered to Lander as a legitimate prisoner of war, Lander swore he would kill on the spot any man who touched Sims. Convinced his words had taken effect, Lander ordered some of the infantry to mount captured horses and pursue Porterfield's men. He then proceeded toward the bridge to bring Dumont's men into Philippi.[20]

Dumont had not seen Lander dart across the bridge as he carefully approached it, apprehensive that a Confederate detachment might be guarding it. As the Hoosiers worked their way across the 300-foot span and entered Philippi, Dumont watched Kelley's men approaching from the heights on the east. But Porterfield's men had achieved the advantage of a good head start and they were safely on their way toward Beverly. The two Federal columns pursued but were too exhausted by their night-long march to close the gap between themselves and the Confederates. Porterfield escaped with only six casualties: one wounded, one wounded and captured, and four others captured—including Sims and Lieutenant

19. FWL to GBM, June 8, 1861, MP 46:372; "Active Service; or, Campaigning in Western Virginia," *Continental Monthly* 2 (March, 1862): 334; Colonel Ebenezer Dumont, Official Report, June 4, 1861, *New York Herald,* June 16, 1861; Kemper, "Seventh Regiment," 123–4; Grayson, *History of the Sixth Indiana,* 24.

20. FWL to GBM, June 8, 1861, MP 46:372–3; First (Union) Virginia soldier to his father, June 7, 1861, *Wheeling (Va.) Daily Intelligencer,* June 12, 1861; "From Grafton. Particulars of the Fight at Phillippi" *Wheeling Daily Intelligencer,* June 6, 1861; "Further Details about the Engagement at Phillippi," *Cincinnati Daily Commercial,* June 8, 1861.

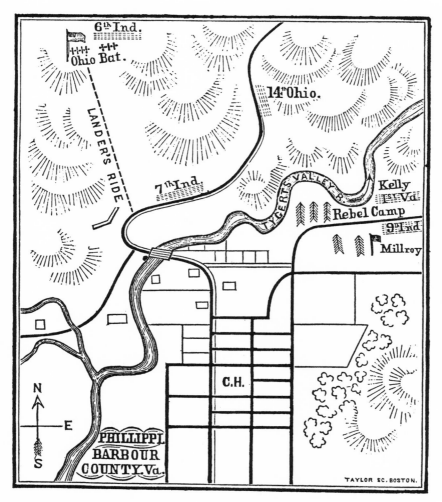

Philippi Skirmish and Lander's Ride, June 3, 1861

From Catherine Merrill, The Soldier of Indiana in the War for the Union *(Indianapolis, 1866), 32*

Colonel William J. Willey, commander of the Thirty-first Virginia, who was too sick to withdraw with Porterfield. Significant stores and supplies fell into Federal hands, including 750 stands of arms, ammunition, wagons, horses, and medical supplies.

Kelley was the most noteworthy of the five Union soldiers who were wounded. Although initially diagnosed as mortally wounded, his injury was deemed not life-threatening by day's end. The only man killed during the expedition was a private in the Seventh Indiana who accidently shot himself in the leg during the night march and subsequently bled to death.[21]

Unable to pursue Porterfield's troops any considerable distance, Dumont returned to Philippi and ordered the Seventh Indiana's flag to be raised over the courthouse, replacing the secessionist banner. Lander handed over William Sims to Dumont, instructing him once again that the Confederate must be treated as a prisoner of war and not be harmed. Dumont called a council of his officers to consider means of preventing his troops from looting citizens' homes. At this time, Lander decided his work was complete and informed Dumont that he would head back to Grafton.[22]

The fifteen-mile return carried Lander over the pike at a much more leisurely pace than he had ridden the previous night. Lander rode into Grafton at 10:30 P.M. as correspondents and military personnel were engaged in fact gathering from the events near Philippi. According to one newsman, Lander was nearly stuporous with fatigue. He was immediately escorted to General Morris's headquarters at the Grafton Hotel, where a growing crowd gathered to hear his news. "He could hardly talk," observed a reporter, "I saw him close his eyes and almost go to sleep twice while stating that our men were pursuing the retreating enemy."[23]

To pull the weary warrior from the crowd, Morris called Lander into

21. Colonel Ebenezer Dumont, Official Report, June 4, 1861, *New York Herald*, June 16, 1861; Martin K. Fleming, "The Northwestern Virginia Campaign of 1861," *Blue and Gray Magazine* 10, August 1993, 15.

22. Colonel Ebenezer Dumont, Official Report, June 4, 1861, *New York Herald*, June 16, 1861; FWL to GBM, June 8, 1862, MP 46:373; FWL to Hon. W. M. Dunn, June 17, 1861, newspaper clipping, LP 10. A ridiculous claim exists and persists that Lander took "French leave" at Philippi and rode on to Washington instead of returning to Grafton. See an Indianan's account in Eva Margaret Carnes, *The Tygarts Valley Line: June–July 1861* (Philippi, W.Va., 1961), 54.

23. "Letter from Phillippi," June 3, 1861, *Wheeling (Va.) Daily Intelligencer*, June 7, 1861.

his private room for a personal report about the mission. Lander gave him the report and also received a telegram from General McClellan directing him to take the first available train to Cincinnati. Lander boarded a train and rode to Parkersburg on June 5 where he completed his earlier mission of setting up reinforcements, then crossed into Ohio and joined his boss at department headquarters a few days later.[24]

The Philippi campaign fell short of expectations. Union success relied on impeccable timing, but the two columns could not coordinate their movements and Porterfield's rag-tag units survived to fight another day. No battle occurred, and the early morning action came to be known appropriately as the "Philippi Races." The only achievement Union participants could claim was pushing back the Confederates farther from Grafton and the B & O Railroad and capturing weapons and supplies. Had the expedition occurred two years later in the war, it would have received little attention and almost no news coverage.

But the Philippi Races claimed the honor of the first land action of the war; this guaranteed overwhelming coverage by the northern press. One of the beneficiaries of that coverage was Frederick Lander. His role in the campaign placed him in newspapers frequently over the next five weeks. *Frank Leslie's Illustrated* featured two sketches of Lander in the Philippi expedition, including "Lander's Ride" and a scene with him directing the Ohio battery opening the contest from Talbott's Hill.[25] The press coverage made Lander's name one of the most recognized among Union participants in the first months of the war.

The Union also achieved a strategic windfall from the Philippi affair. McClellan was pleased with the result, for it allowed him to push more troops and supplies into western Virginia unopposed to renew an offensive. Forwarding his official report of the engagement to Winfield Scott on June 10, McClellan closed the dispatch crediting Lander for his "marked gallantry" on June 3. The fallout from the Confederate withdrawal toward Beverly also precipitated a movement for the western counties of Virginia to separate from the Tidewater region and form their own state. On June 11 the delegates from the mountain counties held a convention in the custom house at Wheeling, where they set up

24. Ibid.; GBM to FWL, June 3, 1862, LP 2:6304; FWL to GBM, June 5, 1861, Department of Ohio Headquarters, Telegrams Received Book; FWL to GBM, June 8, 1861, MP 46:373.

25. *Frank Leslie's Illustrated Newspaper*, June–July 1861.

their own provisional state government and elected Francis H. Pierpont as their governor.[26]

Six days later, Lander seized the opportunity to correct an injustice to the Sixth and Seventh Indiana. Both units were scathed by a correspondent of the *Cincinnati Times* who claimed they vandalized citizens' homes after the Philippi rout. Recognizing overt attempts at posturing by states within the North, Lander corrected the position by claiming "I think the wrong of the article in question is the endeavor to fix the whole blame of the disorderly acts of the volunteers on the Indiana regiments." Lander raged over the newsman's attempt to belittle the Hoosiers' performance. "The movement on Phillippi during the dark and stormy night of June 2d is no subject for ridicule," he seethed. "Nothing but the imbecility of the enemy prevented the march on Phillippi [from] being one of extreme risk to the advance guard."[27] His defense of the Indiana troops was also a defense of himself. The engagement was far from satisfying, but he firmly maintained that the lost opportunity had nothing to do with his or the volunteers' performance.

Western Virginia's maneuvers to free itself from its secessionist neighbors were not lost on Frederick Lander. Afforded some time to rest and reflect in Cincinnati, Lander indicated that he still harbored tremendous resentment over the way he was treated in his efforts to raise a regiment. When he learned that Governor Andrew finally had forwarded arms from Massachusetts to western Virginia, Lander fired off a petulant response to the state house in Boston. "I wish to learn if the arms sent forward by Massachusetts to Western Va. were in response to my request or suggestion?" asked Lander. After recounting his previous service and earlier troubles in raising a regiment, Lander surmised that his unpopularity at Washington was preventing a greater effort for the people of western Virginia. "For these reasons," continued Lander, "as Massachusetts never took occasion to ask my services or tender me the opportunity to lead a portion of their men, I would like to feel assured that I might have been of use in bringing before the Governor the suggestions which led to her aid to Western Virginia."[28]

26. Newell, *Lee vs. McClellan*, 102–4.

27. FWL to W. M. Dunn, June 17, 1861, "The Indiana Troops at Phillippi—Card from Col. Lander," newspaper clipping, LP:10.

28. FWL to Adj. Gen. Schouler, June 17, 1861, Massachusetts Historical Society, Boston.

No time was available to dwell on the recent past. McClellan issued orders for his staff to move their headquarters from Ohio directly to the hill country and advance with the soldiers. It was a momentous event; each time the train stopped at stations between Cincinnati and Marietta, McClellan wrote his wife, "Gray-headed old men & women; mothers holding up children to take my hand, girls, boys, all sorts, cheering and crying, God bless you! I never went thro' such a scene in my life & never expected to get thro' such another one."[29]

As Lander passed through Parkersburg on June 21, he bought an eight-year-old dark chestnut horse for seventy dollars.[30] He still preferred and rode his gray charger, the one that had made such an impression on the men at Philippi. McClellan and his staff disembarked at Grafton on the twenty-second. By this time, Lander's decade-long reputation had garnered him notice from the correspondents who followed the Department of the Ohio. A twenty-four-year-old Ohio newsman named Whitelaw Reid had been hired by the *Cincinnati Gazette* to report on McClellan's army. He sent daily dispatches back to his editor, which were published within a week of Reid's observations.

Having seen the headquarters personnel for the first time, Reid's resulting report gushed at the appearance of McClellan's volunteer aide-decamp, and he made sure his readers understood why.

The General has surrounded himself with an admirable staff, evidently chosen for fighting, not for showing off brass buttons and padded coats to advantage. Foremost among them in the public interest is the redoubtable Col. Lander, the California, Rocky Mountain, grizzly bear, Potter-Pryor man. Of fine physical proportions, tall, "solidly built," with a splendid head, a keen eye, and a face that tells many a deed of daring, and many a scene of trial, Lander is a man to attract your attention anywhere, and force you to exclaim (as I heard a number, wholly ignorant of the name or reputation of the person they were observing, say to-day,) "That must be a remarkable man!" His experience on the plains and in California exactly fits him for the warfare ahead of us in Western Virginia. . . . He knows, by a lifetime's experience, just what guerrilla fighting is; and there isn't, after all, so much difference between the Indians on the

29. Sears, *McClellan*, 83; "Agate" to the editor, June 22, 1861, *Cincinnati Daily Gazette*, June 26, 1861. It is interesting to note that McClellan failed to inform his wife that once he and Lander crossed the river and trotted in front of Union soldiers for the first time, the men mistook the more imposing figure of Lander for their general.

30. Bill of Sale to FWL, June 21, 1861, LP 2:6318.

plain and the rebels of Western Virginia as to require any modification of the treatment.[31]

McClellan disagreed with Reid's characterization of how the southerners would fight him and concentrated his troops against his adversary expecting much more than guerrilla warfare. But he no longer had to contend with Porterfield. General Robert E. Lee, military adviser to Jefferson Davis in Richmond, sent his adjutant to western Virginia to replace him. The new commander was Brigadier General Robert Seldon Garnett, an 1841 West Point graduate who inherited a poorly supplied army of 3,000 men. "They have not given me an adequate force," complained Garnett to his wife; "I can do nothing. They have sent me to my death." Garnett had to split his force into two wings to hold the Staunton-Parkersburg Turnpike at the passes at Rich Mountain and Laurel Hill. Nine miles of rugged terrain separated the two gaps. Within two weeks of taking command, Garnett was heartened by the doubling of his command to 6,000 soldiers.

To counter the Confederates, McClellan had nearly 20,000 men divided into four brigades; however, half of his force was spread out for several miles on detached service. Furthermore, his troops were just as green as their rebel counterparts ("so difficult to get these Mohawks in working trim," McClellan complained to his wife, using a pejorative for Mexican War volunteers). To better ascertain the quality of the force under his control, McClellan ordered Lander to proceed to Clarksburg and instructed him to preserve order in the area and provide him with numbers and quality of arms of the Ohio and Indiana troops stationed there.[32]

McClellan had modeled the campaign after General Winfield Scott's advance against the Mexicans fourteen years earlier. Scott was now general-in-chief of all Union forces, and McClellan wrote to his adjutant, "Say to the General that I am trying to follow a lesson long ago learned from him—i.e. not to move until I know that everything is ready, & then to move with the utmost rapidity & energy." McClellan stressed that he would not depart from his intention of gaining success by maneuver

---

31. "Agate" to the editor, June 23, 1861, *Cincinnati Daily Gazette,* June 27, 1861.

32. GBM to his wife, June 23, 1861, in Stephen W. Sears, ed., *The Civil War Papers of George B. McClellan* (New York, 1989), 34; C. Vann Woodward, ed., *Mary Chesnut's Civil War* (New Haven, Conn., 1981), 176; FWL to GBM, June 25, 1861, MP 46:382–4.

rather than by pitched battle. Noting that Garnett's position mimicked Santa Anna's in 1847, McClellan wished to repeat the success achieved at Cerro Gordo.[33]

Lander remained at Clarksburg, where he was appointed provost marshal on July 4, while McClellan advanced to Buckhannon with 8,000 men and eight cannons. Fifteen miles down the pike rested Garnett's men in their Rich Mountain camp. General Morris advanced his brigade on a parallel route to contest the Confederates at Laurel Hill, where he met stiff resistance on July 7. In the meantime, McClellan plodded southeast with his other brigades until they came within hailing distance of the Confederates on July 9. Lander joined this advance and camped with McClellan and his staff at Roaring Creek.

At Roaring Creek Flats, Lander's fiery temper and insistence on discipline made his presence known. Watching in disgust as the Germans in Colonel Robert L. McCook's brigade invaded neighboring farms to confiscate sheep and hogs for their dinner, Lander sought out the brigadier and dressed him down. McCook, certainly not used to a mere aide-de-camp so vehemently "instructing" him on appropriate military etiquette, fired back at Lander. The altercation continued for several minutes, providing the Ohioans in McCook's brigade with an event that long remained in their memories.[34]

Later that night McClellan decided that a reconnaissance in force should advance to test the strength of the Confederate works at the western foot of Rich Mountain. Lieutenant Orlando M. Poe, McClellan's chief engineering officer, led the mission early on Wednesday morning, July 10. Lander and Colonel Thomas Key accompanied Poe and a brigade of Ohio and Michigan troopers in the cautious advance toward Camp Garnett, the rebel entrenchments housing 1,300 soldiers under the command of Colonel John Pegram. Approaching within 300 yards of the opposing entrenchments, Poe's force bumped into southern pickets, who opened fire,

---

33. GBM to E. D. Townsend, July 5, 1861, in Sears, *Papers of George B. McClellan*, 44–6.

34. S. Williams to FWL, July 4, 1861, LP 2:6319; Fleming, "Northwestern Virginia Campaign," 48–9; Jack Zinn, *The Battle of Rich Mountain* (Parsons, W.Va., 1971), 1–2; GBM to his wife, July 7, 1861, in Sears, *Papers of George B. McClellan*, 49–50; William Kepler, *History of the Three Months and Three Years' Service of the Fourth Regiment Ohio Volunteer Infantry in the War for the Union* (1886; reprint, Huntington, W.Va, 1992), 33.

supported by artillery behind them. One Union soldier was killed and two more wounded, but the advance continued.[35]

Lander, under fire for the first time in the war, dismounted and walked toward the mountain as marksmen directed their fire toward him. One hundred yards later he stopped in the face of his adversary and calmly examined the works in front of him. As the firing momentarily stopped, Colonel Key watched in admiration as Lander took off his hat, bowed to the Confederates, then turned around and walked back toward Roaring Creek as the exchange of musketry resumed. Key considered Lander's exploit the coolest operation he ever witnessed.[36]

Poe captured several pickets, who exaggerated southern strength enough to convince him that the Confederates could not be assaulted in front. The reconnaissance in force returned to the Roaring Creek camp where McClellan called a night council with his staffers and subordinates to determine how to maneuver against the rebels. General William S. Rosecrans, one of McClellan's brigadiers, entered the council having obtained unexpected assistance. One of his regimental officers had detained a young man named David Hart near the picket line. Hart claimed he lived near the summit of the mountain and was returning from a visit with relatives. Satisfied that Hart harbored only Union sentiments, Rosecrans questioned him further and was pleased to learn that the young man was familiar with the Rich Mountain terrain—including all the cattle trails on its slopes. Hart agreed to guide the Union troops toward his father's house (which occasionally served as a tavern for weary travelers) on a path that would circumvent the entrenched Confederate line.

McClellan interrogated Hart, then listened to Rosecrans's proposal. "Let me take my brigade and Hart, and I will start out at three in the morning with a day's rations, and will reach the tavern by half-past ten o'clock," declared Rosecrans. "I will attack and capture the place." McClellan selected the regiments to carry out the plan. Seeking to assure a successful mountain expedition, McClellan offered Rosecrans the services of his aide: "Would you not like to have Colonel Lander?" Rosecrans accepted the offer. The officers finalized the details of the plan, which included McClellan attacking Camp Garnett directly after Rosecrans's force

35. *OR*, 51(1):11–12; William Bickham to the editor, July 14, 1861, *Cincinnati Daily Commercial*, July 19, 1861.

36. [Thomas Key] "Reminiscences of Rich Mountain," March 6, 1862, *Cincinnati Daily Commercial*, March 12, 1862; Shea, *American Nation*, 303.

struck the southerners' flank. After times and forces were decided, the council broke up and the commanders retired for the night.

At 3:00 A.M. of July 11, Rosecrans's command woke and formed line on the turnpike. Four regiments of 1,842 infantrymen—the Eighth, Tenth, and Thirteenth Indiana, and the Nineteenth Ohio—along with seventy-five horse soldiers, comprised Rosecrans's column. Lander and Hart headed the troops. They set off shortly before 5:00 A.M.; on the hour they veered off the pike in front of the Union encampment and marched through the paw paw bushes at the wood line on the eastern slope of the mountain.

Lander resumed the familiar role of pathfinder on the seemingly pathless terrain. Using no axe or other instruments that could alarm the unsuspecting southerners, he worked his way well southeast of the Confederate left flank. A drenching rain commenced at 6:00 A.M. to assure a dark and miserable trek. For Lander, it was the Philippi night march all over again—this time without a road to follow. Clambering over rocks and ravines, it did not take Lander and Rosecrans long to realize that Hart was leading them much farther south than they had originally intended. The slow ascent was marred by the rain, but mostly by the rugged terrain—nearly impenetrable summertime thickets of laurel, grapevine, and greenbrier. The expected three-hour flank march had already passed four hours with no destination in sight.[37]

While Lander attempted to manage the responsibility of moving nearly 2,000 troops into a battle, he was unaware that his superior had apparently decided to call the whole thing off. George McClellan anguished at his headquarters at Roaring Creek throughout the early morning of July 11. Promised hourly reports by cavalry couriers of Rosecrans's progress, McClellan had received none by 9:00 A.M. McClellan decided to recall Rosecrans's troops. He dispatched a courier from the First Ohio Cavalry to deliver his decision to his brigadier, but the horse soldier fell into Confederate hands at the base of Rich Mountain. Intercepting his note, the Confederate commander, Colonel John Pegram, came to the erroneous conclusion that an attempt was in progress to turn his right flank rather than his left one. To counter, Pegram sent more of his troops to increase the force already present at the summit of Rich Mountain. But he planned

37. Zinn, *Battle of Rich Mountain*, 2; *OR*, 2:215; W. S. Rosecrans, "Rich Mountain." *National Tribune*, February 22, 1883.

to position these men on the north side of the turnpike, thus opening a door for Rosecrans to walk through from the south.[38]

Lander had yet to find that door at the summit. At 10:30 A.M. the rain let up a little as Hart and Lander led the men along the west side of a heavily timbered valley. Hart claimed that the counterslope would take them one mile southeast of his father's house. From there the road sloped gently to the Hart farm. Rosecrans dispatched a cavalryman to deliver his only prefight update. Two hours later the column reached the top of the counterslope where Rosecrans ordered the men to bivouac. Rosecrans, Hart, and Lander continued forward to reconnoiter.

Rosecrans deemed Hart too timid to be of continued service and excused him from further duty. Then Lander and Rosecrans rode into an old field to get their bearings. Rosecrans claimed that the field offered them a view far to the right (east) of Beverly where the two could see a line of tents and eighteen wagons. The Hart farm was hidden from view by an intervening wooded ridge; however, a sled road led around the western edge of the field along a ridge. From there a wagon road turned to the north and ran down to the house.[39]

Rosecrans prepared to use this road to form his men. He ordered the Eighth Indiana to form column; behind them the Tenth Indiana took position. But the colonel of the Eighth mistook his orders and marched his men into a ravine to the left of the road. The misalignment was rectified by putting the Tenth in the van with the Eighth behind them, followed by the Thirteenth Indiana, while the Nineteenth Ohio brought up the rear. An hour was lost in reforming the line; the troops set off at 2:00 P.M.

Lander continued to lead Rosecrans's troops, guiding the Tenth Indiana over the crest of the final hill before the one-mile descent to the Hart farm. Rosecrans ordered out his skirmishers, Company A of the Tenth Indiana, led by Captain Christopher Miller. Within minutes of resuming their advance the skirmishers were fired on by southern pickets stationed three-quarters of a mile from the Hart house. The volley took out three Union soldiers (including Captain Miller), but the Federal pickets maintained their position, fired their first shots of the war, and sent the Confederates falling back to the Hart farm. On the north side of the road

---

38. Fleming, "Northwestern Virginia Campaign," 50–1.

39. Zinn, *Battle of Rich Mountain,* 2–6; *OR,* 2:215; Rosecrans, "Rich Mountain," *National Tribune,* February 22, 1883.

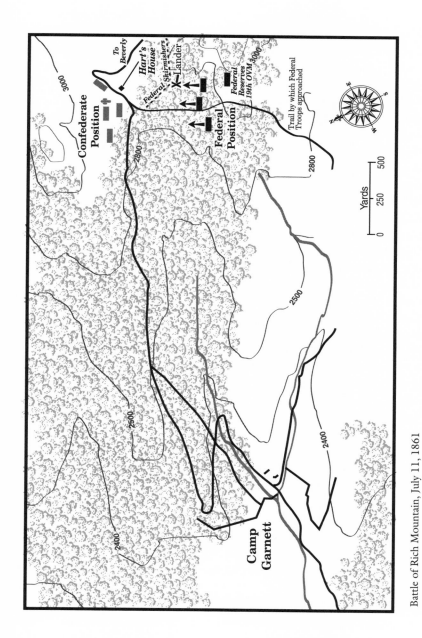

Battle of Rich Mountain, July 11, 1861

Adapted from Orlando Poe's Map, Ezra Carmen Papers, LC

stood the only artillery piece the Confederates had, a six-pound bronze cannon commanded by Lieutenant Charles W. Stratham. As the southern pickets pulled back to the Hart buildings, Stratham cut his fuses to one and one-quarter seconds and frantically fired case shot at the bluecoats, belching rounds at a rate of four per minute. His barrage brought the Union advance to a standstill.[40]

Mounted on his light gray horse, Lander descended the slope directly behind the skirmishers with the Tenth Indiana. Unlike at Philippi, the Confederates had stayed to fight, which is what Lander had hoped for since the war began. But even he could not have anticipated what unfolded in the next minutes. Stratham's artillery blasts wrought havoc on Rosecrans's column. A fragment from one of the Confederate shells slammed into Lander's horse and the wounded animal crumpled beneath its rider.

Extricating himself from his fallen mount, Lander sighted a boulder in front of him. The huge rock protruded conspicuously from the down-slope directly to the right of the Tenth Indiana soldiers, who had flattened themselves onto the ground to escape the artillery rounds. Lander bolted to the rock and climbed on top of it. Clad in his characteristic western trappings—rough overcoat, slouch hat, and breeches tucked into his boot tops—Lander remained on the rock hurling oaths and orders, completely exposed to enemy artillery blasts but showing no concern over the danger. "Why in hell don't the Hoosiers form by platoons," roared "Old Grizzly" from his boulder, urging the soldiers to form a skirmish line and drive out the enemy cannon.

Instinctively, a sergeant on the right flank of the Tenth Indiana line passed his musket to Lander, who quickly aimed his shot and fired at the artillerists manning the southern gun, shouting, "Bang away, you scoundrels! We'll come down there and lick you like the devil directly!" Within seconds, another loaded gun exchanged hands down the Hoosier line and ended up in Lander's hands. He fired the weapon, then received a third one. The scenario was repeated again and again until Lander had fired off half a dozen rifles at his adversary. Before the southern infantry could sight their exposed target, Indiana officers coaxed Lander off his boulder as Rosecrans established an infantry line to advance across the Hart farm.[41]

40. Zinn, *Battle of Rich Mountain,* 12.
41. *OR,* 2:207; *Lafayette (Ind.) Daily Journal,* July 19, 1861; William Bickham to the editor, July 12, 1861, *Cincinnati Daily Commercial,* July 18, 1861; William Bickham to the

A short but vicious fight ensued. By 6:00 P.M. the battle was over. Confederate casualties amounted to eighty-eight killed, wounded, and captured. Union losses totaled twelve killed and sixty-two wounded. Additionally, Rosecrans claimed the capture of two of Pegram's cannons. However, Colonel Pegram and the majority of his 1,300 southerners escaped into the mountain forests. Rosecrans blamed his superior for Pegram's escape and the unexpected concentrated fire at the summit: "General McClellan, contrary to agreement and military prudence, failed to attack."[42]

McClellan's hesitance did not delay Union success for long. Two days after the Rich Mountain fight, Colonel Pegram and half his original command—approximately 600 men—could not escape; after he learned they were surrounded, Pegram surrendered the entire remnant of his force. Later that day the remainder of General Garnett's command, which had abandoned Laurel Hill on the night of July 11, skirmished with three regiments of Union troops at Corricks Ford, a shallow segment of the Cheat River. Garnett and thirteen other southerners were killed in the brief action. Although most of the Confederates retreated and escaped, more than 700 had become casualties in the Rich Mountain campaign.[43]

The aftermath of the battle presented the first war horrors experienced by most of McClellan's soldiers and staffers who were not Mexican War veterans. "Men were torn and mangled in all sorts of ways, and horses killed," wrote Orlando Poe to his wife, adding, "I don't want to witness the effects of another battle." An Indiana infantrymen concurred: "It is truly a horrible sight to see so many such men mangled in this manner, and gives us great proof of the great wickedness of this infernal rebellion." But Lander appeared unfazed by it all. Studying the lifeless Confederate bodies at the summit, he gruffly declared, "God, what good shots I have—every Rebel shot clean through the head!"[44]

editor, July 14, 1861, *Cincinnati Daily Commercial,* July 19, 1861; Rosecrans, "Rich Mountain," *National Tribune,* February 22, 1883; newspaper clipping, LP 10; "An Incident in the Life of General Lander," *Wheeling (Va.) Daily Intelligencer,* March 10, 1862.

42. Fritz Haselberger, *Yanks From the South! (The First Land Campaign of the Civil War: Rich Mountain, West Virginia)* (Baltimore, 1988), 139; *OR,* 2:215–16; Rosecrans to Lorenzo Thomas, June 15, 1865, U.S. Army Generals' Reports of Civil War Service.

43. Haselberger, *Yanks From the South!* 144–5; W. Hunter Lesser, *Battle at Corricks Ford: Confederate Disaster and Loss of a Leader* (Parsons, W.Va., 1993), 14–18, 26 (n. 30).

44. Orlando Poe to his wife, July 12, 1861, Poe Collection, LC; George Rogers diary,

The most important consequence of the Rich Mountain campaign for McClellan was the fact that his Department of the Ohio soldiers had cleared the enemy from the northern portion of western Virginia and had removed a significant threat from the B & O Railroad. Additionally, the western approaches to the Shenandoah Valley lay open for Union advances. The victories could not have been more timely for McClellan, for many of his three-month enlistees neared the end of their terms and subsequently resumed their civilian lives just after the general accomplished his goals.

McClellan, a master of the telegraph, trumpeted his achievements to the U.S. War Department and the northern newspapers, declaring that "secession is killed in this country."[45] He was immediately congratulated and hailed as a hero, an ironic circumstance given his paralyzing caution, his indecision on the battlefield, and his lack of direct involvement in the outcome. Despite the battlefield shortcomings, McClellan's campaign ran smoothly due to fine work by his subordinates to achieve the desired results.

Immediately after the battle Lander followed the headquarters staff to Beverly, the town at the eastern base of Rich Mountain where McClellan had set up headquarters. Taking his meals with the general, Lander's relationship with McClellan was stronger than ever, largely due to the success of the campaign. McClellan thought highly of his volunteer aide, so much so that when he received information of a setback inflicted on one of his subordinates operating near the Kanawha River, McClellan fumed to Scott across the telegraph. "Unless I command every picket & lead every column I cannot be sure of success," he seethed on July 19. "Give me such men as Marcy, Stoneman, Sackett, Lander, etc & I will answer for it with my life that I meet with no disaster."[46]

Despite his superior's praise, Lander remained without an official rank and now was forced to carry on without his prized horse. The gray charger was so badly wounded that the captain of the quartermaster department determined it to be totally unfit for use. Lander mounted the animal he purchased at Parkersburg but still kept the injured horse because he had grown too attached to part with it. By new orders he had his baggage sent to Clarksburg and also sent his horses there.[47]

July 12, 1861, IHS; Betty Hornbeck, *Upshur Brothers of the Blue and Gray* (Parsons, W.Va., 1995), 58.

45. GBM to E. D. Townsend, July 14, 1861, in Sears, *Papers of George B. McClellan,* 56.
46. *OR,* 2:288.
47. Certification by Captain R. Saxton, July 18, 1861, LP 2:6322–3; FWL to Charles

Campaign plans were adjusted at the War Department to gain success in all theaters of Virginia. A large but untested army under the command of Major General Irvin McDowell headed westward from the capital. A smaller force under the command of Brigadier General Robert Patterson headed south into the Shenandoah Valley and had begun to threaten Winchester, a major hub where eight roads converged. General Scott wanted McClellan to cooperate with Patterson by taking his army through one of the unprotected passes in an effort to "bag [Confederate general Joseph] Johnston." Those plans were obliterated on July 21. Southern general Pierre G. T. Beauregard battled McDowell near Manassas Junction. Joined by Joseph Johnston's men (who had slipped out of the Shenandoah Valley without Federal knowledge), Beauregard trounced McDowell and sent his fledgling army fleeing back to the defenses of Washington, thus dashing all Union hopes that the end to a quick and glorious war was close at hand.

General Scott wired McClellan the bad news at 8:00 P.M. "McDowell has been checked," the old general understated. "Come down to the Shenandoah Valley with such troops as can be spared from western Virginia and make head against the Enemy on that quarter." But as McClellan planned to comply with the instructions, the U.S. War Department changed its mind. The capital was in a panic and needed an overall commander to reorganize the army and instill confidence in the troops. The choice was the thirty-four-year-old McClellan—the only victorious department head in the war's early months. Early on July 22, McClellan received his new instructions to "charge Rosecrans or some other general with your present department and come hither without delay." Told not to bring troops, McClellan prepared to comply quickly with his orders. "Meet me in Washington City," he told Lander.[48]

Lander joined McClellan and his other staffers on the railroad journey that took them from Wheeling to Pittsburgh, then through Pennsylvania

---

Tull, July 16, 1861, MP 9:4394. Charles Tull is a mysterious figure associated with Lander. Lander hired him as a citizen spy six months after the Rich Mountain campaign. Tull performed his job well by giving Lander very accurate information. See Edward C. Fishel, *The Secret War for the Union: The Untold Story of Military Intelligence in the Civil War* (Boston, 1996), 168.

48. Scott to GBM, July 21, 1861, MP 9:4845; Sears, *McClellan*, 93–4; GBM to Scott, July 21, 1861, in Sears, *Papers of George B. McClellan*, 65–6; GBM to FWL, July 22, 1861, LP 2:6325.

to Washington. They arrived late on July 26; McClellan was immediately appointed commander of the Division of the Potomac. Lander's return to Washington was marked with uncertainty. Though pleased by the reunion with his wife, he knew that the rare opportunity to lead troops in western Virginia was not likely to be repeated with McClellan in control of a much larger command. His performance at Rich Mountain, though more important and successful than Philippi, received little attention in the press due to the Federal disaster ten days later at Manassas.

Lander's leadership abilities, however, were not lost on those with influence. General McClellan, Rhode Island governor William Sprague, and Virginia senator Robert Carlisle lobbied strongly to win Lander an appointment. Their efforts bore fruit immediately. Lander's flamboyance, loyalty, and patriotism, which were highlighted in his February–April missions, plus his dashing displays of leadership and bravery on the battlefield could no longer be overlooked. On August 6, Frederick Lander was awarded the rank of brigadier general, predated to May 17, 1861.[49]

Lander's promotion was a singular feat. Not since the initiation of hostilities and never again in the war would an unranked and unpaid Union volunteer receive a general's star.

49. Newspaper clipping, LP 10; Commission of Frederick W. Lander, LP 2:6379.

6

"We Need Fighting Men"

Aye, deem us proud, for we are more
　　Than proud of all our mighty dead
Proud of the bleak and rock-bound shore,
　　A crowned oppressor cannot tread.

Proud of each rock and wood, and glen,
　　Of every river, lake and plain;
Proud of the calm and earnest men
　　Who claim the right and will to reign.

Proud that yon slowly sinking sun
　　Saw drowning lips grow white in prayer,
O'er such brief acts of duty done,
　　As honor gathers from despair
　　　　　　　　　　　　—F. W. Lander

Washington appeared safer by August 1. The capital was finally relieved of the threats of a Confederate invasion that followed the Union
disaster at Bull Run, near Manassas Junction. Congress again went about
its business and passed its final legislation prior to its annual summer leave,
including passing a bill to create the Metropolitan Police and also appro-
priating money to carry on the war. The senators and representatives re-
cessed just as General McClellan started to add more stability to the area.
Permits to enter the town were strictly regulated. Undesirables disap-

peared from the city streets as new troops were expected to march in by the thousands. Regiments and military guards appeared to be garrisoned everywhere. "The city . . . has a more martial look," wrote one citizen in his diary. With no imminent threat of an invasion, Washington could go about its business as a wartime capital. Dignitaries felt safe enough to pay a visit, including Prince Napoleon of France, who arrived with his staff to get a personal view of the American war. His was a special trip, marked by state dinners scheduled in his honor at the White House and at Secretary Seward's house.[1]

A day or two prior to Seward's planned reception, one of his invited guests, renowned poet Nathaniel P. Willis, dined at Willard's. The popular hotel still held the reputation as a center of social activity, but in early August it had been heavily garrisoned by officers and troops. Willis had published extensively throughout the past three decades and was entering articles in his own *Home Journal* in the summer of 1861. The artist's eyes, skilled after fifty-five years of noting sights of inspiration, did not fail him at Willard's. While staring at a throng of military personnel in the lobby, Willis fixed his gaze on an officer who appeared to search in vain for someone. The officer passed Willis in the hotel corridor, exited the building and crossed the sidewalk to his horse, then mounted the animal and rode away. It was a scene all too commonplace at the hotel, and Willis later admitted that his attention would have briskly left the officer had it not been for the unique mien of the man. "His movement was very peculiar," observed the poet, "above the middle height, and most powerfully built, he looked both active and indolent—both stately and careless. It was something between the complete soldierliness of a knight-templar and the covert agility of a panther on the prowl." Willis was dumbfounded that no one he asked at the scene could identify the captivating officer.

Attending Prince Napoleon's reception at Seward's house on August 7, Willis caught sight of someone he could identify—Jean Davenport Lander. Knowing the actress from an earlier acquaintance, Willis was happy to meet her again and politely accepted her offer of an introduction to her husband, a man currently lost in a crowd in the secretary's expansive parlor. Willis was aware that the spouse of "Miss Davenport" had been recently promoted to general, but to the best of his recollection he had

1. Leech, *Reveille in Washington*, 108–9; Bruce Catton, *Terrible Swift Sword* (Garden City, N.Y., 1963), 81.

never met the man. Crossing the room several minutes after the actress left his side, Willis searched for her in a sea of people and found her at her husband's side. It was only then Willis realized that the "magnificent specimen" he had seen at Willard's and Brigadier General Frederick Lander were one and the same.[2]

Mrs. Lander was immensely proud of her husband, so much so that she took to calling him "General" in her personal correspondences. After she introduced Lander to Willis, the general informed the bard that they had met before. Lander revealed to Willis his own ambition to be a poet and reminded Willis that he had approached him years earlier for advice and a critique of some of his literary work. Lander then recounted to him how he (Willis) had frankly informed him that poetry was not his trade and advised him to focus his talents elsewhere. To prevent embarrassing the esteemed poet at a public event, Lander thanked Willis for his honest advice and credited him with steering his career in a way that escalated him to a commissioned general's rank in the Union army. "Who will say that 'our country' owes me nothing after this?" boasted Willis later to his *Home Journal* readers, reminding them of Lander's western Virginia accomplishments: "Would 'the Union,' at present rather have Lander a poet, or Lander the twin-hero to McClellan!"[3]

The Union's newest brigadier basked in the accolades earned from the western Virginia campaign. He also enjoyed the monthly $124 salary that came with the commission. Donning his new starred epaulets, Lander posed at Brady's studio for two photographs within days of Seward's reception. Both photographs captured Willis's image of Lander, depicting the general as a determined officer.[4]

Notwithstanding the professional criticism of his literary skills, Lander the soldier refused to dissociate himself from Lander the poet. Inspired by a spectrum of topics, Lander crafted his poems both on the events of the day and of yesteryear. Lander's newest source of inspiration was the war and the sacrifices incurred on the battlefield. That summer in Washington, Lander disregarded Willis's earlier critique and returned to rhyme. Hear-

2. Wilson and Fiske, *Appleton's Cyclopaedia,* vol. 6 (1899), 539–41; Nathaniel P. Willis, "Gen. Lander as Seen on Horseback and in Mr. Seward's Parlor—His Experience as a Poet," LFP.

3. Willis, "Gen. Lander as Seen on Horseback," LFP.

4. Francis A. Lord, *They Fought for the Union* (New York, 1960), 123; Matthew Brady, photographs of Frederick Lander, U.S. Signal Corp photo No. 111-BA-593, NA.

ing stories about the action at Manassas, Lander was taken by the performance of the First and Second Rhode Island Infantry, two regiments from Colonel Ambrose E. Burnside's brigade who were decimated on Matthews Hill. Colonel John Slocum had been mortally wounded leading his Second Rhode Island over a fence. Rhode Island governor William Sprague—a strong proponent of Lander's promotion that summer—had participated in the Manassas fight and watched his men fall in heaps. Heavily influenced by the disappointing loss, the New Englanders' sacrifice, and the Union cause, Lander wrote "Rhode Island to the South," a poem whose final three stanzas highlighted his values concerning the sacrifices needed to preserve the Union.[5]

Lander liked his effort so much that he sent the poem to Nathaniel Willis again, requesting his opinion. For once Willis appeared impressed with what he considered "inspired" prose and published it in his *Home Journal*.[6] "Rhode Island to the South" marked the return of Frederick Lander as a poet. The war dominated Lander's themes, and he began to compose an impressive list of prose relating to military issues.

Lander had the time to attend receptions and write poetry in Washington in August primarily because the new brigadier had yet to be given a force to command. McClellan methodically crafted an organized and trained army by incorporating new regiments into brigades and divisions as they entered the capital. Lincoln issued a second call for troops, this time setting a quota for 300,000 three-year men—a frank admission of the Union's plan for a large and protracted war. Governor John Andrew diligently answered Lincoln's call by sending more than a score of Massachusetts regiments to Washington. Toward the end of September two of those regiments, the Nineteenth and Twentieth Massachusetts, entered McClellan's army as part of Lander's brigade. The Nineteenth in particular was well fitted for Lander; most of its men were recruited from his boyhood home of Salem.

With a promise of Massachusetts regiments to lead, Lander spent a disproportionate amount of effort to incorporate some specialized troops into his command. John Saunders, a carpenter by trade and another hometown acquaintance, had been busy during the summer recruiting a

---

5. Frederick Lander, "Rhode Island to the South," in *The Rebellion Record*, vol. 3, ed. Frank Moore (1863; reprint, New York, 1977), 17. See Appendix 1 for the text to this and all of Lander's poems.

6. Willis to FWL, October 5, 1861, LP 2:6355.

company of soldiers. His was a unique unit. Saunders's recruits were sharpshooters. Saunders had obtained a custom-made, forty-pound telescopic rifle, able to strike a target consistently at 500 yards. The bullet could penetrate a fourteen-inch pine plank at a distance of 200 yards. Saunders showed his rifle to another sportsman, Governor Andrew, who was easily convinced that an entire company of soldiers carrying these guns would provide great benefit to the service—particularly in picking off enemy artillerists.[7]

Lander concurred. Concerned in August that the Confederates were raising battery works near Munson's Hill in sight of Washington, Lander urged having marksmen available to thwart Confederate efforts there. Lander asked his boyhood friend, Boston attorney William D. Northend, to intervene. On August 24, Northend informed Lander that "Saunders has now about 120 men of the right sort." Five days later, the unit grew to 200 and Secretary of War Simon Cameron issued orders to Andrew to send the marksmen—named the Andrew Sharpshooters—to Washington. By this time the Munson's Hill threat had disappeared (and was later found to be a hoax).[8]

On September 6 Lander's brigade, consisting of the Nineteenth Massachusetts, Twentieth Massachusetts, and the Berdan Sharpshooters (an eighteen-company marksmen unit to which the Andrew Sharpshooters were attached) marched into Washington and established a camp on Meridian Hill, in full view of the city and one mile from the domeless Capitol. The Twentieth, dubbed the Harvard Regiment for the numerous elite college graduates in its ranks, was the first one encamped at Meridian Hill. Lander briefly addressed his fellow Bay Staters, leaving a positive impression on the volunteers. Young Lieutenant Oliver Wendell Holmes Jr. judged Lander to be "a first rate man," while Lieutenant Henry Livermore Abbott took comfort in his erroneous belief that Lander was an old army officer. The Nineteenth Massachusetts filed into camp soon afterward, as did several companies of sharpshooters and eventually the Seventh Michigan. On September 12, Lander's brigade settled in its final composition with the two Massachusetts regiments, the Michigan men, the Andrew Sharpshooters (the rest of Ber-

7. "The Target Rifle," newspaper clipping, LP 10.
8. Ibid.; Northend to FWL, August 24, 1861, LP 2:6331; *OR* (Series 3) 1:464; Leech, *Reveille in Washington,* 112, 116.

dan's Sharpshooters remained detached), and Battery B, First Rhode Island Light Artillery.[9]

That same day, Lander received orders to transfer his men to Poolesville, Maryland, where he was to become part of a new division created in the Army of the Potomac. Brigadier General Charles P. Stone, another Massachusetts native who had served ably on General Scott's staff to protect Washington during the war's first months, was awarded command of the Corps of Observation, a three-brigade division designated to cover the Upper Potomac region. Stone's force occupied the Maryland shore to study the movements of Confederate troops stationed across the river in and around Leesburg. On September 14 Lander and his brigade marched into Poolesville, bivouacked for the night, then moved two and one-half miles south of town, where the soldiers settled in on a low treeless plain two miles north of Edwards Ferry, a Potomac crossing at the mouth of Goose Creek. The ground was originally a wheatfield on a farm owned by a man named Williams. It served as a prime site to spread Lander's 2,500-man force.

William Northend accompanied the general for the troop transfer, a rare visit between the two old friends. Lander christened the site Camp Benton in honor of Colonel William P. Benton, an aggressive Indiana commander who impressed Lander at Rich Mountain. Sitting in the most advanced position of Stone's division, Camp Benton pleased the soldiers with its main features—a clear cold brook running in front of it, woodland to the west, and a clear view to the Bull Run Mountains and the Blue Ridge beyond. Taking it all in, a member of the Twentieth Massachusetts considered the camp "a healthy and lovely situation."[10]

But Lander had not brought his men there to admire the landscape. He longed for action and welcomed the opportunity to encamp within

---

9. *OR* (Series 3), 1:475–6, 478; Oliver W. Holmes Jr. to his mother, September 11, 1861, in *Touched with Fire: Civil War Letters and Diary of Oliver Wendell Holmes, Jr., 1861–1864,* ed. Mark De Wolfe Howe (Cambridge, Mass., 1947), 7; Henry Abbott to his mother, September 6, 1861, in *The Civil War Letters of Henry Livermore Abbott,* ed. Robert Garth (Kent, Ohio, 1991), 44; The Nineteenth Massachusetts History Committee, *History of the Nineteenth Regiment Massachusetts Volunteer Infantry, 1861–1865* (Salem, Mass., 1906), 14–15.

10. *OR* (Series 3), 1:478; Nineteenth Massachusetts History Committee, *History of the Nineteenth Regiment,* 15–16; George Bruce, *The Twentieth Regiment of Massachusetts Volunteer Infantry, 1861–1865* (Boston, 1906), 14–17.

three miles of Confederate pickets across the Potomac. He insisted that discipline be enforced at the regular army standard; therefore, extended daily drills sharpened the volunteers. Company, battalion, regimental, and full brigade movements were practiced and repeated every afternoon. It seemed to the soldiers that when they were not engaged in drills, they spent the rest of their time cleaning their brass buttons and shoulder scales. "If any men ever earned thirteen dollars a month we did," claimed Captain John Adams of the Nineteenth Massachusetts. On alternative nights, two companies of infantry accompanied two cannons from the Rhode Island battery to Edwards Ferry as outpost duty. Others got to work constructing military buildings on the towpath that ran between the Potomac River and the Chesapeake and Ohio (C & O) Canal. Northern and southern pickets often exchanged friendly and not-so-friendly banter across the river.[11]

General Lander was often visible to his men, particularly during the night excursions to the ferry. He also presided over numerous brigade inspections to ensure his men looked and drilled to his expectations. Some were impressed by his appearance, describing him as "a fine dashing officer with a horse to match." But Lander's insistence on remaining under arms five days per week and on stumbling around the canal on clammy nights produced some grumblings in Camp Benton.[12] "It seems to be his particular delight to send us off to bivouac on the river when it is actually so cold that the men walk about half the night to keep themselves from freezing," complained Lieutenant Henry Livermore Abbott to his father. "You will judge what kind of man he is in short when I tell you that he has a more violent prejudice against allowing any body in his command to sleep quietly during the time allotted by the Almighty for sleep."[13]

Despite the isolated outbursts of the officers, the volunteers found little to complain about at Camp Benton in its first month of existence. The Union troopers covered the Maryland side of the river with few incidents.

---

11. Capt. John G. B. Adams, *Reminiscences of the Nineteenth Massachusetts Regiment* (Boston, 1899), 13; "Salem" to the editor, September 19, 1861, *Salem Gazette,* October, 1861; Bruce, *Twentieth Regiment,* 17–18.

12. Adams, *Nineteenth Massachusetts Regiment,* 13; Edgar Newcomb to his brother, September 23, 1861, in *A Memorial Sketch of Lieut. Edgar M. Newcomb,* ed. A. B. Weymouth (Malden, Mass., 1883), 27; Oliver W. Holmes Jr. to his mother, September 23, 1861, in Howe, *Touched with Fire,* 8–9; Bruce, *Twentieth Regiment,* 18–19.

13. Abbott to his father, September 25, 1861, in Garth, *Letters,* 51.

Opposing pickets on each side of the river kept an agreement not to shoot at each other. To retain their skills the Andrew Sharpshooters maintained a daily two-hour regimen of target practice. "Most of the men are sure of their man at half a mile," boasted a member of the unit. But as September rolled over to October, no one could be sure whether they would soon be able to test his claim.[14]

Lander's brigade was centered within the Union force opposite Leesburg. General Stone's Corps of Observation watched the Potomac between Nolands Ferry and Seneca. One regiment of unattached infantry covered the shore between Point of Rocks and Harpers Ferry upstream, and Major General Nathaniel Banks's division rested in reserve deeper in the Maryland countryside. Additionally, two divisions of Federal soldiers encamped across Washington on the Virginia side.[15] No threats against this force appeared, and McClellan likewise offered no evidence that he would advance the Army of the Potomac into Virginia.

Lander chafed at the inactivity. He directed much of his ire toward his command, particularly at the Seventh Michigan Infantry and its commander, Colonel Ira Grosvenor. Lander was fed up with Grosvenor's inattention to details, complaining that "he has caused much annoyances to me." It irritated Lander that by date of commission, Colonel Grosvenor, a former militia colonel, outranked Colonel Raymond Lee, a West Pointer leading the Twentieth Massachusetts. Realizing this left Grosvenor in charge of the brigade during the general's absences from command, Lander sought to rectify the hierarchy with General Stone. Members of the Seventh Michigan in turn directed their ire at Lander. After the regiment lost eleven men in ten days to measles, Lander flippantly remarked, "It was no wonder they were all dying, they were so damn dirty." Reports of Lander's insult reached the company officers, leading four disgruntled captains to sit in a tent one night, sharing a pitcher of whiskey while plotting how to kill their brigade commander.[16]

14. Edward Bicknell to the editor, October 1, 1861, *Chelsea (Mass.) Telegraph and Pioneer,* October 12, 1861.

15. Byron Farwell, *Ball's Bluff: A Small Battle and Its Long Shadow* (McLean, Va., 1990), 40.

16. FWL to Charles P. Stone, October, 5, 1861, LP 2:6352–4; "Remarks of Gen. Shafter before the Thomas Post G. A. R., March 18th, 1902," Bentley Historical Library, University of Michigan, Ann Arbor.

Although he was outwardly critical of the Seventh Michigan, Lander harbored doubts about the fighting élan of all of the volunteers within the Army of the Potomac. He maintained that the emigrants and untrained mountaineers he saw in the West were more fit for war than the raw soldiers serving in McClellan's army. Lander felt the policy of "judiciary promotions" would help to rectify the situation.[17] Nothing instilled more confidence, in his opinion, than to reward a volunteer with a commission for valorous performance on a battlefield. After all, he was a model example of such a promotion. But a battle was a prerequisite for the promotion and no hint of one could be detected in the early autumn of 1861.

Lander yearned for action. In the five months between February and July he was constantly on the go, first as a special agent, then as an active participant in the western Virginia campaign. With the passing of the first week of October, Lander realized he had seen much more action as a volunteer aide than he had in his first two months as a brigadier general. This did not sit well with him. Although holding a prestigious position as a brigadier in the largest army in the western hemisphere, Lander never let go of the desire to command an independent force. His forte was mountains and railroads—areas where he could conduct lightning strikes—not the flat and softly rolling pastoral lands where armies encamped and relaxed rather than fought.

Early in October's second week, Lander took leave of his command and rode to Washington. His objective was to convince the Lincoln cabinet to grant him a special command. On the night of October 10, he saw President Lincoln, Secretary Seward, and John Hay leave the White House. Lander joined the group and learned they were on their way to McClellan's quarters. With no time or desire for small talk, Lander spoke about how much he could accomplish with a specialized force. He postured that he would like a good place to die with his force and to set the nation right in the face of the world after what he called the "cowardly shame" of Bull Run. Lander took his leave before the men reached McClellan's. Watching the jingoistic general walk away, Lincoln turned to Seward and Hay and declared, "If he really wanted a job like that, I could

17. FWL to John Hay, December 31, 1861, John Hay Collection, Brown University Library, Providence, R.I.

give it to him. Let him take his squad and go down behind Manassas and break up their railroad."[18]

Lander called on Seward two days later to press his case. Complaining about the futility of watching the Potomac and grieving about the waste of inactivity, Lander offered his former boss his resignation. Lander's soul-searching had engendered the desire to go back to the West—"to begin again," as he explained to Seward. "Be of good cheer," came Seward's sanguine response. He then gave Lander information to cheer about: General Scott was already fixing his orders for exactly the work he wanted to do.[19]

General Scott had always appreciated the savage enthusiasm of the former frontiersman and never forgot Lander's patriotic acts nor his desire to raise and lead a force of loyal Virginians. Scott was still in charge; he requested Lander to meet him at the War Department on Sunday, October 13. When Lander arrived, Scott offered him his greatest opportunity since the commencement of the war. The U.S. War Department had created a new military district named the Department of Harpers Ferry and Cumberland. The command embraced the 120-mile line of the B & O Railroad between Harpers Ferry and Cumberland, covering a thirty-mile-wide swath in Virginia territory. Scott informed Lander that he had tagged him to head this department.[20]

Lander immediately accepted the position and threw himself into his new role. He tendered his resignation in McClellan's army, reminding "Little Mac" that considering his selfless service throughout the fist months of the war, the request should be granted immediately. He then sent an agent to Baltimore to meet with B & O president John W. Garrett and to get his views on how to open the rail line, which had been down for five months. Lander was particularly interested in the citizens' sentiment along the line, map availability, and the quality of forces in Maryland that could be employed. As soon as the agent returned, Lander sent him

18. John Hay diary, October 10, 1861, in Burlingame and Ettlinger, *Inside Lincoln's White House,* 24.

19. John Hay diary, October 12, 1861, in Burlingame and Ettlinger, *Inside Lincoln's White House,* 25. Seward relayed the specifics of his conversation with Lander to Lincoln and Hay later that night.

20. "Agate," "From General Lander's Division," February 7, 1862, *Cincinnati Daily Gazette,* February 13, 1862; Summers, *Baltimore and Ohio,* 104; Edward Lander Sr. to Edward Jr. and Charles, November 10, 1861, LFP.

to New York to obtain rifles. In the meantime, Lander rode to Baltimore and met with Garrett personally. From there he toiled endlessly to round up enough available Maryland troops to incorporate into his embryonic force.[21]

Lander returned to Washington and held a series of meetings with General Scott on October 20 and 21. Scott consulted his protégé about Romney, a town in Hampshire County, Virginia. Romney held strategic importance for the protection of the B & O Railroad since three roads spoked from the hub to various points on the line. The town had already changed hands six times; the current possessor was a small Confederate cavalry detachment that had seized Romney from an Ohio battalion on September 24. As the new department head in charge of reopening the railroad, Lander urged Scott to commit a large enough force to take and hold the town. Lander considered the closest and most logical choice to be Benjamin Kelley, the former First Virginia colonel who was wounded at Philippi. Not totally recovered from his injury, Kelley was nevertheless promoted to brigadier general and commanded a quartet of Ohio and Union Virginia infantry regiments at Grafton. Scott complied by sending orders to Kelley to capture Romney, informing him that he would temporarily head the Department of Harpers Ferry and Cumberland until Lander arrived.[22]

Lander's plans progressed swiftly. His friend and aide, Simon Barstow, had succeeded in acquiring more troops from Maryland's Eastern Shore to add to the ever-growing department. But by the afternoon of Monday, October 21, events upriver from Washington redirected Lander's thoughts and actions. General Stone's Corps of Observation, including Lander's brigade, had crossed onto the Virginia river height known as Ball's Bluff and heavily engaged Confederate forces under the command of Colonel Nathan Evans throughout the day. Promising telegrams sent by General Stone in the morning and early afternoon suddenly turned sour. By late afternoon, the War Department learned that Colonel Edward Baker (whom

21. FWL to GBM, October 13, 1861, LP 2:6369; FWL to B. W. Latham, October 14, 1861, LP 2:6370; Latham to S. F. Barstow, October 25, 1861, LP 2:6381; FWL to "Cols. commanding 7 and 10th Maryland Volunteers," October 16, 1861, LP 2:6372.

22. FWL, Testimony, December 27, 1861, JCCW, pt. 1, 161; Hu Maxwell and H. L. Swisher, *History of Hampshire County, West Virginia, from Its Earliest Settlement to the Present* (1897; reprint, Parsons, W.Va., 1972), 550; Frothingham, *B. F. Kelley,* 17–18; *OR,* 5:625.

Lander knew from their ocean voyage together a year earlier) was killed, and the troops across the river were in trouble. McClellan ordered Major General Banks to move a brigade to support the engaged troops. By early evening a short telegram sent by McClellan's chief of staff was delivered to Lander's home: "The General commanding directs that you proceed at once to report to General Stone at or near Edward's Ferry." By 9:00 P.M. Lander set off to reunite with his former command.[23]

He rode all night through a persistent light rain. Six hours and thirty-six miles later, Lander reached the remnants of his command. Many of the wounded were left on Ball's Bluff. More than 100 had drowned in the Potomac; their bodies would wash up downriver near the city of Washington for days afterward. Another sizable force, over 1,500 strong and under the command of Brigadier General Willis A. Gorman, had formed a bridgehead across Edwards Ferry and remained on Virginia soil overnight. Gorman's force included the Seventh Michigan, one company from the Nineteenth Massachusetts, and the Andrew Sharpshooters of Lander's brigade. "I found my regiments scattered every way," Lander recalled two months later. Collecting all the camp guards and managing to find three organized companies of his brigade, Lander described the men as "tired, beat out, and wet through." He placed them near the riverbank under some haystacks and—acting like a father as much as a general—he told his forlorn troopers to get some sleep.

At the break of dawn, Lander found a doleful General Stone consulting with General Banks around a campfire. Lander greeted the two, then requested permission from Stone to proceed to Harrison's Island in the Potomac River, which had served as the launching point to Ball's Bluff the day before. Lander wished to retrieve the remnants of his Twentieth Massachusetts, which he learned had been terribly chewed up on the Virginia heights across the Potomac. Stone denied the request, preferring Lander to stay and consult with them. Banks asked Lander what he thought the next step should be. Lander responded by asking him what McClellan's most recent orders had been. Told that those orders were to hold their positions "at all hazards" across the river from Edwards Ferry, Lander retorted, "There is nothing to be done but to re-inforce the men there at once." Banks did not appear to wholly support the proposal, ex-

---

23. Col. Edward Wallis to S. F. Barstow, October 19, 1861, LP 2:6375; *OR*, 51(1):500–1; R. B. Marcy to FWL, October 21, 1861, LP 2:6378.

plaining that his brigades had been wearied by extensive marching in cold wet weather. "There is no time to rest," Lander snapped back, reminding Banks that one of his regiments (the Seventh Michigan) stood on Virginia soil without effective weapons and they needed immediate support.[24]

Once Banks sheepishly agreed to cross his men at the ferry, Lander explained, "As I have no brigade, as my regiments are scattered everywhere, I will act as aid, or reconnoitering officer, or anything you choose." Enraged and disgusted at what he interpreted as Banks's indecision and lack of promptness, Lander stormed away from the campfire and headed toward the riverbank. As Lander passed by the beat-up Harvard regiment, a company officer witnessed his brigade commander in a horrible rage, "swearing that the thing is nothing less than murder." The general mounted his horse, galloped to the ferry, and dismounted.[25]

"Old Grizzly" paced the river bank, his concern now for his men across the river. With the aid of a member of the Andrew Sharpshooters, he confiscated one of the three skiffs that was used to transport troops the preceding day. He crossed the river and while moving toward the front met General Gorman, who had taken charge of the troops on Virginia soil. Gorman urged Lander to return to the Maryland side of the river to get General Banks's assistance in pulling the troops back to Maryland. Lander refused, citing that headquarter's orders were to hold the position at all costs. Gorman protested the decision and warned his peer that the area was too risky to plan a defense, but Lander ignored him and continued forward. Knowing that his command was exposed, Lander reasoned, "Having lost one regiment, the 20th Massachusetts, I believed it was about time to save another." Gorman crossed the river to find Banks as Lander advanced to the front.

24. Edward Lander Sr., to Edward Jr. and Charles, November 10, 1861, LFP; FWL, Testimony, December 27, 1861, JCCW, pt. 2, 253–4; Alpheus S. Williams to his daughter, November 5, 1861, in *From the Cannon's Mouth: The Civil War Letters of General Alpheus S. Williams,* ed. Milo M. Quaife (Detroit, Mich., 1959), 24. Banks's testimony differs significantly from Lander's. He claimed that he supported Lander's desire to cross the river: "I said it was my duty" (Banks, Testimony, January 28, 1862, JCCW, pt. 2, 415–16). Major Dwight Bannister's testimony supports Banks by claiming that he was in the process of sending cannons across the river when Lander arrived (Bannister, Testimony, January 9, 1862, JCCW, pt. 2, 285).

25. FWL, Testimony, JCCW, pt. 2, 254; FWL to W. D. Northend, November 6, 1861, Northend Papers, Emory University; Henry Abbott to his father, October 22, 1861, in Garth, *Letters,* 66.

A member of the Nineteenth Massachusetts who had crossed into Virginia the day before watched his careworn general approach. "If I would have been with you," Lander exclaimed, "I would have found a way out of a field before entering it." The field that Lander found had been covered with a fully grown and partially harvested corn crop. A rail fence ran from the river to the woods in front of the field. Captain Saunders and several of his sharpshooters were encamped at the southern end of the fence. A farmhouse stood on the far right on open land. Thick woods outlined the center and eastern portions of the field. Goose Creek also ran through the eastern woods, parallel to the fence. A bridge crossed the creek. Gorman had ordered a company of the First Minnesota Infantry to guard the bridge, where they remained when Lander arrived on the scene.

Lander sent orders back for two more companies to reinforce the westerners, then he ordered the Seventh Michigan to deploy in a ravine. Telling their colonel that the regiment's guns—the Belgian muskets—were worthless, the general instructed the Michigan troopers to watch for attacking enemy cavalry and prepare to give them the bayonet. In the meantime, he took Company K of the Nineteenth Massachusetts (known as the Tiger Zouaves for their colorful uniforms) and deployed them as skirmishers to scour the woods in front. A cold rain pelted the men as the time passed 2:00 P.M.[26]

Suddenly, a shower of leaden balls poured from the woods in front. Captain Saunders, fearing that the Federal companies guarding the bridge had opened on them, shouted into the woods, "Hold on Boys, you are firing at your own men!" His claim was answered by a member of Colonel William Barksdale's Thirteenth Mississippi Infantry. "Now you son of a bitch," the rebel shouted, "we've got you." With that, 500 members of the Thirteenth Mississippi assaulted Lander's force and attempted to drive it into the river.[27]

The Mississippi troops struck the Federals on their left flank and in-

26. Bicknell, "Sharpshooters," 9–10; Annette Tapert, ed., *The Brothers' War: Civil War Letters to Their Loved Ones from the Blue and Gray* (New York, 1988), 28–9; Lander to JCCW, pt. 2, 254; Nineteenth Massachusetts History Committee, *History of the Nineteenth Regiment*, 32–3.

27. Officer in Lander's brigade, "The Fight at Edwards Ferry," *Boston Journal*, November 1, 1861.

stantly drove back the Minnesota company guarding the Goose Creek bridge. Falling back in confusion, they streamed through the left flank of the Andrew Sharpshooters arrayed behind them and drove them back as well. Although the Union troops on the Virginia side of Edwards Ferry numbered more than 2,000, no more than 200 were deployed to resist an assault, and Lander found himself as the only general officer in the area. Gorman and Banks had just crossed over to Virginia in an effort to organize troops to support him. Although he had earlier offered to volunteer his services as an aide to the commanding officer on the field, Lander took control of the exposed force.

Under fire for the first time since the Rich Mountain battle three months earlier, Lander quickly arranged a defense. He saw 2,000 Confederates on the hills in reserve, too far away even for his sharpshooters but close enough to disperse with artillery. Unfortunately, the only batteries offering support remained on the heights in Maryland, lobbing shot and shell over their heads toward the southerners. Lander rushed to the Andrew Sharpshooters. He restored their left flank behind a rail fence that ran east to west below a hill. The sharpshooters held the Confederates in check with their heavy telescopic rifles, which dropped southerners from 400 yards.

Lander wanted the hill in front of him and had decided to use Saunders's men to take it. But as he walked from right to left behind his men to assure his battle line was maintained, one of Barksdale's Mississippians fired at the Yankee general. The musket ball tore into the instep of Lander's lower left leg and dug into his calf, where it buried itself deep in the muscle. As the pain surged through him, Lander reeled and dropped to the ground. He rose again and denied anything was wrong, refusing any aid or to be removed from the front. He hobbled directly behind the sharpshooters, waving his pistol in the air while exhorting the company to hold its ground.

Forty-five minutes passed. Barksdale's men offered no more threat to the line and retired toward Fort Evans near Leesburg. Lander, growing weaker by the minute, then ordered the sharpshooters to fall back toward the river. As they withdrew, an aide found Daniel Hand, the new assistant surgeon of the First Minnesota Infantry, and asked him to examine Lander's wound. The ball had driven Lander's boot strap into his calf. But as Hand pulled the leather strap out of the hole, he recalled that Lander "swore a blue streak, and vowed he would go on to the ferry before having anything done." Complaining about Lander's restlessness, Hand later admitted, "I was rather glad to get him off my hands."[28]

Lander mounted a horse and, supported by two sharpshooters, was escorted to one of the three available boats at the ferry. He was turned over to another surgeon and Major Dwight Bannister, the paymaster of Lander's brigade. They supported the general as the skiff docked on the Maryland side of the river. Generals Stone, Gorman, and Banks greeted Lander at the shore and shook his hand. As Major Bannister helped Lander into a waiting ambulance, Lander called Banks back to him and told him "in rather strong language" to return to his men in Virginia and hold their position, claiming that with appropriate support he could have taken Leesburg. After Banks left his side, Bannister took his seat next to Lander in the ambulance. "There will be no fighting until General McClellan comes up," Lander quietly predicted. With that the two rode back to Poolesville.[29]

At 7:00 P.M. Dr. Bryant, the brigade surgeon, found his most important patient and examined the wound. It was an ugly hole indeed, but Bryant did not note any overt reason for concern. He cleaned out the remaining boot leather, extracted the ball, and dressed Lander's wounded leg. Captain Charles Candy, Lander's assistant adjutant general, quickly telegraphed Jean Lander to inform her of her husband's injury but to assure her all was well—"wound not at all dangerous"—since it had not clipped the bone. Jean Lander rode out to Poolesville the next day and found McClellan paying a respectful visit at her husband's quarters. By that time McClellan had ordered the remaining Union troops to recross the Potomac to the safety of the Maryland shore. The ill-fated campaign was over.[30]

28. Bicknell, "Sharpshooters," 11; Lander to JCCW, pt. 2, 254; Nineteenth Massachusetts History Committee, *History of the Nineteenth Regiment,* 33–4; "The Fight at Edwards Ferry," *Boston Journal,* November 1, 1861; Edward Lander Sr. to Jean Lander, November 8, 1861, LP 11 (letter includes a newspaper clipping describing the wound); Edward Lander Sr. to Edward Jr. and Charles, November 10, 1861, LFP; "A Brilliant Little Fight," October 29, 1861, newspaper clipping, LP 10; Daniel Hand, "Reminiscences of an Army Surgeon," *Glimpses of the Nation's Struggle,* vol. 1 (St. Paul, Minn., 1887): 279–80.

29. Bannister, Testimony, JCCW, pt. 2, 285.

30. W. B. to the editor, October 22, 1861, newspaper clipping, LFP; Charles Candy to Mrs. Lander, October 21, 1861, LP 11; Edward Lander Sr. to Edward Jr. and Charles, November 10, 1861, LFP; Bannister, Testimony, JCCW, pt. 2, 285.

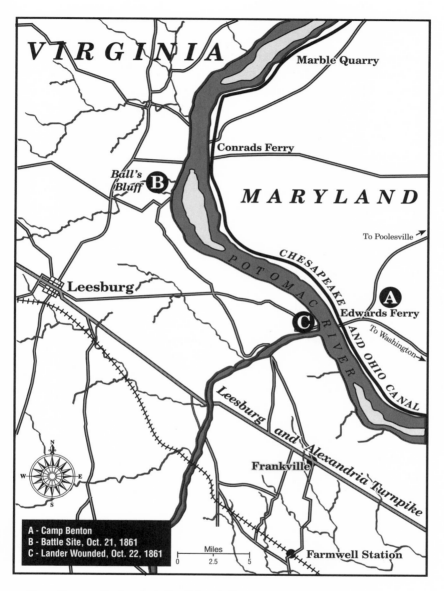

Upper Potomac Region, including Edwards Ferry

Jean stayed with her husband at Camp Benton for three days and took the occasion to visit the camps of his regiments. His wife's arrival did little to curtail Lander's temper. He vented his anger over the entire fiasco that had transpired in the two days of action at Ball's Bluff. Every aspect of the battle irritated him to the core. The poor plan of battle, the wasted sacrifice of human life—particularly in his Twentieth Massachusetts—the lackluster support by Banks, and the apparent lack of aggression by Gorman on the Virginia side of the river fed his fury for days. Lander's oaths were hurled within earshot of his staff members. Lieutenant Edgar Newcomb of the Nineteenth Massachusetts served as Lander's clerk throughout the autumn and paid close attention to the goings-on at Camp Benton the week after the battle. "You have heard of our shameful retreats from Ball's Bluff," Newcomb wrote to his sister. "[T]his time the shame falls wholly on our leaders, who planned the expeditions. Gen. Lander was so disgusted as in the excitement of the moment to say that unless he considered our ultimate success doubtful, he would resign at once. Perhaps, probably his words meant more than he had intended, but the general opinion hereabouts is that this war will be a long one."[31]

McClellan, who had never acted on Lander's October 14 resignation request, officially relieved him from brigade command to convalesce. Lander rode back to Washington with his wife and staff on Saturday, October 26, and returned to his E Street home. Once again, his sister Louisa visited from New York to help Jean and her mother nurse him. His flesh wound was not considered life threatening, but the Confederate ball had caused extensive and painful damage to his calf muscles. His personal physician, Dr. Prince, examined him and restricted him to bed rest for a few weeks to heal his leg.[32]

Restless, impatient, and still angered over the upper Potomac disaster, Lander turned his thoughts to the new command that he had been planning prior to his wounding. On October 27 General Kelley seized Romney with a mixed infantry, cavalry, and artillery force numbering 2,000 men. Although unable to capture the southerners defending the town, his victory succeeded in capturing many of their supplies and removing a direct

---

31. Emerson Bicknell to the editor, October 26, 1861, *Chelsea (Mass.) Telegraph and Pioneer,* November 2, 1861; Edgar Newcomb to his sister, October 31, 1861, in Weymouth, *Memorial Sketch,* 31.

32. Frederick W. Lander, Service Record, RG 94, NA; Edward Lander Sr. to Edward Jr. and Charles, November 10, 1861, LFP.

threat from the B & O Railroad between Cumberland and Hancock. The line was severely damaged, however, with several miles of track destroyed and several bridges burned. Months of work would be required to restore the track in the Virginia segment between Cumberland and Harpers Ferry.[33]

Lander was set to inherit this district from the ailing General Kelley, who convalesced in Cumberland while waiting for someone to take over. Lander brought staff members to Washington from the Corps of Observation to begin work in the Department of Harpers Ferry and Cumberland. His aides and agents worked diligently throughout the final week of October to enlist recruits and service them with new arms. On October 28 Lander sent Simon Barstow to General Scott with some written views on how to improve the department prior to his command there. Calling Kelley "brave to audacity," Lander requested that the general be strengthened immediately with experienced reinforcements, preferably from Rosecrans's force.

Lander had subtly hinted to Scott that undo caution was hampering the Union army. "In the present state of the public mind in Upper Virginia and Western Maryland, growing out of our late defeat at Ball's Bluff," reasoned Lander, "any reverse which might happen to Kelley would have a very bad effect on the success of our proposed recruitments." He stressed the immediate necessity to repair the B & O to provide the Army of the Potomac an open avenue of supplies by more rapid and direct transport than the alternative routes on which the Union currently relied. He reiterated his concerns about Kelley's safety three days later, exhorting, "The danger is now, and not hereafter or when he is reinforced."[34]

But Lander's requests were not a priority. A raging months-long feud had been developing between General McClellan and General Scott concerning how the Union armies should be used. Scott realized he was fighting one of the only battles of his career that he could not win and submitted his resignation prior to the Ball's Bluff campaign. The battle postponed the official change of commands, but Scott openly preferred to promote Henry Halleck rather than McClellan. A careful and immediate

33. Frothingham, *B. F. Kelley,* 17–20.
34. *OR,* 5:630–1; FWL to Simon Cameron, October 31, 1861, Records of the Office of the Secretary of War, RG 107, M221, Roll 196, NA.

investigation of "Little Mac's" role in the Leesburg fiasco would have revealed some culpability in withdrawing Brigadier General George A. McCall's men (his division was advancing up the Leesburg Pike near Dranesville on October 20) without informing General Stone. This led to Stone's surprise at finding the full concentration of southern force and attention focused completely on his movements.

McClellan proclaimed his innocence by stressing that the impetuous Colonel Baker made a fatal mistake. Despite his vaguely worded orders to General Stone, McClellan absolved himself from blame by insisting that he never intended for Stone to cross the river against Evans's army at Leesburg. His insistence paid off; on November 1, General Winfield Scott retired from the Union army, completing a distinguished service spanning five decades. Thirty-four-year-old George McClellan replaced him as general of all northern armies.[35]

"Little Mac's" promotion delivered a tremendous blow to Lander's war career. Within days of assuming overall command, McClellan suspended active recruitments for the Department of Harpers Ferry and Cumberland and terminated Lander's new military department. "I had often observed to the President and to members of the cabinet that the reconstruction of this railway [the B & O] could not be undertaken until we were in a condition to fight a battle to secure it," McClellan later explained. He considered the reconstruction as "very desirable but not vital" and felt that Winchester and Strasburg must fall into his hands to assure that the rails were adequately protected. With the winter season approaching, McClellan felt his army was in no condition to take those towns. General Kelley kept his force at Romney and oversaw workers who set out to repair the Patterson's Creek bridge near Cumberland. McClellan refused to strip troops from other commands and send them into northwestern Virginia to assist Kelley in his endeavors.[36]

Making matters worse, Lander put weight on his lame leg too early and tore the new tissue that had been forming in the wound. Forced to be laid up in his bed longer than originally anticipated, Lander fumed on hearing of McClellan's decision not to support his new command, a decision that severed the relationship existing between the two former railroad expedi-

35. Sears, *McClellan*, 121–5.
36. George B. McClellan, *McClellan's Own Story* (New York, 1887), 192; Summers, *Baltimore and Ohio*, 105. No official orders terminating the Department of Harpers Ferry and Cumberland have been found.

tion men. "This war is a farce," Lander seethed to his boyhood friend William Northend, adding, "bloodless nerves ruin the roast." He seriously entertained thoughts of returning to civilian life, telling Northend, "My intention of resigning is fixed and definite under present leadership. . . . Had I a good brigade and was detached say 4,000 men, two companies of cavalry and six old fashioned smoothbore guns . . . I would beat any 6,000 of them if left alone by superior officers." He wired a ciphered message to Brigadier General Henry W. Benham, who had been ordered by General Scott to reinforce Kelley (an order subsequently reversed), to let him know that he was wounded and was unsure of his future destination. "The report as to my promotion was a canard. Probably resign soon."[37]

The first weeks of November represented the most uncomfortable period of Frederick Lander's career. Two weeks earlier he had enjoyed peak strength and responsibility, and had been handed a department tailormade for his skills and supported by General Winfield Scott, a man who respected Lander. Incapacitated and restricted to bed rest, Lander no longer enjoyed good health, and he no longer had a command. McClellan seemed content to reinforce his army, drill it, and review it, but was in no hurry to send it off to fight. More than 100 days had passed since Lander had participated in the Rich Mountain campaign, and the only notable action had been Ball's Bluff. With the winter season approaching, the prospects of several months of inaction by the Union armies in the east was fast becoming a reality.

To divert his attention and alleviate his discomfort, Lander turned to one of his favorite pastimes—poetry. The heroic sacrifices at Ball's Bluff captured Lander's thoughts, particularly when he read a newspaper account that claimed the Confederates were saying that fewer of the Massachusetts officers would have been killed there had they not been too proud to surrender. The allusion to his native state's soldiers—particularly to his own Twentieth Massachusetts, which lost nearly 200 men on the Potomac bluffs—inspired him to produce a tribute he called "Ours." The acclaimed poem was published in newspapers throughout the North, ending with two stirring stanzas:

37. Newspaper clipping, Scrapbook; FWL to Northend, November 6, 1861, Northend Papers, Emory University; FWL to Henry Benham, November 7, 1861, Telegrams Received by the Secretary of War (unbound), 8:772, M504, NA.

Pride 'tis our watchword; "clear the boats,"
  "Holmes, Putnam, Bartlett, Pierson—Here"
And while this crazy wherry floats
  "Let's save our wounded," cries Revere.

Old State—some souls are rudely sped—
  This record for thy Twentieth Corps—
Imprisoned, wounded, dying, dead,
  It only asks, "Has Sparta more?"[38]

As December rolled into Washington, General Lander had recovered enough to hobble about with the aid of crutches. He no longer talked about resigning, for his future course in the army turned for the better. Although he could no longer raise new regiments for the defunct military department, he still was slated to replace Kelley at Romney once his wound had healed enough for him to endure a winter season in northwestern Virginia.[39]

The promise of action reinvigorated Lander. He went back to work, this time focusing not on a division or a brigade, but a company—the Andrew Sharpshooters. Impressed by their performance at Edwards Ferry, Lander had earlier requested that Governor Andrew give special commendation for Saunders's green-uniformed men because they, "by strict orders, and by a coolness free from that effervescent dash which is too apt to be called courage, kept their cool and held an important position against a segment of the enemy."

Lander reveled in the possibilities the sharpshooters offered with their long-range accuracy, their skills as artisans, and the strength and endurance locked within their large-framed bodies (indeed, thirty men in the company exceeded six feet in height). But Lander realized that the sharpshooters could not survive guerrilla attacks solely with the cumbersome telescopic guns they carried. With the aid of Simon Barstow and William Northend, Lander pushed to have Saunders's men supplied with side arms. "I want the men to have the revolvers," the general maintained, "and it is simply ridiculous, to expose them with a rifle that weighs fifty

38. Holien, *Battle at Ball's Bluff*, 88–9.

39. Willis, "Gen. Lander," March 3, 1862, Scrapbook; Special Orders No. 166, December 2, 1861, extracted copy in PDV. The orders acknowledged that Lander had been assigned to "Special duty in this city [Washington]; this arrangement to date from October 9, 1861."

pounds and has no bayonet, without them." By the first week in December, Lander was fed up with excuses for Governor Andrew's lack of diligence in the matter, so much so that he ranted his frustration to William Northend with animated fury: "For Christ's sake, use your influence to have these men obtain their revolvers, as it is all they will get, and I hope to do much with them as a special corps."[40]

Frederick Lander turned forty years old on December 17. That day, the general and Mrs. Lander took advantage of unseasonably warm December weather (the temperature in Georgetown was fifty-six degrees at 2:00 P.M.) and rode up to Silver Spring, Maryland, to visit Francis P. Blair. At seventy years of age, Preston Blair was a respected antislavery politician who was a moderate voice in the new Republican Party he had helped to form. Lincoln depended on Blair for many area assignments (such as offering Robert E. Lee command of the Union army the previous April). The elderly Blair held Lander in high regard, an admiration the general reciprocated by calling himself "Mr. Blair's general." Blair's namesake son held a colonel's commission in the western theater, but his daughter Elizabeth still occupied the Silver Spring estate while her husband served in the navy. She was home when the Landers arrived.

Elizabeth admitted an interest in the general since he was her father's favorite, but she was fonder of Jean Lander because "she appears to me to be an earnest frank warm-hearted woman & proudly devoted to her husband, but as ambitious as he is." Elizabeth noted the contrast the two presented during their visit: "she is sprightly and plain . . . He has a fine face & is very impatient of the restraints inflicted by his wound." Jean Lander cherished the Blair trip. The two months spent together during Fred's recuperation turned out to be the only protracted time the Landers had enjoyed together since their honeymoon one year earlier.[41]

Only the weather turned mild in Washington as Christmas approached. Two months after the fiasco, Ball's Bluff continued to reverberate in the

40. W. B. to the editor, October 22, 1861, newspaper clipping, LFP; FWL to Governor Andrew, November 3, 1861, LP 2:6417–18; FWL to Northend, December 4, 1861, Northend Papers, Emory University.

41. Temperature readings of the District of Columbia, December 17, 1861, NWR (All temperature readings from December 1861 through 1862 were taken in the Georgetown neighborhood.); Sifakis, *Who Was Who,* 58; Elizabeth Lee to "Phil," December 17, 1861, February 5 and March 3, 1862, in *Wartime Washington: The Civil War Letters of Elizabeth Blair Lee,* ed. Virginia J. Laas (Chicago, 1991), 92, 98, 105.

capital. Congress had reconvened early in December without one of its favorites—the late senator Colonel Edward Baker, who was killed in the fateful action near Leesburg. This, along with McClellan's resistance to advance his army, sparked a series of resolutions that led to a vote of thirty-three to three on December 10 to create the Joint Committee on the Conduct of the War. This seven-member body was formed to investigate the Ball's Bluff disaster and the current state of the Union armies. The committee consisted of three senators (Benjamin Franklin Wade, Zachariah Chandler, and Andrew Johnson) and four congressmen (Daniel Gooch, John Covode, George W. Julian, and Moses F. Odell). All except Senator Johnson and Representative Odell were considered radical Republicans. The committee was chaired by Senator Wade, who held a strong prejudice against West Pointers, Democrats, and those with southern ties.[42]

The Joint Committee invited George McClellan as their first witness. McClellan accepted and was scheduled to participate in the closed session on December 23. But that appointed day came and went without the general in attendance. The committee learned that he had contracted typhoid fever and was confined to his bed, where he would remain for at least the next two weeks.[43] Unable to question the main target of their inquiry, the committee scrambled through the Christmas period to gather other military figures to testify. They summoned General Lander, who learned that he held the dubious honor of being the first witness scheduled to sit before Wade's panel.

On Friday, December 27, 1861, Frederick Lander limped into the senate chambers and testified in front of the Joint Committee on the Conduct of the War. After he was officially sworn in, Senator Wade gruffly pushed Lander through the formalities of detailing his position in the army for the committee's records. Then Wade asked Lander, "I suppose you have reflected upon a plan of the campaign so as to give an opinion of your own in regard to what this army on the Potomac ought to do." "Yes, sir," came Lander's reply. Then Wade politely continued, "If you will give us your opinion, as a military man, upon that subject, I will be obliged to you."

---

42. Keith A. Botterud, "The Joint Committee on the Conduct of the Civil War" (master's thesis, Georgetown University, 1949), 1–13.

43. Sears, *McClellan*, 136.

Given that open opportunity, Lander focused his responses on the importance of the northwestern Virginia theater, an area of operation he was destined to inherit. The general's initial presentation that day, by his own admission, was "poorly stated." He uncharacteristically appeared hesitant and reserved, perhaps uncomfortable, in front of Senators Wade, Chandler, and Johnson—the three committee members who asked him most of the questions that day. Lander duplicated a response at one point and gave unsubstantiated information on two other occasions. Once he stated that a northern branch of the Manassas Gap Railroad ran supplies from Winchester to Confederate General Joseph E. Johnston's army at Centreville (no such rail line existed). He later insisted to Wade that General Jackson's Shenandoah Valley army was drafting blacks to fill its ranks, relying solely on the report of a "very smart negroe" as the source of this misinformation. Lander rambled at times, shifting his focus from operations within the Shenandoah Valley to strategy descriptions of slipping beyond the Confederate left flank at Manassas to relieve the citizens of North Carolina and Tennessee.

Despite what he considered a subpar presentation, Lander likely impressed the Joint Committee by displaying the aggressive nature so antithetical to the personalities of many of the generals who would testify after him. When Wade asked him if the winter season was a practical one for military operations, Lander responded that he did not know if it was feasible for the pampered soldiers of the Army of the Potomac "who are housed and buttered up about Washington, and taught to believe that if they make a march of three miles it will get into the papers." Lander saw the question as an opportunity to hype the unheralded westerners he had led the previous summer. The winter-time campaign "is practicable with 5,000 or 6,000 of our Western Virginia troops, and Ohio and Indiana troops" he boasted, referring to Philippi when he added, "I know the Indiana troops travelled night and day to get into battle, and the only trouble was they did not get there."

Senator Chandler was given an unsolicited lesson about railroad operations, Lander's forte, when he asked the general how he proposed to harass the enemy's left wing. Lander believed an effective railway was vital to supply an army from behind. He offered a temporary solution to counter the Confederate control of the B & O line between Harpers Ferry and Hancock. "I suggested some time ago the laying of a railway on the Chesapeake and Ohio canal towpath," Lander lectured while pointing to a map.

"It would make a connexion [*sic*] between our army here and the extreme right . . . so that at any time, if the enemy attempt to enter Maryland there, we can meet them," he explained. Lander reminded the committee that it was only by his earlier suggestion to General Scott that General Kelley's command occupied Romney, stressing that the Federal position there was key to protecting the western B & O line and strategic for launching a campaign from the Union right.

Lander admitted to the committee members that he lacked knowledge about the strategy of operations in eastern Virginia but pointedly stated that the capture of Richmond should not be the primary war objective. Lander disliked the plan of advancing westward from the Chesapeake Bay and demonstrated its futility: "But if we go on the left simply because we can defend with sloops and steamboats from the sea, how is it?" he asked. "We fight a big battle, and perhaps take their earthworks; perhaps they beat us. Three chances out of five that they beat us." Lander continued the scenario, "But suppose we beat them. They retire a little way, and then fight again. They retire again, and again fight; and so we fight them all the way to the Gulf of Mexico, for they will retire on their system of railways, destroying as they go."

Lander painted an alternative picture of grand strategy, one that shifted canvasses from the Tidewater regions in the eastern lowlands of the Old Dominion to the mountains of western Virginia. This was the finest moment of his testimony. He appeared to enjoy the role of grand strategist, and explained it in the simplest terms to the politicians unversed in war. He focused on turning the Confederate flank by advancing inward from the mountains, sweeping the southerners to the sea. "In turning the [left] every battle we win is a victory," Lander reasoned, "because we dispossess them of the munitions of war . . . cut off their means of transportation, and get their arms, and disperse this army, and they can never raise another army." Lander's explanation of specifics in how to wrest control of the Shenandoah Valley from the Confederates lacked cogency, but the Joint Committee clearly understood that Lander believed the slow plodding to arrive at an advertised battlefield was exactly why General McDowell met with disaster at Manassas in July. Lander believed that the only way to win the Shenandoah Valley and capture the Confederate army there was to quietly and quickly concentrate Federal troops. "The secret of war," Lander professed, "is to find out where the enemy does not expect you, and there mass your troops and beat him."[44]

After he expressed his opinions about general operations in the eastern theater, the Joint Committee shifted its focus to the Ball's Bluff battle. Senator Chandler had Lander review his role in the aftermath, then he asked him whether the Federals across Edwards Ferry could have advanced on Leesburg to hit Evans's southerners in the flank. Referring to the accepted belief that a masked battery stood in their path that day, Lander still maintained that the Edwards Ferry force should have made a junction with Baker's Ball's Bluff men. "You do not consider the [masked battery] insuperable?" asked Chandler. "Not at all," responded the now comfortable and confident witness, "Not by any means."

Lander then informed the committee that he had discussed a plan to take out the Confederate Leesburg force on October 9, nearly two weeks before the battle. He specified that he had wished to advance McCall up the Leesburg Pike, then throw Banks's division across the river to back up McCall. In accordance with Lander's plan, four Union divisions existed within striking distance to envelop and annihilate the Leesburg force. Knowing the battle's consequences looked bad for General Stone, Lander made sure the committee understood that from his perspective, "General Stone was tripped up by circumstances. . . . I regard General Stone, from my communication with him, as a very efficient, orderly, and excellent officer." But Lander insisted the major error existed in terrible river transport, an area that he had much experience with on the western frontier.

Lander closed the day's hearings with a display of unmitigated bravado. When asked again whether the Confederate batteries obstructed any relief efforts for Colonel Baker, Lander once again demonstrated to the politicians that he held a more aggressive view of operations than they would likely hear from any other subordinate of General McClellan. "I told my lieutenant colonel I was of a great mind to steal 3,000 men and take the town of Leesburg," he boasted, "I could have done it, I think. At least that shows I did not think much of their batteries. Batteries are pretty bad things for columns of troops, but not for riflemen and skirmishers."[45]

So ended the testimony of the first witness to the Joint Committee on the Conduct of the War. Lander returned to his E Street home and his

---

44. Lander, Testimony, JCCW, pt. 1, 160–4.
45. Lander, Testimony, JCCW, pt. 2, 253–7.

wife. It had been only five days since his physician examined his leg, and the doctor believed another five days was necessary before Lander could return to active service. Special Orders #339, announced to Lander later that day, would not allow any padding to Lander's recuperation time: "Brigadier General Frederick W. Lander, United States Volunteers, will repair to Romney and assume command."[46]

With the aid of General Rosecrans, more regiments were ordered into Hampshire County, Virginia, to add to Kelley's numbers already entrenched at Romney. The Confederate force at Winchester posed a direct threat to the Federals and the railroad, but General Kelley was too incapacitated to continue to lead. It was only fitting that Lander take over the Federal force at Romney, for his insistence to General Scott was the reason they existed there in the first place. Frederick Lander was returning to the hill country. Elated over his new assignment, Lander offered an optimistic toast that night: "The past for its memories, the present for its occasions, the future for freedom."[47]

The general spent the closing days of 1861 preparing to return to the front. On New Year's Eve Lander informed the still-ailing McClellan that his own health was "sufficiently restored" and that he was now prepared to report. In truth, he was not ready. He had no staff to assist him and no money; even his newly purchased riding horses would be delayed in reaching him. Lander formally applied for $1,000 in gold and specific men to fill his staff needs, and the Andrew Sharpshooters to be sent to him from Poolesville, Maryland—"they are mechanics and artisans and are particularly suited for the class of service I am ordered to perform."

His final request was for formal permission to seize Martinsburg and Stephenson's Depot (three miles north of Winchester) from the Confederates. Lander had no intention of remaining idle at Romney, and he believed the troops there were up to the task of neutralizing the Confederate army guarding the Lower Valley. The qualities the general deemed essential for victorious soldiers were spelled out in a December 31 letter to Abraham Lincoln. "We need fighting men," Lander declared, closing his letter to the president by adding, "Up to the present time have seen so many shaking nerves in this war that I sometimes doubt my eye-sight."[48]

46. Special Orders No. 339, December 27, 1861, LP 3:6450.

47. Toast by F. W. Lander, December 27, 1861, PDV.

48. FWL to GBM, December 31, 1861, LP 3:6455; FWL to Simon Cameron, December 31, 1861, LP 3:6453; FWL to Lincoln, December 31, 1861, ALP 30:13609.

Wednesday, January 1, 1862, dawned under unusual circumstances in Washington. War and winter notwithstanding, the battle fronts were peaceful and the temperature in Georgetown had already reached fifty degrees by 7:00 A.M. Near Romney the mercury rose to a balmy sixty-four degrees late that afternoon.[49]

New division commander Frederick Lander awoke early that morning, spent the entire day completing his preparations, and boarded the B & O car that would take him northward to Baltimore, then westward to the Allegheny theater of operations.[50] Colonel John S. Clark, completing business in Washington as a member of Nathaniel Banks's staff, was awestruck at Lander's fiery determination. The impressed officer wrote Banks, "I pity the rascals if once he gets within striking distance."[51] Lander's eyesight was sharp, his nerves were steady, and his spirit was willing. But as the train rolled away from its D.C. station with its restless passenger aboard, both the general and his wife were well aware that his injured and weakened limb was by no means ready to endure a harsh winter campaign in the mountains of northwestern Virginia.

Beginning on the morrow the daytime high temperatures plummeted forty degrees throughout the region.

49. Temperature readings, District of Columbia and Sheets Mill, Va., January 1, 1862, NWR.

50. B & O Pass, January 1, 1862, LP 3:6479.

51. Clark to Banks, January 2, 1862, BP 18:1.

Superintendent Lander, 1859. Henry Hitchings entitled this sketch
"Oct 1859 Iowa Frederick Lander," an odd label considering that Lander
was never in Iowa in October of that year. Hitchings likely sketched Lander
in the spring of the 1859 wagon road expedition, then finalized the drawing in Iowa.

*Courtesy of Yale University Art Gallery, New Haven, Conn. Gift of
Elisabeth Hitchings Rothschild and daughters Anne DeMunn and Christina
Sekaer*

Lander photographed by Mathew Brady in 1859 or 1860
Courtesy of MOLLUS Massachusetts Collection, USAMHI

Jean Margaret Davenport photographed in 1854,
six years before she married Frederick Lander
Courtesy of Jourdan Houston and A. Fraser Houston

Frederick Lander as seen by the public on the eve of the Civil War. *Frank Leslie's Illustrated Newspaper* published this image, along with a biography of him, on April 6, 1861. This is perhaps the public's first view of the renowned explorer and Indian negotiator.
Courtesy of MOLLUS Massachusetts Collection, USAMHI

ARING RIDE OF COLONEL LANDER AT THE BATTLE OF PHILIPPI.—FROM A SKETCH BY OUR SPECIAL ARTIST ACCOMPANYING MAJOR-GENERAL M'CLELLAN'S COMMAND.—SEE PAGE 102.

Lander's Ride, June 3, 1861. This gravity-defying ride down Talbott's Hill in the opening action of the "Philippi Races" was accomplished "with a temerity rivalling that of the Old Putnam of Revolutionary times." The feat kept Lander in the newspapers throughout the month of June.

Courtesy of Library of Congress

The Andrew Sharpshooters. This specialized unit owed its existence to Lander's efforts. They served under him longer than any other single unit, but lost their identity after Lander's death when they were forced to part with their custom-made rifles and were ordered to be incorporated into the Fifteenth Massachusetts Infantry.

Courtesy of Tom McAuley, Lynn, Mass.

Union evacuation of Romney, January 10, 1862. Lander likely appears on horseback in the lower right-hand corner of this Thomas Nast sketch.

Courtesy of Hampshire County Historical Society, Romney, West Virginia

Lander in 1862. This Brady photograph is believed to have been taken in Paw Paw in February. The general appears gaunt, the result of the debilitating wound he suffered at Edwards Ferry four months earlier.

From CDV, author's collection

"Funeral of General Lander in Washington," captured by Alfred Waud on March 6, 1862. Waud highlights the specialized rifles of the Andrew Sharpshooters in the upper left corner. Lander's "favorite horse" follows the coffin with the general's saddle and boots strapped to him.

M. and M. Karolik Collection of American Watercolors and Drawings, 1800–1875. Courtesy of Museum of Fine Arts, Boston

7

"Is Not War a Game of Risks?"

> Once on New England's bloody heights,
> And o'er a Southern plain,
> Our fathers fought for sovereign rights,
> That working men might reign.
>
> And by that only Lord we serve,
> The great Jehovah's name;
> By those sweet lips that ever nerve
> High hearts to deeds of fame.
> —F. W. Lander

"I shall have a small force to oppose the enemy," Frederick Lander informed a hometown friend on January 3, 1862, highlighting his greatest impediment when he admitted, "and as I can barely move about, anticipate a hard time of it." Lander wrote the letter from Baltimore, where he had stayed to finalize his preparations before he replaced General Kelley at Romney. He boarded his train at the Camden Street depot on the freezing morning of January 4. The New Year's Day heat wave quickly became a memory. Morning temperatures had returned to frigid winter readings, forewarning the general that the hill country would be as damp and cold as originally expected.[1]

1. William Northend to Mrs. Lander, March 4, 1862, LP 11; Temperature reading,

Shortly before noon Brigadier General Lander's B & O Railroad car steamed northward from Monocacy Junction to Frederick. The general's destination was 100 miles away; still, the brief detour was necessary for Lander to meet with Major General Nathaniel Prentiss Banks, the division chief stationed at Frederick. Lander found Banks at his headquarters, where the two discussed operations in their military districts.

The forty-five-year-old Banks, nicknamed "the Bobbin Boy of Massachusetts" for working in a cotton mill at an early age in his home state, had been awarded a major general's commission in May of 1861 despite his lack of military experience. The appointment elevated Banks to the third highest ranking general in the Union army, outranked only by George McClellan and John Frémont. Banks was the quintessential political appointment; the former Speaker of the House of Representatives had also served three one-year terms as governor of Massachusetts. Leaving Massachusetts early in 1861, Banks had barely settled in his new lucrative job as resident director of the Illinois Central Railroad in Chicago when war broke out in April.[2]

Using his political influence, Banks gained his immediate prestigious commission, annoying the West Point graduates he superseded to obtain a division command. Lincoln chose Banks obviously not for his military potential, but ostensibly for his ability to use his political influence to gain recruits, money, and propaganda for the Federal cause. Banks had commanded the Department of Annapolis during the summer of 1861 before shifting to gain control of a division in the Military District of the Potomac, which subsequently was transferred to the newly formed Army of the Potomac in October of 1861.[3] Banks's three brigades stretched between Frederick and Williamsport.

Generals Lander and Banks were both Bay State division commanders, but the similarities between the two ended there. Banks's initial impressions of Lander are unknown; however, Lander harbored acrimonious feelings about Banks stemming from what Lander considered to be his lack of decision and promptness at Ball's Bluff. ("He is a good man. I like

---

District of Columbia, January 4, 1862, NWR. Northend quoted Lander's January 3 excerpt in his March 4 letter. The morning temperature in Georgetown was twenty-two degrees.

2. James G. Hollandsworth Jr., *Pretense of Glory: The Life of General Nathaniel P. Banks* (Baton Rouge, 1998), 42–4.

3. Sifakis, *Who Was Who*, 30–1; Warner, *Generals in Blue*, 17–18.

him. But he is not a soldier," assessed Lander in November).[4] Still, communication between the two was vital to achieve successful Union operations to reopen the B & O Railroad. Banks anchored the right flank of the Army of the Potomac, while Lander's command in the Department of Western Virginia would link with his at an area between Hancock and Williamsport.

Lander's journey via railroad was over for the day. The B & O ran from Frederick to Monocacy Junction, then to Point of Rocks and Harpers Ferry, where it crossed the Potomac River and ran through the northern perimeter of Virginia all the way to Cumberland. In the spring of 1861, Confederate forces had removed all of the double track between Martinsburg and Harpers Ferry along with over seven miles of single track between Martinsburg and Hancock. Without the benefit of a direct rail link to his command post, Lander departed Frederick on the National Turnpike, a freshly macadamized road that had been constructed nearly fifty years earlier to carry travelers and supplies from Baltimore to the Ohio River Valley.[5] Lander's destination was Cumberland, approximately ninety miles west of Frederick. From Cumberland, Lander would cross the Potomac and head twenty miles south to join his new command at Romney.

Lander's riding horses, scheduled to arrive at Frederick, unfortunately were sent from Washington late and would not arrive until the early hours of January 5. (The railroad operator in Baltimore, obviously aware of Lander's short temper, ended the dispatch informing Lander of the delay with the admonition, "Don't swear".) Lander was too impatient to wait. Borrowing horses and a sleigh, he departed Frederick at 2:00 P.M. Lander's route took him through Turner's Gap in South Mountain, then through the towns of Boonsboro and Funkstown. Shortly after passing through the latter, the turnpike crossed Antietam Creek on a thirty-year-old triple-arched stone bridge, then continued its westward course. The sun had set about half an hour prior to his arrival at the creek, denying Lander the opportunity to view the pastoral scene offered by the countryside.[6]

4. FWL to William Northend, November 6, 1861, Northend Papers, Emory University.

5. Festus Summers, "The Baltimore and Ohio—First in War," *Civil War History* 7 (September 1961): 253; Maryland Geological Survey, *Report of the Highways of Maryland* (Baltimore, 1899), 166–8.

6. H. C. Clarke, comp., *The Confederate States Almanac and Repository of Useful*

The general knew he was unprepared for his command. He had been afforded little time since the official announcement, but he also had squandered valuable time before acquiring his essentials—including a decent map of the theater of operations around Romney. He inquired into obtaining a detailed map; however, the one he received was not up to his standards. Newspapers, the same medium that had done so much to elevate his popularity, now worked against him. The day before he left Washington, Lander complained to one of Lincoln's secretaries, "The newspapers have so well apprised the enemy of our movements . . . that I shall have great difficulties to encounter and few successes to chronicle."[7]

Lander also lacked a staff. His choice for aide-de-camp, Captain Charles Candy, who had served him in that capacity at Poolesville, had been promoted to head a new Ohio regiment. Lander's next choice was Simon Forrester Barstow. Lander succeeded in obtaining a captain's commission for his hard-working friend and offered him the staff position. Barstow accepted, but remained in Washington to receive another essential commodity for his superior—money. Since the U.S. War Department was slow to react to Lander's request for gold, Mrs. Lander gave Barstow $800 to deliver to her husband to aid him in the initial stages of the campaign.[8]

Approximately four hours and twenty-five miles after leaving Frederick, the general rode into the old Maryland city of Hagerstown, a Union-loyal community that was celebrating its centennial in 1862.[9] But no celebrations awaited Lander on his arrival there. Instead, he was delivered alarming news from thirty miles upriver at Hancock. Banks had been aware since the early morning hours that a Confederate force had been seen at Bath, a historic resort town six miles south of the Potomac River. Banks immediately relayed the information to his superior, General George McClellan, but he downplayed the news: "Don't think there is serious

---

Knowledge, for 1862 (Vicksburg, Miss., 1861), 4; O. Hobitzell to FWL, January 4, 1862, LP 3:6499; Nathaniel Banks to S. Williams, January 4, 1862, MP 15:7509; Western Reserve Historical Society, ed., *The James E. Taylor Sketchbook* (Dayton, Ohio, 1989), 295–302; S. Williams (Brigadier General Seth Williams) was adjutant general of the Army of the Potomac. All dispatches addressed to Williams in the winter of 1862 were intended for George McClellan.

7. B. H. Latrobe to FWL, January 4, 1862, LP 3:6491; FWL to John Hay, December 31, 1861, Hay Collection, Brown University Library, Providence, R.I.

8. FWL to Simon Cameron, January 1, 1862, LP 3:6480–1; Mrs. Lander to Barstow, January 4, 1862, LP 3:6507.

9. Western Reserve Historical Society, *Taylor Sketchbook*, 295–302.

cause for apprehension." He was wrong. By 3:00 P.M. Banks's aide, Colonel Samuel H. Leonard, wired his superior from Williamsport: "The rebels have attacked us at Bath and our guns at Hancock have opened on them." Banks quickly relayed the information to a recuperating General McClellan in Washington. Once Lander was apprised of the Bath attack when he entered Hagerstown, the general entered the telegraph office there. Knowing that an undersized Union force sat across the river from Bath at Hancock, Lander's first wire, sent at 7:15 P.M., clearly indicated his new mission and intentions: "I shall not leave Hancock, Maryland."[10]

Lander stayed in Hagerstown for two and one-half more hours. During that time he was provided unsubstantiated reports from Banks at Frederick and from Colonel Leonard at Williamsport. By 9:00 P.M. Lander learned that the Union force that was attacked escaped to the Maryland side of the river, that they were armed with cumbersome Belgian .69-caliber rifles, and that an estimated enemy force of 6,000–7,000 men was bombarding Hancock with six artillery pieces.[11]

It was a dire situation for a leaderless command over there. Lander sent a request for materials to pontoon the Potomac. He then wired Banks's adjutant to inform him that "[m]y address is Hancock. Please send a detailed statement of position of forces I can draw on." Knowing that the First Maryland Infantry was the closest regiment to the contested area, Lander added that their colonel, John Kenly, should move his men overnight and assist Lander "if he hears us engaged briskly."[12]

Lander's intentions were inscrutable. He wanted to attack an estimated force, believed to be 7,000 strong, with an unknown number of poorly armed Federals, and he wanted Banks to support the attack with his own infantry. Lander rode from Hagerstown to Williamsport late that evening. Shortly after 11:00 P.M., Lander departed Williamsport for Hancock, a distance of twenty-five miles up the towpath of the frozen C & O Canal.[13]

---

10. S. H. Leonard to R. Morris Copeland, January 3, 1862, BP 18:1; Banks to S. Williams, January 3, 1862, MP 15:7511–12; S. H. Leonard to Capt. Shriber, January 4, 1862, BP 18:1; Banks to S. Williams, January 4, 1862, MP 15:7514; FWL to Dudley Donnelly, January 4, 1862, LP 3:6497. Captain R. C. Shriber was aide-de-camp to General Banks. Major R. Morris Copeland was assistant adjutant general of Banks's division. All dispatches sent to these two officers were intended for General Banks.

11. Banks to FWL, January 4, 1862, LP 3:6502.

12. FWL to Banks, January 4, 1862, 9:15 PM, BP 18:1.

13. Banks to S. Williams, January 5, 1862, MP 15:7525.

Lander arrived at Hancock in the early morning hours of Sunday, January 5, 1862. The temperatures had fallen into single-digit readings, preserving a few inches of snowfall from the day before. Tucked within the slimmest segment (approximately two miles) of Maryland's panhandle region, Hancock was the only Free State community that separated Pennsylvania from Virginia. Previously known as the "North Bend Settlement," a significant frontier trading post, Hancock thrived once C & O Canal construction reached there in 1839. Renamed for a Revolutionary War soldier who had operated a ferry there, Hancock's prosperity was significantly reduced by railroad competition beginning in 1850. It still served as a major stopping point along the National Turnpike and housed several warehouses for canal and turnpike transport.[14] The town had now become the focal point for the U.S. War Department.

Once he arrived at Hancock, Lander set up his headquarters in a store that doubled as a telegraph office. While there he interrogated the main parties involved in the skirmish at Bath the previous day and was briefed about what had taken place over the past two days. He learned that only one regiment, the Thirty-ninth Illinois, along with a two-gun section of Captain Clermont L. Best's Fourth U.S. Artillery, Battery F, and one squadron of cavalry had patrolled the Virginia side of the Potomac River, having crossed there from Maryland two weeks earlier. Companies D, K, and I had moved into Bath while the remaining companies guarded points closer to the river. Their skirmishing force was attacked south of Bath on the evening of January 3, suffering three wounded and eight captured men. The commander of the Thirty-ninth, Colonel Thomas O. Osborn, immediately telegraphed General Kelley for support. Kelley sent out the Thirteenth Indiana by train from Cumberland the following morning and instructed Osborn to call on a new regiment that had just arrived across the river at Hancock from Camp Curtin in Harrisburg, Pennsylvania. The new regiment was the Eighty-fourth Pennsylvania, a unit composed of nine companies of 766 soldiers under the leadership of Mexican War veteran Colonel William Gray Murray. Eight companies of Pennsylvanians crossed the Potomac late on Friday night (January 3) and reinforced Osborn at Bath. Murray ranked

14. Temperature readings, Cumberland, Md., January 5, 1862, NWR; National Park Service, *Chesapeake and Ohio Canal*, Official National Park Handbook, no. 142 (Washington, D.C., 1989), 94; Mason-Dixon Council Boy Scouts of America, *184 Miles of Adventure: Hiker's Guide to the C & O Canal* (Hagerstown, Md., 1970), 35.

Osborn by the date of his commission and took control of the two forces.

Early the following morning, Murray had ordered the entire force around Bath, 820 men, to scale Warm Spring Ridge, which ran in a north-south direction along Bath's western perimeter. They were attacked by a substantial Confederate force later that morning. The enemy hesitated in its approach, and Murray easily repulsed (and stampeded) a militia force that approached his right flank on the ridge. The two Union guns, under the direction of Lieutenant Edward D. Muhlenburg, contested the eastern approaches of the ridge. The guns proved extremely valuable, for the Eighty-fourth Pennsylvania's weapons, shoddy Belgian rifles, were inoperable because the barrels were choked with the tallow they were shipped in. By 3:00 P.M., when the southern force opposing him sent two regiments to attack the hill, Murray pulled in his force and ordered a retreat toward the Potomac.

Late on the afternoon of January 4, the Federals retreated two miles northwestward to the Sir John's Run railroad depot, which was guarded by another Thirty-ninth Illinois company. They met the Thirteenth Indiana there (the Hoosiers had recently arrived by train as promised by General Kelley). With the Confederates closing in toward the river, Colonel Murray believed his force of twenty-three companies was sufficient to repulse them and he ordered the command to prepare for an assault. His plans immediately changed when he learned that the Thirteenth Indiana, eight companies of whom were armed with percussion smoothbores, carried only two rounds of ammunition per man. Ironically, they believed that they would obtain more at Bath.

The Yankees retreated to prevent capture. The Hoosiers reboarded their boxcars and headed back toward Cumberland, while the supply wagons, artillery, and Thirty-ninth Illinois companies crossed the river at the Sir John's Run junction into Maryland. Murray's men hiked five and one-half miles along the railroad to Alpine Station. This railroad depot sat directly across the river from Hancock. Murray crossed his men there while an additional two Illinois companies easily repulsed the feeble Confederate pursuit. Murray's ten-hour defense and subsequent retreat was indeed fortuitous—he lost only one man, who drowned in the Potomac during the dark crossing to Hancock. That night the Confederates were left with some abandoned Union supplies, but little else. Too late to cross the Potomac, the Confederates lobbed artillery shells into Hancock for a couple of hours, then ceased for the night to renew hostilities the next morning.[15]

In addition to the Eighty-fourth Pennsylvania, Thirty-ninth Illinois, one squadron of cavalry, and Muhlenburg's two artillery pieces, the only other unit at Hancock was the 110th Pennsylvania, another new regiment fresh out of Camp Curtin. They, like the Eighty-fourth Pennsylvania, had left training camp without firearms. Lander learned that this unit was one that he could not rely on. Four companies of the 110th were recruited from Philadelphia and the remainder hailed from the mountain country of central Pennsylvania. The heterogeneous mix bred animosity. Add to this the insufficient disciplinary traits of the company and regimental officers, and the result was a disorderly mob. The 110th Pennsylvania had illustrated this on their way to Hancock from Hagerstown at approximately the same time Lander approached the latter town from Frederick on January 4.

The 110th Pennsylvania had camped around Hagerstown since arriving there at 3:00 A.M. on January 3, and many of the men sought a place to assuage their thirst. This resulted in a continuous flow of soldiers into the saloons. Shortly after the men returned to camp, a brief fight developed between the drunken country boys and the equally intoxicated Irish Philadelphians from whom they were trying to steal the regimental flag. When he heard about the attack at Bath, Colonel Leonard had ordered the 110th Pennsylvania's commander, Colonel William D. Lewis, to advance his regiment to Hancock from their camps west of Hagerstown. Placed under guard, the quarreling parties marched along the National Turnpike toward the scene of conflict. The march was interrupted by another intra-regimental brawl. This one turned out to be uncontrollable, as the enlisted men went at each other with fists and feet and pummeled each other with large chunks of limestone picked up from the freshly macadamized road. According to the regimental historian, "Every fellow that had a drink, or any drunken respect for himself, went to work throwing stones at the other fellows." For more than twenty minutes the air "was black with limestone." Regimental officers (several of whom were also drunk) intervened by striking the men with the flats of their swords and their pistols, but by the time any semblance of order was restored, more than forty casualties

15. Gary L. Ecelbarger, *"We are in for it!": The First Battle of Kernstown, March 23, 1862* (Shippensburg, Pa., 1997), 1–5.

could be counted in the force that had yet to fight the Confederates. Lewis finally delivered his new regiment to Hancock at midnight, completing a two-day odyssey filled with adventure and shame.[16]

Lander realized his three-regiment force lacked experience and decent weapons. He had wired a request to have one of his own former regiments, the Nineteenth Massachusetts, sent to him from Poolesville, but this request was denied. His specialized troops, the Andrew Sharpshooters, would also be delayed in reaching him. In an effort to control costs, General Stone had convinced General McClellan on January 1 to transport the company directly by canal to Cumberland rather than by railroad. Stone's idea neglected the effect of winter weather on the function of the C & O. What started out as a thin sheet of ice on January 3 thickened so much in the next twenty-four hours that an ice tug was required to lead the canal boat to prevent it from severing in two. The sharpshooters ran low on food and relied on a keg of New England rum and hot coffee to sustain them. By the time Lander had arrived at Hancock on the morning of January 5, he learned that the sharpshooters were bogged down in ice south of Harpers Ferry, seventy miles and several days away from helping him.[17] His crack troops would be sorely missed, as they were necessary to prevent the enemy from crossing into Maryland or damaging the railroad on the Virginia side of the river.

The size, strength, and availability of the Union force was now well known to Lander. What was still unclear to him was the identity and strength of the southerners across the river. The last intelligence report reduced the estimate of the rebel attacking force from 6,000 to 3,000 with six cannons. It was also believed that the enemy would not attempt to cross the river but would be satisfied with "injuring the railway" and then would subsequently retire.[18] Lander realized that those reports were wholly inaccurate. Looking across the Potomac from his headquarters, he could see a

16. James C. M. Hamilton, "Manuscript History of the 110th Pennsylvania," War Library and Museum, Philadelphia, 5–7; S. H. Leonard to R. Morris Copeland, January 3, 1862, BP 18:1; S. H. Leonard to R. C. Shriber, January 4, 1862, BP 18:1; D. R. Miller to the editor, January 30, 1862, *Shirleysburg (Pa.) Herald*, January 20, 1862; Samuel C. Baker to the editor, January 6, 1862, *Shirleysburg Herald*, January 12, 1862.

17. FWL to GBM, January 5, 1862, MP 15:7526; Stone to S. Williams, January 1, 1862, MP 15:7477; Bicknell, "Sharpshooters," 13–14; H. Tyndale to R. M. Copeland, January 5, 1862, BP 18:1.

18. Banks to S. Williams, January 5, 1862, MP 15:7527–8.

larger force with more cannons positioning themselves on the northern end of Horse Ridge, less than one mile from the town of Hancock.

At 9:30 A.M. Lander saw two southern soldiers approach the river; one of them waved a white flag—a sign of truce—to prevent the U.S. troops from taking a potshot at them. He sent Lieutenant Colonel Orrin L. Mann of the Thirty-ninth Illinois, his appointed provost marshal, with a small detachment to receive the messenger. Mann and his men navigated a ferry boat across the Potomac, picked up one of the Confederates, and returned to the Hancock side of the river. The southern soldier was blindfolded at the river bank, then escorted up the streets of Hancock toward Lander's headquarters. He was identified as Lieutenant Colonel Turner Ashby, the flamboyant commander of the Seventh Virginia Cavalry.[19]

The Union detachment exchanged some polite banter with Ashby as they escorted him across Main Street one block to the paralleling High Street. They led him to Lander's headquarters where the general impatiently awaited the messenger and his information. Once inside, Ashby's blindfold was removed. Lander, Ashby, and Mann initially sat in the telegraph office, but Lander decided to interrogate Ashby in an adjacent room to prevent the Confederate from attempting to decipher the telegraphy that was frequently delivered to the building.[20] By identifying Ashby, Lander already knew that the forces across the river belonged to Major General Thomas J. "Stonewall" Jackson. Ashby handed Lander a dispatch from Jackson. When he opened it Lander realized he was being given an ultimatum:

> Head Quarters, Valley District
> Opposite Hancock
> January 5, 1862
> To the Officer Com'dg
> the United States Forces
> in and near Hancock, Md.
>
> Sir,
>   It is my purpose to cross the river and take possession of the town of Hancock.

---

19. Charles M. Clark, *Yates Phalanx: The History of the Thirty-ninth Regiment, Illinois Volunteer Veteran Infantry, in the War of the Rebellion, 1861–1865,* ed. Frederick C. Decker (1889; reprint, Bowie, Md., 1994), 34; Alexander Read to Martin Watts, January 30, 1862, *Clearfield (Pa.) Progress,* April 9, 1961.

20. Clark, *Yates Phalanx,* ed. Decker, 34.

If in opposing the execution of this purpose, you make use of the town of Hancock, or the citizens of the town aid you in your opposition, I will cannonade the town.

If neither of these things is done, I will refrain as practicable from firing upon it.

An immediate reply to this communication is required.

T. J. Jackson
Maj. Genl. P.A.C.S.
Comdg Valley District[21]

Lander bristled as Ashby warned him that he was tremendously outnumbered by Jackson's force. Ashby also told the general that Jackson would allow two hours to remove the noncombatants from Hancock before bombarding the town. Ashby, who was unaware of Lander's identity, certainly did not expect the emphatic response that the general delivered to him: "Colonel Ashby," Lander began, "give my regards to General Jackson and tell him to bombard and be damned! If he opens his batteries on this town he will injure more of his friends than he will of the enemy, for this is a damned sesech place anyhow!"

Both Ashby and Mann believed that Lander's "Union answer" (as one Pennsylvanian proudly described it) signified the end of the interrogation and they both stood up to leave the room. As Mann attempted to replace Ashby's blindfold over his eyes, Lander stopped them. "Hold on! Take a seat, Colonel Ashby. General Jackson has addressed me in a polite and soldierly manner and it demands a like reply." With that, the general scrawled a more formal response to be delivered to his adversary, handed it to Ashby, and provided his final observation to the cavalier. "General Jackson and yourself, Colonel Ashby, are gentlemen and brave men, without a question," Lander observed, "but you have started out in a God Damn bad cause!"[22]

With that closing, Lander shook Ashby's hand. Lieutenant Colonel Mann covered his eyes again and escorted him to the Confederate side of the river. Ashby quickly found Stonewall Jackson and handed Lander's written response to him. Jackson's Valley District army numbered nearly 11,000 men, over 9,000 of whom had accompanied him to Bath. Those

---

21. Jackson to FWL, January 5, 1862, LP 3:6505.
22. Clark, *Yates Phalanx,* ed. Decker, 34; "H. H. H." to the editor, January 19, 1862, *Altoona (Pa.) Tribune,* January 23, 1862.

men (including cavalry and militia) occupied a triangle between the Great Cacapon River to the west, Alpine Station to the east, and south to the town of Bath. Jackson carried twenty-seven cannons with him; several were ensconced on the northern face of Horse Ridge facing Hancock. Jackson's ultimate destination was Romney; however, he had started the campaign moving northward from Winchester. At first it appeared his mission was dedicated to destroying the railroad. Once he accomplished this, Jackson had the opportunity to capture Hancock, advance across Maryland's panhandle region to Cumberland, then seize Romney by surprising the Union force there from behind.[23]

Stonewall Jackson knew his force dominated the Federals at Hancock and anticipated that the commander there—whoever he was—would surrender the town to him. When Jackson opened Lander's response he learned that he would be given neither the town nor the commander's name:

January 5
Answer to Rebel Jackson
10 1/2
Comdg officer, Confederate Forces

Sir:
    I decline to accede to your request. If you feel justified in destroying the property and lives of peaceable citizens under the plea of crossing the Potomac at a particular point, a crossing which I dispute, you must do so on your own responsibility, not mine.
Very Respectfully,
The Officer Comndg.
The U.S. Forces[24]

As Stonewall Jackson prepared to vent his disapproval of Lander's refusal, the Union commander fumed over the inappropriate support he felt he was getting from General Banks. The flatboats and cable he had requested the previous evening were bogged in the ice that caked the C & O

---

23. *OR,* 5:391, 1026–7. None of Jackson's writings spell out his desire to advance along the panhandle; however, the fact that the extremely devout general was determined to cannonade Hancock on a Sunday adds more credence to the importance he placed on capturing the town to accomplish his mission. It is unlikely that he would have bombarded Hancock on the Sabbath strictly as a diversion for other endeavors.

24. FWL to Jackson, January 5, 1862, LP 3:6661 (copy on reverse side of dispatch).

Canal. The ice continued for four miles north of Harpers Ferry, which made it impossible for Lander's pontoon equipment to arrive. A steam tug was used to break the ice to allow other boats to pass. No new artillery pieces, supplies, or regiments had arrived since the 110th Pennsylvania made its midnight appearance. The Pennsylvanians came unarmed and, like the Eighty-fourth Pennsylvania before them, were forced to settle for the tallow-caked Belgians that sat in the frozen canal boats at one of several warehouses in Hancock. As the 110th Pennsylvania built fires in the streets of Hancock to melt the fat out of their gun barrels, Lander stewed in the telegraph room of his headquarters. He wanted to replace his telegrapher (who inexplicably had disappeared for over two hours the previous hectic evening), but it would take at least one more day for a more able operator to reach Hancock.[25]

None of this sat well with Lander, who wired Banks almost immediately after Ashby returned to Virginia soil. Briefly informing the "Bobbin Boy" about Jackson's ultimatum, Lander listed the greatest obstacles impeding a successful defense: 1,000 rifles frozen in a canal boat, no transportation, and no subsistence. He added, "One thousand men have the Belgian which in its present state cannot be made to go off. Two thirds of them are as badly armed." Lander insisted on a swift supply of reinforcements, material goods, and adequate transportation. He ended by urging Banks to place his force in Jackson's rear—"as I advised last night"—and promised that he would keep Jackson engaged in front as long as he could "to give you a chance south of him."[26]

Without waiting for a response, Lander left his headquarters to prepare for Hancock's impending bombardment. The town's citizens, mostly women and children, were ordered to vacate the premises. No repeat orders were necessary; they shrieked and wept as they scurried through the streets toward Pennsylvania. A few of the elderly male residents shouldered antiquated muskets and offered their services. Lander could hardly refuse—he had only 2,000 available infantry to counter Jackson's 8,700. He ordered two companies of Illinois soldiers to cover the mouth of the Great Cacapon River, ten miles southwest of town, where Confederate

25. W. A. Gorman to Banks, January 5, 1862, BP 18:1; W. A. Gorman to Banks, January 5, 1862, BP 18:1; H. Tyndale to Banks, January 5, 1862, BP 18:1; Hamilton, "110th Pennsylvania," 11–12; Frank Drummond to Banks, January 5, 1862, BP 18:1; Thomas Eckert to Banks, January 5, 1862, BP 18:1.

26. FWL to Banks, January 5, 1862, 10:15 A.M., BP 18:1.

troops had been stationed to burn a bridge the previous night. The Eighty-fourth Pennsylvania was posted on Main Street behind sturdy brick houses. Many carried buckets of water to douse the fire expected to be produced by enemy projectiles. Company D of the 110th Pennsylvania was positioned closest to the river. They took cover in a large brick warehouse and used crossbars and picks to dig loop holes through the walls every few feet. Lander employed the remainder of the 110th Pennsylvania as a ruse. He ordered the regiment to march continuously out of the woods to open ground on the high ground north of town to fool Jackson into believing the town was receiving reinforcements.[27]

Muhlenburg's two cannons also occupied the heights in back of Hancock. He unlimbered his ten-pounder Parrott rifle and a smoothbore in the churchyard shared by an Episcopal church on the west and a Catholic church 100 yards east of it. A cemetery marked the area between and behind the churches; the cannons lay behind it on the crest. The small smoothbore would be ineffective at a mile from Jackson's guns, and Lander learned that the more accurate and powerful Parrott would provide him with limited service—Muhlenburg had only ninety-two rounds left to fire.[28]

By 1:00 P.M., an eerie silence pervaded Hancock. More than three hours had passed since Jackson sent his ultimatum, yet no action had been taken. In the warehouse that covered Company D of the 110th Pennsylvania, two enlisted men who had been students of the ministry prior to the war conducted prayer service. At approximately 2:00 P.M., a puff of blue smoke emanated from Jackson's hill across the river. Seconds later a shell exploded over the warehouse and put an end to religious services. Muhlenburg answered the "opening of the ball" with a salvo thrown by his section. The duel would continue for four more hours with

27. Harvey S. Wells, "With Shields in 1862," *Philadelphia Weekly Times,* March 28, 1885; Harvey S. Wells, "The Eighty-fourth Volunteer Infantry in the Late War," *Philadelphia Weekly Times,* April 10, 1886; Alpheus S. Williams to R. M. Copeland, January 8, 1862, BP 18:1; Hamilton, "110th Pennsylvania," 13.

28. FWL to Banks, January 5, 1862, BP 18:1. Lander apparently wired Banks with this finding shortly after his explanation of Jackson's intentions. All of the available rounds were shells. He requested 100 more rounds: "Forward case shot by all means." In the heat of battle, artillerists could routinely fire two rounds per minute. Assuming conservatively Muhlenburg could fire three rounds every two minutes, then his ammunition would be expended in one hour.

Muhlenburg returning a more desultory fire to conserve his scant supply of shells.[29]

Confederate projectiles ricocheted off buildings and bounced on the streets. Some struck near Lander's headquarters, but he was not observing the action from there. As the Eighty-fourth Pennsylvania cowered behind the houses on Main Street, they watched a lone horseman trotting along the road—General Lander. As Confederate projectiles burst and landed around him, the general coolly soothed his green troops as he passed by. "Soldiers," Lander announced, "do your duty; there is work for you today; meet it bravely; if I am killed, somebody will take my place." The display and speech emboldened the Pennsylvanians. Harvey S. Wells of Company F was much impressed. "There was something about the appearance of the man that indicated he was equal to the station," he wrote to the citizens of Muncy, Pennsylvania, "and there was not a soldier looked upon his countenance, but that felt confidence in his ability."[30]

Jackson continued throwing shells into Hancock until the sun set over the Alleghenies at 5:00 P.M. No casualties were inflicted on Lander's men, but the artillery fire allowed Jackson the opportunity to damage the railroad extensively, while the heavy winds that whipped through the region destroyed the telegraph lines west of Hancock. Lander could not communicate directly with General Kelley in Cumberland, but he had messages transmitted to him through Baltimore to Pittsburgh to Cumberland. Banks had troops and 15,000 rations on the way to Hancock by 6:00 P.M.; however, this did little to calm Lander. He wired Banks at 10:00 P.M. insisting on more Parrotts to counter Jackson's salvos, which were expected to resume early the next day. Lander urged Banks to hurry the guns— "delay will kill us"—and repeated the message he had sent for two days: cross the river and attack Jackson from behind. Lander maintained that it "would be the best movement of the war." He alternatively suggested that if Banks was unwilling to cross the Potomac then he should send "five regiments by force march and I will cross here and beat them." Lander insisted that to stand idle at Hancock would result in disaster: "If I am to

29. Hamilton, "110th Pennsylvania," 13–14; "H. C. W." [Lieutenant H. Clay Weaver] to the editor, January 6, 1862, *Shirleysburg (Pa.) Herald*, January 12, 1862.

30. Jacob Peterman to his father, January 9, 1862, letter in private possession of David Richards, Gettysburg, Pa.; "A Volunteer" [Harvey S. Wells] to the editor, January 8, 1862, *Muncy (Pa.) Luminary*, January 14, 1862.

hold this place with four fords to attend to, . . . the enemy will drive the men out in spite of me."[31]

Banks sent Lander's message to McClellan one hour later. Banks added a note to his superior indicating that his Third Brigade was ordered to Hancock on a forced march along with two Parrott guns, thereby satisfying part of Lander's request. Confident that McClellan would not consent to the bold but reckless endeavor that Lander had suggested, Banks ended his cover note by adding, "[I] have not thought it consistent with my orders to order my Division to cross the River in present condition of affairs, but am ready."[32]

Lander assessed his situation that Sunday night. He needed something to claim in his favor. He had spent a trying day under fire and had withstood the barrage, but he knew that Jackson was not going away. Not satisfied with Banks's responses to his requests, Lander wired his last message of the day directly to the U.S. War Department in Washington. After Lander summarized the events of the day, he relayed what met his gaze from across the Potomac: "Tonight one hundred eighty six camp fires in sight. . . . Had not Banks better cross and get in rear of such a prize? The hillside is covered with tents and wagon trains. If not, may I not be reinforced heavily and ordered across? My command is in advanced state of discipline. I asked you for one efficient Regt., the 19th Mass. as an example and for Provost service on this account."[33] Not expecting a timely response to his queries, Lander retired for the night and took advantage of his first opportunity in two days to get some sleep.

A severe storm of sleet, snow, and hail swept across western Maryland overnight, preventing significant support from reaching Lander early on Monday, January 6. Two more Parrotts had left Sandy Hook near Harpers Ferry at 5:00 A.M. the previous day, but four inches of snow on the roads stalled their progress toward Hancock. Six companies of the First Maryland Infantry had arrived at the outskirts of Hancock at 1:00 A.M. to provide Lander with his only new troops. Lander kept them near one of the Potomac fords east of Hancock to contest any attempt by

31. Clarke, *Confederate States Almanac,* 4; Banks to S. Williams, January 5, 1862, MP 15:7531; FWL to Banks, January 5, 1862, BP 18:1; FWL to R. M. Copeland, January 5, 1862, BP 18:1; FWL to Banks, January 5, 1862, MP 47:85848–9.

32. Banks to S. Williams, January 5, 1862, MP 15:7530.

33. Temperature reading, District of Columbia, January 5, 1862, 9:00 P.M., NWR; FWL to Randolph Marcy, January 5, 1862, MP 47:85317–18.

Jackson to cross there. Lander's pontoon cable had yet to reach him, not because of the weather, but owing to "the blunder of an incompetent" in Banks's command.[34] All in all, the situation had changed little at Hancock since midnight of January 4.

Jackson resumed shelling Hancock at noon on January 6. His men had effectively vandalized the railroad and destroyed a large and long bridge that crossed the Great Cacapon River west of Hancock. They also had ransacked two houses in Bath and burned a few buildings at Alpine Station. By 5:00 P.M. Jackson had attempted to cross the Potomac at Sir John's Run. Lander countered by posting infantry there. By 7:30 P.M. it appeared to Lander that Jackson had begun to withdraw. The Confederates would not capture Hancock during this mission.[35]

Lander had used Muhlenburg's guns again, but he was able to fire only a couple of dozen rounds since he was not yet resupplied with ammunition. Still, the Parrott provided excellent service for Lander; it had fired so accurately that General Jackson was forced from his viewing position atop Horse Ridge to find a safer location for his headquarters one mile closer to Bath. The Confederate gunners adopted the code word "Brown Church" to escape Muhlenburg's Parrott shells; no one moved when "Red Church" was called, the location of Muhlenburg's inaccurate smoothbore.[36] On the Maryland side of the river, Lander's men had no tents and were forced to enter the citizens' homes for shelter. Lander had suffered no losses for a second straight day; however, the neglect of high command to the seriousness of his situation irritated him to the core.

Continuing snowfall failed to cool Lander. Not only was he furious at Banks, but his animosity against McClellan was also growing more fervent with each passing hour. He now believed the only cooperation he would receive would come from General Kelley, an officer whom Lander considered to be superior to any other general in the western Virginia theater. When the telegraph lines went down west of Bath, Lander found it too

34. Temperature readings, Cumberland, Md., January 6, 1862, NWR; John R. Kenly to R. Morris Copeland, January 7, 1862, BP 18:1; H. Tyndale to R. M. Copeland, January 6, 1862, BP 18:1.

35. J. W. Garrett to Samuel P. Chase, January 6, 1862, MP 15:7566–7; S. H. Leonard to R. M. Copeland, January 6, 1862, BP 18:1; S. H. Leonard to Banks, January 6, 1862, BP 18:1; FWL to R. M. Copeland, January 6, 1862, BP 18:1.

36. S. H. Leonard to Banks, January 6, 1862, BP 18:1; Jed Hotchkiss journal, January 5 and 6, 1862, Jed Hotchkiss Papers, Reel 1, LC.

slow and impracticable to transmit telegraph messages by alternative wired routes. He set up a horse relay to transfer dispatches from Hancock to Cumberland. Once Lander saw Jackson withdrawing a large portion of his force from Alpine Station, he grew alarmed that the southerners were now after Kelley's Romney force. Not hearing from Kelley by 11:00 A.M. on Tuesday morning, January 7, Lander yearned to head to Romney to save the force there. He wired headquarters in Washington to get a message to Kelley via Pittsburgh to warn his force. McClellan concurred and complied.[37]

Lander finally received Kelley's horse relay on Tuesday afternoon. Kelley's message had been written over twelve hours earlier, indicating that the ailing general in Cumberland was unaware that Jackson had already pulled back from the railroad. Still, Lander was pleased to learn that Kelley had sent 3,000 soldiers out from Romney down the Northwestern Turnpike seventeen miles to surprise a militia detachment at Blue's Gap, a Cacapon Mountain pass situated at the midpoint between Romney and Winchester. "I have no doubt but that the expedition will be successful," Kelley confidently predicted, "The news will be carried at once to Jackson that I am moving on Winchester or his rear which will cause him to advance on me or to fall back to save Winchester." Advising Lander to watch Jackson's movements closely, Kelley asked a question that Lander had been begging to have answered for two solid days: "Can't you be reinforced from Banks's column to any extent you may require to enable you to cross the river and act offensively?"

Complaining of his own poor health that dated back to his Philippi injury, Kelley admitted as he closed his letter, "I am extremely anxious for you to relieve me. Yet I am extremely thankful and so will the government be that you happened to be at Hancock. The fact of your being there doubtless saved the town. I will send a messenger to you tomorrow giving you an account of the expedition at Blue's Gap."[38]

Lander and Kelley shared the same military mindset. They both believed in attacking the tail of Jackson's army and both were incredulous that McClellan and Banks opposed the idea. Lander agonized over the fact that he had yet to receive orders to support Kelley. He wired Banks with a daring proposition. "Ask headquarters if I may not cross here and

---

37. FWL, Testimony, Pt. 1 JCCW, 161; FWL to R. M. Copeland, January 7, 1862, BP 18:1; GBM to "Comdg. officer at Romney," January 7, 1862, MP 15:7612.

38. Kelley to FWL, January 6, 1862, LP 3:6509–10.

engage the enemy." Lander persisted, "It must be a forced march under scant subsistence but I hope to harass him enough to do some good and will try not to lose the command." Lander stressed how disappointed he was that Banks had failed to cross the river, move to Martinsburg, and draw Jackson away. Mentioning Kelley's mission, Lander explained that the railroad was now lightly guarded and Jackson would surely destroy it if he was not checked. Lander then provided options to either attack Jackson or to take command at Romney. Either option carried risk. Lander realized this and ended his telegraph by coldly admitting, "Shall probably drown or freeze some men."[39]

On receiving the note, Banks's temper shortened. Wiring McClellan and sending Lander's dispatch to him, Banks explained why he did not cross to Martinsburg: "Every intelligence officer here confirms the suggestion that to cross the river will result in failure to intercept the Enemy and place the division in peril." McClellan, finally recovering from his bout of typhoid, wired back to Banks concurring, "I would not run the great risk of crossing the River unless you see certain chances of great success and perfect certainty of being able to recross at Pleasure." For Banks's benefit, McClellan surmised that "Lander is too young a General to appreciate the difficulty of a river behind his Army." He instructed Banks to order Lander not to cross the Potomac, but to move to Romney at once, then fall back to the railroad if he was threatened there.[40]

Banks cheerfully and swiftly relayed McClellan's message to Lander, but he was mistaken if he believed that the direct orders would be effective at quieting him. Lander held the belief that Banks had not completely apprised McClellan of the situation in front of him (indeed, Banks did censor Lander's earlier dispatch).[41] Lander interrogated a slave who had escaped from Jackson's division and learned that Jackson's supply trains lay vulnerable to destruction. Irritated at Banks for not supporting him in a timely manner (Brigadier General Alpheus S. Williams's brigade would not arrive at Hancock until early the next day), and believing that McClellan would support offensive actions against the enemy if he were

39. FWL to Banks, January 7, 1862, LP 3:6514–15.
40. Banks to GBM, January 7, 1862, 11:15 A.M., MP 15:7591–2; GBM to Banks, January 7, 1862, MP 15:7615; GBM to Banks, January 7, 1862, MP 15:7616.
41. Banks to FWL, January 7, 1862, LP 3:6518; FWL to Banks, January 7, 1862, BP 18:1. The line Banks had omitted read: "Headquarters cannot know the state of things here, orders given a week since to Kelley will not do now."

appropriately updated, Lander used this newly acquired intelligence to build a case for attempting to capture his adversary's supplies. But the temperamental general no longer could control his anger. Shunning the politeness and formality that traditionally characterizes dispatches between commanding officers, Lander adamantly spelled out his intentions in an acrid message he transmitted for both Banks and McClellan to read:

> I now demand direct orders. I propose to cross the river tonight with 3,000 men, 4,000 not having yet arrived, fall on the rear of the enemy and have Williams's brigade now on his way here rest 4 hours and then cross to aid me. Our troops are so distributed that they can do little. Gen. Banks should have been moved on Martinsburg. He then would have been ready to help me on the rear of the enemy. How can he reinforce me over 50 miles of country road and snow to aid Kelley and beat the enemy? How can I get to Romney in time to serve any real purpose?
>
> This ought to be read to Genl. McClellan by the officer receiving it, for I cannot believe if he has received my dispatches but what the mistake of Jackson's moving his artillery and baggage [toward Hancock] would have been taken advantage of. And I have not pressed the necessity of reinforcements here from the fact that I believed the commander in chief knowing me well would trust me to hold the enemy here engaged to the last and clearly see what is evident that the real movement was drawing troops from Baltimore and a crossing farther east.[42]

Banks ranted on receiving and reading Lander's note. He would make sure that McClellan was forwarded every single word of it. Along with Lander's dispatch, Banks sent confirmed information—contrary to Lander's insistence—that proved that no railway existed between Winchester and Strasburg, and then sent a wordy dispatch of his own to clarify that his "division will face any possible danger cheerfully and manfully," but since the enemy had appeared to have withdrawn, there was no indication to take such a risk. Banks, knowing the phrases that McClellan liked to hear, informed his superior that he believed that efforts to guard the railroad should be done "at our own time and with full preparation, and especially that we should avoid being drawn into this country by adventitious circumstances, promising no certain good, and having no connection and offering no support to the great work in contemplation." Banks signed off his dispatch by supporting McClellan's methodical develop-

---

42. FWL to Banks, January 7, 1862, BP 18:1.

ment of his plans, believing that he should not allow the impatience of Congress or the people to force him to speed up his schedule. Banks was certain that McClellan would see his side of the argument, and on receiving McClellan's return dispatch, he sent the whole order back to Lander.[43]

In the meantime, Lander impatiently waited to receive the necessary permission from his superior officer. Time was of the essence; every passing minute meant that Jackson's vulnerable wagons were becoming more inaccessible. Although his sojourn in Hancock had been unexpected, Lander still envisioned that the grand strategy to defeat Jackson and Johnston about which he had testified to the Joint Committee in December was still viable. Lander expanded on the plan in his Hancock headquarters. He wrote a five-page plan describing movements in northwestern Virginia. The report called for Banks to cross the Potomac at Sandy Hook and block Snicker's Gap in the Blue Ridge Mountains (with reinforcements from Baltimore supporting his rear) to prevent a linkage between the Confederates in the Shenandoah Valley with Johnston's army entrenched at Centreville and Manassas. Banks would then occupy Winchester and all of its roads leading from the mountains. A reinforced command at Romney would move eastward against an isolated Jackson in the Valley. Even if the Confederate Valley force exceeded 15,000 men, Lander reasoned that if "the leaders capable of making requisitions giving orders in a comprehensive manner, understanding what is required of them and with alacrity executing their parts of the programme, What chance for escape has Jackson?"

Lander's strategy called for the swift destruction of Jackson—"celerity" emphasized—then continuing to hold the mountain passes with 20,000 men. Not only would Johnston's Manassas army have its supply line destroyed, but the Confederates could be destroyed as well by a head-on fight if Johnston attempted to rescue Jackson (at the least he could be lured from his earthworks), or by a timed flank attack if Johnston attempted to cross his Confederates into Maryland. Although Banks wanted to take his time to repair the B & O, Lander placed primary importance on the rebuilding of the railroad: "With ample transportation in the shape of railways, boats, etc., at our command cannot our force be used twice to beat Jackson and then to join the Army of the Potomac?"

43. *OR*, 5:694–5; GBM to Banks, January 7, 1862, MP 15:7608.

Lander felt no reservations at the prospect of sacrificing soldiers to complete the overall objective. He realized his proposals carried risk, but he firmly believed that more risks needed to be taken by the Union army: "Is not war a game of risks, are not fear and doubt states of nervous sentiment which embarrass leaders and prevent results?" Lander felt that he was not healthy enough to head the operation, but he was willing to attempt the most perilous part "by cutting off the Manassas Railroad, though I am not sure that the detachment will not be annihilated . . . But are we less able to penetrate the enemy's country than Jackson to penetrate ours?" Lander closed his holograph with an example of emphasis: "Had I today 4,000 men armed with Sharps breech-loading rifles, 400 mules for a pack train, the authority to use some of the ships and yawls at the navy yard with the aid of the gallant Kelley, I would do the most of [the operation] alone and not lose men or trains if a reverse should unfortunately await me."[44]

Lander had the opportunity to work with Kelley to attempt his objective. Unfortunately, his Sharps were replaced by Belgians (a weapon Lander called "a curse to the army"), his ships and yawls were substituted by flatboats that were iced in a frozen canal scores of miles away. He had no pack mules and commanded only half the men he proposed were necessary to conduct his mountain operations. Banks had not demonstrated the mettle Lander expected of him.

Placing too much confidence in dubious and unconfirmed sources, Lander had been misinformed. No rail line existed between Strasburg and Winchester, the Confederate supply wagons left Bath at the van of the column and not in the rear, and Jackson was not heading through Bloomery Gap as Lander had deduced, but was instead plodding toward Unger's crossroads, several miles southeast of Bath.[45] These misconceptions did not negate Lander's plan; he wanted to attack the vulnerable tail of Jackson's moving division with an overwhelming force and disrupt it. He still expected McClellan to provide positive orders. If he would not force

44. LP 3:6456–60. These five pages of notes are unsigned and undated, but they clearly read as a strategy of operations in the Shenandoah Valley and eastern theater of operations. The order of its appearance in the Lander collection suggests that it was written in December, but the events Lander describes—including his physician's statement about his health and Jackson's presence on "the peninsula"—isolate the timing of the piece to Lander's Hancock defense.

45. *OR*, 5:392.

Banks to cross, McClellan could still allow Lander to attempt his mission, regardless of the risks involved.

McClellan's response, relayed through Banks's headquarters at Frederick, was transmitted to Lander's office in Hancock later in the afternoon of January 7. The three-sentence message struck Lander like a lightning bolt: "Say to General Lander that I might comment very severely on the tone of his dispatches but abstain. Give him positive orders to repair at once to Romney and carry out the instructions I have sent already to fall back on the Railway. It would be folly to cross the river at Hancock under present circumstances, except with a small corps of observation, but not to follow up the enemy." Banks, as a form of revenge, also relayed a parenthetical statement that McClellan had not intended Lander to see: "General Lander is too suggestive and critical."[46]

McClellan used sound military judgment to admonish Lander for his impetuosity. Twenty-five years after the fact, McClellan underscored his comments by admitting that he was "obliged to check Lander rather abruptly for attempting to assume control over troops not under his command," but firmly believed that the incident did not cause any ill feelings toward him.[47]

He was quite mistaken. "Old Grizzly" raged uncontrollably the moment he received the dispatch. The message not only prevented him from attempting to attack Jackson on January 7, it also demonstrated that McClellan's military philosophy of caution and careful planning ran antithetically to his (and Kelley's), and could significantly retard future operations against Stonewall Jackson in the Shenandoah Valley. McClellan was not willing to attempt any movement that had the potential to replay the Ball's Bluff disaster. Lander's strategy called for risk-taking, swift movements, and sacrifice. McClellan, like Banks, had no heart for any part of it in January of 1862.

Lander picked up Kelley's inspiring letter that he had received earlier that day and compared it to what he had just received from headquarters. McClellan cut Lander deeply when he characterized his ideas as "folly." Was not Kelley performing a similar operation? Would McClellan call it "folly," too, if Kelley succeeded?

For his own benefit, Lander refused to allow McClellan to have the

46. GBM to Banks to FWL, January 7, 1862, LP 3:6519.
47. McClellan, *McClellan's Own Story*, 191.

final word on the matter. "This letter shows all the folly," he wrote at the bottom of General Kelley's letter to favorably characterize the Blue's Gap mission. "The country wants folly, asks for folly, common sense and bravery." Lander then provided a lyrical summary of the opportunity that McClellan allowed to slip away: "A demoralized enemy, starving and fearful, believing we are in force, a dark night, a snowy road, I would have stampeded the whole rearguard and burned his wagons."

"I now go to Romney."[48]

48. FWL, Commentary, LP 3:6510. Lander frequently scribbled observations on dispatches, usually on the back or in the margins. The practice may have been a way for the general to vent his anger and frustration. He also may have wished to retain the "exchange" for postwar use, either for a writing project or for a political campaign.

8

"I Will Cross Hell on the Ice"

By pondering our plans and maps,
 Great General George has got the gaps,
But we, who watched this sleepy war
 We got the gaps long, long, before.
      —F. W. Lander

During the late evening of January 7, 1862, General Frederick Lander scrawled his final military communiqué from Hancock, Maryland. The two-page dispatch addressed to Banks's brigadier, Alpheus S. Williams, was not transmitted by telegraph wire but instead was left at Lander's headquarters. Williams had departed Frederick with his Third Brigade to take overall control of Hancock. Although Lander had pleaded for infantry help since Saturday night, Williams would not enter Hancock until noon on Wednesday. Lander did his best to control his temper in this particular letter, most of which was dedicated to stressing the importance of constructing a pontoon bridge across the icy Potomac and protecting it with crude earthworks and the sturdy buildings on Hancock's Main Street. "You will oblige me by transmitting a copy of this communication to Maj. Gen. Banks," scribbled Lander at the end of the message, swallowing his frustration at Williams's superior by closing, "and being guided by his well-attested judgment and discretion receive such orders as he may choose to give in the premises."[1]

As Lander wrapped up his preparations for departure, his horse relay from General Kelley galloped into town. The rider reined in at Lander's headquarters and handed him Kelley's follow-up note concerning the result of the Blue's Gap expedition. Lander read with pleasure as Kelley trumpeted the rousing success his troops had achieved over the Confederates guarding the pass. Kelley's force, 2,000 men under the command of Colonel Samuel Dunning of the Fifth Ohio, had departed Romney shortly before midnight on January 6, marched seventeen miles in seven hours to the gap, and routed the militia force there—"Cleared them out in about twenty-five minutes, captured two guns—all they had . . . burnt their entire camp, killed ten or twelve, and took about fifteen prisoners." Kelley explained that the rest of the enemy force had fled into the wooded hillside, and his detachment (at the time he wrote the letter) was returning to Romney. Kelley believed that Jackson would draw away from Bath and would then come after him. "If he comes toward me," Kelley wished Lander to corner him, explaining, "I can resist him there with much less force than he will bring against me. It is the key to the upper valley and the railroad."

Lander could not control his enthusiasm after reading the note. Folly indeed! Kelley had taken the initiative. His troops marched a round-trip distance of over thirty miles, cleared an enemy stronghold, and added two cannons to their arsenal—all within twenty-four hours. Lander remembered his last admonition from McClellan, who had scolded the Bay Stater for even suggesting to attempt what Kelley had already accomplished. "Who is right now?" Lander wrote across the top of Kelley's dispatch. It was bittersweet news, though. Kelley was working under the false premise that Lander would now attack an unsuspecting Jackson, who would be focused on Kelley's position. Lander did not look forward to informing his friend that he would arrive alone; his regiments would stay at Hancock to await Williams's arrival. Lander's orders were to pull back Kelley's successful troops from Romney toward Cumberland. It was cruel irony for Lander. Those troops existed there by his recommendation to General Winfield Scott; now McClellan controlled matters and negated Lander's strategic objectives. "McClellan orders Romney evacuated,"

1. FWL to Williams, January 7, 1862, BP 18:1.

penciled Lander at the bottom of Kelley's letter. The fact that McClellan's huge army stagnated around the capital for nearly six months did not go unnoticed by the disgusted commander. "See the difference between Kelley and the Army of the Potomac," observed Lander as he scrawled his final line at the bottom of the page, "A little dash is a good element."[2]

After closing with that gratifying commentary, Lander wrapped himself in his buffalo skin (a garment left over from his expedition days) and departed his headquarters. He boarded his horse-drawn sleigh, tugged on the reigns, and glided out of town, disappearing behind Sideling Hill as the horse team pulled the general westward on the National Turnpike across Maryland's panhandle. The troops he left behind had been impressed by the appearance and leadership of the former frontiersman. "He is a gallant Western man—and we were sorry to hear of his leaving us," wrote Jacob Peterman of the Eighty-fourth Pennsylvania.[3] This regiment, along with the unruly 110th Pennsylvania, the Thirty-ninth Illinois, and Muhlenburg's artillery, awaited the arrival of their new commander and an uncertain future.

Cumberland lay at the terminus of the C & O Canal. Despite the convenience of the macadamized road carrying Lander's sleigh the requisite thirty-five miles to arrive there from Hancock, the snow-crusted mountains and arctic conditions made for a miserable ride. The temperature dipped below zero overnight, but the region had warmed thirty degrees by the time Lander reached Kelley's headquarters in Cumberland in the early afternoon of January 8.[4] Congratulating his ailing friend on a job well done, Lander briefed Kelley about his orders to take the Romney force back to the railroad. Twenty miles still separated Lander from the Romney troops he was about to inherit. His ultimate objective, after discussing the area with Kelley, was to ride down to Romney and evacuate all the supplies and men by taking them to suitable ground for protecting the

2. Kelley to FWL, January 7, 1862, LP 3:6520. Kelley ordered 3,000 men to make the attack, but only two out of three soldiers in the designated regiments left Romney. For a description of the skirmish at Blue's Gap, see "Prock" to the editor, January 8, 1862, *Vincennes (Ind.) Western Sun*, January 18, 1862; and "Volunteer" to the editor, January 9, 1862, *Painesville (Ohio) Telegraph*, January 23, 1862.

3. FWL to Barstow, January 8, 1862, LP 3:6526; Jacob Peterman to his father, January 10, 1862, private possession of David Richards, Gettysburg, Pa.

4. Temperature readings, Cumberland, Md., District of Columbia, and Sheets Mill, Va., January 8, 1862, NWR.

railroad. Lander and Kelley agreed that celerity was key. Jackson's force was believed to greatly outnumber the 7,000 Federals at Romney. The Confederates could attack that force within two days.

Lander had yet to receive any staff help, but that problem would partially be resolved within the next twenty-four hours. Captain Simon F. Barstow, the general's new aide-de-camp, was expected to reach Cumberland soon, carrying the $800 in gold that Mrs. Lander had provided him in Washington. Anxious to assess the situation at Romney, Lander left a note for Barstow to obtain a detailed statement of the size and location of the Union force around Romney as well as a description of the road network he could use for the eventual withdrawal from town.[5] Leaving his buffalo skin and sleigh behind, Lander straddled a horse and trotted out of Cumberland.

Twenty miles later, Lander rode into Romney on Wednesday night, January 8.[6] He had slept no more than fifteen hours over the previous five and one-half days, had no staff help, no decent maps, and no idea about the makeup of the forces under his command. The quality of his troops appeared to be the only gratifying element of the campaign. The westerners (named for the westernmost contiguous states they were recruited from and not to be confused with territory and California frontiersmen) consisted of western Virginia campaign veterans: the Seventh, Thirteenth, and Fourteenth Indiana; the Fourth, Fifth, Seventh, and Eighth Ohio; and the First and Seventh (Union)Virginia. They had performed well in their first expedition to Blue's Gap, although they had gone beyond their orders and burned several buildings and slaughtered livestock. Still, Lander was impressed with the speed and efficiency with which they had accomplished their mission.

Lander toiled for two days to plan the monstrous task of evacuating Romney. Unfamiliar with the region, his primary concern was to decide which road network to use to pull back to the B & O. Captain Barstow arrived on January 9 and provided a description from General Kelley. The shortest distance for departure would be to move northward past Hanging Rock to Springfield, then due north to the Green Spring station on the B & O. Kelley advised Lander against attempting that route. He

5. FWL to Simon Barstow, January 8, 1862, LP 3:6526.

6. Hiram R. Treher (5th Ohio) to his parents, January 15, 1862, *Chambersburg (Pa.) Semi-Weekly Dispatch,* January 28, 1862.

feared that Jackson would approach in two westward-moving columns, one traveling from Blue's Gap on the Northwestern Turnpike, the other advancing from Bloomery Gap on a road that led directly into Springfield. Kelley had 1,700 men under the overall command of Colonel James Gavin (Seventh Indiana) posted on the latter road two miles east of Springfield. They guarded the ford over the South Branch River to contest the Confederate advance along that road. Kelley was still apprehensive; if Gavin's men were forced back, Jackson's column could take Springfield and either hit Lander in the flank or trap him from the north and south if he was unfortunate enough to be caught between Romney and Springfield. The other disadvantage of the northern route was the numerous unbridged creeks that traversed the roads.[7]

Kelley preferred an alternate route. The New Creek Road would carry the division westward from Romney then northward to Cumberland. This route was several miles longer than the northern one, but Kelley reasoned that the road was in better shape and had a strong bridge over New Creek. Kelley also stressed that the railroad could be employed for troop transport if he chose this route. Most important, Kelley deemed the New Creek road "the only practicable one" since it carried Lander and his men safely away westward to prevent being struck by one or both of Jackson's columns.[8]

Lander considered Kelley's advice but at the same time entertained other ideas. Acknowledging that his force could not feasiblely defend Romney, Lander expressed his concern to General McClellan over the safety of the railroad. Supplies had already begun moving from Romney to the railroad, foretelling that the troops would soon follow. Lander had sent the Ringgold Cavalry toward Bloomery Gap from Springfield to ascertain Jackson's position. Detailing the numbers of Union forces in all areas around Romney and the railroad, Lander assured the War Department that "I am collecting all the intelligence practicable and shall not, I think, be surprised."[9]

7. Road descriptions around Romney, LP 3:6662; Troop strength and distribution in Romney and vicinity, LP 3:6653; FWL to Barstow, January 8, 1862, LP 3:6626–7.

8. Kelley to FWL, January 9, 1862, LP 5:6699.

9. Fifth Ohio soldier to the editor, January 9, 1862, *Cincinnati Daily Commercial,* January 16, 1862; Samuel C. Farrar, *The Twenty-second Pennsylvania Cavalry and the Ringgold Battalion, 1861–1865* (Pittsburgh, Pa., 1911), 35; FWL to A. V. Colburn, January 9, 1862, MP 47:85864.

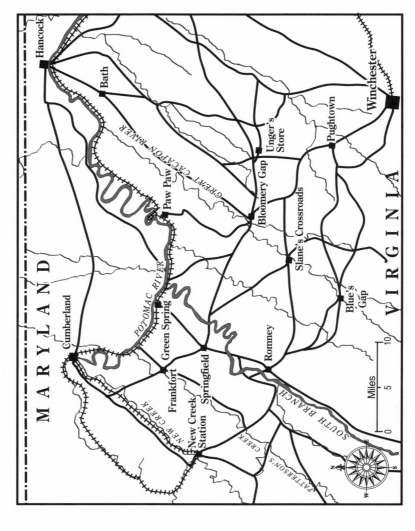

Northwestern Virginia Theater of Operations, January–March 1862

Friday, January 10, opened with a flurry of dispatches ticking across the telegraph lines of western Virginia. Lander was informed that he and his men now belonged to the Army of the Potomac rather than Rosecrans's Department of Western Virginia. He was promised a handful of regiments from western Virginia to add to his command; the three new regiments from Hancock also were ordered to his division (General Williams expressed great delight in being rid of the unruly Pennsylvanians). McClellan, soon after informing Francis H. Pierpont (the governor of the "Restored Government of Virginia") that "I will do the best I can for Romney," sent a message to Lander that suggested something totally antithetical: "Be careful not to be caught. . . . Be sure to fall back in time."[10]

Lander wired Kelley in Cumberland to have fifteen railroad cars ready at New Creek by 9:00 P.M. along with enough ambulance wagons to supply 7,000 men. Additionally, Lander requested that Kelley inform General Rosecrans to send five days' rations for the same number of men. If Kelley believed Lander was agreeable to an uncontested evacuation, the remainder of Lander's dispatch set him straight. Lander had been forming an audacious plan, one that would use the railroad to link with General Williams's Hancock force at Sir John's Run (three miles west of Hancock). Knowing that Jackson had yet to pass through Bloomery Gap from Unger's Store, Lander had made preparations to have canal boats taken to the fordable part of the Potomac at Sir John's Run. "I shall cross the river there and attack the enemy's rear," Lander ordered a surprised Kelley, "Tell Williams to prepare to march to Sir John's Run drawing five days subsistence." Lander reasoned that the combined forces could be used to "beat the enemy and relieve the railroad."[11]

Notwithstanding the success of his own aggressive mission, Kelley was stunned at Lander's request. Although he had indicated to Lander one day earlier that Williams should cross into Virginia and fall on Jackson's rear, the situation had changed dramatically. Kelley learned that the long railroad bridge over the Great Cacapon River had been burned and felled by the Confederates, making a successful link with Williams a difficult task. Kelley worked hard to talk Lander out of any rash actions without setting off his friend's temper. "You will excuse me for this freely express-

---

10. *OR*, 51(1):517–18; Alpheus S. Williams to "Lew," February 3, 1862, in Quaife, *From the Cannon's Mouth*, 55–6; GBM to FWL, January 10, 1862, LP 5:6698.

11. FWL to Kelley, n.d., LP 3:6657.

ing my opinion," relayed Kelley to the irascible general, "Take it only for what it is worth."[12] He eventually convinced Lander that time was too short to link with Williams, indicating that Williams appeared apprehensive about moving his brigade from Hancock. Lander acquiesced, particularly after he found the removal of baggage to be extremely slow that day. He left his headquarters to finalize preparations for the departure.

Lander's presence in Romney on Friday evening did not go unnoticed. An Ohio soldier, like poets and sculptors before him, was impressed by his first look at his new commanding officer. "About 6:00 P.M. I saw Gen. Lander's large and manly person, on the street, personally superintending the arrangements for the guard to the baggage," he wrote to his hometown paper. "He is tall, well built, graceful in his bearing, positive in his manner, and in every way carries the stamp of a soldier."[13]

That Ohio soldier was fortunate not to be within earshot of Lander shortly after he made his observations. Lander's orders to have ambulances made ready to remove the wounded to safety had not been carried out. He discovered shortly after dark that he would be delayed in leaving the area until he could rectify this particular problem. A pious surgeon from the Fourteenth Indiana suffered from bad timing when he asked the irritated general what plans he had made for evacuating the wounded from his regiment. "God damn you, the 14th Regt., the whole army, everybody and everything," roared Old Grizzly, "and if I have forgotten anything, God damn it." Lander eventually delegated the responsibility to an officer with experience in the quartermaster department. No sick or wounded soldiers were to fall into Confederate hands.[14]

It was becoming all too apparent to Lander that time had run out while supplies still remained in Romney. No more wagons were available to remove them. He felt his only option was to deny the Confederates any plunder when they took over Romney. Lander ordered the unevacuated stores to be set afire. For the troops who had participated at Blue's Gap

12. Kelley to FWL, n.d., LP 5:6688; Kelley to FWL, January 9, 1862, LP 5:6691, 6700–1. Kelley's and Lander's undated dispatches were likely transmitted on Friday, January 10.

13. "Boulder" to the editor, January 10, 1862, *(Columbus) Ohio State Journal,* January 16, 1862.

14. Augustus Van Dyke to his father, February 2, 1862, Van Dyke Papers, IHS; "Boulder" to the editor, January 10, 1862, *(Columbus) Ohio State Journal,* January 16, 1862.

three days earlier, this was a welcome order and they wished to burn houses along with supplies; however, Lander posted guards at citizens' residences to prevent a repeat of the Blue's Gap aftermath. A soldier in the Seventh Ohio observed that "everything that could not be taken was hastily committed to the flames. Many tents were thus destroyed, together with blankets, trunks, clothing, provisions accoutrements, and articles of camp equipage,—the flames lighting up a scene of destruction that I hope never to witness again." Another Buckeye claimed that the whole town appeared to be on fire.[15]

With the night sky illuminated by the flaming Union stores, Lander's troops marched toward the B & O Railroad at 9:00 P.M. Lander moved his troops northward—not by General Kelley's cautious New Creek route but by the shortest and most direct path. Sporadic rains accompanied by violent wind gusts buffeted the foot soldiers as they trekked on the rapidly muddying road. Over the next three hours the 7,000 soldiers stretched five miles in columns of fours and the baggage trains in the van added another three miles to the line. The roads had already impaired the marching abilities of the foot soldiers. "Some places it was six inches deep and almost thin enough to run like water," observed Lorenzo Vanderhoef of the Eighth Ohio, "other places . . . stiff enough to pull the boots off a man's feet."[16] Shortly before midnight, the rearguard cut the telegraph lines and evacuated the camp.

The column lurched slowly along Green Spring Road, passing under the "Hanging Rock" and over a wire suspension bridge that crossed the South Branch of the Potomac. An Irish company of the Eighth Ohio had been guarding the bridge; they struck their tents and joined the column. The vanguard marched in ankle-deep mud all the way to Springfield, ten miles north of Romney, and entered the town at 2:00 A.M. Here, Colonel Gavin and his Seventh Indiana guarded the approach from Slane's Crossroads and Bloomery Gap. Lander rode to the front of his column and concluded that the enemy was several hours from them. He decided

15. "Boulder" to the editor, January 10, 1862, *(Columbus) Ohio State Journal,* January 16, 1862; Treher to his parents, January 15, 1862, *Chambersburg Semi-Weekly Dispatch,* January 28, 1862; "Volunteer" [V. E. Smalley] to the editor, January 16, 1862, *Painesville (Ohio) Telegraph,* January 23, 1862.

16. Lorenzo Vanderhoef diary, January 10, 1862, in *"I Am Now a Soldier!": The Civil War Diaries of Lorenzo Vanderhoef,* ed. Kenneth Martin and Ralph Linwood Snow (Bath, Maine, 1990), 78.

to bivouac at Springfield. Gavin gave up his bed to the general, and the rest of the men tore down fence rails. Soon a thousand fires blazed to take the damp chill out of the soldiers' bodies.

Knowing that they would be marching again in a few hours, the men flopped down on any available space. The majority slept in the open, under a rainy sky. Those without ingenuity sank in the mud while others collected unburned rails to shelter themselves from the elements. The temperature dropped from the midforties registered the previous afternoon to below freezing, adding more unpleasantness to the uncomfortable evening.

The march resumed at 8:00 A.M. on Saturday morning, January 11. Those familiar with the region expected to advance by the shortest distance to the railroad by continuing the northern course to Green Spring station. Lander perplexed his men when he had the column depart from the Green Spring Road, which would have carried them eight miles northward to the railroad. Instead they marched on the northwest road toward the dingy and dilapidated village of Frankfort, six miles from Springfield. For two hours the men halted here, stacked arms, and fed their horses. Two roads diverged from Frankfort, one leading northward to the mouth of Patterson's Creek, the other leading northwest to Cumberland. Lander ordered his men to move on the former route, giving the soldiers a clue to their final destination.[17]

The advance from Frankfort was short but harrowing. A cold, misty rain had aggravated the northerners ever since they left Romney. Not only did the water turn the roads into deep quagmires, it had swollen the numerous creeks that Lander's men forded. Most of these so far had been relatively shallow tributaries, but now the men had to conquer Patterson's Creek, the largest feeder of the North Branch of the Potomac River. Lander split his forces based on the knowledge provided him prior to the evacuation. The infantry followed a mountain road northward to the railroad, staying east of the creek until they reached the railroad bridge at its

---

17. "Boulder" to the editor, January 10, 1862, *(Columbus) Ohio State Journal,* January 16, 1862; "Volunteer" [V. E. Smalley] to the editor, January 16, 1862, *Painesville (Ohio) Telegraph,* January 23, 1862; temperature readings, Cumberland, Md., and District of Columbia, January 10–11, 1862, NWR; Oliver Wise to the editor, January 28, 1862, *(Canton, Ohio) Starke County Republican,* February 6, 1862; G. B. Cock to the editor, January 15, 1862, *Starke County Republican,* January 23, 1862; H. J. J. [Henry J. Johnson] to the editor, January 18, 1862, *Wellsburg (Va.) Herald,* January 24, 1862.

mouth. The cavalry, artillery, and baggage wagons stayed on the main road and attempted to cross the rain-swollen creek. The water churned in a swirling torrent—running at the top of the banks—and appeared unfordable.

Lander, who had moved with the cavalry, had reached the limit of his patience. The twenty-mile march had consumed twenty hours, and the general was unwilling to allow nature to impede him any longer. He ordered wagons, pulled by four-mule teams, to be run into the creek. Sixteen animals were swept away attempting this endeavor. Eventually, after enough wagons had been successfully positioned, timbers and planks were laid on them to allow all noninfantry personnel to cross. A cavalry lieutenant almost met the same fate as the mules when his horse was swept from under him; the rider saved himself by grabbing an overhanging limb and holding on long enough to be rescued by his company mates. Lander and his orderly, Ringgold Cavalry sergeant John Elwood, watched the near disaster from the eastern side of the creek. Not having experienced this type of difficulty since his expedition days, Lander uttered loud enough for Elwood to hear, "The next time I undertake to move an army, and God Almighty sends such a rain, I will go around and cross Hell on the ice." His orderly felt certain Lander was drunk that night and assessed the general as a wicked man.[18]

With much difficulty, Lander's section of the column crossed the creek and advanced to the Patterson's Creek railroad station. The infantry, now wading through knee-deep mud, crossed the railroad bridge and entered the station from the east shortly after 9:00 P.M. One soldier sized up the total march as "twenty-one miles in length and from ten to fifteen inches deep." The men quickly sought hay, laid it over the wet ground, and fell asleep under the cool misty sky. They enjoyed what one called a "sound and refreshing a night's sleep as ever blessed tired soldiers."[19]

---

18. Farrar, *Twenty-second Pennsylvania Cavalry*, 35–6; John W. Elwood, *Elwood's Stories of the Old Ringgold Cavalry, 1847–1865: The First Three Year Cavalry of the Civil War* (Coal Center, Pa., 1914), 85–6.

19. Oliver Wise to the editor, January 28, 1862, *(Canton, Ohio) Starke County Republican*, February 6, 1862; G. B. Cock to the editor, January 15, 1862, *Starke County Republican*, January 23, 1862; H. J. J. to the editor, January 18, 1862, *Wellsburg (Va.) Herald*, January 24, 1862; "Volunteer" to the editor, January 16, 1862, *Painesville (Ohio) Telegraph*, January 23, 1862; H. R. Treher to his parents, January 15, 1862, *Chambersburg (Pa.) Semi-Weekly Dispatch*, January 28, 1862.

Sunday morning's light dawned across the Potomac River at approximately 7:15 A.M. on January 12. The soldiers awakened to see their new camp a nightmare. The Patterson's Creek camp surrounded the railroad station on the only low-level ground forming a shallow basin south of the river. The soldiers had encamped west of the mouth of Patterson's Creek. The heavy rains and warm temperatures over the past three days had caused the Potomac to flood over its banks. The result was a wholly unexpected catastrophe. "Mud, Mud, Mud!" cried an Indiana soldier with ample justification. "If all of Virginia had been canvassed a worse place could not have been found," an Ohioan chimed in. A member of the same regiment announced, "The sea of mud, stirred and kneaded by 8,000 soldiers, was altogether indescribable, for only a comparatively small portion was on the top in sight."[20] Patterson's Creek station, sitting six miles east of Cumberland, offered no comfort for the veterans of the previous days' mud march.

Shadow Lawn, a two-year-old brick house standing close to the depot, appeared to be the only solid structure in the area. The Gibson family, who resided there, was restricted to the first floor while all four rooms on the second floor were confiscated for military duties. The medical director's office was located on the first floor. Telegraphers occupied the upstairs rooms across the stairway. Adjutant Barstow's office stood to the right of the telegraph room, and additional staff aides occupied the room to the left. Across from the latter room was the most important military room in the house. Behind this door toiled General Lander.[21]

Lander kept long hours, often receiving and transmitting dispatches well past midnight. His first order of business was to provide sustenance for his hungry men, who had initially christened their miserable site

20. B. F. Kelley to FWL, January 12, 1862, LP 5:6711; Clarke, *Confederate States Almanac*, 3; Temperature readings, Cumberland, Md., January 12, 1862, NWR; John V. Hadley to Mollie Hill, February 4, 1862, in "An Indiana Soldier in Love and War: The Civil War Letters of John V. Hadley," ed. James I. Robertson Jr., *Indiana Magazine of History* 59 (1963): 203; George L. Wood, *The Seventh Regiment: A Record* (New York, 1865), 86; Theodore Wilder, *The History of Company C, Seventh Regiment, O. V. I.* (Oberlin, Ohio, 1956), 21–2.

21. C. W. Dennis, "Suggested Location for Markers for Civil War Blockhouses and Points of Historic Interest on the Cumberland Division of the Baltimore and Ohio Railroad," MS 1856, Maryland Historical Society, Baltimore; *Wheeling (Va.) Daily Intelligencer*, February 13, 1862; "From Gen. Lander's Division," February 3, 1862, *Cincinnati Daily Commercial*, February 6, 1862.

"Camp Nothing To Eat." Supplies began to flow in quickly enough to change the name to Camp Kelley (misspelled as "Kelly" in most of the letters sent from there). Lander also consolidated his troops at the camp by ordering up Colonel James Gavin's men from Springfield and shuttling cannons and equipment from Cumberland.[22]

General Kelley, incapacitated in Cumberland, provided valuable assistance; so much so that he had to remind Lander that he (Lander) controlled all the troops in the area and that Kelley was merely aiding him until he could depart to Grafton to speed his recovery. Kelley had been the one to suggest to Lander initially that he pull the troops back to Patterson's Creek; however, he expected Lander to occupy the high ground on the Maryland side of the Potomac, where the Thirteenth Indiana had entrenched since returning from their Sir John's Run expedition. Lander, less than one week removed from his Hancock defense against Jackson, realized the futility of guarding the railroad if the river flowed between the men and the tracks, and modified Kelley's suggestion. Of the 9,330 infantry available to him, 6,331 stayed on the Virginia side of the river, 1,787 stretched between Cumberland and the North Branch Bridge camps in Maryland, and an additional 612 soldiers (consisting mostly of the Fifth Ohio infantry) guarded the New Creek station in Virginia, twenty miles southwest of Cumberland on the railroad. Lander also had 1,114 cavalry and seventeen cannons spread out on the same points.[23]

The division was dispersed to protect the railroad at its most approachable points. Lander learned on January 14 that his force could be assaulted at any time—General Jackson and his division had begun to occupy Romney (all his forces would be in the town within three days). Jackson, who had apparently yet to learn Lander's identity, wired Confederate secretary of war Judah P. Benjamin (the former Louisiana senator whom Lander had met on their voyage from San Francisco late in 1860): "Through the blessing of God I regard this district as essentially in our possession." Lander believed that Jackson commanded 15,000 men,

22. "Volunteer" to the editor, January 16, 1862, *Painesville (Ohio) Telegraph*, January 23, 1862; James Gavin to FWL, January 12, 1862, LP 5:6715–16; J. M. McKenzie to FWL, January 13, 1862, LP 5:6725–6.

23. B. F. Kelley to FWL, January 14, 1862, LP 5:6729; B. F. Kelley to FWL, January 10, 1862, LP 5:6713. The modern town of Keyser, West Virginia, occupies the site of New Creek.

when his force actually was slightly smaller than that of the Federals. However, Jackson's men were concentrated at Romney, and he prepared to damage the railroad bridges by attacking one of Lander's isolated factions at New Creek. Jackson also desired Cumberland, informing the Confederate secretary of war that the medical stores and other supplies there would be of great value to the Confederacy.[24]

Lander felt that he needed to strengthen his railroad defense with reinforcements. Promised four regiments from western Virginia days before, Lander had yet to see any of them. When the War Department informed him on Thursday, January 16, that the Twenty-ninth, Sixty-second, Sixty-sixth, and Sixty-seventh Ohio were finally ordered to join him, Lander testily scribbled in response, "When can I expect them? It is important for me to know."[25] An insufficient force guarded New Creek, and the War Department was reacting too slowly to accommodate him.

Discipline had been sorely lacking within Lander's division, so much so that the general assessed his command to be "more like an armed mob than an army." Pyromaniacs had set train cars on fire at New Creek; the two Pennsylvania regiments had raced to Cumberland to the point of exhaustion owing to a running bet by the drunken Colonel Lewis of the 110th Pennsylvania and his equally inebriated opponent, Major Walter Barrett of the Eighty-fourth Pennsylvania. Lax officers had allowed their men to plunder private property within pistol shot of headquarters. More than a dozen Federals defected to Confederate lines during the retreat from Romney.

Not surprisingly, the theme of Lander's first series of General Orders to his division centered on disciplinary measures to prevent any further depredations that could exacerbate the demoralization of his command. He informed his men that his patrols would shoot "then and there" anyone guilty of destroying or stealing private property. Lander informed McClellan's chief of staff that he had divided his force into brigades and appointed Colonel John S. Mason of the Fourth Ohio, a West Pointer, as provost marshal of the post. Admitting "the great embarrassment here" to

24. FWL to S. Williams, January 14, 1862, MP 48:85882–3; *OR*, 5:393, 1033; William Allan, "History of the Campaign of General T. J. (Stonewall) Jackson in the Shenandoah Valley of Virginia from November 4, 1861, to June 17, 1862," *Southern Historical Society Papers* 43 (August 1920): 132.

25. A. V. Colburn to FWL (with response), January 16, 1862, LP 5:6733.

General Randolph B. Marcy, Lander also assured the chief of staff that the situation was swiftly shaping up.[26]

Immensely handicapped by the lack of division staffers, Lander welcomed the arrival of his newest handpicked aide-de-camp, Lieutenant Fitz-James O'Brien, at the Patterson's Creek headquarters. O'Brien was a well-known celebrity, being an accomplished poet and writer for *Harper's Weekly*. Lander likely met the Irish bohemian at Annapolis in April of 1861 when O'Brien was a member of the Seventh New York Infantry. Impressed with O'Brien and his poetry, Lander offered him the job after receiving 100 applications for staff appointments. Not expecting the captain to lower his rank to join his staff, Lander was pleasantly surprised when O'Brien accepted the offer. The bard had recently published two critically acclaimed poems, but he had not been successful at finding lasting work in the army until Lander's offer reached him. "I am in harness, and am staff officer of parade, and am already intrusted with the rather arduous but important duty of posting pickets through this devil of the wilderness," wrote O'Brien shortly after arriving at Camp Kelley. He found himself quickly overworked by the burdens of a short-handed division staff.[27]

Lander's ire remained directed at General George McClellan. Lander's relationship with his boss had been crippled by the Hancock admonitions. Hinting for three days that he needed to attack Jackson's tail to impede southern plans, Lander agonized as Jackson safely concentrated his force at Romney. McClellan did not hurry to pull strings to send reinforcements when Lander felt he desperately needed them. The four to six regiments promised him had turned out to be the smaller number, and not one of those regiments had entered Lander's district by January 16.

That same Thursday, when McClellan sent a query to Lander about what he felt should be done within his district, Lander took the open invitation to reiterate his views of strategy. "Strengthen the Army of the Potomac, and troops brought up from the west can be placed along the

26. Samuel Dunning to FWL, January 21, 1862, LP 5:6753; Harvey S. Wells, "The Eighty-fourth Pennsylvania Volunteer Infantry in the Late War," *Philadelphia Weekly Times,* April 10, 1886; "Gen. Lander's Orders," *Cincinnati Daily Commercial,* January 28, 1862; FWL to Randolph Marcy, January 16, 1862, MP 48:85875–6.

27. Fitz-James O'Brien, *The Poems and Stories of Fitz-James O'Brien* (New York, 1968), xxvi–xxvii; Francis Wolle, *Fitz-James O'Brien: A Literary Bohemian of the Eighteen-Fifties* (Boulder, Colo., 1944), 232–5.

railroad here as it is open . . . and a blow given to Jackson," stressed Lander to his superior, summarizing, "in short, an attack made to take [the] Shenandoah Valley from the enemy." Believing that he carried only half the force Jackson had, Lander still planned, when reinforced, to guard the railroad with the incoming regiments and move the rest of his force to the Great Cacapon River on the Virginia side and cross General Williams's Hancock force there. Lander informed McClellan that he had been constructing boats in Cumberland for the sole purpose of getting Williams's men across. Lander had been focused on this movement since the day he left Romney and refused to let the proposal die. He pounded his plan to McClellan, insisting that the combined force could take Bath, Martinsburg, then Winchester. After this Lander wished either to fill the passes of the Blue Ridge or to fall on Leesburg and join General McCall.[28]

Lander felt his forceful response to McClellan's inquiries would set his command in motion. In the meantime, he had General Kelley to aid him in his preparations to take Romney away from Stonewall Jackson. Kelley ordered the construction of four flatboats in Cumberland, two fifty-footers and two thirty-footers. Kelley politely told Lander that they would be finished in five to six days. The ailing commander was set to leave the region in a few days, but until then he continued to assist Lander and skillfully worded his "suggestions" so as not to embarrass or insult his quick-tempered friend. Suggesting that Lander send more infantry to reinforce the New Creek station, Kelley gently added, "Do not get out of patience with me. I take more liberties with you than I would with any other officer because I know you appreciate my motives. . . . My only motive is the success of our cause." A day later, with the boat construction in full swing, Kelley warned, "My Dear General, mature your plans well. Do not make a mistake or a mismove. The eyes, hopes, and prayers of a nation are on and for you. If you cannot see your way perfectly clear—bide your time."[29]

Lander received the dispatches but did little to heed the carefully stated message. The success of his plan required reinforcements (which had yet to arrive) and coordination with General Banks at Frederick and General Williams at Hancock to link with him in Virginia to push toward Winchester and draw Jackson toward them. Lander believed he had the authority from the War Department to send Williams direct orders for assis-

28. *OR*, 5:702–3.
29. Kelley to FWL, January 17–18, 1862. LP 5:6785, 6788–9.

tance. Lander did so on Friday, January 17, telling Williams to be ready at an hour's notice to join him with five days' rations for a tentless bivouac in Virginia. Williams hated the plan because, as he informed his superior, General Banks, much of his command at Hancock was shoeless and frost-bitten. Banks also disapproved of Lander usurping his command and complained to McClellan about it. The incident generated another admonition from McClellan, this time requesting that Lander explain the order and his intentions for the troops.[30]

Realizing that McClellan had conveniently forgotten his heartfelt plan, submitted just one day earlier, Lander testily wired a sarcastic response to McClellan's assistant adjutant general. "Guerilla parties infest the country south of this point as I advance east toward Bath," he pointed out, "I have not troops enough to fully guard my rear, this Railroad, and still be strong enough to meet Jackson who occupies a central position near Bloomery gap. Since the Commanding General's reprimand to me for advising the advance of General Banks on Martinsburg, it is plain that nothing will engage Jackson's attention from the east or dispossess him of supplies or baggage. . . . My mistake in asking [for Williams's assistance] was my misconception of the object I was ordered here for, which I supposed was to open the Baltimore and Ohio Railroad."[31]

Lander refused to let his plans wither away. Working until the early morning hours of January 19, he addressed another dispatch directly to General McClellan. Admitting that he was forced to act against his better judgment to divide his force, Lander claimed that the railroad protection was useless since the Ohio regiments he had requested had not arrived. Lander now wished to concentrate his men for a direct assault on the Confederates. He asked McClellan to have Banks "only show his force" at Shepherdstown to help him divert Jackson's attention so that Lander could carry out his plan. Surprisingly, McClellan put this plan in motion by ordering Banks to demonstrate at either Harpers Ferry or Shepherdstown. Banks used his network near the river to prepare a crossing. General Williams at Hancock was still upset at Lander's persistent requests to unite forces, characterizing Lander as "being in a constant stew." Admitting that he "had no stomach" for such an operation with poorly clothed sol-

---

30. Alpheus S. Williams to Banks, January 18, 1862, BP 18:2; S. Williams to Banks, January 17, 1862, BP 18:2.

31. FWL to S. Williams, January 17, 1862, MP 48:85886.

diers, Williams felt relieved when it appeared to him that higher command had quickly quelled Lander's "quixotic expedition."[32]

Indeed, Lander's plan was suspended again. But this time higher command was not responsible; nature was. Heavy rains and midwinter thaws flooded the Potomac for the second time in eight days. River levels rose as much as six feet in one day. Lander could not use his newly constructed flatboats; however, the freshet also impeded his adversary. General Jackson had pushed his pickets toward New Creek but was unable to cross Patterson's Creek to complete the expedition. Retiring back to Romney, Jackson vented his disappointment at what he deemed the demoralization of Brigadier General William W. Loring's troops and decided to place his division in winter quarters throughout the limits of his district. Leaving Loring's men in Romney, Jackson retired with his Stonewall Brigade back to Winchester beginning on January 23.[33]

General Loring treated the order as punishment. His officers did likewise; they pressured Loring to petition the Confederate War Department to order the command to "some more favorable position." Loring grew concerned that his isolated force of 4,500 effectives stood in grave danger of assault by the Federals around Cumberland. Writing to General Jackson on January 28, Loring provided Stonewall with his estimates of Union strength at the railroad stations and warned his superior, "Within a few hours they can concentrate their entire force at any one of these stations." Jackson disagreed, gruffly stating that "such danger, I am satisfied, does not exist."[34]

Stonewall Jackson underestimated Lander's aggressiveness. Working with a new map prepared by Colonel G. Ellis Porter of the Maryland Home Brigade, Lander learned quickly of Loring's isolation and made preparations to circle around and attack Romney from the east—a strategy that Loring had feared and that Jackson had ignored. Lander explained to McClellan that he would concentrate his men at Slane's Crossroads where he could obtain his supplies from the railroad prior to launching the attack. "Much has been said by experienced parties of subsisting on the

32. FWL to GBM, January 19, 1862, MP 48:85885; S. Williams to FWL, January 19, 1862, LP 5:6818; Alpheus S. Williams to "Lew," February 3, 1862, in Quaife, *From the Cannon's Mouth*, 56.

33. *OR*, 5:393–4; Allan, "Jackson in the Shenandoah Valley," 133–4; Hotchkiss journal, January 1862, Hotchkiss Papers, LC.

34. *OR*, 5:1054–6.

enemy," wrote Lander to McClellan on January 25, explaining his greatest impediments by continuing, "This cannot apply in a country cleared out of subsistence and forage by the opposing force." Lander added a request for mules instead of horses in the winter mountain country and reiterated a wish that had been expressed for three solid weeks: "The propriety of a show of General Banks' force . . . is respectfully submitted."[35]

Lander learned quickly that he would receive little cooperation from Brigadier General Williams at Hancock. Williams had made it clear that he did not share Lander's ardor for winter campaigning. "I certainly shall not willingly expose my command to a long unsheltered bivouac this season of the year unless in a cause of great emergency," explained Williams, curtly surmising that the casualties he would suffer in Lander's endeavors would exceed those incurred in "half a dozen battles."[36]

Others were entirely supportive of Lander's strategy. Brigadier General Robert H. Milroy had taken over Brigadier General Joseph J. Reynolds's Cheat Mountain District in General Rosecrans's army and enjoyed the luxury of observing Lander's persistence without being directly affected by it. Writing to the fiery commander from Huttonsville in western Virginia, Milroy lauded Lander's plans and proclaimed, "We may confidently look for action now!"[37]

"All quiet on the Potomac," chimed a soldier in Lander's division as January turned to February. He was one of nearly 10,000 men who guarded the railroad and appeared to do little else. The troops who had been there from the beginning had become more intolerant of their living situation. "Mud! mud! mud!" complained a member of the First (Union) Virginia; "We walk in mud, we eat in mud, we sleep in mud, we breathe of mud, we dream of mud, and now I write of mud." The newer troops appeared more optimistic. "We are encamped in a very romantic portion of the country, and in a beautiful valley," wrote an impressed soldier of the Sixty-second Ohio who had arrived at the Maryland side of Camp Kelley merely one week earlier. "It is a grand and imposing sight to go up on the

35. FWL to S. Williams, January 25, 1862, MP 48:85929; "Map of the Seat of War of the Upper Potomac," LP 3:6544. Lander obtained secret service funds and employed a network of citizen spies headed by Charles Tull, the mysterious agent who worked with Lander in western Virginia. Tull's spies likely provided Lander with the news of Loring's isolation at Romney (see Fishel, *Secret War for the Union,* 168).

36. Williams to FWL, January 25, 1862, LP 5:6891.

37. Milroy to FWL, January 25, 1862, LP 5:6880–1.

mountain and look down on the tent covered valley below, which is as thickly covered with tents and men as the mountains are with the beauties of nature."[38]

The troops took solace wherever they could find it. The recent Federal victory at the battle of Mill Springs in Kentucky lifted their spirits; many hoped that they would be sharing those honors soon. Although they longed for pitched battle, retaking Romney did not excite them. One of Lander's troopers who was not impressed with the town on his first visit echoed the sentiments of many when he surmised, "What Romney was to us, it is to the rebels—an unnecessary expense."[39]

Lander had prepared to attack Loring for a week but was handicapped by appalling deficiencies. Not only did he lack supplies and transportation, Lander also sorely missed the staff help necessary to direct and control what he had coming in. Captain Barstow and Lieutenant O'Brien appeared to be his only reliable assets, but they were tremendously overworked. Lander had been promised a quartermaster, but that officer had yet to arrive. He had hundreds of sick soldiers hospitalized at Cumberland, yet no competent medical director was there to manage their care. The general strained to get more troops to reinforce his command, sometimes exceeding his authority by pulling them from other districts. Lander somehow managed to secure a brigade of new Ohio troops from Rosecrans's army, a feat that produced another admonition from the War Department.[40]

Lander's patience with the War Department thinned with each passing day. Not only were the authorities slow to fill his requests, it also seemed to him that they were initiating moves to weaken his command. No longer were Williams and Banks ordered to support him; in fact, telegrams began arriving at headquarters requesting Lieutenant Muhlenburg and his two cannons to return to Hancock. Lander ignored those requests since he considered his dependable artillerist as a member of his command

38. "Lovejoy" [Samuel Gillespie] to the editor, February 1, 1862, *(Washington C.H., Ohio) Fayette County Herald*, February 6, 1862; H. J. J. to the editor, February 2, 1862, *Wellsburg (Va.) Herald*, February 7, 1862; Henry Sands to the editor, January 27, 1862, *(New Lexington, Ohio) Perry County Weekly*, February 5, 1862.

39. "Cass" to the editor, January 20, 1862, *(Warren, Ohio) Western Reserve Chronicle*, February 12, 1862.

40. S. Williams to FWL, January 25, 1862, LP 5:6887; S. Williams to FWL, February 2, 1862, LP 6:7014.

and not merely a loan from Banks. McClellan also criticized Lander's choice of Slane's Crossroads as a launching point for his Romney attack, cautioning him on his exposure to an attack by Jackson (although in the same dispatch McClellan admitted being unfamiliar with other major crossroads in the area).[41]

Focused entirely on his division's activities, Lander found little time for anything else—including sending letters to his wife or his friends. He refused to cater to public requests that did not directly impact his men. A Boston publishing firm learned this firsthand when it sent Lander a request to send materials pertinent to his career for a compilation of biographies titled *The Officers of the Union Army and Navy—Their Lives and Portraits*. "I have no time to write history," bluntly replied Lander on January 24. "My public services have been greatly overestimated, and if you could know the very poor opinion I entertain of myself and others now charged with the holy mission of preserving this Republic, you would never ask it."[42]

Inevitably, the friction that developed between Lander and McClellan reached the public's eyes. Lander was unaware that McClellan had openly divulged military information, including select dispatches, to Malcolm Ives, a correspondent to the *New York Herald*. In an effort to enjoy the backing of the nation's largest newspaper, McClellan leaked military secrets to give the *Herald* the advantage over any other publication (he welcomed the antiabolition position of James Gordon Bennett, the paper's editor). McClellan sat for a three-hour interview with Ives on January 14, then briefed Ives regularly concerning operations ongoing in all the military districts in the country.[43]

Lander learned this all too painfully by reading the newspapers that circulated through Camp Kelley. It was common for correspondents' columns from large newspapers to be picked up by smaller daily and weekly publications. Lander was directed to the January 24 piece contributed by an unidentified correspondent to the *New York Herald*, which was republished in another paper. The newsman fabricated the events leading to the Romney evacuation. The report claimed that McClellan had been preparing to reinforce Lander with 12,000 Ohio troops at Romney. They had been scheduled to arrive on Sunday (January 12): "But on Friday night, Gen. McClellan had

41. Clermont L. Best to John Mason, January 26, 1862, LP 5:6890; S. Williams to FWL, January 27, 1862; MP 16:8104–6.
42. FWL to Messrs. L. Prang & Co., January 24, 1862, *Boston Journal*, April 2, 1862.
43. Sears, *McClellan*, 142–3.

received a despatch from Gen. Lander, stating that he had evacuated Romney." The implication that he conducted a pusillanimous retreat against the wishes of his superior aggravated Lander and his adjutant, Simon Barstow, who warned that "if the battlefield is the city of Washington, the arms the purchased pens of newspaper correspondents, the ammunition semi-official garbled orders, and the success in such a strife the criterion of military merit—Gen. Lander will withdraw from the contest." Newspapers quickly published unconfirmed reports of Lander's resignation.[44]

If Lander truly entertained thoughts of resigning, he dropped them early in February. Despite the lack of cooperation from the War Department, division deficiencies, and newspaper controversies, he felt he was ready to assault Loring's troops at Romney on February 2. Meanwhile, Loring had been apprised of the Federal attack plans. Loring's pleas to the Confederate War Department prompted Secretary Judah P. Benjamin to order General Jackson on January 31 to pull the Romney force back to Winchester. (Jackson was so incensed at the interference that he complied with the order and resigned in the same letter; he withdrew the resignation the following week.) The first of Loring's three brigades planned to depart Romney on the evening of February 2.[45]

Although he was unaware of Loring's retreat plans, Lander was set to block Loring's withdrawal because his division would attack Romney from the east. Lander's men received their orders at 9:00 A.M. S. C. Boehm, the B & O agent at Cumberland, had fired up all the available engines since midnight to transport Lander's westerners eastward to French's Store. From this station Lander's men were to march southward to Romney. The regiments encamped near Cumberland had already relocated downriver to Patterson's Creek to consolidate the available infantry. McClellan continued to preach caution, warning Lander not to advance beyond Romney and to beware of Jackson's return from Winchester, for McClellan considered Stonewall "to be a man of vigor and nerve, as well as a good soldier."[46]

Lander remained at headquarters to assure that his plans were carried out. This day, he thought, should represent the turning point of an other-

44. "Our Baltimore Correspondence," January 24, 1862, *New York Herald,* January 27, 1862; Barstow to Salmon P. Chase, February 4, 1862, CP 16:6711–12; "Resignation of General Lander," *Cincinnati Daily Gazette,* February 3, 1862.

45. Allan, "Jackson in the Shenandoah Valley," 135–40.

46. Thomas Clark to his wife, February 2, 1862, CL; S. C. Boehm to FWL, February 1, 1862, LP 6:7017; "Juniata" to the editor, February 5, 1862, *Philadelphia Press,* February

wise fruitless and frustrating campaign. For nearly thirty days he had agonized as opportunity after opportunity slipped away from him. But it now appeared that "Old Grizzly" would finally be released from his cage. His success should convince General McClellan, the U.S. War Department, the Joint Committee on the Conduct of the War, and President Lincoln that Lander's Western Division would succeed in winter operations, notwithstanding inclement weather or the skepticism and sluggishness of upper command.

Thirty-degree temperatures and a clear sky dawned on Sunday morning; weather would be no impediment. General McClellan remained reserved; however, he granted his support for the plan and would not block this movement. But as his division marched off at noon, Lander's newest command threat struck him from within. The symptoms had made their appearance before, but they had never been as menacing as the episode that assaulted him on February 2. The general reeled from a combination of intense pain and violent chills that knocked him off his feet. A physician was quickly summoned, and he sedated the general.[47]

After advancing one quarter of a mile Lander's troops were recalled to their camps, the third time in thirty days that a planned movement had been aborted. That night the first of Loring's three brigades slipped out of Romney. Over the next thirty-six hours the rest of the Confederate force stationed there evacuated town and safely headed toward Winchester along the Northwestern Turnpike. The Confederates encountered no opposition during the orderly withdrawal.[48]

General Frederick W. Lander was down. No one at his headquarters was sure whether he would ever rise again.

1862, LP 6:7017; "Juniata" to the editor, February 5, 1862, *Philadelphia Press,* February 13, 1862; GBM to FWL, February 2, 1862, LP 6:7015.

47. Temperature readings for Cumberland, Md., February 2, 1862, NWR; Simon F. Barstow to Salmon P. Chase, February 4, 1862, CP 16:6711–12.

48. "H." to the editor, February 4, 1862, *Wheeling (Va.) Daily Intelligencer,* February 12, 1862; Brenda Kitzmiller, "The History of the Bridges across the South Branch of the Potomac River on the Northwestern Turnpike (U.S. Route 50), Hampshire County, West Virginia," Handley Library, Winchester, Va.; John H. Worsham, *One of Jackson's Foot Cavalry* (New York, 1912), 63; Marcus B. Toney, *Privations of a Private* (Nashville, Tenn., 1905), 43.

9

"I Am Dying"

The storm stole out beyond the wood,
    She grew the vision of a cloud,
Her dark hair was a misty hood,
    Her stark face shone as from a shroud

Still sped the wild storm's rustling feet
    To martial music of the pines,
And to her cold-heart's muffled beat
    Wheeled grandly into solemn lines.
                —F. W. Lander

A relieved Simon F. Barstow replied to Secretary of the Treasury Salmon P. Chase's request concerning Frederick Lander's health. The forty-four-year-old Barstow had developed a protective bond with his younger boss. General Lander and Captain Barstow shared a few things in common: both were born on December 17 and both entered the world in Salem, Massachusetts. After completing his duties as Lander's liaison to Governor Andrew in the summer and autumn of 1861, Barstow adeptly transformed himself from Boston lawyer to Lander's assistant adjutant general. During a snow squall that fell on Tuesday, February 4, 1862, Barstow answered Secretary Chase in a three-page letter that included a short explanation of what had transpired at division headquarters over the previous weekend. "On Sunday last, the General was seized with one of the congestive chills to which he is subject," wrote Barstow. Pronouncing that the general had made a quick recovery, Barstow admitted the seriousness of his last attack when he described it as "so aggravated in its character, that the medical attendants considered his life in imminent peril."[1]

Rumors concerning Lander's illness spread through Camp Kelley to such an extent as to rival the mud as a topic of conversation. The soldiers fingered a cause to Lander's "congestive chills," one that would influence their opinions of the general for the remainder of his life. "There is a current report that the sudden sickness of Gen. Lander the other day was delirium Tremens," wrote Lieutenant Colonel Thomas Clark, Twenty-ninth Ohio, to his wife. "I neither affirm or deny it."[2] Clark's letter to his spouse was private; however, another soldier publicized the rumor in a witty explanation that identified Lander with an animal far different from the respected grizzly bear. The letter was printed in the soldier's hometown newspaper one week later:

> Well last Sunday was "ground-hog day," and our commander, after taking on a goodly portion of "tangle-foot," felt certain he had force enough to take Winchester, Meen-asses Junction or some other important post . . . but by the time we got 400 yards on our road—it being a very clear day—the old ground-hog saw his shadow and returned to his hole. . . . Just a few minutes ago, when we were all enjoying ourselves hugely, "marching orders" rang from one end of the camp to the other, and curses loud and deep were heaped upon the head of our old "ground-hog" for so grossly deceiving us; but as this is a great country for rye, we acknowledge the "powers that be," and yield a cheerful compliance to the constituted authority.[3]

Rumors that Lander was a hard drinker had begun one month earlier (Ringgold Cavalry Sergeant John Elwood accused him of intoxication on the night the Federals evacuated Romney). Lander had been partially responsible for the camp gossip. His short and erratic temper had prompted accusations from his subordinates. Lander also peppered his language with profanity, a habit that angered the more devout members of his rank and file. An Indiana private spoke for many when—witnessing one of Lan-

1. Maria P. Barstow, Widow's Pension File #372742, RG 94, NA; John Hadley to Mollie Hill, February 4, 1862, in Robertson Jr., "An Indiana Soldier," 203; Simon F. Barstow to Salmon P. Chase, February 4, 1862, CP 16:6711–2.

2. Thomas Clark to his wife, February 5, 1862, CL.

3. "H." to the editor, February 4, 1862, *Wheeling (Va.) Daily Intelligencer*, February 12, 1862.

der's obscenity-filled tirades—he assessed him to be "one of the most wicked men I ever saw. Profanity seemed to him a recreation and no time or place was sacred from his oaths."[4] Lander had made it easy for members of his division to link his unorthodox behavior with a fondness for the liquor bottle.

Lander's forceful personality and tendencies made it impossible for the men in the ranks to develop a universal opinion about him. His gruff and acrid nature induced his troopers to write to loved ones to either praise him or denounce him. Soldiers within the same regiment provided conflicting assessments of their leader. "General Lander . . . is just the man for this place," a member of the Fourteenth Indiana wrote approvingly to his hometown newspaper. "We all love him—the 14th boys think he is a *bully fighter,* and I think they would storm hell if he desired them to." Augustus Van Dyke of the same Hoosier regiment disagreed. "General Lander is a man in whom I have not much confidence," he complained to his father. "He is too head strong and swears too much and drinks entirely too much whiskey."[5]

Perhaps the most disagreeable decision Lander authored at Camp Kelley was issuing whiskey rations for his troops. The controversial policy had turned heads in the War Department in mid-January when Lander insisted on a steady alcohol supply for his soldiers. When he was informed that his request was "not customary except to men in fatigue or other hard duty," the general insisted that his entire division was broken down and exhausted, thus qualifying them for the rations. Although more common in malarial regions, Lander firmly believed that one-half gill (two ounces) whiskey rations every two days, laced with quinine, had medicinal properties essential to troops performing in any inclement conditions.[6]

Lander met with resistance from all quarters of potential opposition. Pockets of strict temperance existed within the ranks of his division, the hometowns from where the soldiers hailed, and in the civilized centers that existed within his district of operations. Representatives from all areas voiced their disapproval. An influential citizen in Wheeling obtained permission from General Rosecrans to halt the removal of liquor from the

4. Augustus Van Dyke to his parents, March 4, 1862, Van Dyke Papers, IHS.

5. K. M. D. to the editor, January 31, 1862, *Cincinnati Daily Commercial,* February 4, 1862; Augustus Van Dyke to his father, February 2, 1862, Van Dyke Papers, IHS.

6. Randolph B. Marcy to FWL, January 15, 1862, LP 5:6734; FWL to R. B. Marcy, January 16, 1862, MP 48:85875; Thomas Clark to his wife, January 23, 1862, CL.

town's custom house. Even more demonstrative was a contingent of forty women in Cumberland who sent a petition to Lander urgently requesting "that speedily efficient means be employed to put a certain stop to the traffic that is so sadly injurious to the bodies and souls of our soldiers."[7]

Although the teetotalers in the ranks grumbled about how alcohol would adversely affect discipline, other soldiers welcomed the "whiskey and bark" rations. For his part Lander took measures to prevent his men from exceeding their allotments by closing all taverns and saloons near Camp Kelley. This measure failed to prevent his soldiers from obtaining intoxicating amounts of liquor; sentries stole the supply from the quartermaster and freely distributed it to the men.[8]

Lander's illness nullified his best opportunity to win an impressive battle victory over a significant portion of General Jackson's Valley District division. The lost opportunity was not caused by delirium tremors or drunkenness, notwithstanding the claims of the opinionated members of his ranks. The acute attack was a symptom of a more serious and chronic condition. By his own admission Lander had taken command in the field before his Edwards Ferry wound had sufficiently healed. The combination of injury, harsh weather, a winter camp likened to a pigsty, and long restless hours slowly ate away at Lander's health. His circumstances and symptoms were characteristic of an infection that invaded the bone near his flesh wound. From here the bacteria penetrated soft tissue and eventually produced episodic events marked by pain, fevers, and convulsive chills. It appears that Lander suffered from contiguous focus osteomyelitis, a fatal disease for which there was no cure.[9]

7. Thomas Hornbrook to FWL, n.d., LP 3:6554; Ladies of Cumberland to FWL, n.d., LP 3:6671–2.

8. "S." to the editor, January 29, 1862, *Cincinnati Daily Commercial*, February 2, 1862; John Hadley to Mollie Hill, February 4, 1862, in Robertson Jr., "An Indiana Soldier," 202; Ambrose Thompson to FWL, February 6, 1862, LP 6:7084–5.

9. Jon T. Mader and Jason Calhoun, "Osteomyelitis," in Gerald L. Mandell, John E. Bennett, and Raphael Dolin, eds., *Mandell, Douglas, and Bennett's Principles and Practice of Infectious Diseases*, 4th ed. (New York, 1995), 1039–43. The author is indebted to Dr. Thomas LoRusso and Dr. Depak Soni, physicians who practice at INOVA Fairfax Hospital (Falls Church, Va.). In separate interviews, each doctor provided the same diagnosis when Lander's symptoms were described. Lander's "congestive chills" were likely episodes of rigor that seized his body during the infectious process. Other septic sources are possible, but given the site of his Edwards Ferry injury, the wound near the bones in Lander's lower leg likely seeded the infection.

The severity of his most recent attack indicated that Lander's days were numbered. Simon Barstow, his loyal aide, was closest to him and appeared to be denying the gravity of his commander's illness. Only Lander and his physicians understood the implications of the "congestive chills." Four days after Barstow matter-of-factly described Lander's malady to Salmon P. Chase, the general also wrote the secretary, explaining how he believed his relationship with McClellan was being misinterpreted by the press. Whereas Barstow had clung to the naive belief that Lander's near-fatal attack had been the result of "mental anxiety brought on by heavy responsibilities," Lander wrote frankly to Secretary Chase. After rambling for two pages about his lack of supplies and his transportation deficiencies, the general provided an eye-opening revelation to Chase: "But as I am dying, . . . my health gone, I fear, for all time—why complain?"[10]

Lander did not feel compelled to write to Secretary Chase to evaluate his health, but to extinguish the flames of controversy that were ignited by enterprising correspondents who worked for big-city newspapers. The subject had been Lander versus McClellan at Hancock and Romney, and Lander bristled at what he considered to be a misrepresentation of the facts. He was particularly livid at the initial reports written by the Baltimore correspondent of the *New York Herald*. Lander also had been accused by other newsmen of criticizing President Lincoln and making absurd requests that involved military impossibilities. Both Barstow and Lander had successively provided their explanations to the secretary. Lander denied criticizing the president and believed that the correspondent had access to McClellan's dispatches and had altered the wording in his submission. "If I was critical, it was on the 'have beens,'" explained Lander, "I said Banks 'should have crossed as I said three days ago' not Banks 'should cross.'" Barstow had provided a similar argument, claiming the documents he possessed as Lander's adjutant proved "the worthlessness of the statements on which [the reporter's] comment is based."[11]

Lander admitted that he had no time for newspaper controversies and downplayed the difficulties of his relationship with McClellan to quell the stories. He stretched the truth considerably when he wrote Chase that "Gen'l McClellan has no better friend than I am."[12] To placate his subor-

10. Barstow to Chase, February 4, 1862, CP; FWL to Chase, February 8, 1862, CP 11:12872–5. The original letter had no punctuation in this phrase of admission.
11. Ibid.
12. FWL to Chase, February 8, 1862, CP.

dinate, McClellan had made several overt attempts at smoothing Lander's ruffled feathers during the latter weeks of January and early February. The commander cautiously supported Lander's maneuvers, although he treaded all too slowly when it came to upgrading Lander's transportation deficiencies. Once the Federals learned that Loring's men had escaped back to Winchester, McClellan sent an appeasing telegram to his disappointed subordinate. "Am sorry enemy has escaped you," he wrote to Lander, "but am sure it was no fault of yours and that you would have succeeded had it been possible. I thank you for your energy." McClellan had also hinted to Lander of a special duty once the Army of the Potomac advanced in the upcoming spring season. "I would like to give you a picked corps of light troops," explained McClellan, evoking memories of the successful summer of 1861: "So as you did at Rich Mountain, so [I] want you [to] do for me in an advance."[13]

Lander's friends in Washington would not allow him to accept McClellan's olive branches. They kept Lander's suspicions about his superior alive by reiterating accusations of McClellan's hidden motives. Several days after McClellan offered his condolences, Lander received a letter from Washington. "From what I have heard in and around Congress, there seems to be an impression that McClellan will make an effort to get you on his staff—or under his immediate control," wrote the friend. "This it is thought, is not for your benefit, but to keep you from a fairer field where your name will shine out in victory. Our friends are apprehensive that duplicity and cunning may succeed in tempting you from the mountains of western Virginia where you will have the opportunity to annihilate the left wing of the rebel army—to the center where your efforts and your acts would be covered up by 'superiors' or be noticed by such faint praise as to drive you from the service of your country."[14]

Lander needed no influence from his Washington sources to feed his mistrust of General McClellan. Not only did he have the memories of Hancock and Romney to keep his suspicions alive, but he also enjoyed the company of partisan correspondents who frequented his camp. Lander placed his trust in two newsmen, both of whom worked for Cincinnati newspapers. Whitelaw Reid, the young *Cincinnati Daily Gazette* corre-

13. GBM to FWL, February 6, 1862, LP 6:7091; GBM to FWL January 15, 1862, LP 5:6885.

14. A. W. Thompson to FWL, February 9, 1862, LP 3:6558–9.

spondent who had written so fluently about Lander during the summer campaign in western Virginia, arrived at Lander's camp in early February to cover Lander and his men. The *Cincinnati Daily Commercial* sent their own correspondent, F. B. Plimpton, to report on Lander's movements. At forty-seven, Plimpton was twice as old as the youthful Reid. Both men, employed by papers that constantly criticized each other, ironically worked on the same mission—to favorably present General Lander and his Western Division, composed in the main of Ohio regiments, to their readers.[15]

Reid prided himself as an experienced and gifted correspondent. He also had become enamored with Lander's exploits, many of which he had witnessed the previous summer. Nearly seven months had distanced the Rich Mountain campaign from Lander's current winter campaign. Reid was disappointed to see a paler and limping commander at Patterson's Creek, compared to the striking leader who had evoked "that-must-be-a-remarkable-man" accolades half a year earlier. Witnessing the restless general at headquarters, Reid took note of Lander's leadership trademarks, which included snapping short explanations to his officers with quick forcible directions, and his tendency to "denounce some negligence in office with a round energy of expression that would startle his chaplain." Relieved that some things never change, the newsman affirmed that "he is still the same Lander that those who were at Phillipi or Rich Mountain will remember forever."

Writing his dispatches under the pen-name "Agate," Reid took great pains to interpret the Lander-McClellan controversy to Lander's advantage. Whereas other newspapers appeared to be pro-McClellan on the Hancock and Romney issue, the Agate dispatches strongly defended Lander. He pointed out to his readers the erroneous information that other publications held as truth. For example, Reid clarified that Lander had been building flatboats in Cumberland to convey General Williams into Virginia for a combined attack on Jackson, and not to use the boats to withdraw his own men to Maryland as some papers had incorrectly surmised. Reid understood that his readers appreciated aggressiveness in commanders, and Lander was a fitting subject to satisfy their desires. His

---

15. James G. Smart, ed., *A Radical View: The "Agate" Dispatches of Whitelaw Reid, 1861–1865,* vol. 2 (Memphis, Tenn., 1976), 1–2, 4, 11–12; M. D. Potter to FWL, January 30, 1862, LP 3:6549; "P." (F. B. Plimpton) to the editor, February 3, 1862, *Cincinnati Daily Commercial,* February 6, 1862.

pro-Lander, anti-McClellan dispatches gained wide readership throughout the North in February as other newspapers picked up his frequent contributions. The soldiers in camp also learned much about Lander from Agate. His columns were read in both the *Cincinnati Daily Gazette* and the *Wheeling Daily Intelligencer*.[16]

The *Cincinnati Daily Commercial* was not as intensely partisan as was the *Gazette;* however, F. B. Plimpton's dispatches were also very favorable to Lander. Using the simple pseudonym, "P.," Plimpton's first report about Lander was written February 3 and published three days later. His contributions appeared almost daily in the newspaper for the next ten days. Plimpton focused on the disadvantages that Lander worked with as well as the care of the multitudes of sick soldiers in Cumberland. Though not as anti-McClellan, Plimpton, like Reid, corrected the misinformation in the infamous *New York Herald* account by stressing to his readers that Lander had retreated from Romney against his will and was the commander who would gain victories once he was allowed to fight. Plimpton was impressed with "Lander's coolness in observation and impetuosity in action," although his first observations of the general were noted shortly after his illness. On February 9, he informed his readers that Lander had been physically disabled by the attack for a week and looked extremely thin and careworn. "I shall get better," Plimpton reported Lander as exclaiming to him, "as soon as I can get on my horse and take exercise." Plimpton added that Lander could be held to his word, "for he is a Centaur in his habits."[17]

Most of the newspaper correspondents in Lander's camp were not professional reporters, but soldiers contributing letters to their respective hometown papers. Many soldiers-turned-correspondents adopted unique pseudonyms. "Volunteer," a member of the Seventh Ohio, wrote weekly for the *Painesville Telegraph;* "Lovejoy," a First Ohio cavalry bugler, did likewise for the *Fayette County Herald,* as did "Old Town," Eighty-fourth Pennsylvania, for the *Raftsman's Journal,* published in Clearfield, Pennsylvania. Other less inventive writers signed off their contributions with their own names or initials. The uncensored reports were usually pub-

---

16. "Agate" to the editor, February 5, 1862, *Wheeling (Va.) Daily Intelligencer,* February 13, 1862; "Agate" to the editor, n.d., *Wheeling Daily Intelligencer,* February 15, 1862; Smart, *Radical View,* 61–6.

17. "P." to editor, February 3, 4, 5, and 9, 1862, *Cincinnati Daily Commercial,* February 6, 7, 8, and 15, 1862.

lished within a week after submission, providing the hometown citizenry in Ohio, Indiana, Pennsylvania, Illinois, and western Virginia with valuable information about the life of a soldier in Lander's division.

During the first week of February the general's illness restricted him to his headquarters. Although his physicians stressed the importance of resting, Lander refused to stay bedridden, often jumping from his bed to storm into the telegraph room or Barstow's office to push his orders through. Whitelaw Reid (one of the few "outsiders" who witnessed Lander that week) noted the general's weakened appearance. "Just now a great deal depends on Lander's health," wrote Agate to his readers, "and I regret to say that it is yet far from established."[18]

After Loring's troops evacuated the area, the reoccupation of Romney became anticlimactic (Plimpton called it "a trifle"). During the sleeting night of February 6, the leading elements of Lander's division swept in southwestward from Green Spring station. Lander, still ailing from his illness, remained at his Patterson's Creek headquarters, where he received and relayed the announcement of Romney's takeover at 10:00 P.M. He informed McClellan that seven prisoners were captured and that the wire suspension bridge over the South Branch River west of Romney had been downed by the Confederates. Although disappointed at the missed opportunity to bag Loring's men, Lander did not consider the possession of Romney as a trifle. He trumpeted his accomplishments to Secretary Chase. "Now look at this campaign," he wrote on February 8. "I hold the Baltimore Road to Big Cacapon Bridge. I hold the entire country south from Romney to [the] Big Cacapon." In the whole, Lander had good reason to feel proud. His objective to protect the railroad in his district now appeared to have been achieved without imminent threat from Jackson's forces.[19]

Lander continued to rail about his division deficiencies, informing Secretary Chase two days after Romney was retaken that he still lacked transportation. He highlighted the fact that over 1,000 men lay sick in the Cumberland hospital and predicted that many more would be cut down by exposure for the want of wagons to haul tents and subsistence. The di-

18. "Agate" to the editor, February 8, 1862, *Cincinnati Daily Gazette,* February 12, 1862.

19. "P." to the editor, February 5, 1862, *Cincinnati Daily Commercial,* February 8, 1862; FWL to GBM, February 6, 1862, MP 48:85954; FWL to Salmon P. Chase, February 8, 1862, CP 11:12872–5.

vision sick list grew astronomically, so much so that special attention was necessary to accommodate the bedridden members of his ranks. The general harbored strong opinions on how to ease their care. Complaining that the crowded hospital buildings added to the rampant sickness, Lander wished to procure large hospital tents, fitted with floors and stoves, to shelter the sick while still providing them with "the pure open air." He was not granted this wish, but he was provided with a medical director. The Army of the Potomac's Special Orders Number Thirty-five tagged Dr. George Suckley as Lander's preeminent physician. Suckley, the idealistic and eccentric naturalist who accompanied the Isaac Stevens's expedition in 1853, was a welcome addition. His experience was necessary to handle the multitude of ill soldiers that hampered the division's effectiveness.[20]

Dr. Suckley soon received a very important patient. Captain Barstow had overexerted himself performing the work of at least two staff aides throughout January and early February. During the second week of February, Barstow continued to cling to his duties despite rapidly failing health. He later learned that he had contracted measles. His condition required him to be quarantined in Cumberland. Barstow's hospitalization left a tremendous void of experience in Lander's staff.[21]

Lander had begun to receive needed personnel prior to Barstow's departure. In addition to Fitz-James O'Brien, Captain Ambrose Thompson, formerly employed in Major General Irvin McDowell's division, transferred to Lander to serve as his quartermaster. He took over his duties on February 2. Thompson was the son of a Washington, D.C., friend.[22]

Lander also brought on Lieutenant Henry ("Harry") G. Armstrong of the Fifth Ohio, an Irish-born officer and former employee of the *Cincinnati Daily Gazette*. He was reassigned to headquarters as was Major Dwight Bannister, the paymaster who had helped Lander immediately after he was wounded at Edwards Ferry. Lander reverted to nostalgia when he requested that fifty-two-year-old Frederick A. Barton, his former mentor at Phillips Academy, join his staff as an additional aide-de-camp. Barton was serving as chaplain in the Tenth Massachusetts at the time, the

20. FWL to Salmon P. Chase, February 8, 1862, CP 11:12872–5; FWL to Edwin Stanton, n.d., LP 3:6666; Special Orders No. 35, LP 6:7036.

21. "Agate" to the editor, February 12, 1862, *Cincinnati Daily Gazette,* February 17, 1862.

22. S. Williams to FWL, February 2, 1862, LP 6:7025.

same regiment in which his namesake son led as a captain of Company E. It was twenty-year-old Captain Frederick Barton, not his father, who arrived at Patterson's Creek as a new staffer for Lander. Major John Frothingham rounded out the staff as Lander's chief engineering officer. All of the new staff men were in place and performing their duties during the first week of February.[23]

Lander was fortunate to receive the staff help when he did. Realizing that his district appeared to be cleared of the enemy, Lander had planned simultaneous movements both to reoccupy Romney and to move the remainder of his men down the railroad to new campgrounds. The new destination was Paw Paw, a cleared railroad station approximately twenty-five miles downriver from Cumberland. Named for the fruit trees indigenous to the region, Paw Paw offered Lander's men a cleaner environment for winter encampment. It also fulfilled McClellan's orders to pull his men closer to Banks's division, where a combined movement against Jackson at Winchester could be managed. The railroad was repaired all the way to Paw Paw; subsequently, Lander sent Colonel Jeremiah C. Sullivan there with the Thirteenth and Fourteenth Indiana regiments on Friday, February 7. Sullivan sent word through the chain of command that a rebel force of unknown strength was fifteen miles south of the station at a mountain pass known as Bloomery Gap. Sullivan believed that the enemy outpost had sent scouts to Paw Paw less than one week before, but the station was currently unoccupied.

Lander ordered his men to move to Paw Paw. Using the railroad to transport men and supplies, Lander's division quartermaster performed masterfully in just his first few days of active service. Captain Ambrose Thompson stationed himself at French's Store, a B & O station east of the mouth of the winding South Branch River (Green Spring station sat west of the river), where he coordinated the trains to operate on the single line of tracks that existed between Patterson's Creek (eleven miles upriver)

23. Fitz-James O'Brien Service Record, NA; Henry G. Armstrong Service Record, NA; "Agate" to the editor, February 12, 1862, *Cincinnati Daily Gazette,* February 17, 1862. Lander had requested "that Capt. Fred A. Barton, now chaplain of the 10th Mass. . . may be detailed to serve with me" (FWL to GBM, January 1, 186[2], Frederick Barton [Jr.] Service Record, NA). But the captain and the chaplain were two different Fred Bartons. Either Lander's confused request resulted in the younger Frederick Barton's reassignment, or the older Fred Barton, who resigned as chaplain of the Tenth Massachusetts due to ill health in May of 1862, was deemed too sick to serve on his former student's staff.

and Paw Paw (seven miles downriver). Thompson oversaw trains that stretched for over a mile. He emptied troop-filled boxcars to pack them with supplies, which were subsequently sent to Paw Paw. At the same time the young quartermaster ferried cavalry and artillery across the river from Maryland to Virginia at French's Store. He exhibited a take-charge attitude from the moment he stepped into his role and apparently held a low regard for the volunteer soldier awarded with commissions in Lander's division. Improvising with a broken line to anchor his ferry to bring across the cavalry, Thompson vented his disapproval at what he witnessed at the station. "For heaven's sake, don't send me volunteer officers—I can do better alone," he remonstrated to Captain Barstow. Thompson's performance did not go unnoticed by brigade commanders in Lander's division. "I thank you for Captain Thompson," wired Colonel Nathan Kimball after watching the young quartermaster in action at French's Store. "He is a noble and efficient officer. God Bless him."

Thompson made it clear that at least one of Lander's regimental commanders was not fit to lead troops. Colonel Otto Burstenbinder, Sixty-seventh Ohio, had caused much grief within minutes of his regiment's arrival in Lander's district. While Lander transferred his command eastward from Patterson's Creek on February 6, Thompson lost his patience over Burstenbinder's conduct. The colonel interrupted the division's train schedule after insisting that his men would not disembark from their boxcars without written orders, and then decided on his own to change the division's countersign. Thompson reported him for neglect of duty but later withdrew the charge. "I am not overworked," he explained to Captain Barstow after enduring the Burstenbinder incident, "[I'm] only annoyed at the bad behavior of the officers."[24]

Colonel Kimball commanded Lander's First Brigade and was responsible for placing troops at Paw Paw to secure the ground for the remainder of the division's arrival. Late on February 8, Kimball positioned six infantry regiments there. Kimball sent scouts southward to ascertain the size of the enemy force at Bloomery Gap as well as their exact dispositions there. He also discovered that the whiskey ration policy had backfired at Paw Paw. After watching his men illegally gaining access to the stores of liquor, Kimball poured out the whiskey. "It was doing harm," Kimball ex-

24. Thompson to Barstow, February 8, 1862, LP 7:7133–35; Kimball to Barstow, February 8, 1862, LP 7:7144; Ambrose Thompson to FWL, February 9, 1862, LP 7:7199.

plained, informing Lander that the men were getting drunk on the unauthorized rations. In addition to maintaining discipline, Kimball also impressed Lander with his aggressiveness. To prevent reinforcements from reaching the rebel outpost at Bloomery Gap, the brigade commander proposed an immediate assault by initiating joint movements from Paw Paw and Bath. Kimball notified Lander on February 9, "I think a move on Bloomery tomorrow night would gain us much advantage."[25]

Notwithstanding Colonel Burstenbinder's folly, Colonel Kimball had demonstrated to Lander that quality officer material was available in his district of operations. Lander thought highly of both Colonel Erastus B. Tyler, Seventh Ohio, who commanded his Third Brigade, and Colonel James Gavin, Seventh Indiana, for their "energy and vigor" in the movement toward Romney. Colonel Samuel Dunning, Fifth Ohio, commanding the Second Brigade at New Creek, also had shown very capable leadership skills. Lander's chief of artillery, Colonel John S. Mason of the Fourth Ohio, and Colonel Samuel S. Carroll of the Eighth Ohio were two West Point officers who also caught Lander's eye. The four new regiments that Lander "borrowed" from Rosecrans's army were brigaded under the command of Colonel Orlando Smith of the Seventy-third Ohio. Although Lander harbored some trepidations concerning his new regiments, he appeared satisfied overall with the western foot soldiers under his command. His infantry force consisted of twenty regiments organized into four brigades, a force that exceeded 12,000 men.

Lander offered mixed reviews on his cavalry. His greatest complaint about his horse soldiers was the condition of their weapons. Very few of his cavalry carried carbines, the arm most associated with this wing of the army. Lander had a modest cavalry force; only one full cavalry regiment, the First (Union) Virginia, served him in northwestern Virginia. The remainder of the cavalry consisted of two companies (A and C) of the First Ohio Cavalry, an independent squadron of Maryland cavalry, and two squadrons of Pennsylvania cavalry. Lander favored Captain John Keys of the Ringgold Cavalry (a squad recruited from Washington, Pennsylvania), rating him as "my best cavalry officer."[26]

25. Kimball to Simon Barstow, February 8, 1862, LP 7:7143–4, 7147; Kimball to FWL, February 9, 1862, LP 7:7184–5, 7187–8.
26. FWL to GBM, February 6, 1862, MP 48:85954.

It was an honor the captain enjoyed over the colonel of the First (Union) Virginia Cavalry, Henry Anisansel, a French-Swiss immigrant who had been a teacher in Canonburg, Pennsylvania, prior to the war. Although Lander had yet to see Colonel Anisansel personally, the cavalry officer apparently did not endear himself to his division commander after his first weeks of transmitting dispatches to Lander. Lander was put off by Anisansel's presumptuous advice; for example, while planning his movement into Romney, the colonel responded to Lander's request to follow the rest of the command into Romney by writing, "I will start very early and overtake you. Cavalry in the rear of an Army is of no use. Could not possibly start before noon from New Creek." An Ohio lieutenant considered the "chattering" Anisansel to be "absolutely useless for any purpose except to draw [his] pay and to wear gold braid."[27] Lander would have the opportunity to make his own conclusions about the foreigner's worth within the next two weeks.

Lander's artillery was at best an impediment. He counted twenty-five cannons in his division; fewer than half of them were rifled pieces and four of those had no horses to pull them. Lander's favorite artillery officer was Lieutenant Edward D. Muhlenburg, the artillerist who had manned the two-section battery so masterfully at Bath, then at Hancock. Lander had Muhlenburg train the other artillerists in the division, but was furious to receive continuous requests from Banks to have Muhlenburg return to Frederick. The request became official orders on February 9. With no option, Lander watched Muhlenburg depart. Then the general took six of his own cannons and sent them to Cumberland. Lander reasoned that these cannons were too inefficient to use actively as they would require infantry support and he had none to spare. He was far from satisfied with the active artillerists in his division. "My artillery can hit nothing," he groaned.[28]

Headquarters at Patterson's Creek turned chaotic as Lander and his staff prepared to transfer their camp to Paw Paw. Whitelaw Reid was privy to the activity on the second floor of Shadow Lawn:

27. Henry Anisansel Service Record, NA; Anisansel to FWL, February 5, 1862, LP 6:7051; W. L. Curry, comp., *Four Years in the Saddle* (Jonesboro, Ga., 1898), 234.
28. FWL to Preston Blair, February 16, 1862, LP 3:6566–7; FWL to S. Williams, January 20, 1862, MP 48:85938; Alpheus S. Williams to FWL, February 9, 1862, LP 7:7171; S. Williams to FWL, February 9, 1862, LP 7:7200; *OR*, 51(1):534.

Behind a table, heaped with dispatches that none but the staff must touch, sits the Adjutant General of the division, signing orders, hearing reports, sending messages, giving directions—overwhelmed with a maze of business. The room is filled with his business for the staff to transact his suggestion or request. . . . The telegraph operator enters with a dispatch, "Road clear to Paw Paw." "Start that train at once." An orderly hurries down, and in a moment you hear the shouts and the rattle of drums mingling with the whistle of the locomotive and the hoarse jarring of the cars as the train moves on. "Tell Colonel so-and-so to load his regiment immediately." And away goes another courier.[29]

In the midst of moving the equivalent of a city population by rail, the general was greatly irritated by any personnel who impeded the process. When a wagon master, summoned to headquarters after a careless error that delayed operations, tried to explain away his faux pas, "Old Grizzly" refused to hear it. "Off with you," Lander growled, "I want none of your excuses; but if this occurs again, I'll have you tied to one of your own wagons and horsewhipped!" Needless to say, the wagon master vowed never to repeat the error.[30]

Shortly afterward, Lieutenant Colonel Orrin L. Mann was called to headquarters. His regiment, the Thirty-ninth Illinois, was to remain at Patterson's Creek to guard the bridge and send off railroad construction material. Lander reiterated to the temporary commander (Colonel Osborn was sick in Cumberland) his published order that strictly prohibited marauding and insisted that the order be obeyed by the Thirty-ninth Illinois. Mann snapped his hand to his forehead and proclaimed, "General, I will try and see your order's obeyed." Lander exploded on hearing the indefinite response—the same one that Norwich University prided as its motto. "Try! God damn your soul to hell!" swore the general, stamping his foot to emphasize his anger. "Try! What in the hell do you mean, Sir, by such talk? Is that any language for a soldier to use, damn you!" Lander stamped his foot again and again, increasing the intimidation for the unfortunate officer. Mann respectfully saluted him again and clarified, "General Lander, your orders shall be obeyed to the letter!" Pleased with the correction, Lander softened his posture, warmly

29. "Agate" to the editor, February 12, 1862, *Cincinnati Daily Gazette*, February 17, 1862.
30. Ibid.

grasped the shaken lieutenant colonel's hand, and said, "That is right, Colonel; that is soldierly! I bid you good bye, and hope we shall soon meet again."[31]

Lander arrived at Paw Paw on February 8 and took over a home previously occupied by two secessionist women. The general spent only a handful of hours each day in the house to sleep. Much of his time was spent in a simple log cabin on the side of the railroad tracks just outside the camp perimeter. It had served as a schoolhouse prior to their arrival; now it was the telegraph office. The operator took over the lone bench in front of the fireplace. Staffers dragged the wires through a broken window pane. For hours on hours Lander would stand in front of the operator dictating dispatches and receiving replies.[32]

Although impressed with Kimball's proposal to attack Bloomery Gap immediately, Lander realized he was not ready for the endeavor. The general's greatest impediment in early February of 1862 was not the quality of his personnel, but lack of a means to supply them. Lander complained of deficiencies in all aspects of his division, not the least of which was food. Colonel Tyler's brigade had been encamped on high ground a few miles south of French's Store. Appropriately, they dubbed their bivouac "Camp Starvation."[33] After twenty-four hours without a morsel at the crossroads camp, Colonel Gavin ordered his Seventh Indiana to scour the countryside. "There was at once a general stampede," recounted a private in the unit. "In less than 15 minutes boys were seen with guns in their hands scaling the mountains in every direction in quest of prey. An hour had elapsed when they came flocking in with a perfect cargo of meat such as beef, pork, and muten [sic]. . . . We tore the meat into peices [sic], laid it into the fire, covered it up with ashes, and when it was partly cooked, we took it out and devoured it as greedily as starving Wolves."[34]

31. Clark, *Yates Phalanx,* ed. Decker, 46–7.

32. "Agate" to the editor, February 12, 1862, *Cincinnati Daily Gazette,* February 17, 1862.

33. Harry G. Armstrong to Simon Barstow, February 8, 1862, LP 7:7153; FWL to Salmon P. Chase, February 8, 1862, CP; Lawrence Wilson, *Itinerary of the Seventh Ohio Volunteer Infantry, 1861–1864, With Roster, Portraits, and Biographies* (New York, 1907), 119.

34. John V. Hadley to Mollie Hill, February 18, 1862, in Robertson Jr., "An Indiana Soldier," 204.

Lander had worked fervently in early February to solve his division's supply woes. He negotiated a contract with two entrepreneurs to keep a steady supply of beef available to his troops. With the promise of six and one-half cents per pound of beef in monthly payments, Lander's men were to receive high-quality meat without interference from politicians. The contract assured that 100 head of cattle would be attached to his supply trains at all times.

Unfortunately for Lander, he could not afford to supply his men appropriately. Given $10,000 for all purposes, the general committed most of it for the beef cattle, leaving him with fewer than $2,000 for other supplies. He was informed on February 10 that at least 100 four-horse wagons existed in Wheeling for a reduced price of $105 per wagon, but Lander had to decline the offer for lack of funds. In an inventive effort to obtain more money, Lander sold off 100 government horses deemed unfit for service. The condemned animals drew a slew of speculators to Cumberland from as far away as Ohio, who purchased the horses for prices ranging from five to fifty-three dollars. Receiving an average of thirty-five dollars for each animal, Lander used the cash to purchase approximately half as many healthy horses to ameliorate his transportation woes.[35]

With little money available to keep his men well-fed for continued operations in northwestern Virginia, Lander lacked confidence that the War Department would send him timely funds and looked for other means to feed his men. He had set his sights on Moorefield, a town forty miles south of Romney where he had learned that hundreds of cattle grazed. The beef supply was guarded by one of Stonewall Jackson's Hardy County militia outposts commanded by Colonel W. H. Harness. "[I] would very much like to go to Moorefield and capture those cattle," pleaded Colonel Samuel Dunning at New Creek on February 9. Lander could not agree more and sent positive orders for Dunning to break up the "guerilla haunt" there.[36]

Colonel Dunning gathered a force consisting of the Fifty-fifth Ohio (600 men), the Seventy-third Ohio (400 men), the Fifth and Sixth (Union) Virginia Militia (400 men), three companies from the First (Union)

35. Beef contract, February 1, 1862, LP 3:6552–3; H. W. Crowther to FWL, February 10, 1862, LP 7:7223; Batelle and Evans to FWL, February 10, 1862, LP 7:7250–1; P., "Sale of Government Horse Frames," February 7, 1862, *Cincinnati Daily Commercial,* February 11, 1862.

36. Dunning to FWL, February 9, 1862, LP 7:7191; *OR,* 5:405.

Virginia Cavalry (200 men), and a two-gun section from Battery I, First Ohio Light Artillery, commanded by Captain H. F. Hyman. The men departed Camp Lander at New Creek at noon on Monday, February 10. The morning had been unusually cold, with the temperature at Cumberland registered at ten degrees. By evening they reached Burlington, where they bivouacked for the night. The march was resumed on Tuesday morning, and Dunning's 1,600-man force reached within three miles of the ferry crossing by 9:00 P.M. Guided by an elderly citizen, Dunning found himself at Gibson's Ford, surprised to see the ferry boat split in two and sunk. Moorefield sat one mile away from the eastern bank of the South Branch.

Unable to cross his force, Dunning planted the cannons on a commanding hill and sent a communication across to Colonel Harness of the Hardy County militia. The message was brief and reminiscent of the Hancock ultimatum: "Sir—I will give you fifteen minutes to surrender your command. If you refuse to do so, take the women and children out of the town and I shall bombard it." Harness responded much like Lander had done to Jackson, refusing to surrender the town and warning Dunning that his men would contest any attempt at a takeover.

Dunning ordered Captain Hyman to lob a few rounds of solid shot at the town. The projectiles scattered the militia while Dunning brought his infantry to the riverbank. Unexpectedly, a hidden company of southern sharpshooters opened on the Yankees from thickets on the eastern bank, wounding three. Dunning sent out skirmishers to drive out the rebels, while his infantry crowded into empty supply wagons and floated across the river with the aid of his cavalry. Once on the Moorefield side, the Federals seized the town. For the first time since the commencement of the war, the Stars and Stripes cast its shadow on the Moorefield courthouse.

The Hardy County militia fled over the hills beyond Moorefield. Regimental commanders in Dunning's force detailed squads to arrest all male inhabitants of the town. Approximately fifty men, many from the Hardy Blues, which had been paroled by McClellan after Rich Mountain, were led across the river. Dunning was disappointed to learn that the large stock of supplies he expected to capture had been taken out of Moorefield the previous day. Still, 230 head of cattle were confiscated once the soldiers recrossed the river, thus achieving the main object of the mission.

The Federal soldiers-turned-cattle-herders returned toward New Creek beginning Wednesday, February 12; the trek required two days. Dunning's second expedition, like the first at Blue's Gap, succeeded in dispersing one of Stonewall Jackson's military strongholds. Dunning had again been disappointed by southern militia that fled instead of fought, but he had demonstrated that even the greenest of Union troops would march and fight if led properly. At Blue's Gap he had completed a thirty-five mile mission (round trip) in twenty-four hours. Despite the obstacles that impeded his Moorefield expedition, his force accomplished the task by averaging nearly twenty miles per day.[37]

While Dunning's men marched to New Creek from Moorefield, his division commander toiled at Paw Paw headquarters. Lander had yet to learn the results of Dunning's expedition, but other events had drawn his attention. Railroad trestles over the Great Cacapon had been nearly completed; however, reports from General Williams announced that Confederate troops appeared to be threatening Hancock again. Lander appeared pleased about the threat for it meant that he could activate his stagnant division. If the reports were true, the Great Cacapon Bridge would become a prime target for Jackson's men. "If they would only attack us at the bridge tonight," exclaimed the confident general, "wouldn't they confer a favor on us!"

But the rumors never panned out, leaving Lander disappointed at the prospect of continued inactivity. He turned to his division correspondents, Reid and Plimpton, and told them, "I can't promise you much fighting, soon, if you stay, or even any; though I hope there may be a little." The Cincinnati newsmen understood the hint of inactivity and departed Camp Chase within the next twenty-four hours.[38]

Lander rushed through his staff work on Thursday, February 13. The telegraph lines clicked away at headquarters to inform him that General Ulysses S. Grant had captured Fort Henry and currently was surrounding Fort Donelson in Tennessee. General Ambrose Burnside was threatening

37. Samuel Dunning to FWL, February 14, 1862, LP 8:7441–2; "J." to the editor, February 15, 1862, *Cincinnati Daily Commercial,* February 19, 1862; "Unknown" to the editor, February 16, 1862, *Cincinnati Daily Commercial,* February 20, 1862; H. F. Hyman to the editor, February 20, 1862, *Cincinnati Daily Commercial,* February 25, 1862.

38. Alpheus S. Williams to FWL, February 12, 1862, LP 7:7278; Captain Rodger to FWL, February 12, 1862, LP 7:7289; W. E. Porter to FWL, February 12, 1862, LP 7:7285; "Agate" to the editor, February 12, 1862, *Cincinnati Daily Gazette,* February 17, 1862.

Roanoke in North Carolina. Notwithstanding these successes in other theaters of operation, General McClellan appeared to be doing nothing with his army. Lander wanted so badly to attack Winchester, to act, to move. None of his previous requests had been granted, so Lander addressed his next dispatch to a higher authority—the new secretary of war, Edwin M. Stanton. Secretary Stanton had replaced the corrupt Simon Cameron in January. Having met Lander at functions sponsored by the Washington Art Association, Stanton had been well acquainted with Lander since the 1850s.[39]

After predicting that the railroad would be repaired as far as Hancock within a day, Lander poured out his frustrations to Stanton, asserting that the War Department and "the orders of weak men" were greater obstacles to his success than the acumen of the enemy. Lander did not mince words, shunning any concern over the perception of his acrid opinions. "Genl. Williams is an ass. Genl. Banks is a failure," flared Lander with unbridled animosity. "With faith in God and the American Republic I will beat the enemy forces with half their numbers and continue to do it. My enemy is your department, not in front. I detest and despise all behind me, but will move continually on the front. And if I had been provided [the] means [I] would never be beat." Lander realized this would raise eyebrows at the War Department, and continued by challenging Stanton with phrases that teetered toward insubordination: "You will regard this as disrespectful," he acknowledged, "I hope you may. I am not here for promotion or emolument."[40]

Lander soon learned more about the only enemy stronghold remaining in his district. The force at Bloomery Gap had been most recently estimated to be 500–600 strong, with the potential to receive reinforcements from General Jackson at Winchester. This information had been obtained from Colonel Gavin on February 12. Lander decided to remain idle no longer. He would send out a force to break up the "rebel's nest" fifteen miles away from him and personally lead this expedition. Not only would clearing Bloomery Gap remove an imminent bushwhacking threat to his district, it would also divert attention away from General Williams's force

---

39. F. B. A. David to FWL, February 12, 1862, LP 7:7257; *Washington (D.C.) Daily Union,* January 15, 1859.

40. FWL to Edwin Stanton, n.d., LP 3:6665–70. Lander made a copy of the letter, which exists in his papers. Since the envelope also was retained, no evidence is available to confirm that he actually sent this letter.

at Hancock, much like General Kelley had done for him with the Blue's Gap expedition six weeks earlier.[41]

"Expect my first fight near Bloomery," Lander revealed to a staffer later that day. "I shall hardly go to Winchester, but [will] go to the limits of my department." He designed the expedition to produce more than a battle. It was a message to send to Washington to show the War Department the difference between himself and what he called "weak men"—those officers unwilling to conduct significant winter operations. "I detest the quibbles and fears of West Point always thrust under my nose," opined Lander. "I go where the word can't is continuously introduced."[42]

Lander's greatest obstacle in this planned movement was his health. Whether it was chronic or another attack of "the congestive chills," the pain was back and increasing in its intensity. Eleven days earlier it had struck him when he was idle and he had required morphine to overcome it. This time Lander needed to be active to keep him aware and awake.

Knowing that he was dying, Frederick Lander would do what was necessary to achieve glory. Time—his most precious commodity—was not on his side.

---

41. James Gavin to FWL, February 12, 1862, LP 7:7279–81; *OR,* 5:405.

42. FWL to Dwight Bannister, February [13], 1862, private collection of Amos and Virginia Pearsall, Des Moines, Iowa. Virginia Pearsall is the granddaughter of Bannister. The letter is misdated as February 14. Lander sent the letter to Washington from Paw Paw, not knowing that Bannister would arrive at Camp Chase in time to join the expedition.

10

"Follow Me!"

Come, my cold mate, kneel, 'tis an awful hour,
    Put thy hand in mine, we will kneel to God,
He can guard us well, and His holy power
    Make the blue sea firm as the old green sod.

Here's a parting thought for the ones we love
    Here's a steadfast look at the wave below,
Here's a humble prayer to the God above,
    May He guard us well, for we need Him now.
                      —F. W. Lander

The mundane refrain "All Quiet on the Potomac" ended abruptly at Camp Chase on the afternoon of February 13. The long roll beat at 3:00 P.M., interrupting a quiet afternoon of letter writing and rest. Captain Marcus Spiegel of the Sixty-seventh Ohio managed to finish a letter to his wife when he heard the parade roll. He closed the letter by asking her to tell their little boy that "Pa Pa is at Paw Paw." Private Hiram Treher of the Fifth Ohio had only begun his letter to his hometown newspaper when he heard the drum. The letter would have to wait. Two days later, Treher had a much more exciting story to tell.[1]

1. Marcus Spiegel to his wife, February 13, 1862, in *A Jewish Colonel in the Civil War: Marcus M. Spiegel of the Ohio Volunteers,* ed. Jean P. Soman and Frank L. Byrne (Lincoln,

The soldiers formed on the parade ground at 4:00 P.M. One hour later they were in line and ready—destination unknown. Five infantry regiments, most from Colonel Nathan Kimball's First Brigade, formed the bulk of the line consisting of the Fifth Ohio, Eighth Ohio, Sixty-seventh Ohio, Seventh (Union) Virginia, Thirteenth Indiana, and the Fourteenth Indiana. A section of artillery and 100 horse soldiers from the First Ohio (Company C) and Ringgold (Pennsylvania) Cavalry also added to the strength of the force. In all, 3,000 soldiers waited to embark on their mysterious mission.

General Lander rode up to the parade ground shortly after 5:00 P.M. Some of his staffers, including Lieutenant O'Brien, Major Frothingham, Lieutenant Armstrong, and Major Bannister accompanied him. The general sat atop Katy Lu, the horse that poet N. P. Willis had considered so much a part of Lander. He trotted to the center of the line and faced his men, who had lined up in their "present arms" position. As usual, the general's presence was awe inspiring. Lander raised his cap, evoking spirited cheers from his troops. An Ohioan stated that all in the ranks "felt they stood in the presence of a soldier." Lander spoke a few minutes with his aides, passed to the right of his line, and set his column in motion.[2]

While Lander and the infantry marched out of Camp Chase, another body of troops trudged eastward to join their division mates who remained at Paw Paw. Colonel Erastus B. Tyler's Third Brigade, which bivouacked at miserable Camp Starvation, responded with cheers after they received their orders to join the rest of the division at Paw Paw. They had endured freezing temperatures without tents, cooking utensils, and rations; they even lacked paper and envelopes to write home and complain to loved ones. All of that changed at noon on Friday. Marching with a bounce in their step, the infantrymen reached the railroad, marched to the Little Cacapon River, turned to the east, and rested. Rails and other wood rose in piles and were set ablaze. Soon every one took a cup of hot coffee, a piece of hard tack, and a piece of fatty meat. "This we called supper,"

Nebr., 1995), 39; Hiram Treher to the editor, February 15, 1862, *Chambersburg (Pa.) Semi-Weekly Dispatch,* February 25, 1862.

2. Hiram Treher to the editor, February 15, 1862, *Chambersburg (Pa.) Semi-Weekly Dispatch,* February 25, 1862; "Prock" [William Landon] to the editor, February 20, 1862, *Vincennes (Ind.) Western Sun,* March 1, 1862; Nathan Kimball to FWL, February 16, 1862, LP 8:7443. Kimball's letter is a revealing and unpublished report of the Bloomery Furnace expedition.

wrote a member of the Seventh Indiana, "and [we] enjoyed it." After they finished their meal, the soldiers resumed their march. They reached Paw Paw that night.[3]

While the infantry from Tyler's brigade bivouacked near the Little Cacapon railroad station, Company A of the First Ohio Cavalry thundered past them toward Paw Paw. They arrived at Camp Chase expecting to rest for the night. They had barely dismounted and fed their horses when they learned that they were added to the mission. In the meantime, Colonel Henry Anisansel delivered eight companies of Union Virginia horse soldiers to Paw Paw (they had departed from the mouth of the South Branch River several hours earlier). The First Virginia companies added their numbers to the Ohio and Pennsylvania cavalry who had not embarked southward, but had been ordered to do so once they were in full force. The mixed cavalry rode out to join the expedition shortly after 11:00 P.M.[4]

Bloomery Furnace, the object of Lander's mission, stood slightly over one-third of the way between Winchester and Camp Chase, fourteen miles southeast of Paw Paw. Most recent estimates placed more than 500 Confederate militia there. Lander planned to surprise the force in a pre-dawn attack and capture not only the rebels, but also their supplies. They were believed to be encamped near a cluster of buildings that stood on the north side of Winchester Road, near the iron ore furnace for which the area was named. The furnace, which produced wrought-iron blooms, had been operating since 1833. The heirs of S. A. Pancost became the proprietors after Pancost died in 1857. They routinely rafted the blooms to eastern markets on the Cacapon River.[5]

Bloomery Furnace and its operating houses were tucked between two mountain passes. Bloomery Gap, which took its name from the furnace, stood one mile west of the furnace. Here, the northward-flowing Little Cacapon River squeezes between Castle Mountain to the south and Little

3. Billy Davis diary, February 11–13, 1862, in *The Civil War Journal of Billy Davis,* ed. Richard Skidmore (Greencastle, Ind., 1989), 101–2; J. Hamp Se Cheverell, *Journal History of the Twenty-ninth Ohio Veteran Volunteers, 1861–1865* (Cleveland, Ohio, 1883), 36.

4. "Lovejoy" to the editor, February 20, 1862, *(Washington C.H., Ohio) Fayette County Herald,* February 27, 1862; "Uno" to the editor, February 17, 1862, *Wheeling (Va.) Daily Intelligencer,* February 20, 1862.

5. Hamill Kenny, *West Virginia Place Names* (Piedmont, W.Va., 1975), 119; Maxwell and Swisher, *History of Hampshire County,* 534.

Mountain to the north. The North River meets with the Little Cacapon one-half mile north of the gap, forming an area appropriately called the Forks of the Cacapon. From the fork the Great Cacapon serpentines northeastward through the Cacapon Mountain chain until it empties into the Potomac at a point halfway between Paw Paw and Hancock.

Bloomery Run Gap stood one mile east of Bloomery Furnace.[6] This smaller pass, within the same mountain range, allowed room for Bloomery Run to flow into the Cacapon River. Winchester Road also crowded through the opening, stretching in both directions beyond. Seven miles east of Bloomery Run Gap was Unger's Store. Winchester stood nineteen miles south of this crossroads.

Lander had been studying the roads leading to Bloomery Gap since he took over Kelley's force at Romney. Winchester Road, which Jackson's men had used to pass through the gap when they occupied Romney early in January, ran from east to west through the gap from Unger's Store to Slane's Crossroads. Three roads approached the pass from the B & O Railroad. One road began at the mouth of the Little Cacapon River, wound through Spring Gap, and emptied into Winchester Road to the west of the Forks of the Cacapon. This route added several unnecessary miles to an advance. The most direct and passable route was Winchester Pike, which ran from Paw Paw to the Forks of the Cacapon. This road crossed the North River before it ended at Winchester Road. As tempting as this road was for quick and easy transport of division wagons and men, Lander ruled it out because it required a crossing of the Cacapon River at the gap and therefore was likely to be heavily picketed.[7]

Another north-south road ran from the mouth of the Great Cacapon River to Winchester Road. This mountain road, running on a parallel track approximately four miles east of Winchester Pike, led directly to the furnace and buildings. Although this road was a greater threat to the Confederates, no pickets were placed here, probably because it was a poor road that ran entirely east of the Cacapon. No Union troops had been stationed or seen on this side of the river throughout the winter season. There was no reason for the Confederates to believe that General Williams's

---

6. "Bloomery Run Gap" is the author's designation for an otherwise unnamed opening in the hills.

7. John Frothingham to FWL, January 19, 1862, LP 5:6538; Lander's Campaign Map, LP 5:6544; U.S. Department of the Interior, Geological Survey Map, Paw Paw and Largent, W.Va., Quadrangles.

men at Hancock—the closest force to the northern entrance of the road—would venture into the area, particularly when Confederates patrolled Bath to watch their movements.

Lander wanted to use the mountain road although he had yet to see or test it. He planned to cross his men to the road from the parallel Winchester Pike at a point about four miles south of Camp Chase. Lander felt confident that advancing southward on the mountain road would offer the surprise attack he sought by sweeping directly into the enemy camps. His biggest obstacle was the Great Cacapon River, a formidable moat that separated the two roads. Rather than cross the river directly in front of the enemy camp, Lander wished to ford it several miles north of the furnace. Earlier, on February 13, the general and a small scouting party had ridden to the river bank to lay a pontoon bridge across it prior to the expedition. The group was fired on by Confederate pickets and driven away.[8] Reasoning that the small southern party posed no threat and the Confederates were unlikely to patrol the river bank at night, Lander revised his plan. His frontier expedition skills would be called into action, for he would pontoon the river when his troops arrived there and not before—a feat that required the rapid construction of a 180-foot wagon bridge in the dead of night.

The sun disappeared half an hour after Lander and his men departed Camp Chase. Temperatures that had exceeded fifty degrees throughout northwestern Virginia had begun to cool, but they had already done their damage. The unusually warm day had muddied the roads and turned the several inches of snow that had blanketed the region into slush. Lander and his men found that swift movement would become an arduous task. The first two miles of the expedition were abominable. The soldiers in front of Lander's column loosened the mud, which initially was one to six inches deep. By the time the rearguard slopped through the quagmire, the muck had reached their knees. It felt like the Romney retreat all over again.

Fortunately for Lander, Winchester Pike improved two miles south of Paw Paw. Here the road was passable, but the slush still slowed the soldiers. The column of men, wagons, horses, and cannons did not get to enjoy the improvement for long. Lander led the men off the pike and

---

8. "Younger" to the editor, n.d., *Wheeling (Va.) Daily Intelligencer,* February 26, 1862; Soldier to the editor, February 15, 1862, *New York Tribune,* February 20, 1862.

marched them on a narrow, rough, newly constructed road that carried them toward the river. Unlike the pike, this perpendicular road returned the force to awkward steps as they trudged two abreast through darkened woods. The men scaled Sideling Hill, a three-and-one-half-mile chore that carried them 1,500 feet above sea level. "[A]n awful hill," complained Captain Spiegel of the Sixty-seventh Ohio, who noted the "high Rocks and Scattered Pine and Spruce trees and on the other Side the grandest precipice down, down, as far as men could see, with an awful rolling of Water which at first sight, would naturally stop a person and make him look, admire, and chill at the awful, romantic and fearful sight."[9]

The "awful rolling of water" that Captain Spiegel described was the Great Cacapon River. Lander ordered the Thirteenth Indiana and Sixty-seventh Ohio to countermarch back to the turnpike. They were to form near Winchester Road west of the Cacapon River to cut off a westward rebel retreat. The remainder of the force continued toward the river. After they descended Sideling Hill, Lander halted one mile from the river bank. The soldiers built campfires and boiled coffee while Lander and his staff rode to the bank with wagons and pontoon boards.[10]

The time approached 10:30 P.M. The poor roads had slowed the Federals to a meager eight miles in over five hours, and an hours-long respite was necessary to allow the engineers to bridge the river. To strike the gap before daylight required crossing the men, then marching them another seven miles—all in less than nine hours.

Lander's short temper flared at the river bank. Time was working against him, and he did not want to hear any excuses about why his plans could not be carried through. When Major Frothingham expressed some doubt about pontooning the swollen river with the supplies at hand, Lander, in the words of an Ohio officer, "stormed, swore and out-roared the roaring flood." Jonathan Fuller, the Eighth Ohio's wagon master, stepped up and informed the headquarters staff that he had engineering expe-

---

9. Temperature readings, District of Columbia, February 13, 1862, NWR; Clarke, comp., *The Confederate States Almanac,* 5; Marcus Spiegel to his wife, February 17, 1862, in Soman and Byrne, *Jewish Colonel,* 40–1; "Prock" to the editor, February 20, 1862, *Vincennes (Ind.) Western Sun,* March 1, 1862; "One of the Boys" to the editor, February 15, 1862, *Wheeling (Va.) Daily Intelligencer,* February 22, 1862.

10. Nathan Kimball to FWL, February 16, 1862, LP 8:7443; Spiegel to his wife, February 17, 1862, in Soman and Byrne, *Jewish Colonel,* 40; "Frank M. D." to the editor, n.d., *Wheeling (Va.) Daily Intelligencer,* February 21, 1862.

rience from his circus work prior to the war. Despite his own wealth of experience, Lander still welcomed the expertise and, with Fuller and Frothingham, he directed the placement of the wagons. Several mules were hitched to a wagon tongue; from there, they pulled a heavily ballasted wagon into the river. The swift-flowing current reached half way up the animals' sides, but none were lost as they dragged the wagon to the opposite side of the river. The mules were detached to repeat the procedure with another wagon, then another, and another. In a few hours twenty wagons spanned the river in a single line. Planks were laid across the wagon beds to complete the bridge.[11]

At 2:30 A.M. Lander sent orders to the men to retrieve their stacked arms and come to the river. His infantry arrived promptly to witness, in the moonlight, a 180-foot bridge. The impressed soldiers crossed three abreast; in half an hour they all reached the eastern side. Lander learned here that the mountain road that would carry his force to Bloomery Furnace was a poor one, so he ordered his heavy equipment to remain behind. This included the artillery pieces, ambulance, and supply wagons. Lander's load had been lightened considerably in both number and weight.[12]

The 2,000 remaining infantrymen filed onto the mountain path and marched southward. "Dark as hell," complained a member of the Fifth Ohio, who also noted that the mud was knee-deep again, as it had been on the other side of the river. The road led them up one mountain, then down to a valley and up another mountain, slowing Lander's advance to five miles in three hours. By 6:00 A.M. first nautical light (the light prior to sunrise) had made its appearance in the region, but Lander was still two miles shy of his destination.[13]

The similarities of this night march to the one conducted on the Philippi campaign were too striking to be considered mere coincidence.

11. Franklin Sawyer, *A Military History of the 8th Regiment Ohio Vol. Inf'y: Its Battles, Marches, and Army Movements* (Cleveland, Ohio, 1881), 32; *OR,* 5:405; Soldier to the editor, February 15, 1862, *New York Tribune,* February 20, 1862.

12. Sawyer, *History of the 8th Regiment,* 32; "Frank M. D." to the editor, n.d., *Wheeling (Va.) Daily Intelligencer,* February 21, 1862; Nathan Kimball to FWL, February 16, 1862, LP 8:7443.

13. Matthew Schwab to his brother, February 17, 1862, Cincinnati Historical Society, Cincinnati, Ohio; "One of the Boys" to the editor, February 15, 1862, *Wheeling (Va.) Daily Intelligencer,* February 22, 1862; Hiram Treher to the editor, February 15, 1862, *Chambersburg (Pa.) Semi-Weekly Dispatch,* February 25, 1862.

Lander patterned the two-column movements on those conducted the previous summer. Unfortunately, the marches were too similar; once again it appeared that he had failed to reach his destination in time.

Lander heard hoofbeats behind him; his cavalry had finally arrived. The 400 horse soldiers had covered the same twelve miles in six fewer hours. Henry Anisansel, the bespectacled colonel of the First (Union) Virginia Cavalry, headed the column. They had already suffered one casualty before the pending attack. Joseph E. Abell of the Ringgold Cavalry lost an eye when a comrade in front of him accidently released a tree branch into his face while they were passing through the woods.[14]

Lander ordered the cavalry to pass the infantry. His element of surprise was still intact since the sun had yet to rise. The general and his staff rode at the head of the cavalry. The infantrymen behind the horse soldiers were ordered to double-quick to support the pending assault. Colonel Samuel Carroll of the Eighth Ohio rode in the vanguard with Lander and his headquarters officers.[15]

Lander turned to Colonel Anisansel and gave him the plan. The rebel officers were quartered in the furnace houses on the north side of Winchester Road, Lander explained to his cavalry chief. He wanted the cavalry to surround the houses with a detached portion to hold the gap until the infantry came up. Anisansel threw out an advanced guard and the column rode on. In the meantime the Sixty-seventh Ohio had reached its destination on the western side of the Cacapon River, two miles from the furnace, and waited. The Thirteenth Indiana marched in close behind to strengthen the blocking force west of the furnace.[16]

The assaulting column of Federals crept to within one-quarter mile of their destination shortly before 7:00 A.M. Lander saw the cluster of houses in the distance. Someone claimed to hear an enemy picket fire a shot ahead of them. Lander's blood was up; he bellowed "Charge!" to his horse-

14. Farrar, *Twenty-second Pennsylvania Cavalry*, 38. Farrar states that Abell's injury occurred "on the night of February 14th, while on this march to Bloomery Gap." He refers to the early morning hours of February 14. Abell never recovered from his injury. Continuously suffering from intense pain, he committed suicide forty years later.

15. Hiram Treher to the editor, February 15, 1862, *Chambersburg (Pa.) Semi-Weekly Dispatch*, February 25, 1862; Samuel Sprigg Carroll, Testimony, HA, 10.

16. Harry G. Armstrong, Testimony, HA, 39; Spiegel to his wife, February 17, 1862, in Soman and Byrne, *Jewish Colonel*, 42; William M. Starr to his father, February 18, 1862, *Bryan (Ohio) Union Press*, February 28, 1862.

men and galloped toward Pancost's house—the building that was believed to quarter the southern officers who guarded the gap. The Federals surrounded the Pancost house in the clearing but were disappointed to find it empty. So were the other buildings: a log house, a barn, and an old mill.

Lander was furious. Not only was he disappointed to have his painstaking plan fall apart within minutes, but he also was incredulous to have his orders disobeyed by his cavalry chief. Inexplicably, Anisansel and most of his horse soldiers did not keep up. The general found himself accompanied by only a couple of companies, his staff officers, and Colonel Carroll. "I think that the greater portion [of Anisansel's force] did not try to keep up," admitted Carroll, who was equally disappointed at the spiritless effort by the horse soldiers. Lander had always been fond of Captain Keys of the Ringgolds, but that officer was sick in Cumberland. His replacement to lead the cavalry was not performing to Lander's standards.[17]

Had the enemy disappeared? Lander approached Private John J. Cannon of Russell's Independent Company of Maryland Cavalry and said, "I want you to take a lantern and find out which way they went." Cannon was a twenty-five-year-old Virginia refugee, having deserted from the Confederate service. Fetching a lantern and ten men, Cannon rode eastward on Winchester Road for approximately one mile to Bloomery Run Gap. The heights that formed the pass continued to block the light from the rising sun. This did not prevent Cannon from seeing rebel pickets, who approached him on Winchester Road. He quickly wheeled his horse and took his scouts back to the furnace buildings to report his discovery to Lander.[18]

The general had learned of the enemy's position prior to Cannon's return. He interrogated a miller and a boy who both told him that the Confederates were in the area, 400 strong, two miles east of the Pancost house. The Confederate militia had received information about Lander's advance earlier in the day and had pulled back their troops and sent their wagons to safety behind the soldiers.[19]

17. Carroll and Armstrong, Testimony, HA, 10, 40; "Uno" to the editor, February 17, 1862, *Wheeling (Va.) Daily Intelligencer,* February 20, 1862.
18. Carroll, Testimony, HA, 11; John J. Cannon, Testimony, HA, 5–6; "Younger" to the editor, n.d., *Wheeling (Va.) Daily Intelligencer,* February 26, 1862; Soldier to the editor, February 15, 1862, *New York Tribune,* February 20, 1862.
19. John B. Frothingham, Testimony, HA, 21; Thomas Mahon, Testimony, HA, 34; Armstrong, Testimony, HA, 40; *OR,* 5:406.

Several minutes had passed when Colonel Anisansel finally arrived at the junction of the two roads. Lander, riding toward the Pancost house, took no time to argue with Anisansel about his hesitance. He firmly held to the principle of surprise, which he felt was essential to bag the enemy force and their wagons. Lander ordered Anisansel to take his men and advance them eastward on Winchester Road. His mission was to engage the enemy and capture their baggage. Lander promised him infantry support if it was deemed necessary. As Anisansel rode out with 125 men, Private Cannon returned with his information for Lander. The general sent Cannon to guide Anisansel to where he had seen the enemy pickets.

Anisansel and Cannon fronted the horsemen and advanced them for approximately half a mile until Lander galloped up from behind and ordered them to halt. Lander expected much from his horse soldiers and wished to leave nothing to chance. He asked Anisansel if his men were properly equipped with both carbines and sabers. Anisansel answered in the affirmative, prompting Lander to add that the colonel would be wise to place his best swordsmen in front. Satisfied that the charging portion of his column was prepared and advancing, Lander rode back toward the Pancost house to organize his incoming infantry. The foot soldiers had arrived minutes earlier and were moving into a cleared field north of the furnace buildings to rest and await orders.[20]

No sooner had Lander left Anisansel's column than the cavalry came under attack. Anisansel commanded a mixed force of Maryland, Ohio, Pennsylvania, and western Virginia companies. They trotted another 300 yards after Lander left, slowing down at Bloomery Run Gap, where their view was obstructed. Anisansel ordered pickets forward, but they met oncoming Confederate infantry, who fired on them and sent the skirmishers back to the main column. Anisansel ordered a halt as soon as he heard his scouts fired on. A rearward captain rode up to his cautious colonel and asked what he planned to do. Anisansel responded that he would wait for Lander to bring up infantry. In the meantime he sent orders back for all men carrying breech-loading weapons to push to the front of the column to engage the enemy.[21] Anisansel concluded that the saber offered no opportunity for success this morning.

20. Cannon, Testimony, HA, 6–7; Armstrong, Testimony, HA, 40; Frothingham, Testimony, HA, 21; "Frank M. D." to the editor, *Wheeling (Va.) Daily Intelligencer,* February 21, 1862.

21. Cannon, Testimony, HA, 7–8; William C. Carman, Testimony, HA, 24–5; Mahon, Testimony, HA, 34.

Captain Nathan Menkin of the First Ohio Cavalry, Company C, impatiently waited in the rear of Anisansel's force. He expected to hurl his men at the enemy and could not understand why they were not advancing. Menkin lost all confidence in Anisansel's leadership. Knowing that Lander would handle the situation differently, Menkin detached Sergeant Charles W. Florence to head back to Bloomery Furnace and apprise the general.[22]

Lander and his staff had headquartered themselves at the Pancost house for approximately ten minutes when Sergeant Florence reined up at the front porch. Lander listened in disgust as the courier relayed Menkin's information. Lander stormed out of the house, sent orders to bring up the Seventh (Union) Virginia and Fourteenth Indiana Infantry, then mounted Katy Lu. With staff in tow he galloped eastward to the stymied cavalry.[23]

The tail of the cavalry column stood three-quarters of a mile east of the Pancost house and stretched for nearly 100 yards to the thinnest segment of the creek gap. Lander trotted to the north side of the road, passing each company and swearing, "Why in hell and damnation don't you charge!" A company captain in the midst of the stagnant force quickly pointed to Colonel Anisansel in the front. Lander rode up to Anisansel and, ignoring the enemy fire directed at him from sixty yards away, exploded, "Why in the hell did you stop?" Anisansel attempted to answer that he had expected to receive infantry support, but Lander could not wait for his explanation. The enemy, led by Thirty-first Virginia Militia colonel Robert F. Baldwin, had begun to rally in front. Baldwin cheered his men on to take position on the hillside. If he were successful, his troops and the limiting terrain could hold up Lander's men indefinitely and allow Baldwin's baggage wagons to escape.

Lander refused to allow a hesitant subordinate to jeopardize his plans. He wheeled and faced his cavalry. With no time for long inspirational speeches, Lander announced, "My men, my men, what are you staying here for? Why don't you go on? Come ahead and follow me!" Lander bellowed "Charge!" loud enough for the rearward companies to hear, shouldered Katy Lu eastward, and galloped through the gap. He veered to the left and charged toward the Confederates who were rallying on the hill.

22. Nathan Menkin, Testimony, HA, 36–7.
23. Irvin Redpath, Testimony, HA, 30; Frothingham, Testimony, HA, 22; Armstrong, Testimony, HA, 40–1; "Frank M. D." to the editor, n.d., *Wheeling (Va.) Daily Intelligencer,* February 21, 1862.

Lieutenant Armstrong, Lieutenant O'Brien, and Major Bannister of his staff followed faithfully. Captain William Carman of the First (Union) Virginia Cavalry also charged. The only other horseman who rode forward with Lander was the ubiquitous Private John Cannon. Colonel Anisansel and the rest of his men lagged behind at the gap.[24]

Overcome by impetuosity, Lander, a division commander, had taken the initiative but was leading a reckless cavalry charge headlong against an unknown number of Confederates lining the hillside in front of him. He would afterward admit to his wife that "it was death or surrender for me" as he spurred Katy Lu 400 yards toward his destiny. To Lander's relief the Federal quintet shocked the unsuspecting Confederate militia and put most of them to flight. As the southerners scrambled up the hillside to escape, Lander headed for Colonel Baldwin and a contingent of his subordinates while the other attacking Federals rode down isolated rebel officers and men. Lander was on top of Baldwin before he could react. "Surrender, Gentlemen," he ordered. "You are completely surrounded and cut off." He then coolly dismounted from his horse. The five rebel officers offered no resistance and handed Lander their swords. The other Union horsemen subdued nine more men.[25]

Higher up on the hill, rebel militia took cover behind trees and opened fire on Lander and his staff; one ball grazed Lieutenant Armstrong's neck. Federal cavalry thundered up the hill to their relief. The horsemen, mostly from the First Ohio Cavalry, had worked their way to the front when Lander ordered the charge. The limiting terrain, primarily the thin pass, delayed them considerably. Once they became engaged, they produced satisfying results. The Buckeyes had served as Lander's headquarter's guard prior to the expedition, and they continued to provide valuable assistance at Bloomery Run Gap. Captain Carman's men from the First (Union) Virginia Cavalry also appeared, as did scattered squads from other companies. Colonel Anisansel rode up with other members of the First Virginia. At this point the fight turned into a melee. Private John Dickey of the First Ohio rode up to a boulder, behind which waited six armed southern militia. "But I got the drop on them," Dickey remembered,

24. Armstrong, Testimony, HA, 40–1; Redpath, Testimony, HA, 30; Cannon, Testimony, HA, 8; FWL to his wife, February 15, 1862, LP 3:6564.

25. FWL to his wife, February 15, 1862, LP 3:6564; "Younger" to the editor, n.d., *Wheeling (Va.) Daily Intelligencer*, February 26, 1862; Armstrong, Testimony, HA, 41; Cannon, Testimony, HA, 7–8.

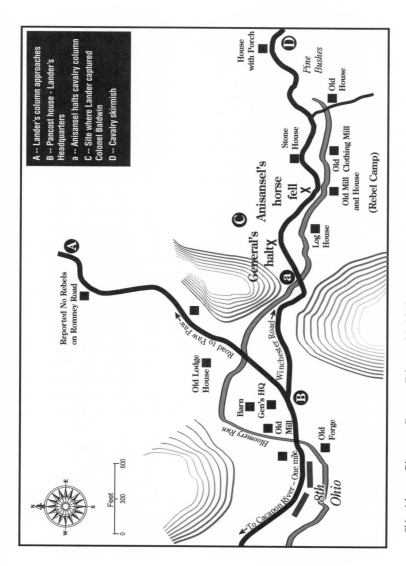

Skirmish near Bloomery Furnace, February 14, 1862

Adapted from evidence map, Henry Anisansel Court-Martial Papers, NA

"when they stacked their arms and . . . I marched them in to General Lander."

The general relinquished some of his captures to other guards and was leading Colonel Baldwin personally back to Winchester Road. He saw a soldier arguing with a southern officer who still held onto his sword. Lander ordered his soldier to disarm the officer. The Ohio private complained, "He says he will never give his sword to a Yankee." Lander dismounted, walked up to the armed officer, and seized him by the shoulders. "Old Grizzly" shook the rebel mercilessly and snarled, "Then you'll give it to me!" The intimidated officer unbuckled his sword and sheepishly handed it over to him. Lander then turned to the Union soldier and snorted, "If you find another man like this, don't multiply words with him." The general then remounted his mare and returned to his own prisoner.[26]

Although Lander had taken out the infantry leaders, his mission had not been completed. Confederate wagons were escaping toward Winchester two miles east of the gap. Lander entrusted this mission to Colonel Anisansel and the Union cavalry. The general and four of his staffers (Major Frothingham had recently come up) halted on Winchester Road near the gap, where Anisansel and about 200 cavalrymen also stood. Lander ordered the horsemen to pursue the enemy and take their baggage. No one budged. Incredibly, the same man who persuaded five officers to surrender their swords to him had been unsuccessful in getting his own men to move. Lander repeated the order with more rage and forcefulness, again with no response. Lander had had enough. He repeated the order, this time threatening to shoot anyone who did not obey. To demonstrate he was true to his word, Lander drew his pistol and fired a shot in the air.

Twenty horse soldiers took off eastward on the road, led by Colonel Anisansel. The remainder of the cavalry either stayed on the road or reined their horses up the embankments on each side to pursue fleeing southern militia. A member of the attacking cavalry claimed that his party

---

26. "Lovejoy" [Samuel Gillespie], *A History of Company A, First Ohio Cavalry, 1861–1865: A Memorial Volume Compiled from Personal Records and Living Witnesses* (Washington C.H., Ohio, 1898), 50–1. In recounting this anecdote, Gillespie claimed that the southern officer was Colonel Baldwin. Considering the overwhelming evidence identifying Lander as the one who apprehended Baldwin, the officer was likely another commissioned commander.

"dashed up every road, ravine, and mountain side, routing, shooting and capturing the flying rebels. It was one continual charge for five miles distance."[27]

In the meantime Lander, his staff, and several of their prisoners rode toward the Pancost house. Colonel Kimball had come up with two of his regiments, the Seventh (Union) Virginia under Colonel James Evans in the lead and the Fourteenth Indiana, Kimball's former regiment now led by Major William Harrow, following close behind. The troops had double-quicked from the houses where they had been set to rest and eat breakfast. They unslung the heavy baggage from their backs, including blankets, haversacks, canteens, and other accoutrements, which were left littering the roadside. They passed Lander and his cortege at the double quick to take part in the action.[28]

The infantrymen trudged through mud "as thick as well worked mortar." They passed Bloomery Run Gap and the area just east of it where Lander had led his men to capture the militia officers. They continued to slosh eastward along Winchester Road in the direction in which Anisansel and his men had gone to capture the enemy wagons. One mile beyond the original skirmish area William Landon of the Fourteenth Indiana, who was a correspondent for his hometown newspaper, slowed down, pulled out his notebook, and jotted down the following observations:

Old man, about seventy, standing in a meadow a short distance from the pike, surrounded by a squad of the 14th who were questioning him. Exasperated cavalryman comes dashing back, leading the horse of his comrade who had just been killed—saddle and horse covered with blood. "Stand away, boys, and let me shoot the damned old rebel." But the old man's life was spared

A little boy was crying as though his heart was broken. "Oh! they have killed my brother, and they are going to kill my father, too!" His brother, like all these "bush-whackers," had fired on our men and then undertook to save his cowardly life by throwing away his gun and running into a house, but an Enfield bullet had overtaken him in his flight.

Two women, the wife and mother of a sesesh Captain of bush-whackers, were filling the air with their cries of despair and grief over his body—refusing

27. Samuel B. Fuller, Testimony, HA, 15; Frothingham, Testimony, HA, 22–3; "Uno" to the editor, February 17, 1862, *Wheeling (Va.) Daily Intelligencer,* February 20, 1862.
28. "One of the Boys" to the editor, February 15, 1862, *Wheeling (Va.) Daily Intelligencer,* February 22, 1862; "Frank M. D." to the editor, n.d., *Wheeling Daily Intelligencer,* February 21, 1862; Nathan Kimball, Testimony, HA, 19.

to surrender his weapons when twice called upon to do so. A cavalryman had nearly severed him in twain by a blow from his sabre.[29]

Colonel Kimball led the two regiments to Sherrard's brick house two and one-half miles east of Bloomery Furnace. The infantry had heard firing in their front, but Kimball was surprised to see a mud-covered Colonel Anisansel with several of the cavalry standing on the road. When Kimball asked Anisansel for an explanation as to why he was not advancing, the hard-luck colonel replied that he had hurt himself when his horse tumbled onto Winchester Road. Kimball could see that Anisansel was in great pain (he suffered from a hernia) and realized that he would be of no service for the rest of the day. Anisansel had sent an officer back to headquarters to inform Lander that his men had been repulsed. They had initially succeeded in capturing two wagons, but no support had come to their aid and in five minutes the Sixty-seventh Virginia Militia and Company A of the Eighty-ninth Virginia Militia advanced on the hills on each side of the road and opened fire. They killed two Union cavalrymen and forced the rest from the wagons. The Virginia militiamen were still in position when Kimball's men marched up the road.

Anisansel strode westward toward the furnace buildings, yielding the front to Colonel Kimball and his infantry. Kimball threw the Seventh (Union) Virginia to the right where Anisansel had experienced the heaviest resistance. Colonel Evans led his Union Virginians up a hill on the right of the road, captured ten wayward militia, but saw no other enemy force. Two companies of the Fourteenth Indiana scaled the hill on the left of the road to scour the woods there, finding nothing. In the meantime, Kimball advanced the rest of the Fourteenth Indiana on Winchester Road toward Unger's Store. They chased fleeing militia for two miles but were unable to retake the wagons. The southerners retreated to Pughtown (a few miles northwest of Winchester), losing a few more stragglers but carrying their supply wagons to safety. Kimball and his infantry occupied high ground for approximately one hour, then the small force retired to the furnace buildings.[30]

29. "Prock" to the editor, February 20, 1862, *Vincennes (Ind.) Western Sun,* March 1, 1862.

30. Kimball, Testimony, HA, 19–21; Nathan Kimball to FWL, February 16, 1862, LP 8:7443; Fuller, Testimony, HA, 15–16; *OR,* 5:406; J. Chapman, "Reminiscences of Bloomery Gap," Virginia Historical Society, Richmond, Va.; "One of the Boys" to the editor, February 15, 1862, *Wheeling (Va.) Daily Intelligencer,* February 22, 1862.

Anisansel straggled back to the Pancost house, muddied, pained, and dejected. Likening the fire that stopped his men to the fight in the streets of Paris during France's revolution, Anisansel conceded that he had been injured and that the enemy had escaped. Lander would take no more. He ordered Anisansel arrested for "misbehavior before the enemy." Two specifications illustrated Lander's greatest points of contention: not attacking the Confederate infantry at the gap, and allowing the wagons to get away, particularly after capturing two of them.[31]

It was still midmorning when Colonel Carroll, inactive since he had aided Lander in surrounding the furnace buildings two hours earlier, was called on for assistance again. Anisansel repeated the claim of his courier; both insisted that they were repulsed because a large force, supposed to be Jackson's advanced guard, had fired on them from solid fortifications along the road. Major Armstrong delivered new orders to Colonel Carroll: "go out upon the Winchester Road and see if there were any fortifications or enemy and learn something definite." Carroll collected his Eighth Ohio and advanced them eastward on Winchester Road, a soupy thoroughfare softened considerably by hundreds of infantry and cavalrymen passing on it before the Buckeyes. Carroll advanced his men eight miles to Unger's Store, the limit of Lander's district, passing Kimball's men, who were returning after their very limited success. Carroll saw no enemy, save for one straggler. He believed the fortifications that Anisansel and his courier insisted they had seen was merely a rock projection.[32]

While Lander's infantry marched to within twenty miles of Winchester, the general stayed at his headquarters with his prize capture. Colonel Baldwin, a Winchester native, was the most noteworthy of seventeen commissioned officers bagged by Lander, his staff, and the leading elements of his cavalry. Lander permitted Baldwin to write his wife a letter that would be passed through the lines to her. "I am a prisoner of War having been captured by Gen'l Lander this morning," penned the captive. "The Gen'l and his officers have so far treated us with the greatest deference and respect and I have no doubt we will [be treated] as well as possible under the present circumstances." Lander was pleased with the compliment, so much so that he requested Baldwin to make

31. Frothingham, Testimony, HA, 23; General Orders No. 109, HA.
32. Carroll, Testimony, HA, 11–12.

him a copy of the same letter to send to his wife.[33] Baldwin was in no position to refuse.

Kimball's two regiments returned to the furnace area after completing their eight-mile round-trip reconnaissance (Carroll's troops were to double that distance in the following three hours). For the Seventh (Union) Virginia, the skirmish against the militia provided them with experience and news to relay to their hometown family and friends. Not all the incidents they witnessed were ones to be proud of, however. A candid member of Company C admitted that a Unionist was accidently killed by a member of another company when he did not heed the order to halt (it was discovered afterward that he could not follow orders from behind—he was deaf).

The witness also claimed that the cavalry accidently killed a boy, but he did not specify whether the child was active in the Confederate militia.[34] One of the captured rebels was a twelve-year-old staunch southerner. He reportedly killed one of the Union cavalry and fired three shots at an officer before he was finally compelled to give up. He still had thirty rounds in his possession on surrender.

The Federals killed and wounded thirteen and captured sixty-five Confederates. Most belonged to the Thirty-first and Fifty-first Virginia—militia units heavily recruited from Winchester and Frederick County. The captured men intrigued their captors. "The prisoners seem to have good humor, taking the matter as a good joke," admitted a private in the Fifth Ohio. "They conversed freely with our boys, told them if they had come a little earlier they would have found a warm breakfast. Most of them are of the opinion the North cannot conquer the South, say they will fight as long as one of them is alive." Some northerners saw Confederate money for the first time. Ordering their prisoners to empty their pockets, the Federal soldiers noted the abundance of "twenty-five cent shinplasters, payable at Winchester." In addition to the prisoners, a booty of corn, rice, coffee, sugar, molasses, whiskey, and flour fell into Federal hands.[35]

33. Robert F. Baldwin to his wife, February 14, 1862, LP 3:6562–3.

34. "Frank M. D." to the editor, n.d., *Wheeling (Va.) Daily Intelligencer,* February 21, 1862.

35. Ibid.; "Prison Diary of Lieutenant Richard L. Gray," in Winchester-Frederick County Historical Society, *Diaries, Letters, and Recollections of the War Between the States* (Winchester, Va., 1955), 45–6; Hiram Treher to the editor, February 15, 1862, *Chambersburg (Pa.) Semi-Weekly Dispatch,* February 25, 1862; *OR,* 5:405; "Prock" to the editor, February 20, 1862, *Vincennes (Ind.) Western Sun,* March 1, 1862.

Colonel Carroll returned to Bloomery Furnace from Unger's Store at about 1:00 P.M., reporting no sign of enemy forces in the area. Lander had already ordered another pontoon bridge constructed, this one across the Little Cacapon south of its junction with the North River where Winchester Road met the water's edge at Bloomery Gap. Lander collected his forces, his prisoners, and his other captured commodities. He moved his men to the bridge and crossed them. The participants were so tired from the strenuous marching, fighting, and sleepless night that some of the cavalrymen stole a nap in their saddles. Lander reached the intersection of Winchester Road and Winchester Pike and headed northward up the latter at 3:00 P.M., picking up the Sixty-seventh Ohio and Thirteenth Indiana along the way. They waded the frigid North River and trudged back to Paw Paw.

By 10:00 P.M. the vanguard of Lander's infantry reached Camp Chase, completing a twenty-nine-hour sojourn that had inflicted seventy-eight casualties on their opponent with a loss to themselves of two killed and three wounded. The unengaged troops had marched thirty miles in that time; the engaged infantry and cavalry had completed a thirty-eight-mile mission. Colonel Carroll and his Eighth Ohio totaled an astounding forty-three miles over what Nathan Kimball called "disgraceful" roads.[36]

The soldiers staggered into camp footsore and weary. Sergeant David E. Beem of the Fourteenth Indiana finagled a horse for the final fifteen miles of the mission, providing the "foot" soldier the opportunity to note that the skirmish took place on Valentine's Day. "Don't you think that Cupid gave it up for once, at least in our case?" he quipped to his hometown sweetheart. "Instead of shooting arrows of love, he shot bullets of lead through the heart, killing some, and doubtless making the hearts of others sad for life." Hiram Treher, the Fifth Ohio soldier whose letter to his hometown newspaper was interrupted a day and a half earlier, claimed he felt "like an old man of seventy-five" on his return to Camp Chase. He planned to send a captured gun to the newspaper as a trophy, but he nixed the idea because he was so tired he could barely carry his own weapon.[37]

Captain Marcus Spiegel dragged himself to his quarters. He could tell

36. "Younger" to the editor, n.d., *Wheeling (Va.) Daily Intelligencer*, February 26, 1862; "Lovejoy" to the editor, February 20, 1862, *(Washington C.H., Ohio) Fayette County Herald*, February 27, 1862; "Prock" to the editor, February 20, 1862, *Vincennes (Ind.) Western Sun*, March 1, 1862; Nathan Kimball to FWL, February 16, 1862, LP 8:7443.

37. David E. Beem to Hala, February 17, 1862, Beem Papers, IHS; Hiram Treher to the editor, February 15, 1862, *Chambersburg (Pa.) Semi-Weekly Dispatch*, February 25, 1862.

his young son that "Pa Pa is at Paw Paw" again, but he could not enjoy the comforts of the same bed he used before the expedition. Spiegel was disappointed to find a cavalryman occupying his bunk. It was Colonel Anisansel, who had arrived hours earlier and was receiving medical attention for his rupture. A court-martial was pending to allow him the opportunity to tend to his wounded reputation.[38]

Katy Lu carried her ailing rider back to the telegraph office shortly before 8:00 P.M. on Friday. Frederick Lander dismounted and wearily entered his office to read the dispatches that had been transmitted over the previous thirty hours. Lander learned that Grant had captured Fort Donelson in Tennessee. In addition, he received Colonel Dunning's report of his success at bringing off the 230 head of cattle from Moorefield. Dunning's accomplishment, in addition to his own, meant that all known opposition had retreated from Lander's district of operations. Lander was also pleased to learn that the B & O Railroad had been opened all the way to Hancock.

Lander assessed both his own and his men's performance at Bloomery Furnace. The expedition had occupied his thoughts throughout the return trip to Camp Chase. He believed that Anisansel had failed him, preventing the capture of the wagons. Still, Lander's chief objective—to break up the Confederate outpost—had been met. His men proved that they could march tremendous distances in the midst of a harsh winter in the mountains. Perhaps General McClellan would learn a valuable lesson when he was apprised of the distance that Carroll and the rest of his men covered over thoroughfares that barely resembled roads. When compared with the action at Manassas, the casualties he inflicted on his opponent were too small to call the affair near Bloomery Furnace a battle, but the Confederate losses exceeded those at Philippi and approached the numbers inflicted on July 11, 1861, at Rich Mountain. Lander's daring charge through Bloomery Run Gap superseded his performance at Philippi, an event that the newspapers were certain to spread for days to come.

It had been a memorable Saint Valentine's Day, indeed, but the toll had been excessive. Lander had been ailing prior to departing Paw Paw. Morphine had relieved him two weeks earlier; this time adrenaline carried Lander through the expedition. But its effects dissipated on Friday night, leaving the general more physically spent than he had ever felt before.

38. Spiegel to his wife, February 13, 1862, in Soman and Byrne, *Jewish Colonel*, 42–4.

After forty uninterrupted hours of activity, Lander needed deep sleep, but before he could go to bed duty required him to transmit a summary of the events of the day to the War Department.

At 8:00 P.M. he wired McClellan. "The railroad was opened to Hancock this morning," Lander began. "Broke up the rebel nest at Bloomery Gap. Ran down and caught 17 commissioned officers . . . Led the charge in person . . . Papers taken and my own reconnaissance south prove the country clear and Jackson and Loring in Winchester."

Lander summarized the results of Dunning's expedition, then decided to close his report. He enjoyed transmitting this information to McClellan to prove that active winter campaigning could be successful. The Bloomery Furnace fight should illustrate to high command that Winchester could and should be assaulted immediately. But Lander had come to the conclusion that he could not lead this charge. His failing body convinced him that he could not endure a field command if McClellan continued to hold him back, which Lander felt was inevitable. Helping to convince him of McClellan's continued recalcitrance was a directive that he had just received from the War Department directing him to send the three Ohio regiments and Hyman's Battery back to Rosecrans.[39] He had opened the railroad, which was McClellan's goal, and although Lander wanted to do much more, he realized that McClellan would refuse to allow it. Pain and fatigue dictated the closing lines of Lander's first and last dispatch of February 14:

> As the work intrusted to me may be regarded done and the enemy out of this department, I most earnestly request to be relieved. If not relieved, must resign. My health is too much broken to do any severe work.[40]

39. *OR*, 51(1):531.
40. *OR*, 5:405–6.

11

"Shall I Disobey Orders?"

Before we yield the holy trust
  Our old forefathers gave,
Or wrong New England's hallowed dust,
  Or grant the wrongs ye crave—

We'll print in kindred gore so deep
  The shore we love to tread,
That woman's eyes shall fail to weep
  O'er man's unnumbered dead.
                                    —F. W. Lander

"Your conduct is just like you," wired back General George Mc-Clellan after obtaining Lander's Bloomery Furnace dispatch. "Don't talk about resigning."[1]

Lander's soldiers wagged his February 14 exploits as "Lander's Midnight Bloomery Dash." The accolades from peers and superiors poured in beginning the next day. Congratulatory telegrams came in from Generals Rosecrans, Kelley, and Milroy. Rosecrans, who was pulling troops away from Lander's command, was quite impressed with his "capture of those rogues" on Valentine's Day. "[I] hope they find you a rock," he wired to Lander, "a rock such against they will split wherever it moves." Secretary

1. *OR*, 51(1):531.

of War Edwin M. Stanton sent his congratulations and mentioned that President Lincoln was also pleased with Lander's performance. In an obvious approval of Lander's winter operations, Stanton went on to favorably compare Lander's success with McClellan's inactivity by adding, "You have shown how much may be done in the worst weather and worst roads, by a spirited officer, at the head of a small force of brave men, unwilling to waste life in camp when the enemies of their country are within reach."[2]

The skirmish at Bloomery Furnace produced extra work at Paw Paw headquarters, where the captured southern militia were processed for transportation. The prisoners were confined to an old storehouse while hundreds from the Western Division gratified their curiosity by peeping at and conversing with the Confederates through a window. Desirous to send samples of Confederate money home to family and friends, the U.S. soldiers exchanged silver and gold for the worthless southern scrip. Lander quickly released those who convinced him that they were Union sympathizers forced into Confederate service. He then sent the remainder from Camp Chase in Paw Paw to Camp Chase in Ohio. Before they departed, Colonel Baldwin wrote Lander a note to thank the general for his generosity. "Yesterday the fortunes of War made me your prisoner," explained Baldwin. "I am glad, sir, as I had to yield up my sword . . . to an officer who not only bore himself so gallantly upon the field, but who could so fully appreciate the feelings of a gentleman so painfully situated. I assure you, sir, I shall ever remember the delicate attention of yourself and the officers of your staff."[3]

Although proud of the success achieved near Bloomery Gap, Lander was disappointed at his cavalry's lackluster performance. On February 15 he wrote his wife for the first time since he retook Romney and described the skirmish to her. Saying nothing about his failing health nor his attempt at resigning, Lander pointedly criticized his cavalry chief—"Col. Anisansel of the cavalry refused to charge and I had hard work to get the men up"—but he used most of his letter to agonize over the lack of support he had been receiving in his district. Complaining that McClellan was pulling regiments away from him and that Williams refused to cross

---

2. Rosecrans to FWL, LP 3:6570; Stanton to FWL, February 17, 1862, LP 3:6571.
3. "A Volunteer" to the editor, February 18, 1862, *Muncy (Pa.) Luminary,* March 4, 1862; Robert Baldwin to FWL, February 15, 1862, LP 3:6565.

the Potomac, even though the railroad had been opened below him, the exasperated general announced, "What a farce this whole affair is!"[4]

Benefitting from some rest, Lander felt much stronger within forty-eight hours of returning to Paw Paw. He had decided by this time not to resign, although his health still concerned him. Writing to his influential friend Preston Blair, Lander recounted the successful expedition but emphasized the frustration he felt at having key elements of his division removed from his jurisdiction. Soul-searching found its way into Lander's letter:

> Until I make a mistake or am beaten, why am I not allowed to pass out of this department and take Winchester and Martinsburg? I have opened the B & O Railroad to the limits of my division of the grand Army of the Potomac and now must set down for a winter quarters. I am broken down in health, yet for an advance, could ride forty miles tomorrow. My hour will come when, before the American people, I will recapitulate my past—a poor history of this war. Caution, caution, caution. Never a blow.
>
> Forgive me, my old friend and do not suppose me *always* a grumbler, but weaker men than I would have done much here if the means had been given. I have never advised to a mistake, yet why am I held back? I have done all I can. The railroad is open to the limits of my command.
>
> Shall I disobey orders and go farther?[5]

Unknown to the elderly Blair, Lander had already put in motion efforts to recapitulate his past. Lander had prided himself as a man of action and had basked in the accolades he received for his role at Philippi eight months earlier. His role in the battle of Rich Mountain, however, had never received the attention he felt it deserved, even though epaulets adorned his shoulders as a result of it. Knowing that the battle at Manassas overshadowed the western Virginia Union victory, and also dissatisfied at Rosecrans's official report of that engagement, Lander took advantage of the lack of public knowledge of this battle and decided to tell the story the way he saw it. He tested his story on Colonel Jeremiah C. Sullivan, formerly commander of the Thirteenth Indiana at Rich Mountain and currently heading one of Lander's brigades. On hearing Lander's fanciful report of the Rich Mountain battle, Sullivan tried to correct his superior. The result was a heated altercation that put Sullivan in his place.

4. FWL to his wife, February 15, 1862, LP 3:6562–3.
5. FWL to [Preston Blair], February 16, 1862, LP 3:6566–7.

Lander submitted the account anonymously to the *New York Evening Express*. In it he heaped a disproportionate amount of responsibility on himself to the detriment of General Rosecrans; in fact, his account criticized Rosecrans for being negligent in carrying out his orders. Not surprisingly, Rosecrans bristled when he read the story. Receiving confirmation that Lander had indeed authored the piece, Rosecrans complained to his wife that Lander's "slanderous tongue is therefore the prisoner of the public mind in Washington." Knowing that McClellan continued to laud Lander's Rich Mountain performance, Rosecrans seethed, "[McClellan] is either a hypocrite or a much poorer judge of human nature than I supposed."[6] Rosecrans's anger was justified, for Lander's uninhibited and vainglorious quest for self-promotion was his most notorious character flaw.

General Grant's capture of Fort Donelson and its 15,000 defenders was the greatest Union success in the early months of 1862. Surprisingly, Lander's Bloomery expedition still received great attention from peers, subordinates, and the public. Secretary Chase boasted of Lander's accomplishments to a Cincinnati editor, calling him "a man of the noblest temper and of equal genius." Newspapers throughout the North, starving for heroes in Virginia to brag about to their readers, reported at length about Lander's gallant dash. "Lander Drives The Rebels" headlined one paper's printed copy of Lander's telegram to McClellan. The editors ended the dispatch with Lander's line: "The enemy has thus been driven out of this department," and omitted his resignation request. Other writers contrasted the War Department's reaction to Lander's success with the Lander-McClellan controversies they had highlighted one month earlier. "Decidedly fighting is getting popular in Washington," wrote one. "The Secretary of War, instead of reprimanding Gen. Lander for his brilliant dash of Thursday last, has thanked him for it. . . . Gen. Lander is an earnest man, and not only believes in fighting the rebels, but knows how to do it. It is cheering to see such men encouraged."[7]

It was not cheering to Brigadier General Alpheus S. Williams in Hancock. Williams stewed at all the attention heaped on Lander. Reporters

6. Rosecrans to his wife, April 22, 1862, in Rosecrans Papers, UCLA; "Gen. Lander and the Western Virginia Campaign," *Wheeling (Va.) Daily Intelligencer,* March 19, 1862. The Wheeling paper published the *New York Evening Express* account.

7. Chase to M. D. Potter, February 17, 1862, in *The Salmon P. Chase Papers*, vol. 3, ed. John Nivens (Kent, Ohio, 1996), 135; newspaper clippings, LP 10.

were not placing Banks's silent division in a favorable light. This aggravated Williams, who could keep his animosity silent no longer. "I see that Gen'l Lander, in his own report and in the newspaper reports from his Head Quarters, is striving to harvest a very large amount of small fame," Williams complained to General Banks. "To those who know the facts," Williams added, "these high sounding reports and complimentary General Orders are simply ridiculous." Claiming that his own outposts had prevented Jackson from attacking the railroad since he occupied Hancock in January, Williams also belittled Lander's "daring and successful reconnaissance," insisting that it was performed against a disaffected militia force that could not have exceeded 300 men. "I confess to be much irritated with this small puffing," Williams continued, "which, not contented with blowing enormous blasts of self glorification, seeks to gain additional eclat by innuendos of what might have been done if some other General had come to his aid or heeded his far seeing suggestions."[8]

Notwithstanding their mutual disrespect, the B & O Railroad forced Lander and Williams to work closer together. Accompanied by the Andrew Sharpshooters, Lander took the first train to Hancock on Sunday, February 16, to meet with Williams. The train sped so fast that pine forests looked like solid stockades to Lander's bodyguard. Once they crossed the river at Alpine Station, Lander and the sharpshooters were escorted to Williams's headquarters, but Banks's brigadier was absent. Lander left word that he intended to extend his division to cover the railroad to Alpine Station opposite Hancock. Williams, seeing the opportunity to escape Lander's pretentiousness as well as his uncomfortable surroundings, asked Banks to move his brigade toward Hagerstown.[9] The request was denied.

While Lander conducted his round-trip railroad journey to Hancock, another expedition embarked on Bloomery Gap again. Lander's aide-de-

8. Williams to Banks, February 19, 1862, BP 18:4. Writing to his daughter on the same day, Williams declared that "I belong to Gen. Banks' division of the Army of the Potomac. Gen. Lander commands a division of the Army of Western Virginia" (Williams to his daughter, February 19, 1862, in Quaife, *From the Cannon's Mouth*, 60). Williams's ignorance of command structure (both Banks and Lander commanded divisions in McClellan's Army of the Potomac) was exceeded only by claims that he had played the largest role in opening the railroad and had been forbidden to cross into Lander's district. These statements were contradicted by his own dispatches sent to Lander and Kelley one month earlier.

9. Bicknell, "Sharpshooters," 19; A. S. Williams to R. M. Copeland, February 16, 1862, BP 18:4.

camp, Lieutenant Fitz-James O'Brien, led a party of thirty-three horse soldiers from the First Ohio Cavalry on a return mission to confiscate 100 head of cattle reportedly remaining in the area. They departed at 4:00 A.M. that frigid Sunday (the temperature was recorded at sixteen degrees in Cumberland) and retraced the hoof steps that had blazed the trail they used two days earlier.

The Union troops reached the battleground shortly after daybreak and viewed the scene of action that had occurred on the fourteenth. The scouting party then rode eastward on Winchester Road until they viewed some suspect-looking riders ahead. The Federals fired their carbines, which drove the southern horsemen back and out of view around a bend in the road. "Now, boys, go in and do your duty," yelled O'Brien as he led the Federal column forward. Once the Union scouting party rounded the bend, they could see the same horsemen returning, followed by a cluster of twenty cavaliers, all wearing blue overcoats, heading toward them. Neither O'Brien nor his men were fooled by the color of the coats, and they stood in the road as the rebel column approached. When within shouting distance, the southerners halted as well. Colonel Turner Ashby headed the southern squadron, and it was he who made the first gesture.

"Who are you?" he bellowed.

"Union troops, God damn you!" came O'Brien's reply.

Pistol cracks immediately filled the air. O'Brien reeled backwards in his saddle from an ugly bullet wound in his left shoulder. Comrades escorted him rearward while the two bodies of horsemen engaged in a running cavalry duel, which lasted several minutes until the Ohioans fled westward to the Cacapon. The Confederates did not offer an aggressive pursuit, allowing the Union troops to return safely to Paw Paw at sundown. O'Brien was the only casualty; however, two members of the First Ohio took the opportunity to desert from the army. A reward of twenty-five cents worth of tobacco was offered for one of them. The other was deemed even more useless.[10]

Lander was both saddened and angry to see his aide ride into camp

10. "Lovejoy" to the editor, February 20, 1862, *(Washington C.H., Ohio) Fayette County Herald,* February 27, 1862; Temperature readings for Cumberland, Md., February 16, 1862, NWR; Curry, *Four Years in the Saddle,* 234–5. Ashby's service record indicates that he was officially commissioned colonel on February 12, but this may have been pre-dated from a later promotion.

with such a serious wound. No cattle were found, and the pass that he had fought over two days earlier belonged to the Confederates again.

Even the original Bloomery Gap fight had proved to be far from satisfying, particularly the behavior of his cavalry. Lander had earlier asked the War Department what to do about Colonel Anisansel. He believed the options would be to send him off to Governor Pierpont (who had appointed him), call a court-martial, or allow him to resign. The response he received from Secretary Stanton indicated how seriously the War Department considered the matter: "If General Lander is satisfied that Col. Anisanzel [*sic*] was guilty of cowardice and of misbehavior before the enemy he may be tried on the spot, and if found guilty, a sentence of death may be executed on the spot; or he may be cashiered by his commanding general at the head of his regiment. The former course is recommended as the preferable one. Cowardice in an officer exhibited on the field of battle should receive the swift punishment of death."[11]

Stanton's caustic response was quickly snatched up by newspapers throughout the North. The extreme stance shocked the soldiers, who had not expected a sentence of death to be recommended. Not surprisingly, Camp Chase became polarized. There was a strong body of support for Anisansel and an equal show of support for Lander in the matter. The newspaper reports detailing Lander's exploits on February 14 did so in a manner that reminded Lieutenant Colonel Franklin Sawyer (Eighth Ohio) of Napoleon at the bridge of Lodi. Others could see no wrong in their commander. "Gen. Lander is a trump," wrote an Ohioan to his brother. A Pennsylvanian in the ranks concurred. Describing the Bloomery expedition to his Philadelphia friends, a Keystoner used a new name for Lander: "Old Fear Naught."[12]

The strongest voices of disapproval came from the cavalry. They praised Anisansel for halting his command at the gap "to feel the enemy as a careful man should." Some considered Lander to be too harsh. Rumors once

---

11. FWL to GBM, February 16, 1862, MP 48:85960–2; Stanton to GBM, February 16, 1862, MP. Stanton's response was unusual for early in 1862, but would be more common as the war dragged on.

12. *Chambersburg (Pa.) Valley Spirit*, February 26, 1862; Sawyer, *History of the 8th Regiment*, 33; Matthew Schwab to his brother, February 17, 1862, Cincinnati Historical Society; "Keystone" to the editor, February 17, 1862, *Philadelphia Press*, February 25, 1862.

again ripped through Camp Chase that alcohol had led Lander's charge at Bloomery Furnace. "No one doubts General Lander's bravery," wrote a member of Anisansel's regiment to the *Wheeling Daily Intelligencer*, "and he has a kind of savage enthusiasm, well calculated to lead men in battle." The soldier continued with a strong allegation: "but of his fitness, at times, to have command of an army, and especially on the morning of said fight, many who saw him have serious doubts. And the public, we have no doubt, will arrive at the same conclusion if he holds his present position any length of time."[13]

Regardless of the split opinions at Paw Paw, Lander was determined to carry through Colonel Henry Anisansel's court-martial. Official charges were printed at the War Department on Monday, February 17, and officers at Camp Chase received orders to report and testify. It would require approximately one week for the court to convene. In the meantime, Lander's exploits at Bloomery earned him a special invitation from Montgomery Blair to go to Washington for a special George Washington's Birthday celebration for the upcoming Saturday. Lander turned down the invitation due to his workload at division headquarters and his ill health.[14]

Lander had illustrated his contempt for those who did not support his charge near Bloomery Gap. At the same time the general saw to it that those who acted courageously were rewarded for that desired trait. Lander relished his first examples of "judicious promotions." Through the approval of Governor Hicks of Maryland, Lander rewarded John Cannon, the private who charged with the general on February 14, with the commission of lieutenant of cavalry. Harry G. Armstrong was promoted from lieutenant to major for his performance. The promotions were presented at camp as Special Orders Number Twenty. After the promotions were an-

13. Elwood, *Stories*, 88; Aungier Dobbs to his children, February 17, 1862, in *Dear Esther: The Civil War Letters of Private Aungier Dobbs*, ed. Ralph Haas (Apollo, Pa., 1991), 64; "W. S." to the editor, February 28, 1862, *Wheeling (Va.) Daily Intelligencer*, March 5, 1862. The strong accusations against Lander make it impossible to discount the possibility that he was drunk during some portion of the twenty-eight-hour expedition. However, it should be noted that all of the accusers make their observations based on hearsay. None of the accusers appear to have taken part in the expedition, nor did they ever claim to actually have seen Lander drinking. No mention of Lander's "fitness" appeared in the forty-three pages of transcript generated form the Henry Anisansel court-martial case.

14. S. Williams to FWL, February 17, 1862, LP 8:7333–34; Montgomery Blair to FWL, February 17, 1862 LP 3:6572–4.

nounced, the soldiers listened as Lander's promise was read to them: "The General Commanding desires this army to know that his eye is on them. He will always lead them into battle. The humble private in the ranks will receive his commendation and support with the highest office when real true and active duty is done."[15]

Still ailing, Lander shored up his division's position while waiting for what he believed to be the inevitable move to Winchester. He spread his force to cover the railroad for sixty miles—from Cumberland to Hancock. Ten percent of his 12,000-man force lay sick at the Cumberland hospital. Lander procured an assistant surgeon to aid Dr. Suckley there. The help was needed immediately; five soldiers died each day and the medical staff was sorely tested. Overall, the healthiest thing that happened to the Western Division was transferring them from Patterson's Creek to Paw Paw.[16]

Those who worked every day with Frederick Lander in February were forced to endure his tirades more frequently than they ever had before. Lander had chosen his staff to consist of a mix of experienced professionals, friends and sons of friends, and literary artists to provide him with the camaraderie he had experienced on the frontier. He never enjoyed that level of comfort during the war. His responsibilities now covered 10,000 people, not the fifty to sixty stalwarts he had led in the late 1850s, the same number he planned on using for daring lightning strikes when the war commenced. Injuries and illnesses within his staff also soured the general's disposition. Believing him to be a heathen, a staffer was surprised one day to see Lander holding a Bible in his hand. He asked Lander if he ever searched the scriptures. The general responded with an anecdote from his cherished days out West:

My mother gave me a Bible, which I have always carried with me. Once in the Rocky Mountains I had only fifteen pounds of flour. We used to collect grasshoppers, at 4 o'clock in the day, to catch trout for our supper at night. It was during the Mormon war, and my men desired to turn back. I was then

15. "Younger" to the editor, n.d., *Wheeling (Va.) Daily Intelligencer,* February 26, 1862; "From Gen. Lander's Division," February 19, 1862, newspaper clipping, LP 10; Special Orders No. 20, February 19, 1862, John Cannon Service Record, NA.

16. George Suckley to FWL, February 15, 1862, LP 8:7294 and LP 8:7452; "From Gen. Lander's Division," February 19, 1862, newspaper clipping, LP 10; George Suckley to S. F. Barstow, February 20, 1862, LP 8:7361; FWL to R. B. Marcy, February 20, 1862, MP 48:85965.

searching for a route for the wagon road. "I will turn back if the Bible says so," said I, "and we will take it as an inspiration." I opened the book at the following passage:

Go on, and search the mountains, and the gates of the city shall not be shut against you.[17]

Lander's staff was finally convinced that their commander put great faith in the Good Book.

Lander's temper exploded on a rainy Wednesday, February 19. Having occupied Paw Paw for nearly two weeks, the general fumed at not receiving definitive orders to move. Late that night, a gale blew across camp. Tents were uprooted, stoves toppled over, and papers flew in the gusts. The sounds of angry curses and axes pounding tent pins resonated throughout Camp Chase.[18] Lander also stormed across the telegraph lines that night. When General Marcy at the War Department gave him an opening by asking him about preparations to take Winchester, Lander fired back two petulant responses. He pleaded for 4,000 more infantry to assault Winchester; then he appended the request by stating, "If you can't spare them order me to take Winchester and give me authority to burn it." Lander claimed that he had five days of forage readily available and stressed that the C & O towpath should be used as a wagon road (he abandoned the earlier concept of laying railroad tracks across it).

Complaining to Marcy that "Caution rules the hour," Lander offered some suggestions to overhaul the flawed system. Lander longed for the men who accompanied him on the wagon expeditions. He requested the services of Lieutenant James Snyder and Lieutenant George Butler, as well as Colonel Cuvier Grover. "Make Grover a brigadier and give him Williams's command to cooperate with mine. And if I don't take Winchester, hang me," offered Lander. "I am fighting for my country and speak plainly. . . . If you send nothing, still order me on. If I run into a hornets nest, will still give a good account of this command. Tell Genl McClellan that I am all to him that I ever have been, and shall be glad to

17. "From Gen. Lander's Division," February 19, 1862, newspaper clipping, LP 10. Lander did carry his Bible on the frontier, but he did not open it to that particular passage, for no form of it exists in either the Old or New Testaments. He may have embellished the long-forgotten passage in relaying the story, or he may have fabricated the entire anecdote.

18. Thomas Clark to his wife, February 20, 1862, CL; Nathaniel Parmater diary, February 20, 1862, OHS.

obey his orders to the front as in times past—lame leg and ill notwith-standing"[19]

Major Dwight Bannister caught wind of Lander's dispatch in Washington. The staffer was in the capital conducting business for his boss when he learned of Lander's rantings across the telegraph lines. "Keep quiet," Bannister warned his antsy superior, informing him that he would soon be able to run his department as he intended. But Lander could not wait. Shortly before midnight, he wired Secretary Stanton a telegram that was reminiscent of what Marcy had received from him earlier that night. "Give me, sir, men and means, orders to go on, without complimenting for minor successes. Hold me strictly responsible for failure," Lander postured. He implied that his time was running out when he added, "I am never so sick as when I cannot move."[20]

Lander's dispatches became more erratic as his health deteriorated with each passing day. He was convinced that no army could beat his marching, but he also was discouraged to see the men take the complimentary newspaper reports too seriously. Lander became paranoid about the newspapers, believing that political influences dictated their actions. This extended into army operations. "There have been awful stealings in the quartermaster and commissary department here," Lander informed the War Department on February 20. "The officers are prominent Republicans and editors of newspapers. Shall I hang one or two of them or not?"

Politics was responsible for Lander's inactivity—at least as far as he was concerned. In this aspect he sympathized with General McClellan, a fellow Democrat. Lander had earlier warned Secretary Stanton that "the enemy is in my rear, not in my front," referring to the political influences that controlled army operations. The general had been infuriated early in the month by false newspaper accusations that he had criticized President Lincoln. But three weeks later he openly implicated the president as a propagandist when he insinuated to General Marcy that Lincoln wanted the Republican editors to steal from the commissary departments to support their papers. He also criticized Lincoln for not executing former secretary of war Simon Cameron for his derelict activities. Lander no longer appeared concerned about what he transmitted over the telegraph lines. "I do not worship any man," he haughtily explained to McClellan's chief of

19. FWL to Marcy, February 19, 1862, MP 48:85967–8; *OR*, 51(1):534.
20. Bannister to FWL, February 19, 1862, LP 8:7358; *OR*, 51(1):533.

staff. "[I] am free spoken."[21] His messages proved that, but they also exhibited strong evidence of an ill and exasperated commander.

The soldiers in the Western Division did not appear to share the general's frustration. The Bloomery Furnace affair, with its abundant newspaper coverage, appeared to satisfy them for the present. Additionally, the news from the West heartened them considerably. Lander's men were well informed—even the illiterate ones. Most were encamped within two miles of the railroad station. A volunteer from each company could pick up the Wheeling and Columbus papers there just one day after their publication; the Cincinnati, Pittsburgh, and Philadelphia papers were retrieved two days after they came off the presses. The papers were immediately taken from the station into soldiers' tents, where a comrade would read the news aloud while his tent mates cheered.

The Union successes at Forts Henry and Donelson and at Roanoke produced noisy enthusiasm at Camp Chase. Additionally, the victories in the West were formally announced in patriotic style. Regimental commanders read the dispatches to their respective units. An Ohioan in Lander's division represented the sentiment of the majority when he wrote, "[T]he capture of Fort Donelson perfectly electrified us with joy, for we saw the importance of it to our army, and it also demonstrated to the boasting, chivalrous Southerners the fact that the Yankees can fight, and that Secession is played out." The victory also heightened the significance of the Union flag to the soldier. "I really felt proud of the Stars and Stripes, the banner which had been loved and honored by all nations," one of the patriots professed.[22]

Lander ordered the information to be passed to his men and saw to it that the Union successes achieved the greatest impact possible. He placed a premium on morale and realized that a strong feeling of honor and patriotism in his men produced stronger and more focused soldiers. This was particularly important during a winter encampment where complacency hindered success. Although the mid-February inactivity agonized the general, his division rank and file never sensed their commander's frustration nor his illness. Lander refused all serenades and never ventured out

21. FWL to R. B. Marcy, February 20, 1862, MP 48:85965–6.
22. Oliver Wise to the editor, February 24, 1862, *(Canton, Ohio) Starke County Republican,* March 13, 1862; "G. B. C." to the editor, February 20, 1862, *Starke County Republican,* March 6, 1862; "D. G. S." to the editor, February 17, 1862, *Portage County (Ohio) Democrat,* March 5, 1862.

of his headquarters when one was tendered. He did make it a habit to ride to his outposts and visit his pickets. Without fail, the general was greeted with cheers from his men in each of those isolated incidents. Most of the division, however, had yet to see the general in person.[23]

All of that would change on Washington's Birthday. On Friday night, February 21, Lander passed orders for his men to receive their formal division review. Lander chose the anniversary of the birthday of the country's first president to enhance the patriotic atmosphere associated with a grand review. Without negating the importance of Union successes in the West, Lander wished to instill fighting spirit in his men by proving to them that they could not be beat. Granted no permission to steel his men with battle experience, Lander settled on the division review as a panacea for the doldrums that infiltrate a winter encampment and dull the spirit of the volunteer soldier.

"The sun rose beautifully this morning and shone pleasantly over our encampment," wrote Lieutenant Colonel Thomas Clark in his daily letter to his wife. Clark and the other regimental officers brushed their horses, coats, and pants for the official 11:00 A.M. review while others decorated the level campground between the railroad tracks and the river. A salute was fired by one of the batteries at sunrise. High above the cannons, at the top of Grindstone Mountain near Paw Paw, sat four members of the First (Union) Virginia Infantry who, according to one of the quartet, scaled the highest terrain near camp earlier that Saturday morning "to celebrate in a proper manner so important an anniversary as Washington's birthday." The Union Virginians enjoyed a majestic view of the mountainous region around Camp Chase and could see for miles in all directions until the snow-clad peaks blended with the skies near the horizon. One of the infantrymen-turned-mountaineers claimed to hear the distant thunder of General Williams's cannons near Hancock firing their holiday salute into the still air thirty miles away.[24]

The First Virginia foursome clambered down the mountain in time to eat breakfast and participate in the grand celebration. The selected ground was the camp of the Seventh Ohio Infantry. By midmorning it was

23. "From Gen. Lander's Division," February 19, 1862, newspaper clipping, LP 10; Thomas Clark to his wife, February 22, 1862, CL; FWL to R. B. Marcy, February 20, 1862, MP 48:85965.

24. Thomas Clark to his wife, February 22, 1862, CL; "H. J. J." to the editor, February 23, 1862, *Wellsburg (Va.) Herald,* March 7, 1862.

finely trimmed up in evergreen. Arches and mottoes hung over the camp streets. Companies vied with each other for the best decorated quarters. An evergreen "Washington" festooned the main arch near the officers' quarters, surrounded by two national flags. Decorative pine branches laid over the white canvas background of division tents spelled out the names of prominent Civil War field officers. The atmosphere reminded one soldier of a fourth of July celebration.[25]

The festivities had just begun. At 11:00 A.M. each regiment in Lander's division formed and marched across the railroad tracks into the fields near the river. The temperature had warmed into the forties as the brigade commanders briefly addressed their respective units to initiate the celebration. Then the cavalry galloped into camp, wheeled into line on the right, and positioned themselves in the rear of the infantry. Following this dashing display, the order to file by right of companies rear into column was given, initiating the parade. Nearly 10,000 bayonets glistened in the late-winter morning sun. The regimental colors enhanced the spectacle, but the brass bands and the thunderous discharges of artillery defined it as a military pageant. After the short parade, the columns were drawn up in line in anticipation of their division commander and his words of inspiration. At this point Camp Chase fell silent.

Shortly before noon the Twenty-ninth Ohio on the left of the line announced the general's arrival by firing a thirteen-volley salute, each volley followed by a one-minute interval. A few minutes after the final discharge, Frederick Lander appeared on his groomed white mare with his staff trotting close behind him. The commander passed the division line in review. His soldiers were awed at Lander's tall and muscular frame with broad shoulders and finely trimmed beard. Lander rode down the front line, then up the rear line. After passing the left rear of his division the general took position at his designated post while the regiments formed in column by company, each one parading past their general. One of his First (Union) Virginia foot soldiers, passing in front of him, could not forget "the gaze of his eagle eye, which seemed in its fiery brightness to almost look a man through." A member of the Seventh Ohio echoed the observation by describing Lander's "eyes of piercing brilliancy" fixed on the men. The cavalry followed the infantry past the general's reviewing stand.

25. Nathaniel Parmater diary, February 22, 1862, OHS; "Volunteer" to the editor, February 24, 1862, *Painesville (Ohio) Telegraph,* March 6, 1862.

The artillery brought up the rear of the parade. After the field pieces rolled past Lander and his staff, the infantry completed a new formation; they realigned from column by companies into solid squares, waiting to be addressed by the general.[26]

Lander had continuously maintained to the War Department how proud he was of his men and that he believed they were the best material in the entire army. He had now created a perfect atmosphere to let them know it. Lander approached each regiment to personally address them. His speeches, characterized by his punctuated but enthusiastic style, brought home the theme of glorious victories awaiting the men on the horizon. Lander told them that he was pleased with the looks of the men and that there was not one in all of that body of men before him, down to the humblest private, that he did not love, honor, and respect. He promised to do what was right by them, and he asked in return that they obey him. "All I ask is that you follow me where I lead," Lander explained, "and if any are killed, this is just as good a time to die as we can ever have."

Lander continued by highlighting recent Union successes. "Our friends in Tennessee and Kentucky had marched out 50,000 strong and captured 15,000 of the enemy," he reminded the men. He then complimented his division for their soldierly bearing and the firmness with which they had stood up under their recent fatiguing marches. Lander insisted that the Western Division would exceed the accomplishments achieved across the Alleghenies. Rather than march 50,000 against 15,000, the general provoked his men with a proposal to march 20,000 Union troops against an equal number of an entrenched enemy. Even with the diminished odds, he did not expect to fail. "I want every man to stand up to the work and not run as long as an officer was left to command," preached the general, "and if officers and all are killed, except one or two, then they could go home, tell the women they had seen some

---

26. Lorenzo Vanderhoef diary, February 22, 1862, in Martin and Snow, *"I Am Now a Soldier!"* 85; C. J. Rawling, *History of the First Regiment Virginia Infantry* (Philadelphia, 1887), 52; Temperature readings, District of Columbia, February 22, 1862, NWR; "H. J. J." to the editor, February 23, 1862, *Wellsburg (Va.) Herald,* March 7, 1862; "D. G. S." to the editor, February 24, 1862, *(Ravenna, Ohio) Portage County Democrat,* March 12, 1862; Wilhelm H. Styer to his parents, February 23, 1862, Marietta Ohio Public Library; "Volunteer" to the editor, February 24, 1862, *Painesville (Ohio) Telegraph,* March 6, 1862; Nathaniel Parmater diary, February 22, 1862, OHS.

mighty good fighting, seen some good men killed, and had come home to help cry for them."[27]

As Lander completed each speech to the regiments, he was acknowledged by thunderous cheers that "shook the very hills of old Va. and echoed from hill to hill." When Lander addressed the regiments that participated in Colonel Dunning's Blue's Gap expedition in January, he seized the opportunity to illustrate to the men the incidents of their past that he did not want to see repeated. "In this war for the Union, we must respect rights and not go about killing stock and burning houses," declared the general. He went on the stress that the Union army had not left "mothers and sisters at home in tears to come out here and frighten women, but to correct those poor misguided people who had been led astray by designing politicians." He then admonished, "Low and degraded must be the soldier who would willfully and maliciously charge bayonet on a hog, and then dodge behind a stump to hide from his general." Lander warned them that he had issued an order against this kind of behavior, and any man caught violating it would be hanged.

The Bloomery Furnace expedition influenced Lander's speech to his horse soldiers. Lander addressed the cavalry in a short and severe speech that informed them that they held the post of honor, and he was going to give them a chance to retrieve the credit they had lost on February 14. Lander said that he wanted no faltering or holding back; he wanted them to go forward when ordered to do so and not to stop and count the probabilities of being killed or wounded. "Your colonel," said Lander, referring to Henry Anisansel, "is under arrest and will have to answer for the recent want of courage displayed by the men at Bloomery." Lander promised fairness: If Anisansel was found guilty, he had to shoulder the responsibility, and if innocent, he would be cleared.[28]

The Sixty-sixth Ohio and Sixty-seventh Ohio were treated with kinder

27. H. J. J. to the editor, February 23, 1862, *Wellsburg (Va.) Herald,* March 7, 1862; D. G. S. to the editor, February 24, 1862, *(Ravenna, Ohio) Portage County Democrat,* March 12, 1862; "Volunteer" to the editor, February 24, 1862, *Painesville (Ohio) Telegraph,* March 6, 1862; Lorenzo Vanderhoef diary, February 22, 1862, in Martin and Snow, *"I Am Now a Soldier!"* 85; "Quill" to the editor, March 5, 1862, *Cincinnati Daily Commercial,* March 10, 1862; Elijah H. C. Cavins to his wife, March 2, 1862, in *The Civil War Letters of Col. Elijah H. C. Cavins, 14th Indiana,* Barbara A. Smith, comp. (Owensboro, Ky., 1981), 53; William Clohan to his parents, February 24, 1862, Clohan Letters.

28. Nathaniel Parmater diary, February 22, 1862, OHS; H. J. J. to the editor, February 23, 1862, *Wellsburg (Va.) Herald,* March 7, 1862; D. G. S. to the editor, February 24,

words from their commanding general. Theirs was a special ceremony because Lander was presenting the regimental colors to their colonels. He first addressed the Sixty-seventh in stirring words that moved Lieutenant Colonel Alvin C. Voris to write, "General Lander is a very fine speaker. He possesses in a high degree many of the qualities of an orator. . . . He has the power of electrifying those he commands with his own courageous spirit. He is truly a gallant and dashing officer."[29]

Lander delivered his final speech of the day to the Sixty-sixth Ohio. Lander's former aide, Charles Candy, had recently been elected colonel of the new regiment, and took the regimental flag from the general. "You have asked me to present to you this regimental flag," began Lander, "this emblem of the hopes, prayers, and devotion of those at home. Do not soil such memories, do not betray such a trust." As the general continued his words of inspiration, one who stood in the ranks of the Sixty-sixth Ohio studied him closely. "He halted just in front of where I was standing," wrote the soldier. "In every look and word, and gesture, he revealed the force of that iron will and restless energy which had driven the last armed traitor band from his department. There was a significant compression of his lips, a clear, steady directness of his eye. His words were few, but they touched the heart."[30]

Using the example of former private and new lieutenant John Cannon, Lander illustrated to the Buckeyes that if they had faith in themselves, their bravery would also be recognized. Formally transferring the flag to Colonel Candy, Lander ended his last speech of the day with stirring words: "Never desert it. Rally around it while you are alive. It shall wave over you when dead; and if each one of you were to live a thousand years, believe that you can find no nobler opportunity to die than beneath its folds for liberty and the rights of free government, and the cause it represents."[31]

Hurrahs and cheers greeted Lander after he completed his final speech at approximately 4:00 P.M. The general strode back toward his headquarters office while his troops returned to their camps shortly after their respective brigadiers addressed them. The soldiers continued the festivities

1862, (Ravenna, Ohio) Portage County Democrat, March 12, 1862; "Volunteer" to the editor, February 24, 1862, Painesville (Ohio) Telegraph, March 6, 1862.

29. Alvin C. Voris to his wife, February 23, 1862, Alvin C. Voris Papers, Virginia Historical Society, Richmond.

30. "P." to the editor, March 3, 1862, Cincinnati Daily Gazette, March 10, 1862.

31. Newspaper clipping, LP 10.

after dark. They lit bonfires. Large crowds collected around the flames to hear the bands discourse their best patriotic selections. In the camp of the Seventh Ohio, the Buckeyes burned Jefferson Davis in effigy as a unique commemoration of his inauguration as president of the Confederate States of America.[32]

The pageantry and atmosphere had made this day memorable for the soldiers in Lander's Western Division. Lander had never looked better in their eyes, and the men were unified in their praise for their commander. "Every man was proud of his gallant leader," wrote one, "and longed to follow him into battle." A member of the Sixty-seventh Ohio concurred. "He is a man whose appearance and style of speech commands the respect and best wishes of all the men, and one whom we would all be ready to follow into battle."

Even the cavalry, at least the Ohio portion of it, gained more respect for Frederick Lander. "He left no doubt as to his fighting spirit," wrote Samuel Gillespie of the First Ohio, "or that we would see plenty of it while he was in command." The reminders of Union successes and promises of more to come left many to believe that the end of the war was close at hand. The day affected one of Lander's soldiers so much that when he wrote a letter to his sister exactly one year later, he made a point to remember February 22 not as Washington's Birthday, but as the day General Lander held his grand review at Paw Paw.[33]

Lander trotted back to the old schoolhouse immensely proud of what had transpired on the parade ground of Camp Chase. He was particularly confident about his infantry, the arm of his division he described as "gallant" to General McClellan. "If you had seen their faces," explained Lander in writing to McClellan, "you would trust them anywhere."[34]

32. Billy Davis journal, February 22, 1862, in Skidmore, *Civil War Journal,* 103; "H. J. J." to the editor, February 23, 1862, *Wellsburg (Va.) Herald,* March 7, 1862; "D. G. S." to the editor, February 24, 1862, *(Ravenna, Ohio) Portage County Democrat,* March 12, 1862; Thomas Clark to his wife, February 22, 1862, CL.

33. "P." to the newspaper, March 3, 1862, *Cincinnati Daily Gazette,* March 10, 1862; "Jeff" [J. Jeff Parsons] to the editor, February 24, 1862, *Weekly Perrysburg (Ohio) Journal,* March 3, 1862; [Gillespie], *History of Company A,* 55; "Volunteer" to the editor, February 24, 1862, *Painesville Ohio) Telegraph,* March 6, 1862; Joshua Winters to his sister, February 22, 1863, in *Civil War Letters and Diary of Joshua Winters: A Private in the Union Army Company G, First Western Virginia Volunteer Infantry,* ed. Elizabeth Davis Swiger (Parsons, W.Va., 1991), 58–9.

34. FWL to GBM, February 23, 1862, MP 48:85970–1.

Lander maintained that hard marching improved his soldiers' health. Within hours of his grand review, his attention was diverted by the opportunity to march his men and battle his adversary. Colonel Francis B. Pond of the Sixty-second Ohio sent word from his Great Cacapon River outpost that Jackson's division was heading for Bath again. Claiming that two scouts viewed the enemy encamped a mere fifteen miles from the resort town, Pond added that his intelligence informed him that the Union citizens living along the Winchester-Bath road were taking to the woods in great numbers.[35]

The prospect of battle stirred Lander's passion, which was already close to peaking from the inspirational atmosphere fostered by his grand review. "If [Jackson] is ass enough to do this," warned Lander concerning Stonewall's offensive action, "I will move on his rear via Bloomery Furnace and beat him to death." But the opportunity to act out his promise never materialized. Pond's information turned out to be erroneous, for Jackson apparently had no intentions of venturing north. In fact, his Martinsburg outpost had evacuated their stations and returned to Winchester. Unsubstantiated reports also claimed reinforcements arriving from Manassas to strengthen Jackson's position in the Lower Shenandoah Valley. Disappointed, Lander settled back into the prospect of prolonged inactivity.[36]

On Monday morning, February 24, eleven officers entered Lander's headquarters and began their proceedings in the court-martial trial of Colonel Henry Anisansel of the First (Union) Virginia Cavalry. Anisansel faced two charges of "misbehavior before the enemy." Two witnesses testified the first day, and four more took the stand the second day to bolster the prosecution's case. Despite the presence of Colonel Kimball and Colonel Carroll to support his claims, Lander realized that he would not win the case. His prize witness, Lieutenant Fitz-James O'Brien, lay in Cumberland with a shattered shoulder and would be unavailable to testify.[37]

Conspicuously absent from the first day of the trial at headquarters was the commanding general. Another attack of the "congestive chills" forced Lander to his bed. He languished there all of that Monday, reeling from an excruciating headache. Lander's deteriorating health had become more

35. Pond to FWL, February 22, 1862, LP 8:7392
36. FWL to GBM, February 22, 1862, MP 48:85969; *OR*, 51(1):535; FWL to GBM, February 24, 1862, MP 48:85972.
37. HA; FWL to his wife, February 25, 1862, LP 11.

disconcerting to those who worked with him. The episodic attacks were more frequent and appeared to be more violent. Despite suggestions from his staff, the general had refused to ease his schedule and continued to keep late hours at the telegraph office, transmitting messages into the early morning hours. His schedule and the stress of his responsibilities had exacerbated his symptoms.[38]

Somehow Jean Lander received word in Washington about her husband's latest setback. Feeling much better the next morning, Lander attempted to assuage her fears. "Don't worry so—ride your horse, and be cheerful," he wrote. Predicting Anisansel's acquittal to her in the same letter, Lander proved prophetic. Without having to call any defense witnesses, Anisansel was found not guilty of both charges on February 27.[39]

Lander did not dwell over the result of the proceedings, for the War Department had ordered another movement for his division. Facing overwhelming pressure from the Lincoln administration, McClellan sent orders for Banks's men to cross the Potomac at Harpers Ferry to begin an advance toward Winchester. Lander received instructions to hold his command at Paw Paw until Banks's crossing was completed. Then the Western Division was to advance east of Hancock to cover the B & O Railroad while it was reconstructed from Hancock to Harpers Ferry. The final stage of the plan was for Lander and Banks to advance on Winchester together.[40]

Lander welcomed the news. He had recently received a letter from John Garrett, president of the B & O Railroad, who informed Lander that Secretary Stanton was prepared to place Lander at the head of an independent department. Lander was further intrigued by McClellan's hints of an important role in the eastern theater, including the Urbanna Campaign. Promising Lander a full share in the pending operations, McClellan went on to discuss what would happen after he captured Winchester. "When this affair is over I shall wish to take you with some of your best troops on a far more important expedition," wrote McClellan on February 25. But he left Lander in the dark about the specifics of the mission.[41]

38. *New York Herald,* March 6, 1862, Scrapbook.

39. HA; F. W. Lander to Mrs. Lander, February 25, 1862, LP 11.

40. *OR,* 5:725–6; *OR,* 51(1):535–9.

41. Garrett to FWL, February 19, 1862, Garrett Letters, MS 1816, Maryland Historical Society, Baltimore; *OR,* 51(1):539. It is possible that Garrett and McClellan were dis-

Preston Blair filled in the gaps left by McClellan. Blair's letter provided a belated response to Lander's heartfelt pleas sent one day after his return from the Bloomery Furnace expedition. Blair lifted Lander's spirits by unmasking the mission that was to be enacted after Richmond was captured. "If we win a great battle and disperse the rebels," revealed Blair, "then your partisan skills will be brought into requisition. You will have a separate command." Blair continued that Lander would be given a special assignment "to overhaul and destroy the fragments of the broken army to catch and bring to judgement the vile leaders who plotted the ruin of our noble republic."

Lander was undoubtedly pleased at the news. The administration had earlier denied him the opportunity to organize a semiguerilla force composed of his wagon road men; now they had turned completely around to allow Lander to use his special talents in an important scavenger operation. But Lander could not afford to look ahead. Conquering Winchester and the Shenandoah Valley remained a major obstacle for the general and his division. Blair was aware of another complicating factor—Lander's health. "You ought not chafe under the obstacles to your immediate progress," Blair told Lander, "but to nurse your impaired strength."[42]

As February waned through its final days, Harpers Ferry became the focus of Union operations. In addition to Banks's planned crossing McClellan had ordered up two other divisions, commanded by Brigadier Generals Erasmus Keyes and John Sedgwick, to head up the Potomac and cross behind Banks. Concomitantly, Joseph Hooker's division was ordered to move downriver to effect a crossing into the tidewater region of Virginia.[43] McClellan's two-pronged effort was designed to force Confederate general Joseph E. Johnston to move from his Centreville and Manassas defenses and commit his troops either to the Valley or toward Richmond to counter the dual threat.

---

cussing two different future roles for Lander. Garrett referred to a B & O command on February 19; six days later McClellan appeared to see Lander as a better fit in southern Virginia.

42. Blair to FWL, February 26, 1862, LP 3:6611–12.

43. Sears, *Papers of George B. McClellan*, 192–5. It is noteworthy that McClellan's movements could have played out the strategy Lander presented to the Joint Committee on the Conduct of the War in December; i.e., occupying the gaps in the Blue Ridge Mountains and pressuring the Confederates in Virginia from the west. No evidence exists to suggest that McClellan's Shenandoah Valley force was designed to stay there after they maneuvered General Johnston out of his Centreville and Manassas trenches.

Lander's role was spelled out on Wednesday night, February 26. Not only was McClellan conducting a dual movement in Virginia, he was attempting a two-pronged thrust toward Winchester. General Marcy instructed Lander to march his men through Bloomery Gap and approach Winchester from the northwest. McClellan would personally escort Banks's men southward through Charlestown to strike at Winchester from the north. A regiment of cavalry and four batteries of heavy artillery were ordered up to add to the Federal firepower at the mouth of the Valley. With Keyes's and Sedgwick's men in tow, the Federal plan to wrest Winchester from Confederate control appeared to be a foregone conclusion.

An unconscionable blunder obliterated the plan. McClellan supervised the crossing of two brigades of Banks's division, 8,500 soldiers, along with eighteen field pieces late in the afternoon of February 26. Canal boats were floated northward on the C & O to provide stable bridge supports for the heavier supplies and the remainder of the force. It seems that the engineers who sent the boats never measured the width of the lift locks near Harpers Ferry. The locks turned out to be six inches too narrow to allow the boats to pass through. An embarrassed McClellan canceled all movements in the early afternoon of February 27. The War Department was incredulous. "If the lift-lock is not big enough why cannot it be made big enough?" naively asked Secretary Stanton. Informed that the locks' walls needed to be knocked out and reconstructed, Stanton acceded to McClellan's revision to hold his forces already in Virginia north of Winchester until the railroad behind them was repaired.[44]

Intensifying the Union's embarrassment, a detachment of Confederates burned the railroad bridge near Lander's old camp at Patterson's Creek. The damage was slight and the span was repaired by midnight. The destruction of his former headquarters did not upset Lander nearly as much as McClellan's change of plans. "Little Mac" led Banks's men into Charlestown on the morning of February 28 but had no immediate designs to attack Winchester. Returning to Sandy Hook near Harpers Ferry, McClellan informed President Lincoln that he merely planned on supplying his troops in Virginia and it would be "many days" before he endeavored to take Winchester. He instructed Lander to move his men to Martinsburg and focus his attention on rebuilding the railroad. "Cause re-

44. *OR*, 5:730–1.

pairs of railroad to be pushed as rapidly as possible," wrote McClellan to Lander, "so as to draw your supplies from the West." Lander also was informed that General Williams would meet him at Martinsburg, then Lander was to move eight miles southward to the hamlet of Bunker Hill. "Get free of this business," wired McClellan to his subordinate, hinting to Lander the future role Blair had already revealed to him. "I want you with me in another direction."[45]

Lander studied the dispatches at the telegraph office with his friend and adjutant, Captain Simon F. Barstow, who had recently recovered from his bout of the measles. While Barstow's health was improving, Lander's was worsening; his gaunt and pale appearance was striking. Lander was in obvious pain but he refused to rest; too much responsibility rested on his weakening shoulders. Studying the maps, he was still lucid enough to understand that McClellan's instructions invited an attack by Jackson's force around Winchester. He would march his 11,000 men through Bloomery Gap, advance his division eastward on Winchester Road to Unger's Store, then take Martinsburg Pike and head northward to Martinsburg. Believing the rumors that Jackson had been reinforced at Winchester, Lander wired McClellan that he expected Jackson to move on his exposed flank as he advanced to link with Williams.

Later on the night of February 28, Lander appeared to relish the possibility of being attacked. Wiring a midnight message to McClellan, Lander expected his movement to initiate a battle. "I will fight my way to the point you name," proposed Lander, "clearing the country as I go and getting in south of Martinsburg so as to catch some of the Rebels if I can. . . . You will oblige me by telling General Banks that if he hears heavy firing near Mills Gap on March 3d—it is my column. My rear will be changed to Cherry Run. It will take 10 days hard work to open railroad to Martinsburg. My tents and baggage will go by rail to Cherry Run, thus if the enemy gives me a battle enroute he will gain nothing but a hard brush. Start early tomorrow."[46]

45. Ibid.; *OR*, 51(1):543–4; McClellan, *McClellan's Own Story*, 195. The exact role that McClellan had intended for Lander has never been elucidated. It is clear that McClellan's reference to "another direction" intended Lander to work with him in some capacity on the Peninsula Campaign. One can speculate that given Blair's letter and McClellan's dispatch, Lander could have been involved in an independent mission for the Army of the Potomac—perhaps a rapid flank movement to come in toward Richmond from the west.

46. FWL to GBM, February 28, 1862 (2), MP: 48:85978, 85980.

Lander did not understand his superior's intentions. McClellan no longer entertained the plan of a quick thrust at Winchester, since the possibility existed that General Jackson had been receiving reinforcements. Four days earlier Lander had desired to pit his 10,000 men against what he believed to be 12,000 Confederates, exclaiming, "I think our Western troops would like nothing better than to engage an equal or superior force." It is what he promised his men during the Washington's Birthday review. Not knowing that Jackson had merely 4,000 men in and around Winchester, McClellan believed Stonewall was reinforced to nearly 20,000 men. Still, with Banks's, Sedgwick's, and Lander's divisions, McClellan had a Federal counter strength of 32,000 officers and men present for duty with seventy-five cannons. But McClellan preferred to wait. Taking every precaution, he wished Lander to arrive at Martinsburg by rail rather than sweep his men north of Winchester and risk a fight.[47]

Buglers woke the westerners early on Saturday morning, March 1. The soldiers were greeted by clear skies and temperatures in the teens. Receiving orders the previous night to have three days' cooked rations packed in their haversacks with sixty rounds of ammunition, Camp Chase bustled with the early morning activity. Two brigades were scheduled to march off in the afternoon; the rest would join them later. At 4:00 P.M. Colonel John Mason's artillery brigade set off with twenty-four cannons, the Fourth and Eighth Ohio, and the Ringgold Cavalry. They headed southward on Winchester Pike, heading straight for the Forks of the Cacapon where they would cross onto Winchester Road and head eastward toward Unger's Store. Following Mason's men were Tyler's five regiments. They veered off to the east a few miles south of camp and retraced Lander's February 14 route to Bloomery Furnace; the pontoon bridge was in place across the Great Cacapon River. Tyler's men encamped at the river bank that night and awaited orders.[48]

---

47. FWL to GBM, February 24, 1862, MP 48:85872–3; *OR* 5:732. McClellan quickly recovered from the lift-lock disaster to concentrate a formidable force in the northern Shenandoah Valley. It would take another week before information from deserters convinced him that Jackson never received reinforcements. Understandably, McClellan did not want to risk any battle until that information was obtained and sent Lander orders: "The route I wished you to take was by railroad to Hancock and Sleepy Creek, thence direct to Martinsburgh [*sic*]" (GBM to FWL, March 1, 1862, LP 3:6626).

48. Lorenzo Vanderhoef diary, March 1, 1862, in Martin and Snow, *"I Am Now a Soldier!"* 87; Temperature records for March 1, 7:00 A.M. Cumberland, Md., and the

Kimball's men stayed at Paw Paw, assured that they would soon be following their division mates. Believing Lander's division was a part of a grand movement by the Federals south of the Potomac, a confident Captain Elijah H. C. Cavins of the Fourteenth Indiana pulled out a pencil and paper and wrote his wife, "I have no doubt of the results. The enthusiasm of the soldiers, increased by our recent success in the west, will cheer us on to victory. If this movement is as extensive as I think it is, and we achieve a perfect success, I think the rebellion will soon be crushed, and we can return to our homes, and enjoy the smiles of those we love." Cavins asked his spouse to ease his mother's worries. Harking back to the memorable division review, he reminded her, "As Gen. Lander said to us a few days ago (the 22nd Feb.) we could not die in a better cause, if it becomes necessary for us to die."[49]

Captain Cavins was destined for a sorrowful disappointment. He was not informed of McClellan's desire to sit and wait for the railroad to be repaired. Despite the change of plans, the greatest threat to Union success in northwest Virginia was not McClellan's caution. Cavins did not realize it, but the greatest obstacle to "a perfect success" occupied a house 100 yards away from the captain's tent. The house was Frederick Lander's headquarters. In it, the general lay incapacitated in his bed.

The "congestive chills" had returned for the final time.

District of Columbia, NWR; Thomas Clark to his wife, February 28 and March 1, 1862, CL; "H. J. J." to the editor, March 7, 1862, *Wellsburg (Va.) Herald*, March 14, 1862; "Quill" to the editor, March 5, 1862, *Cincinnati Daily Commercial*, March 10, 1862; *OR*, 51(1):545. Lander's Bloomery Gap route was in direct violation of McClellan's March 1 telegram (see ref. 48). Did Lander recklessly disobey orders from his superior? Subsequent events may indicate that Lander did not receive the telegram in time. A February 25 dispatch from Lander to McClellan (M504, NA) proves that the rail route was previously discussed. At that time, Lander noted his concerns with this approach: "Railroad transportation being very slow, whatever they may say to the contrary, and no wagon road along the river I can take. The country is stripped of forage and grows worn as we go east and south." McClellan still preferred this route but apparently did not make this clear to Lander until March 1, perhaps after Lander had already begun to advance toward Bloomery Gap.

49. Elijah H. C. Cavins to his wife, March 1, 2, 1862, in Smith, *Civil War Letters*, 53–5.

12

"Bravest of the Brave"

Has it then come for me—the fatal moment
    When I must know the idol feet are clay,
When I must feel thou owest me atonement
    For having held my worship for a day.
                —F. W. Lander

Captain Simon Barstow was not comfortable in his unexpected role as a division commander. At noon on March 2 he was forced to make a second difficult decision. The first one had taken place at 5:00 P.M. on March 1, merely one hour into the movement out of Camp Chase. As Colonel Mason and Colonel Tyler led their brigades southward, Lander had sickened to the point of delirium. At the advice of two brigade surgeons, Barstow agreed to sedating the general with morphine, realizing that this would incapacitate him for several hours. Accordingly, Barstow sent couriers to Tyler and Mason at midnight to inform them of Lander's illness and tell them to hold their positions until the general was lucid enough to join them. Barstow expected his friend to wake with the same energy and exuberance he displayed after his previous bouts with the "congestive chills."

But this time close to a day had passed and Lander remained unconscious. Making matters worse was the weather; three inches of snow had fallen over the region and the gray skies indicated that it was not likely to let up. Barstow had refrained from informing the War Department about Lander's health, hoping against hope that he would recover quick enough to render alarming them unnecessary. Then Barstow read a wire that McClellan transmitted to Banks, one that wondered where Lander and his men were because they should already be at Martinsburg. It had finally dawned on McClellan that Lander may have taken the direct road to Bunker Hill from Bloomery Gap rather than the northern rail approach. Fearing the same danger that Lander had invited, McClellan expressed his desire to recall his wayward subordinate.[1]

At 1:00 P.M. the War Department learned that Lander was not wayward after all. "General Lander has been sleeping under the influence of morphine for twenty hours," came Barstow's shocking message across the wires. Describing the storm that struck the region, Barstow declared that he would order Mason and Tyler back to camp with their men if he did not receive contrary orders.[2]

Lieutenant Colonel Thomas Clark, an officer in Tyler's brigade, commanded the Twenty-ninth Ohio in place of the ill Colonel Lewis P. Buckley. Up since 4:00 A.M., Clark was with his command near the Great Cacapon River when he received word that Lander was ill. Always accusing his commanding general of being a hopeless drunk, Clark remained unsympathetic at the news. "It's a cursed shame that Gen Lander is sick every time there is anything on hand," he complained in a noon-time note to his wife. Two hours later, an impatient Clark wrote another short slip to her. "Hold on," he continued, "Here's a messenger horse all in a foam. Orders to march from Gen. Lander. But darn it all, it's to countermarch. Thunder!"[3]

The orders did not come from Lander, but rather from Simon Barstow. Still clinging to some optimism for the general's recovery, he wired General McClellan again at 2:00 P.M., this time telling him of the recall. Acknowledging that Lander was likely to be incapacitated "for many days," Barstow nevertheless remained deluded about his friend's prognosis. "Lander has so much determination and energy, that he may rise from his sick bed to-day and take command," he declared. However, with the general unconscious for twenty-two hours, hope was fading fast. George

1. *OR*, 51(1):544.
2. *OR*, 51(1):544–6.
3. Thomas Clark to his wife, March 2, 1862, CL.

Suckley, the naturalist and division medical director, arrived from Cumberland and quickly made his way to Lander's room. Looking down on the shadow of what once was a vibrant explorer, he was shocked and disappointed. He told Barstow there was no chance for Lander's recovery and supplied him with a probable timetable of his death. As Tyler's and Mason's commands trekked back to Camp Chase, Barstow wired another message to McClellan with a simple prognosis: "Lander cannot last an hour."[4]

The few who were privy to the information were stunned at the news wired from Paw Paw. The general had complained about his health for one month, yet the War Department believed the illness to be sudden. Jean Davenport Lander was well aware of the progress of the disease. She was taken to Secretary Chase's house, where a friend informed her of the condition of her husband. Wanting to be with him in his final moments, Mrs. Lander desperately attempted to gain transportation to Camp Chase.[5]

The headquarters staff awaited the inevitable. Barstow remained at the schoolhouse to man the telegraph. He informed Colonel Nathan Kimball to stand by, for he was about to inherit a division. Lander's force, 5,000 soldiers in and around camp, with an equal number returning to Paw Paw, had not known how sick the general was. An air of resentment existed about the timeliness of the illness. Lieutenant Colonel Thomas Clark returned to camp before the rest of Tyler's Brigade and learned that Lander was dying. Not understanding the course of the general's sepsis, the teetotaling Clark had maintained that Lander's health problems were linked to the bottle. "It is known that he was drunk yesterday," the misinformed officer wrote on hearing the news, "and today Delirium Tremens as usual." Captain J. H. Robinson's company of First Ohio Cavalry waited outside of the headquarters building. Their horses had been hitched with saddles on since the morning. By late afternoon, all were aware that they were going nowhere.[6]

Dr. Suckley stayed with the general in his room, where he kept a silent vigil. He and Barstow were two of only a few at Paw Paw who had known Lander during the days he was the dominant presence known as "Old

4. *OR*, 51(1):546.

5. Newspaper clippings, LP 10.

6. Thomas Clark to his wife, March 2, 1862, CL; "Lovejoy" to the editor, March 4, 1862, *(Washington C.H., Ohio) Fayette County Herald*, March 13, 1862.

Grizzly." But the disease had ravaged Suckley's patient. It had sapped his strength, consumed his muscle, paled his skin, and deflated his cheeks. A weaker man would have succumbed weeks before, but Lander had somehow hung on. Perhaps the promise of action, battle, and success had carried him to the extent of his physical limits.

Suckley watched Lander move in his bed shortly after 4:30 P.M. Lander had overcome tremendous obstacles time and time again. His work was not complete; he still had much to do. He had pulled himself out of a similar state one month earlier, but it could not happen again—this time the infection had conquered his body. The rally was cut short as Lander lapsed into a deep and irreversible coma. His vital signs diminished rapidly. The promises made to him had been broken. There was no need to fight anymore. At 5:00 P.M., Lander surrendered.[7]

Dr. Suckley announced Lander's death to Barstow at the telegraph office. Barstow was beside himself with grief, but he was also bitter. Why didn't the War Department allow Lander to resign? They had talked him out of it two weeks earlier. They did not take Lander seriously; now it was too late. He could not forgive Washington for its cavalier approach to Lander's complaints, for neglecting his department, for impeding the success he had earned. A loyal adjutant to the last, Barstow's bitterness accompanied his next message transmitted across the wires:

> From Paw Paw, 5 P.M.
> Major Genl G. B. McClellan
>   Genl Lander has just died without suffering. This campaign killed him for he held on in spite of failing health and strength, to the last. I have turned over the command to Col. Kimball.
>   I would respectfully ask that I may be permitted to accompany the remains of my old friend and commander to their final resting place.
> signed
> S. F. Barstow
> A. A. G.[8]

Barstow then wired the news to Thomas Key to deliver to Jean Lander. Another family friend, G. H. Penfield, volunteered as the liaison. Fifteen minutes earlier he had broken the news to her that her husband would not live one more hour. Shortly after 5:00 P.M. he announced Lander's death

---

7. Barstow to GBM, March 2, 1862, MP 46:85981; *OR,* 51(1):546.
8. Barstow to GBM, March 2, 1862, MP 47:85986.

to her. "Mrs. L. takes it hard," wired Penfield to Barstow. Other intimates of the general appeared equally shocked. Thomas Key spoke collectively for them when he telegraphed Barstow, "I have lost a true friend. The country has lost its bravest soldier."[9]

At Paw Paw, Lander's death was announced by hanging a banner, looped with black crape, outside his window. The news stunned his soldiers. Captain Elijah H. C. Cavins of the Fourteenth Indiana was encamped close to headquarters the whole time and never knew that Lander was even ill. "A great man has fallen!" he announced to his wife, with none of the sanguine optimism of a quick end to the war that he had felt one day earlier. "I feel the whole program on the Potomac will be retarded by his death," he sorrowfully predicted. A member of the same regiment felt the same shock, telling his wife that it is "hard to realize that the strong man we had seen dashing along the front of our line in every word look and act a warrior was now helpless in death, that the light of those cold, piercing eyes has gone out."

"Eyes filled with tears as we silently returned to our old quarters," claimed a member of the Fourth Ohio in Tyler's brigade. "We had first known him at Rich Mountain, as the noble, brave, daring and fearless Lander. A great and noble man has fallen." Captain Marcus Spiegel of the Sixty-seventh Ohio was in the middle of writing a letter to his wife when a messenger entered his tent and announced the news. "Such is life," continued the philosophical officer, "8 days ago he presented a flag to our regiment and reviewed 20,000 troops, spoke to all of them and as he came charging along our lines upon his noble steed, erect, powerful, and manly, respected and loved by all, one would have thought, O but for a glorious career of glory as the General may expect and all would be well, and today he is no more."[10]

Spiegel was incorrect in his assertion that Lander was loved by all. "He is gone with no regrets by me," wrote a member of the Ringgold Cavalry, adding "and I am not alone." Lieutenant Colonel Clark concurred. "If a

9. Barstow to Key, March 2, 1862, LP 3:6633; Penfield to Barstow, March 2, 1862, LP 3:6629; Key to Barstow, March 2, 1862, LP 3:6637.

10. "Lovejoy" to the editor, March 4, 1862, *(Washington C.H., Ohio) Fayette County Herald*, March 13, 1862; Elijah H. C. Cavins to his wife, March 2, 1862, in Smith, *Civil War Letters*, 55; Augustus Van Dyke to his wife, March 4, 1862, Van Dyke Papers, IHS; Kepler, *Fourth Ohio*, 58; Marcus Spiegel to his wife, March 2, 1862, in Soman and Byrne, *Jewish Colonel*, 52.

great military display is called for at his funeral, I'm afraid I shall be reported unfit for duty," he informed his wife. Following the camp rumor that Lander was a hopeless alcoholic, a private in the First (Union) Virginia shrugged off his death by informing his family, "I think that he had probably been drunk as usual." A member of the Sixty-sixth Ohio shunned all emotion in describing the incident to his wife. "I am very sorry to lose such a good man," wrote John Rathborn to his wife, "but we all must die sooner or later." A semiliterate private in the Eighty-fourth Pennsylvania followed the cue of the Buckeye's detachment when he told his girlfriend, "Our General took sick and dide and spolt all the fun."[11]

Since he was an unknown entity to most of the Confederates, Lander's death produced little impact in the South. In Winchester, the town that had been Lander's objective since he entered the western Virginia theater in January, Lander's death received no notice in the town's papers, but he did receive mention in at least one citizen's diary. One of the town's secessionists was Kate Sperry, an eighteen-year-old belle who lived with her grandparents in Winchester while her father, Warden Warren Sperry, served in the Confederate army. Kate had known Lander during the 1850s; according to her diary, "he and pa were quite intimate before the war." When she received intelligence of Lander's death, she noted the irony produced by civil warfare by claiming that he "*always* swore that he was a good Southerner and then accepted a Brigadier generalship in the Federal Army—he was from Mass. and a splendid looking man—over 6 ft. high and so handsome . . . —to think of his being so near us with a hostile force."[12]

News of Lander's death trickled into northern papers beginning on the morning of March 3. Nathaniel P. Willis, the poet who was mesmerized by Lander's dominating presence, took a seat at the breakfast table at Willard's Hotel that Monday morning. Engaging in what he called "war talk" with an impatient and ambitious young officer, Willis playfully suggested that he attempt to gain a position on General Lander's staff. Explaining to the young soldier Lander's admirable attributes, the old poet glanced

11. Aungier Dobbs to his wife, March 3, 1862, in Haas, *Dear Esther,* 67; Thomas Clark to his wife, March 2, 1862, CL; William Clohan to his parents, March 4, 1862, Clohan Letters (private collection); John N. Rathborn to his wife, March 3, 1862, in Rathborn Letters, United States Army Military History Institute, Carlisle, Pa.; Henry E. Kyler to Maggie Welch, March 4, 1862, Kyler Letters, Clearfield County Historical Society, Clearfield, Pa.

12. Kate Sperry diary, March 7, 1862, Handley Library, Winchester, Va., 138–9.

down at the half-opened morning paper and immediately ceased his conversation. A headline made his entire discussion obsolete: "Death of
Brigadier General Lander."[13]

One of Lander's closest friends and confidants was overcome with grief
when he heard the news. William D. Northend had shared years of his
childhood with Lander hunting and trapping after school. The friends
kept in close contact through frequent correspondence during the first
year of the war. Northend had kept such a close interest in Lander's activities that tallying his course, acts, and successes, Northend said, had given
him "as much pleasure and pride as if he had been my only brother." He
traveled that Sunday from Boston to Salem where the bells tolled for
General Lander and a special session of the legislature was called to pass a
resolution of sympathy to be sent to Jean Lander.

Northend traveled to Edward Lander's home on Summer Street where
he called on Fred's grieving father and sisters. He spoke to the sisters of a
letter their brother had sent him on Lander's last birthday and went on to
describe that Lander had noted in the margin that he was thirty-nine years
old. The women were startled at their brother's pronouncement and
pulled out the family bible to demonstrate to Northend that Fred was actually forty years old. Northend then realized that his boyhood chum had
held secrets that lasted his lifetime.[14]

On Sunday morning, March 3, 1862, Lander's division at Paw Paw
paid their last respects to his remains. While the 11,000 soldiers formed
two lines near the railroad tracks, Lander's headquarter's staff dressed his
body and finished their preparations to send him by train to Washington.
The general's size denied him a suitable coffin; the worthy one procured
was too small, so the general was placed in a simple pine box. A photogra-
pher took a final picture of the dead warrior. "I have just now turned away
from looking at him as he sleeps in death; with his gray locks resting upon
his pillow, and limbs straightened to go down the dark valley," limned one
witness in Paw Paw headquarters. "But even in death, he wears the in-
signia of power and heroic self sacrifice that gave him that mastering influence that charmed every patriot in his division."[15]

13. N. P. Willis, "General Lander," March 3, 1862, *Home Journal,* clipping in Scrapbook.
14. Northend to Jean Lander, March 4, 1862, LP 11.
15. Thomas Clark to his wife, March 3, 1862, CL; "P." to the editor, March 3, 1862,
Cincinnati Daily Gazette, March 10, 1862.

A chilling rainstorm pounded the Western Division soldiers as they stood silent in formation across Camp Chase. Their two lines stretched for approximately three-quarters of a mile from the general's quarters to the railroad tracks. They were ready by noon but remained in line two hours with the temperature in the midthirties, as Lander's last appearance was delayed. "I hope they will not have any general die soon and if they do I would like for them to die and be buried on a warm day," grumbled Captain Spiegel of the Sixty-seventh Ohio.

Inside headquarters, the chaplain completed his anointment and the coffin was closed. Someone wrapped an American flag around Lander's box, then adorned it with his hat and sword resting on top. Eight regimental officers picked up Lander's coffin and carried him out the door of his headquarters. A solitary cannon initiated the outdoor ceremony with a round from the brow of a nearby hill. The procession was led by two bands playing Webster's "Funeral March." They were followed by the pallbearers while the Andrew Sharpshooters and the Seventh Ohio marched behind the coffin with guns in their respectful "reverse arms" position.

The procession slowly marched between the two lines of silent soldiers—over 5,000 men on each side of the road—toward a waiting train. The rain never let up, symbolic of the stormy last days of the deceased. Slowly the cortege marched with measured tread to the railroad cars. The bands struck up the melancholy and majestic tune "Old Hundred" as the pallbearers lifted the general's coffin into one of the cars. Captain Barstow, twenty members of the Andrew Sharpshooters, and other staff members filed into empty seats. The steam engine of the locomotive drowned out the soft dirges played by the bands. In minutes, Lander's remains and his escorts rolled eastward on the tracks, through the railroad tunnel, and out of the soldiers' view. "Farewell brave Lander, Farewell," closed a newspaper correspondent who witnessed the event.[16]

16. Thomas Clark to his wife, March 3, 1862, CL; Billy Davis, March 3, 1862, in Skidmore, *Civil War Journal*, 109; Temperature readings, District of Columbia, 2:00 P.M., and Cumberland, Md., 7:00 A.M., March 3, 1862, NWR; Marcus Spiegel to his wife, March 4, 1862, in Soman and Byrne, *Jewish Colonel*, 56–7; "H. J. J." to the editor, March 7, 1862, *Wellsburg (Va.) Herald*, March 14, 1862; "Lovejoy" to the editor, March 4, 1862, *(Washington C.H., Ohio) Fayette County Herald*, March 13, 1862; George Wood diary, March 4, 1862, OHS; Oliver Wise to the editor, March 4, 1862, *(Canton, Ohio) Starke County Republican*, March 16, 1862; "P." to the editor, March 3, 1862, *Cincinnati Daily Gazette*, March 10, 1862.

Lander's destination was Washington. His cortege rode along the B & O line to Hancock where the reconstruction of the tracks had been completed. From there his coffin was placed on a wagon and taken to Frederick. Lander's body reversed the steps it took two months earlier; this time returning to Washington on the B & O by way of Baltimore. In the meantime, many of his division soldiers wrote home about what had transpired at Paw Paw over the past two days. Many offered brief reflections about their late general to their family, friends, and hometown neighbors. George Washington Lambert of the Fourteenth Indiana, who claimed that the men around him reacted to the news of Lander's death with joy rather than sorrow, closed his last journal entry concerning Lander on March 3: "Thus ended the career of one of the most daring and strong headed men the world ever knew."[17] Captain George Wood of the Seventh Ohio felt just the opposite of Lambert's mates on hearing the fateful news. Fascinated by Lander's commanding appearance and resolute leadership while living, the general's loss moved Wood to enter his own eulogy in his diary:

> Lander was a brave man and an able commander. In his death the service has lost one of its best men. In battle he exposed himself, disdaining to stand back and see his brave soldiers fall without meeting the same dangers himself. He was very eccentric in his habits and required the utmost promptness on the part of those around him—rewarding the brave and manly whether under shoulder straps or a musket, and punishing those severely who were negligent in performing their duty or who displayed cowardice in any way whatever. He despised little things. In the army he was rough and unpolished but I am told that at home he was a polished gentleman. In his speech he was short and to the point, never using any but the plainest terms. In stature he was tall and slender, with sharp features and a piercing black eye—long hair which hung in slight curls on his neck. I esteemed him a great man and general.[18]

Lander's coffin reached Washington on Wednesday, March 5, at 2:00 A.M. After a mortician embalmed Lander's corpse, it lay for public viewing at Secretary Salmon Chase's home on the corner of Sixth and E Street, where it remained for the rest of the day and throughout the morning of March 6. As members of the Andrew Sharpshooters stood guard over their fallen leader, hundreds of visitors entered Chase's parlor to pay their

---

17. George Washington Lambert journal, March 3, 1862, IHS.
18. George Wood diary, March 4, 1862, OHS.

final respects to Lander. President Lincoln, his cabinet, and Generals McClellan, McDowell, McCall, and Silas Casey were among the prominent officials who entered Chase's mansion to view Lander's body dressed in full uniform with a sash tied around his waist and sword at his side.

Lander's coffin closed at noon to expose a silver tablet on the lid inscribed with four lines. Lander's name, rank, and date of death appeared on the first two lines; his refuted age of thirty-nine years took up the third line. The fourth line bore a title that few could dispute—"Bravest of the Brave." Once again, an American flag draped the coffin. A wreath and Lander's cap and sword decorated the top. Specially selected pallbearers collected around the general, including General Marcy, with whom Lander had corresponded frequently during the winter campaign; Colonel Thomas Key, who had befriended Lander during the western Virginia campaign; and Congressman John F. Potter, for whom Lander had offered to stand in as second in the much-publicized duel with Roger Pryor two years before. They carried the coffin out of the mansion and placed it on a caisson. Lander's remains were taken to the Church of the Epiphany on the corner of Thirteenth and G Streets. "The sidewalks along the route of the procession are thronged with spectators," noted a Washington reporter who covered the event, "and at the church there was a perfect jam."[19] Lander was the first Union general to die in one of the eastern armies, and his was the first funeral for a general held in the city during the war. All who turned out that day were well aware that his would not be the last.

Bishop Thomas M. Clarke of Rhode Island performed the funeral ceremony, evoking memories of Lander's exploits in the West and in the first year of the war. Remembering that Lander was also gifted in the arts, the bishop cited Lander's unique traits and values. The ceremony was relatively short; Clarke closed the funeral by looking at Lander's coffin and declaring, "Brother, go home; for thee the field is won." The packed church then filed out with the coffin to take Lander to the railroad station for his journey home to Salem.

By this time the crowds lining the streets numbered close to 20,000 by one reporter's estimate. With heads bare to show their respect, the throng watched Lander's two-mile long procession slowly advance along Penn-

19. "Funeral of Brigadier General Lander," *Washington (D.C.) National Republican,* March 7, 1862.

sylvania Avenue, led by the 104th Pennsylvania Infantry and followed by the same dignitaries who had paid their last respects at Chase's house. A weeping Mrs. Lander clung to Secretary Chase's arm. President Lincoln looked careworn, not yet recovered from the sudden death of his child two weeks earlier. McClellan appeared equally troubled, showing signs of strain from the mounting criticism of how he was leading the Army of the Potomac. Riding several paces behind the hearse, McClellan turned to Major General William B. Franklin and muttered that he wished he was in the coffin instead of Lander.[20]

The most conspicuous member of the funeral procession trotted directly behind the hearse. Lander's famous gray charger—the horse that seemingly defied gravity at Philippi only to be permanently disabled by a shell fragment at Rich Mountain—followed the caisson with his master's boots bouncing from the saddle to which they were fastened. William Bickham, a Cincinnati reporter who covered Lander's exploits at Rich Mountain, was so overcome by the poignant scene that he ended his column with angst: "Alas noble Lander; we shall ne'er look upon his like again!"[21]

Lander's pallbearers lifted his coffin onto a waiting train, the engine tastefully trimmed for mourning. The Andrew Sharpshooters took their seats in the car behind their fallen general; the next car contained congressmen and select members of Lander's staff. The fourth and final occupied car carried Jean Lander and her mother. Leaving Washington at 5:00 P.M., the train arrived in New York City eleven hours later. Too early on Friday morning for recognition by city officials, twenty sharpshooters escorted Lander's remains to the New Haven Railroad depot where the cortege left the unusually quiet town four hours after they arrived. At 7:00 P.M. on March 7, the coffin reached the Worcester Depot in Boston. After a brief and dignified ceremony, a hearse carried Lander to the Eastern depot. From there, a train took him to his final resting place at his hometown of Salem.[22]

A large crowd gathered at Salem's railroad depot that night waiting for

20. Ibid.; newspaper clippings, Scrapbook; George Meade to his wife, March 18, 1862, in George Meade, *The Life and Letters of George Gordon Meade,* vol. 1 (New York, 1913), 253.

21. William Bickham to the editor, March 6, 1862, *Cincinnati Daily Commercial,* March 12, 1862, Obituary Scrapbook, LP 9.

22. Newspaper clippings, Obituary Scrapbook, LP 9.

their martyred hometown hero. The general's remains entered the depot at 9:00 P.M. From there the throng followed his coffin and cortege to city hall. Once again the sharpshooters guarded the body overnight. Throughout the following morning, thousands of Salem's citizens lined up in front of city hall to pay their final respects, ignoring the cold and slush offered by the late winter Massachusetts weather. At noon the stores closed just as Governor John A. Andrew arrived by special train from Boston.[23]

Lander's third and final funeral ceremony was the most personal event honoring his remains. Hometown family and friends, as well as members of Lander's former commands, formed the cortege at 1:00 P.M. William D. Northend took his position as a pallbearer to his dear friend. They escorted Lander through streets packed with mourners to the South Church, a house of worship filled to capacity that Saturday afternoon. "The life of stirring and animated adventure is ended," lamented Reverend G. W. Briggs. He recounted Lander's life of sacrifice and devotion to his country. His sermon closed with an admission shared by many in his audience: "We almost wish today that this brave son of our state and city had possessed a courage a little less daring, a resolution a little less determined, a spirit a little less controlled by Spartan heroism under physical weakness and pain, so that life might have been a little longer, and he might have helped to render our coming triumph doubly sure."[24]

After a benediction, the procession reformed to escort Lander to his final resting site. Crowds lined Chestnut, Flint, Summer, and Broad streets; the same avenues along which the lad with so much potential had swaggered more than twenty-five years before. Guns were fired each minute, and the town's bells tolled throughout the final procession. Late that afternoon the general was carried to the Broad Street Cemetery, where his pallbearers brought him to the tomb of the West family. Lander had requested that he be buried next to his mother, and unlike other desires that were denied in the last months of his life, this request was granted. The Reverend George D. Wildes conducted a brief burial service. When it was

---

23. Ibid.

24. "Funeral of Brig. General Lander, of Salem," *Boston Journal,* March 10, 1862; Leland, "Death and Tributes," in *Frederick West Lander: A Biographical Sketch (1822–1862),* ed. Joy Leland (Reno, Nev., 1993), 236–7.

concluded, Lander's friends deposited his coffin in the West family tomb, next to the coffin of his mother. The Andrew Sharpshooters fired three volleys over the grave, then all in the cortege walked away.[25]

As memorial tributes to Frederick Lander rolled off the newspaper presses throughout the North, Thomas Bailey Aldrich—destined to become a legendary American poet, fiction writer, essayist, and editor—lamented the loss of his friend. Lander had been a source of inspiration and respect to him, so much so that the twenty-five-year-old writer had applied for a position on Lander's staff in December of 1861. Lander, well acquainted with the young bard and impressed with the volume of poetry he published while still a teenager, sent a confirming telegram to Aldrich to his hometown in Portsmouth, New Hampshire, but Aldrich had left for New York before it arrived and never saw it. Ironically, Aldrich's friend, Fitz-James O'Brien, was hired in his stead (leading one acquaintance to wag, "Aldrich was shot in O'Brien's shoulder").[26]

Lander's death deeply sorrowed Aldrich, but it also inspired him. Taking a break from his editorial work for various New York periodicals, he focused his thoughts to pay a final tribute to "Old Grizzly" with his and Lander's favorite medium—poetry. Powerful and melodious lines of emotion and imagery flowed from Aldrich's mind through his pen to produce a poem that may not have been the most memorable work of what would prove to be a prolific half-century career, but it likely ranked as one of the most personally satisfying odes he ever wrote:

LANDER.

Close his bleak eyes—they shall no more
    Flash battle where the cannon roar!
And lay the battered sabre at his side,
    (His to the last, for so he would have died!)
Though he no more may pluck from out its sheath
    The sinewy lightning that dealt traitors death.
Lead the lone war-horse by the plumed bier—
    Even the horse, now he is dead, is dear!

Take him New England, now his work is done:
    He fought the good fight valiantly—and won.
Speak of his daring. This man held his blood

25. "Funeral of Brig. General Lander, of Salem," *Boston Journal,* March 10, 1862.
26. Wolle, *O'Brien,* 232; O'Brien, *Poems and Stories,* xxvi–xxvii.

Cheaper than water for the nation's good.
Rich Mountain, Fairfax, Romney—he was there—
    Speak of him gently, of his mien, his air;
How true he was, how his strong heart could bend
    With sorrow, like a woman's, for a friend:
Intolerant of every man's desire;
    Ice, where he liked not; where he loved, all fire.

Take him New England, gently. Other days,
    Peaceful and prosperous, shall give him praise.
How will our children's children breathe his name,
    Bright on the shadowy muster roll of fame!
Take him New England, gently; you can fold
    No purer patriot in your brown mould.
So, on New England, Let him lie,
    Sleeping awhile—as if the Good could die![27]

27. Thomas B. Aldrich, "Lander," March, 1862, LCR.

Epilogue

In General Lander, a brave magnanimous and heroic man has died. He was full of reckless daring, of rough manners, but possessed a kind and generous heart. Perhaps he was not a great General, but he was a noble soldier.
—Lieutenant Colonel Alvin C. Voris, Sixty-seventh Ohio Infantry

The day after Frederick Lander died, his division was placed under the command of Brigadier General James Shields, a fifty-six-year-old Irish immigrant, Mexican War veteran, and former senator from two states. Shields appeared as aggressive as his predecessor. On March 12 he marched his troops into Winchester, the morning after Stonewall Jackson evacuated it. General Banks was elevated to command the new Fifth Corps of the Army of the Potomac and took overall charge of his and Shields's divisions. Beginning on March 21, Banks sent his former troops, under the command of General Alpheus S. Williams, out of the Shenandoah Valley toward Centreville. Shields stayed in Winchester with Lander's westerners to patrol the northern Shenandoah Valley.

Stonewall Jackson reacted to the movements and attacked impetuously on March 23, 1862. Shields lay in Winchester, wounded in a skirmish the previous afternoon and totally oblivious to the action transpiring four miles south of him near the Valley Turnpike hamlet of Kernstown. Lander's winter campaign subordinates, led by Colonel Nathan Kimball, surprised Jackson's troops in a ten-hour heated contest. By the time darkness enveloped the field, Jackson and his men were sent streaming southward in retreat. It was the first loss Stonewall had experienced in his military career—and the Union victory at Kernstown would be a rare success achieved in the Virginia theater east of the Alleghenies for the next two years of the war.[1]

The action at Kernstown was redemption time for those troops who had caught Lander's ire one month earlier. The First Virginia Cavalry performed a successful operation at the close of the day, one that collected more than 100 southern prisoners at the cost of nine killed or wounded horse soldiers. Colonel Henry Anisansel was not at their helm that day. The hernia he suffered near Bloomery Gap had incapacitated him so much that he was eventually forced to resign.[2]

Lander's operation to protect and construct the B & O Railroad did not go for naught. On March 29 the line opened from Wheeling to Baltimore for the first time in ten months. Union supplies in previously logjammed boxcars rolled immediately on the tracks. More than 3,000 cars crossed the Harpers Ferry bridge the first day the line reopened.[3]

Fitz-James O'Brien was in Cumberland when the first trains rolled westward from Baltimore to the Ohio River Valley, but he was in no condition to rejoice in the moment. After receiving his shoulder wound near Bloomery Furnace on February 16, O'Brien suffered considerably in a Cumberland hospital. "I hope to God you never have to go through what I have experienced," he complained to a friend late in March, but he knew the worst was still to come, for he had agreed to have his surgeon attempt to resect his shoulder joint. The surgery was performed on the day of the Kernstown battle. Although O'Brien survived it, he did not fare well postoperatively. "I almost died," he admitted in a letter dated April 1. "My breath ceased, my heart ceased to beat, pulse stopped. However, I got through." Tetanus set in and O'Brien continued to weaken.

On Sunday morning, April 6, 1862, O'Brien seemed a little better and sat up on the side of his bed. Two of his literary friends were riding from Baltimore on the unobstructed B & O to visit him. This picked up his spirits considerably. He took a glass of sherry offered him by his physician.

1. Ecelbarger, *"We are in for it!"* 49–75, 173–231. Stonewall Jackson had a minor role in the ill-fated Confederate assaults at Malvern Hill on July 1, 1862; therefore, this can also be added as the only other loss on his record.

2. Henry Anisansel Service Record, RG 94, NA.

3. Summers, *Baltimore and Ohio,* 115–6.

While slowly sipping it, O'Brien turned pale and fell back onto his bed. Again, his breath ceased, his heart ceased to beat, and his pulse stopped. This time, O'Brien did not "get through."[4]

Around the time of O'Brien's death, publication of eulogies to Frederick Lander in northern daily and weekly newspapers began to wane. One of Lander's final poems, a whimsical piece titled "Under the Snow," was published in the May issue of the *Atlantic Monthly* magazine.[5] Submitted anonymously, the stanzas were imbued with Lander's tell-tale style (he also used a line verbatim from an earlier poem). By the middle of May, news of the gargantuan battle of Shiloh and McClellan's advance toward Richmond bumped Lander from the papers forever.

Most of Lander's surviving staff officers remained in his division as aides to General Shields. Shields's division was ordered out of the Shenandoah Valley early in May to join Major General Irvin McDowell's corps near Fredericksburg. They left through Manassas Gap on May 16. By this time, one of Lander's favorite soldiers was out of the war. Lieutenant John Cannon, the former private whom Lander promoted for bravery at Bloomery Furnace, found himself overmatched as a commissioned company officer. Deemed "incompetent to attain any influence over his men," Lieutenant Cannon was also troubled by undisclosed family matters. He was honorably discharged on April 29.[6]

The Western Division joined McDowell's men at Falmouth, Virginia, on May 22, where they were reviewed by President Lincoln the following day in anticipation of the grand movement to Richmond set to begin on May 26. But Lander's suspicions about General Nathaniel Banks's abilities appeared to be borne out the same day as Lincoln's review. Commanding an 8,000-man division in the Lower Valley, Banks left a poorly supplied force at Front Royal under the command of Colonel John Kenly and nine companies of his First Maryland Infantry, one of the first units Lander had wanted for his short-lived Department of Harpers Ferry and Cumberland. Banks failed to provide Kenly with any cavalry to scout the roads of the Luray Valley south of town. Stonewall Jackson and his reinforced southern army took advantage of Banks's error and annihilated Kenly's force. Two days later, Jackson swept Banks from Winchester and sent his army fleeing across the Potomac River.

4. Wolle, *Fitz-James O'Brien,* 243–6.
5. [F. W. Lander], "Under the Snow," *Atlantic Monthly,* 9 (May 1862): 625–6.
6. John Cannon Service Record, RG 94, NA.

The new southern threat in the Shenandoah Valley changed Lincoln's plans. Shields's men were sent back to the Valley, this time as a part of McDowell's newly created Army of the Rappahannock. Major Dwight Bannister, formerly on Lander's staff, heard of the drastic turn of events in the Shenandoah Valley while attached to General McClellan's army on the Yorktown Peninsula. The news prompted him to write to Mrs. Lander, evoking her late husband's exploits and lamenting how the situation would be different had he survived. "Had he been in command of Banks's men, poor brave Col. Kenly and his heroic Marylanders would not have been massacred," Bannister opined.[7]

The Western Division chased after Stonewall once they entered the Shenandoah Valley only to be routed by him at the Battle of Port Republic on June 9. Two weeks later, Lander's former division was dissolved, half being sent to join McClellan east of Richmond, the other half attached to a new northern army under the command of Major General John Pope. The latter force lost an early advantage and became fodder for Jackson in August at the Battle of Cedar Mountain.

Harry G. Armstrong, the second example of Lander's "judicious promotions" for bravery at Bloomery Furnace, proved worthy of Lander's commendation. Lander had promoted the Irish captain to major and kept him on his staff in the winter of 1862. By summertime Armstrong had risen to a lieutenant colonel's rank and was back with the Fifth Ohio, the regiment with which he had enlisted in 1861. He took a bullet below his left knee at Cedar Mountain and was soon discharged for the disability. Armstrong returned to his hometown of Cincinnati, where he worked as a foreman for the *Cincinnati Gazette*. But his injury bothered him considerably. Like Lander, the leg wound bred a blood infection. His infection eventually abated, but not before it reached his heart and damaged that vital organ. Harry Armstrong died from heart failure at the age of forty-four years.[8]

Though devoid of a legacy in the American Civil War, Lander's influence in western explorations bore fruit in 1862. On July 1, 1862, President Lincoln signed the Pacific Railroad Act, legislation adopted by the twenty-five state Union Congress without southern representation to oppose it. Sacramento was chosen as the western terminus with four branch

7. Bannister to Mrs. Lander, May 30, 1862, LP 11.
8. Harry G. Armstrong Pension Record, RG 94, NA.

lines, including an Iowa branch chosen by Lincoln. Lincoln selected Council Bluffs as the eastern terminus for the Union Pacific line, requiring the three other branches under the supervision of private railroad companies to link with the government branch using their own funds. Thus, Lincoln's solution—placing the route of the government branch through the Platte River Valley and setting the terminus far beyond existing railroad companies—was the same plan suggested by Lander in the mid-1850s.[9]

Another of Frederick Lander's special projects was dissolved the same year. The Andrew Sharpshooters were denied special status as a sharpshooter unit. Incorporated into the Army of the Potomac, the sharpshooters were forced to part with their custom-made rifles (the weapons were too cumbersome to bear on extended marches). Without his unit's independent identity, Captain John Saunders led his company through the East Woods at the Battle of Antietam not as a distinct sharpshooter unit, but as a company of the Fifteenth Massachusetts Infantry. Saunders was killed there, one of more than 22,000 casualties incurred on the bloodiest day of American history.[10]

Lander had not been alone in castigating George McClellan for his methodical leadership of the Army of the Potomac. Fed up with McClellan's half-hearted pursuit of the Confederate army after the Battle of Antietam, President Lincoln relieved him of command and replaced him with Major General Ambrose Burnside. The new army commander's only battle—at Fredericksburg, Virginia, on December 13—was a Union disaster. More than 12,000 Union soldiers fell dead or wounded with absolutely no gain. Colonel Edward J. Allen, who had been a long-time Lander confidant since their first meeting on the Northwest Coast in 1853, began the battle in charge of the 155th Pennsylvania, a regiment he recruited near his hometown of Pittsburgh. Because of attrition, Allen finished the day heading the brigade of the Fifth Corps in which his regiment fought. Chronic illness forced him to leave the service with an honorable discharge early the following year.[11]

The staff officers who worked for Lander in 1862 took on elevated responsibilities the following year. Captain Barstow became assistant adju-

9. Vance, *North American Railroad*, 170–1.

10. Bicknell, "Sharpshooters," 35–52.

11. Edward J. Allen, Service Record, RG 94, NA.

tant general of the First Corps, Army of the Potomac, in March of 1863. Ambrose Thompson, formerly Lander's division quartermaster, carried the same position for the entire Army of the Potomac while it was under Major General Joseph Hooker's command. But Captain Fred Barton did not fare as well. Returning to head a company in the Tenth Massachusetts after Lander died, Barton was slightly injured at the Battle of Gettysburg. He returned to a brigade headquarters position as assistant adjutant general near Chantilly, Virginia. Here, Barton suffered the humiliation of capture by John Singleton Mosby and his guerilla force in October, close to where Brigadier General Isaac Stevens (who headed the 1853 railroad expedition to the Pacific Coast) had been killed in battle one year earlier. Barton spent the rest of the year in a southern prison, awaiting exchange.[12]

Jean Davenport Lander refused to wallow in the loneliness of a widow. Soon after her husband's death, Jean and her mother volunteered their services as nurses and headed to Port Royal, South Carolina. In 1863, Jean Lander was in charge of the entire hospital department there. Major Dwight Bannister worked there as paymaster. John Hay, Lincoln's secretary and admiring fan of Mrs. Lander, dined with her in May of 1863.[13]

Jean Lander took leave of her duties late in the year to spend a few days in Washington as a bridesmaid to Miss Kate Chase, the only daughter of Secretary of the Treasury Salmon P. Chase, who was to marry Governor William Sprague on November 12. Prior to the wedding, Mrs. Lander visited Mount Vernon and also took in a play at Ford's Theater. *The Marble Heart* played there on Monday, November 9, starring a captivating young tragedian named John Wilkes Booth. President Lincoln watched the performance with his wife and two secretaries. "Rather tame than otherwise," wrote John Hay in his journal.[14]

12. Pension Records of Maria Barstow, Ambrose Thompson, and Fred Barton, RG 94, NA.

13. John Hay diary, May 19–23, 1863, in Burlingame and Ettlinger, eds., *Complete Civil War Diary of John Hay,* 57–8. Clara Barton did not share Hay's ardor for General Lander's wife. Considering her insufferably arrogant, Miss Barton refused to sit at the same table with Jean Lander when the two nurses were confined to the same ship off the Carolina coast (Stephen B. Oates, *A Woman of Valor: Clara Barton and the Civil War* [New York, 1994], 187, 204).

14. John Hay diary, November 9–12, 1863, in Burlingame and Ettlinger, eds., *Complete Civil War Diary of John Hay,* 110–1.

Six days after the Sprague-Chase wedding, Abraham Lincoln took a train to commemorate the soldiers' cemetery at Gettysburg, Pennsylvania. Mistakenly believing that the president would divert his trip on the B & O line toward Cumberland, secessionists planted explosives underneath the tracks. On November 18, the southerners set off the bombs, causing slight damage to a train; Lincoln, however, had taken a different route to Pennsylvania. The explosion occurred near Paw Paw, where Frederick Lander had died twenty months earlier.[15]

Since joining Lander's 1859 expedition, Albert Bierstadt kept busy converting his landscape sketches to canvas paintings. In 1863 he unveiled his grandest work to date: *The Rocky Mountains—Lander's Peak*, a name that eventually was shortened by removing the reference to Lander. Bierstadt exhibited the painting, depicting an Indian encampment with the majestic peaks towering behind it, in a well-advertised national tour late in the year. He entered his work in the New York Sanitary Fair exhibition in April of 1864, an event designed to raise proceeds to aid wounded soldiers. Six hundred paintings hung in the spacious gallery, but the prime attractions of the show became Bierstadt's American West scene pitted against Frederick Church's immense painting *Heart of the Andes*. Although Church's 1859 South American scene was a marvelous exhibit, Bierstadt's American image, linked with the name of a Civil War martyr, easily won the competition.[16]

Had Frederick Lander reappeared two years after his death to witness the final year of the war, he would have been startled at the enormity of the battles. Day-long casualty tallies of 10,000–15,000 had become commonplace, and the devastation produced in more than one hour of fighting at Rich Mountain in 1861 was routinely topped by single volleys in 1864 encounters. The personnel associated with Lander took diverse paths that year. George McClellan ran against Abraham Lincoln for the presidency of 1864 and lost. His platform was supported by the extreme wing of the Democratic Party called the Copperheads. William Northend was a leader of the movement. Staunch Confederate Jacob Thompson, who had employed Lander for four years in the late 1850s, worked behind the scenes in a desperate attempt to disrupt Union operations, including

15. C. W. Dennis, "Suggested Location for Markers for Civil War Blockhouses and Points of Historic Interest on the Cumberland Division of the Baltimore and Ohio Railroad," MS 1816, Maryland Historical Society, Baltimore.

16. Goetzmann and Goetzmann, *The West of the Imagination*, 154.

getting involved in a plot to burn New York City. Roger Pryor, the Virginia politician who had backed out of a duel with John F. Potter and Lander in 1860, entered the Confederate service as a colonel, rose immediately to a brigadier general, resigned when his command was broken up, then finished the war as a private.

Captain Simon F. Barstow remained an assistant adjutant general, but he performed the duties for General George Gordon Meade, the final commander for the Army of the Potomac. Barstow eventually was breveted brigadier general for his efficient service. Another one of Lander's former aides, Colonel Charles Candy, led a brigade in the Atlanta campaign, also earning a brevet of brigadier general for his leadership. Brevets aside, no fewer than eleven underlings who encamped with Lander at Patterson's Creek and Paw Paw received a general's commission by the close of the war. They participated in all theaters of operation and came out victorious in the spring of 1865.

Five days after Robert E. Lee surrendered his Confederate army to U. S. Grant, Abraham Lincoln was assassinated in Washington, D.C. Benjamin Ficklin, one of Lander's key subordinates in the 1857 wagon road surveys, was suspected of taking part in a conspiracy to kill the president and was arrested but was quickly released for lack of evidence. He was to suffer an inglorious death from choking on his dinner at Willard's Hotel in 1873.

Boardinghouse operator Mary Surratt was arrested for plotting with John Wilkes Booth to kill Lincoln. She was hanged in July with three other conspirators. Included in the team of lawyers who unsuccessfully defended her was Fred Aiken, the young attorney who extolled Frederick Lander's virtues to *Frank Leslie's Illustrated* in 1861 and worked with Lander as William H. Seward's agent in the early months of the war.[17]

During the war and within a few years after its close, several books were published that hailed Frederick Lander's exploits and honored his service for the first year of the conflict. J. T. Headley released the first of two volumes of *The Great Rebellion* in 1866, an impressive history of the Civil War, considering its early publication. Headley mentioned Lander several times in the volume, and eulogized him by claiming, "What to other men seemed impossibilities, [were] to him the proper way to conduct a campaign." Two other anthologies were published to honor the Union mar-

---

17. Champ Clark and the Editors of Time-Life Books, *The Assassination: Death of a President* (Alexandria, Va., 1987), 148, 162.

tyrs of the war; each included a brief biography of Lander. Even the Virginian Addy Markinfield's 1864 book, *"Old Jack" and his Foot-Cavalry,* honored Frederick Lander as "one of the bravest and most energetic officers, and one who had given the highest promise of valuable service to the Union."[18] But all subsequent postwar anthologies understandably directed their emphasis toward the years 1862–1865, the time frame in which most of the great battles were fought and grand movements were conducted. Lander's name no longer figured in the pages of Civil War historiography.

Frederick Lander's dedicated service on the frontier received posthumous awards. A bill sponsored in the House of Representatives became an official act exactly three years after Lander died. Congress finally settled its accounts with Lander's independent exploration of 1854. His widow became the benefactor when she was awarded $4,750 for her late husband's services and expenses. Jean Lander had moved back to "Greystone" (her estate in Lynn, Massachusetts) a few months before the war ended. She decided to return to the stage and traveled the circuit once again, retiring for good in 1877. By this time, she had adopted a son. She named him Frederick Lander.[19]

Lander's lasting impact would remain in the West. A city, a mountain, and two creeks in Wyoming, as well as a county in Nevada took his name. Lander's cutoff proved to be a valuable detour from the Oregon Trail and bore the weight of extensive emigrant traffic throughout the latter half of the nineteenth century.

Lander's protégé, Grenville Dodge, was appointed chief engineer of the Union Pacific Railroad in January of 1866. Three years later he completed 1,086 miles of transcontinental rail. Joining with the wealthy Jay Gould organization in 1873, Dodge oversaw the construction of more than 9,000 miles of road during the following ten years. This included Lander's initial concept of peripheral lines that entered the grand trunk at several points. In 1884 the Oregon Short Line Railroad was completed to a junction with the Oregon Railway and Navigation line that had been

18. John T. Headley, *The Great Rebellion,* vol. 1 (Hartford, Conn., 1866), 289; Shea, *American Nation,* 299–306; Frank Moore, ed. *Heroes and Martyrs: Notable Men of the Time* (New York, ca. 1864), 175–7; Addy Markinfield, *"Old Jack" and His Foot Cavalry* (New York, 1864), 50.

19. "An Act for the Relief of Jean M. Lander," LP 12; Pugh, *Biographical Sketch of Mrs. F. W. Lander,* 3–6; Shahrani, "Lander Family," 12.

projected eastward across the Blue Mountains. The first passenger train steamed from Omaha to Portland on January 1, 1885. Thus, the Oregon line provided the Union Pacific with a vast field for development in the Pacific Northwest. It also confirmed Frederick Lander's forecast of a desirable route for the transcontinental railroad thirty years after he had independently surveyed it.[20]

Veterans North and South dedicated their efforts to recounting their Civil War observances throughout the final two decades of the 1800s and for three decades in the 1900s. Inevitably, those who had worked with Lander early in the war offered their opinions about him. William S. Rosecrans, who was infuriated with Lander's attempt to embellish his own role in the Rich Mountain campaign, appeared to forgive him and actually lauded him when he provided his version of the battle in an 1883 issue of the *National Tribune,* a weekly organ of the Grand Army of the Republic.

George McClellan published his memoirs four years later. He briefly recounted Lander's role in the winter campaign against Stonewall Jackson, then went on to provide a brief explanation about the exchanges between himself and Lander that the newspapers had published in 1862. "On some occasions during this brief campaign I was obliged to check Lander rather abruptly for attempting to assume control over troops not under his command, and to initiate some very rash movements," McClellan explained, believing that a combination of inexperience and illness fostered Lander's impetuous behavior. "These occurrences did not change my feelings toward him," McClellan continued, "and I doubt whether they influenced his [feelings] for me."[21]

Although Lander had ill feelings toward McClellan, his own style and wartime philosophy were far from sound, a fact that was not lost in the memories of those who had served under him. "I am disposed to think that General Lander possessed few of the qualities, except courage, requisite for one charged with the conduct of a great campaign," opined former artillery captain James Huntington: "He was too rash and impulsive; as a leader of light cavalry he would have been in his element."[22] Few ob-

20. Warner, *Generals in Blue,* 128; Vance, *North American Railroad,* 201.

21. Rosecrans, "Rich Mountain," *National Tribune,* February 22, 1883; McClellan, *McClellan's Own Story,* 191.

22. General James Barnett Manuscript, "History of Battery H, 1st Ohio Light Artillery," Western Reserve Historical Society, Cleveland, Ohio. The artillerist's 1880s analysis was in-

jective historians could argue with Huntington's assessment, and Lander himself would have heartily agreed with the latter part of it. Ironically, it had been Lander's desire to lead the small light force for which Huntington and others envisioned him to be a perfect match.

The last published tributes to Lander by those who knew him were released around the turn of the century. William Ellis, the historian for Norwich University, diligently sought out Lander's family and associates to confirm his story for a commemorative history of the university and its cadets. Ellis wrote to Lander's brother Edward, living in Washington, D.C., in 1898, to obtain information from him. The historian quickly realized that Lander had never told his family that he had attended Norwich. Maintaining that his brother was working on railroads instead of training at the school, Edward replied, "It seems to me hardly possible that he should have given up his profession and abandoned [his career] at 26–7 or 8 years of age to have become a cadet." Years later when Ellis and Grenville Dodge teamed up for a more comprehensive three-volume history of the school, they were puzzled once again when Lander's sister, Louisa, continued to question his attendance at Norwich. "There is no doubt in the world but that your brother was a cadet," came Ellis's emphatic rejoinder to her denial.[23]

The surviving Lander siblings refused to accept the change in their martyred brother's name. Short biographies appeared in various anthologies, including *Appleton's Cyclopaedia*. Mysteriously, Frederick W. Lander's middle name was entered as "West" rather than "William." A few years prior to Jean Lander's death in 1903, the executors of her estate donated Lander's official writings and memorabilia, 1,250 items, to the Library of Congress. Once again, the name of the collection was attributed to Frederick "West" Lander. For the next ninety years, "West" replaced "William" in all references to Frederick Lander's middle name.

Perhaps Edward Lander was irritated at the name change as well as learning that his brother's life story contained chapters of which he had no knowledge. Throughout the latter half of the nineteenth century and into the early years of the twentieth century, Edward labored to keep his

---

tended to be part of a book about the Ohio light artillery during the Civil War, a book that never was published.

23. Edward Lander to William Ellis, January 31, 1899, and William Ellis to Louisa Lander, May 24, 1910, EC.

brother's name alive. Edward granted several interviews about him, and he was quick to correct any misstatements in reminiscences about Fred's exploits. "It is partly in defense of a man who gave his life to his country," explained Edward to one editor, "and left no children to defend his memory; a memory cherished and held dear by his friends and relatives."[24] It must have been pleasing to Edward to see one of his nephews, Josiah Pierce Jr., follow in Fred's footsteps as a civil engineer on the Northern Trans-Continental Survey, but by 1902 even he was gone. Fred Lander's influence appeared to die with him.

In 1904 Edward composed an eight-page biography of his brother for the Essex Institute in Salem. He took pains to carve out Fred's life story the way he remembered it. He noted his middle name to be "William," and never mentioned Norwich University in his version of Lander's education. He embellished his brother's height ("He was as tall as Lincoln"), was one year off on the date of his birth and marriage, and may have fabricated Fred's last articulate words: "Don't sound the bugle!" But Edward's tribute was heartfelt, even with the passage of eighty-eight years, for his essay demonstrated an enduring love for his brother with an equal degree of pride in his achievements. "He was remarkable for the adaptation of means to ends," the old judge noted with keen insight, "and moving with rapidity upon the object sought."[25]

But Edward had become aware that his brother's place in history was slipping away with each passing year after Lander's death, forty-two of them to date; time filled with stirring events in American history in which his brother could not participate. He was one of the last survivors who really knew Fred and what he had accomplished. He grudgingly acknowledged that his brother's legacy had become overshadowed. New generations of Americans would grow up in Lander, Wyoming, and Lander County, Nevada, and have no idea why the regions were named that way. No passenger boarding a train in Portland, Oregon, could look out his window at some of the most rugged railroad country on the continent and name the person most responsible for its existence; the person who half a century earlier had the wisdom, foresight, strength, and persistence to survey the thoroughfare that eased the life of subsequent generations of

24. Newspaper clippings, PDV; Edward Lander to Editor of Republican, December 16, 1882, PDV.

25. Judge Edward Lander, "A Sketch of General Frederick W. Lander," *Historical Collections of The Essex Institute* 40 (1904), 313–20.

Americans. A visitor to Lander Post Number Five in Lynn, Massachusetts, the largest Grand Army of the Republic museum in the country, will look at the few items on display there—a pair of well worn leather boots, buttons from a coat, a saddle, and a headquarters flag—and have no understanding or appreciation of the memorabilia. The general they once belonged to did not fight at Shiloh, Antietam, Gettysburg, or Spotsylvania. Those are the enduring names of Civil War sites, not Philippi or Rich Mountain. Few could cite what happened at Hancock and Edwards Ferry, or even locate Bloomery Gap on a map.

"As a General, he was successful in whatever he undertook," Edward said admiringly as he began to close his essay; "as a soldier, too careless of his own safety; as an explorer, the history of the great plains is his monument; as a Civil Engineer, his standing may safely rest on his reports upon the Pacific Railroad." It was a tribute based on forlorn hope. General Lander's successes had been pushed aside by greater Civil War achievements. The history of the Great Plains was dominated by the Indian Wars and typified for many Americans by Wild West gunfights glorified in dime novels.

Edward tried to end his piece in a positive tone. He raved about Fred's intellect, his speeches, his essays, and his poetry. A promising political career seemed inevitable in 1860. Now it was all gone. Frederick Lander's legacy in the history of a nation for which he sacrificed his life had faded away, and Edward could not correct the injustice. Lamentation over what could have been dictated the closing lines of his tribute to Frederick W. Lander, a man who has since been defined as one who embodied the romantic vision of nineteenth-century America:[26]

> To him Nature had been bounteous in her gifts, and his early death closed a career short indeed but full of a promise not to be fulfilled.[27]

26. Definition of Lander provided by Kent D. Richards in Garraty and Carnes, eds., *American National Biography*, 13 (1999), 103.

27. Edward Lander, "Sketch of General Frederick W. Lander," 320.

Appendix 1: The Poetry of Frederick W. Lander

Inspired first by the news of the day, and later by an escalating war, Frederick Lander expressed his thoughts and creativity in verse. Although many of his poems were published in newspapers, others stayed in his private possession. Two were published in the leading magazines of the mid-1800s. Eleven poems written by Lander are extant; at least one more poem, a work called "Inspired," has yet to be found.

The following poem, written in Boston on November 8, 1850, heads the Lander bound collection at the Library of Congress. The poem was never published. It was kept by Jean Lander for forty years, and one can assume that she—as an aspiring young actress at the time—inspired her future husband to create the poem.

FAIR GIRL

With all that Fame accords,
    Wilt thou not claim a gentler part?
A name that rests with hallowed words
    Traced on the tablets of the heart?

Thou should not scorn it;—portals wide
    For sympathies thou spirits know;
Who climb ambition's mountain side,—
    And gaze upon their kind below.

But shouldst thou scorn the earnest thought
    Within one manly breast enshrined:—

It is a tribute, rarely bought
　　By those who traffic in the mind.

Thou art no spirit of a dream,
　　Like the bright things from heaven that light
The rapture of the Poet's scheme;
　　Then fade to leave a deeper night.

But when the form of light appears
　　Supreme o'er each attendant soul,
And eyes grow dim with burning tears,
　　And the heart's rapture bursts control.

To him whom aspiration feeds,
　　Thou art the guerdon of the lot
That gathered from immortal deeds,
　　The glory mortal hand hath wrought.

A voice, a spirit voice, is heard
　　To whisper then of pride and power;
And the cold worldly thought is stored
　　By the wild passions of the hour.

A spirit voice, that cries, behold!
　　Ere thou shalt bid its hope depart,
A prize, for which thy youth may mould
　　Each sterling purpose of the heart.

Behold! thou wretch without an aim,—
　　Is there no trust before thee now?
Go! gather from the lists of fame
　　A wreath to deck your lovely brow.

"Stanzas on the Destruction of the Light-House at Minot's Ledge, and Death of the Two Under-Keepers"

This poem was found in a newspaper clipping in the Lander collection at the Library of Congress. Written in Boston on April 18, 1851, the piece was submitted by Lander under the pseudonym "Fretus." On the clipping, in his characteristic handwriting, Lander jotted his initials next to the pseudonym and signed his name below it.

First Voice

'Tis a perilous home, but it is anchored fast,
    It is anchored fast in the sea below;
We are safe in this nook of the iron bound mast;
    Let the strong waves beat and the tempest blow!

We may mock at the waves, at the white haired waves,
    They have beat on the gristly rocks ere now—
They would sweep us away to our ocean graves,
    But we're anchored fast—let the tempest blow.

Come! my cold mate, gaze on the light above;
    How it laughs in the face of the blinding storm—
'Tis a beaconed trust for a seaman's love;
    Keep thy dull fears close, and thy heart as warm.

Second Voice

Oh, my brother, it is not an idle fear,
    For we are *alone* on the rock—*alone;*
Can the pale lamp laugh, where it shines so clear
    While the grinding base gives that hollow groan?

We are shut in a tomb, we are coffined close;
    'Tis the third long day, and the night comes on;
And hark! how the raging storm still blows—
    How the shaking rock gives a hollow groan!

Let me gaze in peace o'er the ghastly sea—
    Let me look beyond, to the blue lined shore,
Where there's many a heart that is warm for me,
    Full many a heart, I shall meet no more.

First Voice

They will write fair tales, they will sing brave songs,
    They will cherish us well if we perish so—
Keep a true man's heart where his faith belongs—
    Let the rock groan on, and the tempest blow.

I've a wife and a babe on the blue lined coast,
    I've a wife and a babe—my joy and pride;
Let the lamps shine on, that my boy may boast
    When the years have flown, how his father died.

Come, my cold mate, kneel, 'tis an awful hour,
    Put thy hand in mine, we will kneel to God,

He can guard us well, and His holy power
　　Make the blue sea firm as the old green sod.

Here's a parting thought for the ones we love
　　Here's a steadfast look at the wave below,
Here's a humble prayer to the God above,
　　May He guard us well, for we need Him now.

When the stars went out, and the night grew dim,
　　And the grey dawn peered from her misty hood,
He had gathered the souls that trusted Him,
　　And his wild waves swept where the light-house stood.

In a eulogy to Frederick Lander written two days after his death and published in the *Pittsburgh Daily Evening Chronicle* on March 6, 1862, Edward J. Allen, one of Lander's closest friends, submitted the untitled and undated poem below. "The following fragment, which I find among some manuscripts he gave me," wrote Allen to introduce Lander's work, "was written upon seeing a slight notice in a New York paper of a poor Magdalen, who, driven out by the 'scorn of the world which had little charity,' was found upon the outskirts of the city, frozen to death. It is incomplete; but the few verses show poetic power as well as kindliness of heart":

They did not think her wholly good,
　　Some stealthy glances gathered more,
And when she sold her shawl for food
　　They drove her from the open door.

Her startled senses reeled and slid
　　Like phantoms—o'er the frozen pool
Of worldly precepts—seldom hid
　　From such as faint and starve by rule.

She strove to shape some words of prayer,
　　Oft broken by the doubts that chase;
The fingers of her own despair
　　Wrote shame's red letters on her face—

The cautious creatures of the air
　　Looked out from many a hidden place,
And saw the ambers of despair
　　Flush the grey ashes of her face.

Still sped the wild storm's rustling feet
    To martial music of the pines
And to her cold heart's muffled beat
    Wheeled grandly into solemn lines.

And there like old cathedral saint,
    Niched low to guard some cloistered ground,
This hidden nun with earthly taint
    Held up her prayer without a sound.

And when the holy angel bands
    Saw this lone vigil lonely kept,
They gathered from her frozen hands
    The prayer, they folded, and they kept.

Some snow-flakes wiser than the rest,
    Soon faltered o'er a thing of clay,
First read this secret of her breast,
    Then gently robed her where she lay.

There, dead, dark hair made white with snow,
    A still, stark face, two folded palms,
And (mothers breathed the secret low)
    An unborn infant—asking alms.

God kept her counsel, cold and mute
    His steadfast mourners closed her eyes
Her headstone is an old tree root,
    Be mine to utter—"Here she lies."

And so she passes from earth to Heaven—
    Some worldly people called it death—
Heaped snow the storm's kind which had driven,
    Scarce hid her from their mocking breath.

"The Falls of the Shoshonee"

In the first weeks of his 1854 independent railroad survey, Frederick Lander saw the majestic Shoshone Falls on the Snake River. The natural wonder inspired him to write this poem late that summer, while he rested in Salem. He likely sent it to his friend, Edward J. Allen, in Olympia, who subsequently submitted the poem to the *Washington (D.C.) Union* late in 1854 (under the pseudonym "Amicus"). Lander introduced the work by mislocating the position of his inspiration: "Stanzas written on first contemplating the Great Falls of the Shoshonee, situated on the main branch of the Columbia River, in Western Oregon, a thousand miles from the haunts of civilization. The river flows through the black fire-scathed masses of lava, apparently upheaved by some terrible convulsion of Nature. The bed of the stream is more than six hundred feet beneath the surrounding surface. The foaming waters shut in by the perpendicular walls of the chasm, after the first leap of the cataract, are thrust towards the foot of the fall in a whirl of foaming rapids. The river was swollen by the great freshets of the mountains, and the whole scene was one of desolation and of grandeur."

> Thou record of the young earth's overthrow,
>   When mountain strove with mountain, and the ocean
> Dashed his wild billows o'er the nations. Lo!
>   Thy face reveals that dark hour's deep emotion
>   When the green hill tops knelt in their devotion,
> Endowing thee with being; tempest-hurled
>   Through plains and forests heaving with commotion,
> Thy torrents hissed, and flaming billows curled
> Around the broken dregs and chaos of a world.

> Thy birth-crown'd desolation—in the ire
>   Of the fierce elements thy fate was signed;
> The waters wrestled with the powers of fire,
>   And, in the gloomy caverns, with the wind
>   That lifts the pent volcano; when the rind
> Of the strong earth was broken, and aghast,
>   Fair nature shrank from what her power designed;
> Thou, caldron of the wilderness, wert cast
> From out her flaming womb—the haggard and the last.

> Then sank and rose again the flaming torch
>   Of the old mountains; flickered and grew dim
> The stars that shuddered at high heaven's porch,
>   While laughing Tumults shook thy foaming brim.
>   Havoc has ceased his pastime, and the rim
> Of the volcano crumbling to the soil,
>   Thy first leap like an avalanche; and the grim
> And awful crags, that shut thy fierce recoil,
> Are all that now remain, or recollections foil.

Roll on in all their majesty, to wear
    In adamantine walls thine impress deep
To fling unto the morn thy snowy hair,
      Glittering i' th' sun; to wake or sleep
      As He who bade thy foaming current's sweep
Shall breathe upon thee, from thy depths below;
      Thy "voice of many waters" calls to keep
His counsel with the thunder and the snow,
Who placed thee in the wild—"a marvel and a show."

Yet in the murmur of thy feeblest sighs
    There is an uttered language, and a word
For those who gaze upon thee; for there lies
      Meaning in earnest thought, that is not heard,
      Yet speaks, and tells its tale by ripples stirred
Upon that silent pool, like a woman's eyes—
      Deepest when most at rest: (that have not erred
When formed to sweet conclusion that they despise
All attitudes but trust, which language most defies.)

A power of meditation audible
    In the free rapture that the hour confers;
A whispered transport we hear not so well,
      When memory lingers o'er the spot, and stirs
      The soul less concentrated, that demurs
By worldly knowledge; but the moment can
      Wring from the voices of the messengers
That God hath sent into the heart of man
A truth beyond the words his faltering lips would plan.

Those whispers of the spirit so sublime,
    Whate'er our language makes them; that go forth
To battle with the sophistries of time,
      As sprang the soakings from the key North;
      Startling the breast that feels their mystic birth,
Lighting the longings of a chilly soul
      In every spark that warms its being's dearth,
And quickens it to glory and the goal
That dwells beyond where storms and thick'ning waters roll.

Speaking in thoughts whose radiance can reveal
    A dim and outworn majesty of form;
Mocking the ardor of the poet's zeal

And artist's pencil in a fiercer storm
Of things inanimate that can conform
To mortal breasts till thus grown strangely near—
Pierced by the lightning of its power to warm,
When dazzled not by glory we can hear
The angel tones that woo to startle not the ear.

Oh! had we words to speak them—Oh! to speak
Thoughts that were food for nations ere they fail
The burning halo o'er such hours to "wreak
Into expression" plainly, but the sail
We shake out in the tempest's rising gale,
Torn from the mast, soon leaves us what we are—
The fallen creatures from a kingly pale
And we but mock the meteor and the star
With thoughts, whose gathered rays our mortal meanings mar.

"Virginia Dare"

The sculptress Louisa Lander, Frederick's younger sister, carved a figure
of Virginia Dare while in Rome in 1859–1860. The marble figure, repre-
senting the first child of English parentage born in the New World in
1587, depicts Virginia Dare as a young woman had she lived to maturity.
As a favor to his sister, Frederick Lander wrote the accompanying four-
stanza tribute to the statuette. The poem was published in the *Boston
Advertiser* in the summer of 1861. The statue suffered a strange fate. It
sunk in the ocean off Spain when Louisa attempted to ship it to Boston.
Recovered from the ocean floor two years later, the work was purchased
by Louisa, who restored it and exhibited it in Salem and Boston. A gallery
fire in Boston nearly destroyed it. Eventually, Louisa willed it to the state
of North Carolina, and in the 1950s the statue was displayed in the
Elizabeth Garden on Roanoke Island, where it stands today near where
Virginia Dare was allegedly born.

She stands before us like a thing of dreams;
    The glory of her thought is on her face;
And brokenly the tender sunlight streams
    O'er the rapt wonder of her virgin grace:
Lo! the clasped hand; the faint and shadowy trace
    Of bashful thought through all her woodland guise;
Pure, starborn dewdrop, that some floweret's vase

Holds up to heaven beneath the morning's eyes.
That, trembling first, grows calm in softened, sweet surprise.

Hist! 'twas the carol of some wakeful bird,
    Or Nature's voices wooing in the low
Sweet tone of flowers her loitering foot has stirred;
    Or winds are wailing o'er the buds that glow
In chosen glades, and fear lest she may go;
    Or from the brook her Indian lover quaffed,
(More chill to him than Sewell's mountain snow
    Since beauty passed) the rival zephyrs waft
O'er echoing waves his sighs that young Virginia laughed.

No, 'tis the magic of a holier thought;
    Fixed in new wonder by fonder memories given,
Home, and the song her English mother taught,
    Float with the sound, and lift those eyes to heaven;
So the fair Eve, on earth's bless'd day of seven,
    Stood forth betwixt young Adam and the morn,
Ere mortal touch, or taint of earthly leaven,
    Or that sad sense from evil knowledge born,
Had frayed the enraptured soul that thrilled her to adorn.

Ye arbiters of calling and true fame,
    Translators of divinities ye blend
From faith and hope in Freedom's household name;
    Ye judges stern, whom sophistries offend,
Here view the grace that woman's hand can lend
    To all ye love; who, where eternal Rome
Bids artist souls to loftier themes ascend,
    Could mould the tale of dear Virginia's home,
And love her native land beneath a foreign dome.

"The Union"

This unpublished and undated poem was probably written near the outbreak of the Civil War in the first months of 1861. It illustrates the theme
that Lander espoused in his lecture to the Washington Art Association three
years earlier—that American passions were linked to patriotic sentiments.

        Why droop the eagle's wings?
        Has Freedom's heart no fire—
           Strike nerveless things,

The sounding strings,
And tune her sacred lyre.

Our stars still gleam on high,
    Our country's flag unfurled;
Flung out to fly, against the sky,
    Still one, the startled world.

Salt tears we well have shed
    Tears that the false may feign
We weep the dead that nobly bled
    On freedom's southern plain.

Old stormy battle frays
    Old sires and mothers meet;
Still let us raise for former days
    One shout before we meet.

Then death to all who dare
    Assail what those have won
They will not wear a shroud so fair
    Beneath the morning sun

They fought the British crown
    They toiled and won the strife
They trampled down in field and town
    The old usurpers' life

And now by Marion's fame
    By Sergeant Jasper's act
We dare to name our rightful claim
    And consecrate the fact.

O'er all this broadened land
    From our far western wave
Prepared to stand and hand to hand
    Keep what our fathers gave.

"Rhode Island to the South"

Published first in Nathaniel P. Willis's *Home Journal,* and subsequently in the *Rebellion Record,* Lander's tribute to the Union effort in the first Battle of Manassas received critical praise and national circulation. Lander likely wrote the poem in August of 1861, shortly after he received his general's commission and while he awaited the arrival of his troops in Washington.

> Once on New England's bloody heights,
>   And o'er a Southern plain,
> Our fathers fought for sovereign rights,
>   That working men might reign.
>
> And by that only Lord we serve,
>   The great Jehovah's name;
> By those sweet lips that ever nerve
>   High hearts to deeds of fame;
>
> By all that makes the man a king,
>   The household hearth a throne—
> Take back the idle scoff ye fling,
>   Where freedom claims its own.
>
> For though our battle hope was vague
>   Upon Manassas' plain,
> Where Slocum stood with gallant Sprague,
>   And gave his life in vain;
>
> Before we yield the holy trust
>   Our old forefathers gave,
> Or wrong New England's hallowed dust,
>   Or grant the wrongs ye crave—
>
> We'll print in kindred gore so deep
>   The shore we love to tread,
> That woman's eyes shall fail to weep
>   O'er man's unnumbered dead.

"Ours"

Lander's tribute to the Twentieth Massachusetts's sacrifice at the Battle of Ball's Bluff became his most recognized effort. He wrote the poem in Washington in November 1861, while recuperating at his E Street home from the leg wound he received at Edwards Ferry the day after the Ball's Bluff battle. Inspired by a newspaper account that claimed that Confederates were saying "fewer of the Massachusetts officers would have been killed had they not been too proud to surrender," Lander begins his poem with statements of New England pride.

Aye, deem us proud, for we are more
    Than proud of all our mighty dead
Proud of the bleak and rock-bound shore,
    A crowned oppressor cannot tread.

Proud of each rock and wood, and glen,
    Of every river, lake and plain;
Proud of the calm and earnest men
    Who claim the right and will to reign.

Proud of the men who gave us birth,
    Who battled with the stormy wave,
To sweep the red man from the earth,
    And build their homes upon his grave.

Proud of the holy summer morn
    They traced in blood upon its sod;
The rights of freemen yet unborn;
    Proud of their language and their God.

Proud that beneath our proudest dome
    And round the cottage-cradled hearth,
There is a welcome and a home
    For every stricken race on earth.

Proud that yon slowly sinking sun
    Saw drowning lips grow white in prayer,
O'er such brief acts of duty done,
    As honor gathers from despair.

Pride 'tis our watchword; "clear the boats,"
    "Holmes, Putnam, Bartlett, Pierson—Here"
And while this crazy wherry floats
    "Let's save our wounded," cries Revere.

Old State—some souls are rudely sped—
    This record for thy Twentieth Corps—
Imprisoned, wounded, dying, dead,
    It only asks, "Has Sparta more?"

"On Taking the Gaps in the Blue Ridge"

Lander dated this unpublished poem November 5, 1862. It was likely written close to the time he authored "Ours." A poem about McClellan, this one-stanza creation hinted at the strategy that Lander would elaborate on before the Joint Committee for the Conduct of the War seven weeks later.

> By pondering our plans and maps,
> > Great General George has got the gaps,
> But we, who watched this sleepy war
> > We got the gaps long, long, before.

"Under the Snow"

A March newspaper clipping found on page 40 of Lander's obituary scrapbook claimed "General Lander, a short time before he died, wrote a poem, which, during his last illness, he desired his wife, in the event of his death, to send to the *Atlantic Monthly*." Published in the May issue of that nationally renowned magazine, Lander's posthumous poem was described as "striking, both in thought and diction." Lander borrowed several stanzas from the incomplete poem about the waif who died in New York City and reused them in this effort.

> The spring had tripped and lost her flowers,
> > The summer sauntered through the glades,
> The wounded feet of autumn hours
> > Left ruddy footprints on the blades.

> And all the glories of the woods
> > Had flung their shadowy silence down,—
> When, wilder than the storm it broods,
> > She fled before the winter's frown.

> For *her* sweet spring had lost its flowers,
> > She fell, and passion's tongues of flame
> Ran, reddening through the blushing bowers,
> > Now haggard as her naked shame.

> One secret thought her soul had screened,
> > When prying matrons had sought her wrong,
> And Blame stalked on, a mouthing fiend,
> > And mocked her as she fled along.

> And now she bore its weight aloof;
> > To hide it where one ghastly birch
> Held up the rafters of the roof,
> > And grim old pine-trees formed a church.

'Twas there her spring-time vows were sworn,
    And there upon its frozen sod,
While wintry midnight reigned forlorn,
    She knelt, and held her hands to God.

The cautious creatures of the air
    Looked out from many a sacred place,
To see the embers of despair
    Flush the gray ashes of her face.

And where the last week's snow had caught
    The gray beard of a cypress limb,
She heard the music of a thought
    More sweet than her own childhood's hymn.

For rising in that cadence low,
    With "Now I lay me down to sleep,"
Her mother rocked her to and fro,
    And prayed the Lord her soul to keep.

And still her prayer was humbly raised,
    Held up in two cold hands to God,
That, white as some old pine-tree blazed,
    Gleamed far o'er that dark frozen sod.

The storm stole out beyond the wood,
    She grew the vision of a cloud,
Her dark hair was a misty hood,
    Her stark face shone as from a shroud

Still sped the wild storm's rustling feet
    To martial music of the pines,
And to her cold-heart's muffled beat
    Wheeled grandly into solemn lines.

And still, as if secret's woe
    No mortal words had ever found,
This dying sinner draped in snow
    Held up her prayer without a sound.

But when the holy angel bands
    Saw this lone vigil, lowly kept,
They gathered from her frozen hands
    The prayer thus folded, and they wept

Some snow-flakes—wiser than the rest—
    Soon faltered o'er a thing of clay,
First read this secret of her breast,
    Then gently robed her where she lay.

The dead dark hair, made white with snow,
    A still stark face, two folded palms,
And (mothers, breathe her secret low!)
    An unborn infant—asking alms.

God kept her counsel; cold and mute
    His steadfast mourners closed her eyes,
Her head-stone was an old tree's root,
    Be mine to utter,—"Here she lies."

Perhaps the last poem Frederick Lander ever wrote, the following untitled piece was never published. The emotional work was found in his personal papers and was eventually donated to the Library of Congress within a bound collection of dispatches, letters, and other writings.

Has it then come for me—the fatal moment
    When I must know the idol feet are clay,
When I must feel thou owest me atonement
    For having held my worship for a day.

Must my poor heart so soon be disenchanted,
    Finding too little where it sought too much
Must the sewed germ which loves own hand had planted
    Become a stinging nettle to my touch?

Then I protest against life's hollow seeming—
    Protest against its empty days and years!
If love must ever be delusive seeming,
    Baptise its birth, and not its death, with tears!

Appendix 2: One Sentence, Several Questions

"Colonel Lander failed to come but I shall see him this evening and bring him over to see you." Secretary of State William H. Seward sent these nineteen words to Abraham Lincoln; they referred to a planned meeting between the president and Lander—at that time one of Seward's special agents. Two copies of the note exist in Lincoln's papers. One was dated Sunday afternoon, March 10, 1861; the other, also on a Sunday, was dated March 24. Substantiating documentation that places Lander in Austin, Texas, on March 29 eliminates March 24 as a possible date and thus confirms Sunday, March 10, as the day Seward wrote the note.[1] Although the date can be clarified, several other questions are raised by Seward's single sentence.

Neither Lincoln, Lander, nor Seward recorded the meeting or discussed it with their respective confidants. Consequently, no evidence exists to confirm that Lander and Seward ever met with Lincoln on the evening of March 10. Lander fell ill, either with diphtheria or a similar debilitating malady, about this time; on March 11 he admitted, "I am confined to my room."[2] It is quite possible, therefore, that he was incapacitated before March 11 and "failed to come" to Seward's house at the appointed time on March 10 because he was too sick to meet with the president.

1. Seward to Lincoln, March 10, 1861, ALP 18:7959.
2. FWL to C. E. Mix, March 11, 1861, LP 1:6167.

Regardless of whether Lander, Lincoln, and Seward met on the evening of March 10, the intrigue raised by Seward's note surrounds the reasons for bringing the president and Lander together. Without factoring in Lander's illness, a direct read of Seward's sentence is highly suggestive of his anticipation of Lander's return from an important mission, one that Lincoln wished to be briefed about. The documentation of Lander's poor health at this time fails to label this scenario as impossible.

If the planned March 10 meeting was in response to a completed mission by Lander, then what was the location and nature of that mission? The last known document from Lander is dated February 24, from Washington.[3] The next one is also written from the capital on March 11.[4] This leaves a two-week gap in the paper trail that follows Lander in his role as Seward's agent. This in itself is highly suggestive that Lander was out of town for at least a portion of the two weeks, perhaps on a mission for Seward.

An unidentified Washington diarist with close ties to William H. Seward enhances this possibility. On March 6, an excerpt of the diary reveals, "a messenger enjoying the direct personal confidence of Mr. Seward—left Washington for Richmond this morning with positive assurances as to the intentions of the new Administration that no attempt should be made to either to reinforce or to hold Fort Sumter."[5] Although several of these messengers were employed by the State Department, Lander would be a logical guess as the identity of this messenger, particularly when he had been hand-picked by Seward to monitor action at the Richmond convention two weeks earlier. This possibility also dovetails well with Seward's and Lincoln's anticipating Lander's return on March 10: they would have been eager to learn about the reaction to the information that he took with him to Richmond. But without confirming documentation, this scenario remains purely speculative.

The same Washington diarist penned another curious entry that might relate to Lander. On March 9, three days after mentioning the messenger sent to Richmond, the diarist wrote that Seward had been asked "to receive and give audience to a certain Colonel ————, who had a matter of

---

3. FWL to Seward, February 24, 1861, SP.

4. FWL to C. E. Mix, March 11, 1861, LP 1:6167.

5. "Diary of a Public Man," *North American Review* 29 (1879): 487; Roy N. Lokken, "Has the Mystery of 'A Public Man' Been Solved?" *Mississippi Valley Historical Review* 40 (1953), 427.

great national importance." (It should be noted here that Lander was often honored with the title "Colonel" at this time even though he held no military distinction.) The diarist continued to claim that Seward asked him to see the anonymous colonel instead, "as he did not wish to do so." The diarist never names the officer in the entry, but he continues to discuss a March 10 morning meeting with "Mr. Seward's Colonel ———" (the same man Seward refused to see), who proposed a wild scheme to unite the country with a transcontinental railroad through the Southwest. "Is it possible . . . in times of great national trial," concluded the bewildered diarist after hearing the proposal, "that madness becomes a sort of epidemic?"[6]

Could the unidentified colonel have been "Colonel" Lander? Although it is possible, it is highly unlikely. Lander was a strong proponent of a transcontinental railroad, but not through the South. The diarist noted that the unidentified colonel sent a letter of introduction; having worked effectively for Seward for one month, Lander would not likely have required such a formality. Nor would Seward inform Lincoln that he was awaiting Lander's arrival on the afternoon of March 10 if he knew Lander had arrived the day before, as was the case of "Mr. Seward's Colonel ———" reported by the diarist. Seward's refusal to see this colonel the night of March 9 suggests that he did not want to be bothered by what he must have expected to be trifling information. This eliminates the likelihood that the messenger that Seward sent to Richmond on March 6 and the unidentified colonel on March 9–10 in the diary were the same man.

If Lander had indeed embarked on a late February–early March mission, it may have taken him to a region far removed from Richmond. Whitelaw Reid, the young reporter for the *Cincinnati Daily Gazette*, traveled with Lander's division for two weeks in February of 1862 and became a confidant of Lander's during his stay at division headquarters. In a report published by the paper on February 13, 1862, Reid discussed Lander's theretofore unpublicized special-agent work: "As the special representative of the Government, Lander . . . twice crossed the whole extent of the seceded states, in the spring, to see Governor Sam Houston, in Texas, bear to him the messages and inquiries of the administration, and learn the exact condition of the affairs in the State."[7]

6. "Diary of a Public Man," 491–2.

7. "Agate" [Whitelaw Reid], "From General Lander's Division," *Cincinnati Daily Gazette,* February 13, 1862.

Was Reid's use of the word *twice* in describing Lander's journey a reference to an out-and-back trip, or did he actually mean two separate trips to Texas? The former may very well be his meaning, since traversing the South two times is not the assumed way to travel to Texas from Washington in 1861 (one could return by steamer through the Gulf of Mexico, for example). Still, the scenario of Lander completing two distinct trips to Texas is an intriguing one. Sending Lander back to Texas late in March after he returned from the same destination earlier in the month would not be an illogical decision by Lincoln or Seward. Each of them would have felt more comfortable with a messenger who knew the quickest and safest way to reach that state with news of import.

Since Lander can be confirmed to be in Washington on February 24 and on March 11, could the fifteen days between those dates have been enough time for him to travel to Texas and back? Lander's documented late March mission from Washington to Austin exceeded 1,500 miles. He completed the trip in approximately nine days. Lander signed for funds in Washington on March 19, then wrote a letter from Austin on March 29. Since no time of day is recorded in either note, one can reasonably assume at least a day of inactivity between the two documents. The only practical way that he could have accomplished the journey in this time frame was by train, but continuous railroad transportation from Washington in 1861 abruptly ended in northwestern Louisiana. This would have left Lander 400 miles short of his destination of Austin, a journey limited to stagecoach or other horse-style transportation. Given that he impressively completed the entire one-way trip in less than ten days, he must have driven his horse teams at a maddening pace of 65 miles per day. If Lander made a similar trip one month earlier, he could not have ventured inland from the eastern border of Texas (Austin is 300 miles from the Texas-Louisiana boundary), since the trip time was reduced to a maximum of eight days. This enhances the possibility, since he would have reduced horse travel to 200 miles in four or five days versus the 400 miles he covered in six days later in the month. Lander's illness does not eliminate this possible scenario; he could have become debilitated during his return ride on the rails to Washington.

Two documents authored by Lander relate to Texas. One was a summary of his meeting with Sam Houston spelled out in a March 29 letter to Colonel Carlos A. Waite.[8] The other was an undated proposal to bridge

8. *OR*, I:551–2.

the Green River, an obstacle to the cutoff from the Oregon Trail that he had dedicated the previous four years of his life to. In the latter, Lander included the following: "Having just arrived from a tour through the Border State of Texas and home via the seceding States, I am convinced that if Forts Sumpter [*sic*] and Pickens are reinforced, civil war will ensue and the Union party of Texas and the Border States [will] join the Secessionists."[9] One scholar concluded that Lander wrote the bridge proposal on April 10, since he describes a trip to Texas completed on April 9 in a proposal that was rejected by official documentation on April 11.[10]

Several existing circumstances and factors render it implausible to date Lander's bridge proposal to one of two possible days in April of 1861. First is the assumption that Lander wrote a proposal, sent it to the state department, had it reviewed and officially refused within twenty-four to forty-eight hours. It is difficult to imagine the government and delivery service worked so swiftly during a pending national crisis. Lander's characterization of such an important and swift mission as a "tour" raises questions about what trip he was describing. Lander's concern about the Union party of Texas joining the secessionists is a curious one, since Texas had already officially seceded in the first week of March. Lander would have to have known this in April—particularly since he was in the heart of Texas in the last days of March—making it a wonder that he would write his worry of a possibility that was already a fact

It was also uncharacteristic of Lander to be diverted from a pending national crisis and to be thinking instead about the West, as he obviously was at the time he wrote the Green River bridge proposal. In an April 11 letter to Secretary Seward, Lander focused on the preservation of the Union and expressed his desire "to meet the secession movement and secret organizations by counter action."[11] He only had to wait a day to lock in his focus on the crisis; Fort Sumter was fired upon on April 12 and surrendered one day later.

Lander's thoughts did indeed aim westward during the second week of March. He received letters from acquaintances in Nevada and California at this time, and was also rumored to be appointed territorial governor of

9. FWL, "Statement as to a contract to bridge Green River," n.d., LP 8:7540
10. Westwood, "President Lincoln's Overture to Sam Houston," 137 n. 26.
11. FWL to Seward, April 11, 1861, SP.

Nevada or New Mexico.[12] On March 11, Lander wrote to Commissioner Charles E. Mix about settling the Paiute conflict. "I go to reside on the Pacific Coast," he revealed in the letter.[13]

It would have been entirely in character, therefore, for Lander to have authored the Green River bridge proposal in the second week of March, the same period that the West was known to dominate his thoughts. This allows one month for the proposal to be reviewed and rejected, a more reasonable timetable than the aforementioned two-day scenario.

Isolating the date of Lander's undated proposal to the second week of March requires acceptance of a separate trip to Texas completed ten days prior to embarking on the Austin mission. That Lander arrived in the same part of Texas three days sooner than a messenger sent by Scott who left before him is testament to Lander's rugged constitution and notorious reputation as one who jaded his horses. But it also lends credence to the notion of benefitting from an earlier trip to the state, resulting in swifter and more efficient travel the second time around. Lander's concern, revealed in the proposal, about Texas seceding from the United States would now be a reasonable one since the official news of the secession may not have been known to him if he left the state in the first days of March.

Until more documentation can be uncovered to substantiate Lander's whereabouts between February 24 and March 10, 1861, his itinerary as a special agent for the Lincoln administration cannot be further elucidated. Lincoln, Lander, and Seward planned to meet on March 10, and the trio must have held discussions sometime between March 10 and March 19, the period prior to Lander's departure for Austin. William Seward's brief March 10 note to Abraham Lincoln raises many important questions about secret missions conducted at the time of Lincoln's inauguration, but unfortunately provides no answers.

12. Captain William Weatherlow to FWL, January 26, 1861, LP 1:6158–9; "Col. Lander Again." *New York Herald*, March 20, 1861; "The Governorship of Nevada," *New York Herald*, March 21, 1861; Newspaper clippings, Scrapbook.

13. FWL to C. E. Mix, March 11, 1861, LP 1:6167.

Bibliography

MANUSCRIPTS

Bentley Historical Library, University of Michigan, Ann Arbor
"Remarks of Gen. Shafter before the Thomas Post G.A.R. March 18, 1902."

Brown University Library, Providence, R.I.
Hay, John. Collection.

Cincinnati Historical Society, Cincinnati, Ohio
Schwab, Matthew. Letters.

Clearfield County Historical Society, Clearfield, Pa.
Kyler, Henry. Letters.

Essex Institute, Salem, Mass.
Endicott Family. Papers.

Handley Library, Winchester, Va.
Kitzmiller, Brenda. "The History of the Bridges across the South Branch of the
    Potomac River on the Northwestern Turnpike (U.S. Route 50), Hampshire
    County, West Virginia."
Sperry, Kate. Diary.

Houghton Library, Harvard University, Cambridge, Mass.
Lander, F. W. Letters.

325

Bibliography

Indiana Historical Society, Indianapolis
Beem, David. Letters.
Lambert, George. Diary.
Rogers, George. Diary.
Van Dyke, Augustus. Letters.

Illinois State Historical Library, Springfield
Lincoln, Abraham. Collection.

Kreitzberg Library, Norwich University, Northfield, Vt.
Ellis, William. Collection.
Lander, F. W. *Report of the Examinations and Surveys for a Railroad Route, for the Franklin and Kennebec Railroad Co.* Farmington, Maine, n.d.

Library of Congress, Washington, D.C.
Andrew, John. Papers.
Banks, Nathaniel P. Papers.
Chase, Salmon. Papers.
Hotchkiss, Jedediah. Papers.
Lander, Frederick W. Papers.
McClellan, George B. Papers.
Poe, Orlando. Papers.
Reid, Whitelaw. Papers.
Seward, William Henry. Papers.
Stanton, Edwin M. Papers.

Marietta Public Library, Marietta, Ohio
Styer, Wilhelm. Letters.

Maryland Historical Society, Baltimore
Garrett, John. Papers.
    Dennis, C. W. "Suggested Location for Markers for Civil War Blockhouses and Points of Historic Interest on the Cumberland Division of the Baltimore and Ohio Railroad."

Massachusetts Historical Society, Boston
Bicknell, Luke Emerson. "The Sharpshooters." 1883 (microfilm copy).
Lander, F. W. Letter.

National Archives, Washington, D.C.
Court Martial Records. Henry Anisansel Case File. Record Group 153.
Compiled Service Record of Edward Lander, War of 1812.

Department of Ohio Headquarters, Telegrams Received Book, Volume 178, Record Group 393.

Letters Received by the Secretary of War. RG 107, M221.

Records of the Adjutant General's Office. Record Group 94.

    Compiled Records of Harry G. Armstrong, Henry Anisansel, Dwight Bannister, Simon Barstow, Fred Barton, John Cannon, Frederick W. Lander.

    U.S. Generals' Reports of Civil War Service, 1780s–1917.

Records of the Secretary of the Interior relating to Wagon Roads, 1857–1887. M95. 8 reels.

Telegrams Received by the Secretary of War (Unbound). 1861–1862. M504.

U.S. Signal Corp photographs.

National Weather Records, Asheville, N.C.

Temperature Readings for the District of Columbia, Cumberland, Md., and Sheets Mill, Va., 1861–1862.

Ohio Historical Society, Columbus

Parmater, Nathaniel. Diary.

Wood, George. Diary.

Private Collections

Clark, Thomas. Letters in possession of the author.

Clohan, William. Letters in possession of Scott Clohan, Chicago.

Peterman, Jacob. Letters in possession of David Richards, Gettysburg, Pa.

Stanford University Libraries, Palo Alto, Calif.

Lander Family. Papers.

UCLA Libraries, Los Angeles

Rosecrans, William S. Collection.

Special Collections Department, University of Nevada–Reno Library, Reno

McDonnell, Anna [Lander]. Collection.

State Historical Society of Wisconsin, Madison

Potter, John F. Papers.

U.S. Army Military History Institute, Carlisle, Pa.

Rathbun, John. Letters.

Virginia Historical Society, Richmond

Chapman, J. "Reminiscences of Bloomery Gap."

Voris, Alvin C. Papers.

Bibliography

War Library and Museum, Philadelphia
Hamilton, James C. M. "Manuscript History of the 110th Pennsylvania."

Western Reserve Historical Society, Cleveland, Ohio
Barnett, James. Papers.

Robert W. Woodruff Library, Emory University, Atlanta
Northend, William Dummer. Papers.

Yale University Library, New Haven, Conn.
Coe, William Robertson. Collection.
Pierce-Dahlgren-Vinton Family. Papers.

OTHER UNPUBLISHED WORKS

Botterud, Keith A. "The Joint Committee on the Conduct of the Civil War." Master's thesis, Georgetown University, 1949.
Riley, Ben A. "Frederick W. Lander: Secret Agent for the Lincoln Administration." Paper presented to the West Virginia Historical Association, Philippi, April 28, 1984.

GOVERNMENT DOCUMENTS

U.S. Department of the Interior, Geological Survey Map, Paw Paw and Largent, W.Va. Quadrangles.
U.S. Congress. House. *Executive Document No. 56: Reports, Explorations and Surveys to Ascertain the Most Practicable and Economical Route from the Mississippi River to the Pacific Ocean, 1853–55.* 36th Cong., 1st sess.
———. *Executive Document No. 64: Maps and reports of the Fort Kearney, South Pass, and Honey Lake Wagon Road, by F. W. Lander.* 1861. 36th Cong., 2nd sess.
———. *Executive Document No. 70: Practicality of a Railroad through South Pass.* Transmitted February 13, 1858, by F. W. Lander to Secretary of the Interior J. Thompson. 35th Cong., 1st sess.
U.S. Congress. Senate. *Executive Document No. 29: Report of the Secretary of War Communicating Copies of All Reports of the Engineers and Other Persons, Employed to Make Explorations and Surveys to Ascertain the Most Practicable and Economical Route for a Railroad from the Mississippi River to the Pacific Ocean, that have been received at the Department.* 1855. 33rd Cong., 1st sess.
———. *Executive Document No. 36: Report and Map of the Central Division of the Fort Kearney, South Pass, and Honey Lake Wagon Road.* 1859. 35th Cong., 2nd sess.

————. *Executive Document No. 78, vol. 1: Report of Explorations and Surveys to Ascertain the Most Practicable and Economical Route for a Railroad from the Mississippi River to the Pacific Ocean, Made under the Direction of the Secretary of War in 1853–1854.* 1855. 33rd Cong., 2nd sess.

————. Executive Document No. 78, vol. 2: *Synopsis of a Report of the Reconnaissance of a Railroad Route from Puget Sound via South Pass to the Mississippi River.* Transmitted by F. W. Lander to the Secretary of War, November 23, 1854. 1855. 33rd Cong., 2nd sess.

United States Congress. *Report of the Joint Committee on the Conduct of the War.* Washington, D.C., 1863.

U.S. War Department. *War of the Rebellion: A Compilation of the Official Records of the Union and Confederate Armies.* 128 vols. Washington, D.C., 1881–1902.

NEWSPAPERS

Altoona (Pa.) Tribune, 1862.

Boston Herald, 1861–1862.

Boston Journal, 1859, 1861–1862.

Boston Evening Transcript, 1860.

Bryan (Ohio) Union Press, 1862.

(Bryan, Ohio) Williams County Leader, 1862.

(Canton, Ohio) Starke County Republican, 1862.

Chambersburg (Pa.) Semi-Weekly Dispatch, 1862.

Chambersburg (Pa.) Valley Spirit, 1862.

Chelsea (Mass.) Telegraph and Pioneer, 1861.

Cincinnati Daily Commercial, 1861–1862.

Cincinnati Daily Gazette, 1861–1862.

Cincinnati Daily Times, 1861.

Clearfield (Pa.) Progress, 1961.

(Clearfield, Pa.) Raftsman's Journal, 1862.

Clearfield (Pa.) Republican, 1862.

(Columbus) Ohio State Journal, 1862.

Council Bluffs (Iowa) Bugle, 1854.

Frank Leslie's Illustrated Newspaper, 1861.

Harper's Weekly Illustrated Newspaper, 1860–1862.

Lafayette (Ind.) Daily Journal, 1861.

Marysville (Calif.) Daily National Democrat, 1860.

Muncy (Pa.) Luminary, 1862

(New Lexington, Ohio) Perry County Weekly, 1862.

New York Herald, 1861–1862.

New York Times, 1860.
Painesville (Ohio) Telegraph, 1862.
Philadelphia Press, 1862.
Philadelphia Weekly Times, 1885–1886.
Pittsburgh Daily Evening Chronicle, 1862.
(Ravenna, Ohio) Portage County Democrat, 1862.
Sacramento Daily Bee, 1862
Sacramento Daily News, 1860.
Sacramento Daily Union, 1860.
Salem (Mass.) Gazette, 1861.
San Francisco Daily Alta California, 1859–1860.
San Francisco Daily Evening Bulletin, 1860.
San Francisco Daily Times, 1860.
San Francisco Weekly Herald, 1860.
St. Joseph (Mo.) Gazette, 1859.
St. Joseph (Mo.) Journal, 1858.
St. Louis Herald, 1858.
Shirleysburg (Pa.) Herald, 1862.
Vincennes (Ind.) Western Sun, 1862.
(Warren, Ohio) Western Reserve Chronicle, 1862.
(Washington C.H., Ohio) Fayette County Herald, 1862.
Washington (D.C.) Evening Star, 1857.
Washington (D.C.) Daily Intelligencer, 1857.
Washington (D.C.) National Republican, 1862.
(Washington, D.C.) National Tribune, 1883.
Washington (D.C.) Union, 1854, 1859.
Weekly Perrysburg (Ohio) Journal, 1862.
Wellsburg (Va.) Herald, 1862.
Wheeling (Va.) Daily Intelligencer, 1861–1862.

ARTICLES, CHAPTERS, AND PAMPHLETS

"Active Service; or, Campaigning in Western Virginia." *Continental Monthly* 1 (March 1862): 330–8.
Allan, William. "History of the Campaign of General T. J. (Stonewall) Jackson in the Shenandoah Valley of Virginia from November 4, 1861, to June 17, 1862." *Southern Historical Society Papers* 43 (August 1920): 111–295.
Allen, Edward J. "A Grizzly Bear-Hunt." In *Knickerbocker,* June 1854, 642–4.
Baldrica, Alice. "Lander and the Settlement of the Pyramid Lake War." In *Frederick West Lander: A Biographical Sketch (1822–1862),* edited by Joy Leland, 151–190. Reno, Nev., 1993.

Branch, E. Douglas. "Frederick West Lander, Road-Builder." *Mississippi Valley Historical Review* 16 (September 1929): 172–87.

Cooper, John S. "The Shenandoah Valley in Eighteen Hundred and Sixty-Two." In *Military Order of the Loyal Legion of the United States, Illinois Commandery: Military Essays and Recollections,* vol. 4; 36–60. Chicago, 1907.

Daggett, George Henry. "Those Whom You Left Behind You." In *Glimpses of the Nation's Struggle: Papers Read before the Minnesota Commandery of the Military Order of the Loyal Legion of the United States, 1897–1902,* vol. 5; 332–44. St. Paul, Minn., 1903.

"Diary of a Public Man. Unpublished Passages of the Secret History of the American Civil War. Part 4." *North American Review* 129 (November 1879): 484–96.

Fleming, Martin K. "The Northwestern Virginia Campaign of 1861." *Blue and Gray Magazine,* no. 10 (August 1993).

Fuller, W. G. "The Corps of Telegraphers Under General Anson Stager During the War of the Rebellion." In *Sketches of War History, 1861–1865: Papers Read Before the Ohio Commandery of the Military Order of the Loyal Legion of the United States,* vol. 2; 392–404. Cincinnati, 1888.

Glad, Paul W. "Frederick West Lander and the Pacific Railroad Movement." *Nebraska History* 35 (September 1954): 173–92.

Hand, Daniel. "Reminiscences of an Army Surgeon." In *Glimpses of the Nation's Struggle: A Series of Papers Read before the Minnesota Commandery of the Military Order of the Loyal Legion of the United States,* vol. 1; 276–307. St. Paul, Minn., 1887.

Houston, Alan Fraser, and Jourdan Moore Houston. "The 1859 Lander Expedition Revisited: 'Worthy Relics' Tell New Tales of a Wind River Wagon Road." *Montana: The Magazine of Western History,* no. 49 (summer 1999): 50–70.

Idol, John, and Sterling Eisiminer. "Hawthorne Sits for a Bust by Maria Louisa Lander." *Essex Institute Historical Collections* 114 (October 1978): 207–12.

Kemper, G. W. H. "The Seventh Regiment." In *War Papers Read before the Indiana Commandery, Military Order of the Loyal Legion of the United States,* 117–31. Indianapolis, 1898.

Lander, Edward. "A Sketch of General Frederick W. Lander." *Historical Collections of the Essex Institute* 40 (October 1904): 313–20.

Lander, Frederick W. *Remarks on the Construction of a First Class Double Track Railway to the Pacific.* Washington, D.C., 1854.

———. *Report of the Examinations and Surveys for a Railroad Route, for the Franklin and Kennebec Railroad Co.* Farmington, Maine, n.d.

[Lander, Frederick W.] "The Trail, the Trace, and the Wagon-Road; Being Sketches of Wild Life West of the Missouri." *Putnam's Monthly,* no. 9 (May 1857), 449–63.

[Lander, Frederick W.] "Under the Snow." *Atlantic Monthly*, no. 9, May 1862, 625–6.

Leland, Joy. "Death and Tributes." In *Frederick West Lander: A Biographical Sketch (1822–1862)*, edited by Joy Leland, 233–46. Reno, Nev., 1993.

———. "The Northern Pacific Railroad Explorations." In *Frederick West Lander: A Biographical Sketch (1822–1862)*, edited by Joy Leland, 13–60. Reno, Nev., 1993.

Lokken, Roy N. "Has the Mystery of 'A Public Man' Been Solved?" *Mississippi Valley Historical Review* 40 (1953): 419–40.

Mackinnon, William P. "The Buchanan Spoils System and the Utah Expedition: Careers of W. M. F. Magraw and John M. Hockaday," *Utah Historical Quarterly* (1963): 127–50.

Mader, Jon T., and Jason Calhoun. "Osteomyelitis." In *Mandell, Douglas, and Bennett's Principles and Practice of Infectious Diseases*, 4th ed., edited by Gerald L. Mandell, John E. Bennett, and Raphael Dolin, 1039–53. New York, 1995.

Maryland Geological Survey. *Report of the Highways of Maryland*. Baltimore, 1899.

Mason-Dixon Council Boy Scouts of America. *184 Miles of Adventure: Hiker's Guide to the C & O Canal*. Hagerstown, Md., 1970.

National Park Service. *Chesapeake and Ohio Canal*. Official National Park Handbook, no. 142. Washington, D.C., 1989.

National Park Service. *Salem: Maritime Salem in the Age of Sail*. Official National Park Handbook, no. 126. Washington, D.C., 1987.

"Prison Diary of Lieutenant Richard Gray." In *Diaries, Letters, and Recollections of the War Between the States*, vol. 3, edited by Winchester-Frederick County Historical Society, 30–45. Winchester, Va., 1955.

Riley, Ben A. "The Pryor-Potter Affair: Nineteenth Century Civilian Conflict as Precursor to Civil War." *Journal of West Virginia Historical Association* 8 (spring 1984): 30–9.

Robertson, James I. Jr., ed. "An Indiana Soldier in Love and War: The Civil War Letters of John V. Hadley." *Indiana Magazine of History* 59 (September 1963): 189–215.

Shahrani, Mavis. "The Lander Family." In *Frederick West Lander: A Biographical Sketch (1822–1862)*, edited by Joy Leland, 3–12. Reno, Nev., 1993.

———. "Wagon Roads—1857 Season." In *Frederick West Lander: A Biographical Sketch (1822–1862)*, edited by Joy Leland, 61–102. Reno, Nev., 1993.

———. "Wagon Roads—1858 Season." In *Frederick West Lander: A Biographical Sketch (1822–1862)*, edited by Joy Leland, 103–20. Reno, Nev., 1993.

———. "Wagon Roads—1859 Season." In *Frederick West Lander: A Biographical Sketch (1822–1862)*, edited by Joy Leland, 121–50. Reno, Nev., 1993.

Summers, Festus P. "The Baltimore and Ohio—First in War." *Civil War History* 7 (September 1961): 239–54.

Westwood, Howard C. "President Lincoln's Overture to Sam Houston." *Southwestern Historical Quarterly,* 88 (April 1984): 125–44.

BOOKS

Adams, John G. B. *Reminiscences of the Nineteenth Massachusetts Regiment.* Boston, 1899.

Amesbury, Robert. *Nobles' Emigrant Trail.* Susansville, Calif., 1967.

Anderson, Nancy, and Linda S. Ferber. *Albert Bierstadt: Art and Enterprise.* New York, 1990.

Angel, Myron, ed. *History of Nevada.* Oakland, Calif., 1881.

Bancroft, Frederic. *The Life of William H. Seward.* 2 vols. New York, 1900.

Basler, Roy P., ed. *The Collected Works of Abraham Lincoln.* 8 vols. New Brunswick, N.J., 1953.

Briant, C. C. *History of the Sixth Regiment Indiana Volunteer Infantry.* Indianapolis, 1891.

Bruce, George. *The Twentieth Regiment of Massachusetts Volunteer Infantry, 1861–1865.* Boston, 1906.

Burlingame, Michael, and John Ettlinger, eds. *Inside Lincoln's White House: The Complete Civil War Diary of Jon Hay.* Carbondale, Ill., 1997.

Carnes, Eva Margaret. *The Tygarts Valley Line: June–July 1861.* Philippi, W.Va., 1961.

Catton, Bruce. *The American Heritage Picture History of the Civil War.* New York, 1982.

———. *The Coming Fury.* Garden City, N.Y., 1961.

———. *Terrible Swift Sword.* Garden City, N.Y., 1963.

Chase, John A. *History of the Fourteenth Ohio Regiment, O. V. V. I.* Toledo, Ohio, 1881.

Comstock, Jim Ed, *The West Virginia Heritage Encyclopedia* (supplemental series), vol. 20. Richwood, W. Va., 1974.

Cooling, Benjamin F. *Symbol Sword and Shield: Defending Washington during the Civil War.* 2d ed. Shippensburg, Pa., 1991.

Clark, Champ, and the Editors of Time-Life Books. *The Assassination: Death of the President.* Alexandria, Va., 1987.

Clark, Charles M. *Yates Phalanx: The History of the Thirty-ninth Regiment, Illinois Volunteer Veteran Infantry, in the War of the Rebellion, 1861–1865.* 1889. Reprint, edited by Frederick Charles Decker, Bowie, Md., 1994.

Clark, Emmons. *History of the Seventh Regiment of New York, 1806–1889.* 2 vols. New York, 1890.

Clarke, H. C., comp. *The Confederate States Almanac and Repository of Useful Knowledge, for 1862.* Vicksburg, Miss., 1861.

Curry, Richard Orr. *A House Divided: A Study of Statehood Politics and the Copperhead Movement in West Virginia.* Pittsburgh, Pa., 1964.

Curry, W. L., comp. *Four Years in the Saddle.* Jonesboro, Ga., 1898.

Davis, William C., and the Editors of Time-Life Books. *Brother Against Brother: The War Begins.* Alexandria, Va., 1983.

―――. *First Blood: Fort Sumter to Bull Run.* Alexandria, Va., 1983.

Ecelbarger, Gary L. *"We are in for it!": The First Battle of Kernstown, March 23, 1862.* Shippensburg, Pa., 1997.

Ellis, William, ed. *Norwich University, 1819–1911: Her History, Her Graduates, Her Roll of Honor.* 2 vols. Montpelier, Vt., 1911.

Elwood, John W. *Elwood's Stories of the Old Ringgold Cavalry, 1847–1865: The First Three Year Cavalry of the Civil War.* Coal Center, Pa., 1914.

Essex Institute. *Vital Records of Salem, Massachusetts.* 4 vols. Salem, Mass., 1924.

Farrar, Samuel C. *The Twenty-second Pennsylvania Cavalry and the Ringgold Battalion, 1861–1865.* Pittsburgh, Pa., 1911.

Farwell, Byron. *Ball's Bluff: A Small Battle and Its Long Shadow.* McLean, Va., 1990.

Fehrenbacher, Don E., comp. *Abraham Lincoln: Speeches and Writings, 1859–1865.* 2 vols. New York, 1989.

Fishel, Edwin C. *The Secret War for the Union: The Untold Story of Military Intelligence in the Civil War.* New York, 1996.

Frothingham, John B. *Sketch of the Life of Brig. Gen. B. F. Kelley.* Boston, 1862.

Fuess, Claude M. *An Old New England School: A History of Phillips Academy, Andover.* Boston, 1917.

Garraty, John A., and Mark C. Carnes, ed. *American National Biography.* 20 vols. New York, 1999.

Garth, Robert, ed. *The Civil War Letters of Henry Livermore Abbott.* Kent, Ohio, 1991.

Gobright, L. A. *Recollections of Men and Things at Washington, During the Third of a Century.* Rev. ed. Philadelphia, 1869.

Goetzmann, William. *Army Exploration in the American West, 1803–1863.* New Haven, Conn., 1959.

―――. *Exploration and Empire.* New York, 1966.

Goetzmann, William H., and William N. Goetzmann. *The West of the Imagination.* New York, 1986.

Grayson, Andrew. *History of the Sixth Indiana Regiment in the Three Months' Campaign in Western Virginia.* Madison, Ind., ca. 1875.

Haas, Ralph. *Dear Esther: The Civil War Letters of Private Aungier Dobbs.* Apollo, Pa., 1991.

Hammond, Otis G., ed. *The Utah Expedition, 1857–1858: Letters of Jesse A. Gove,*

10th Inf., U.S.A., of Concord, N.H., to Mrs. Gove, and Special Correspondence of the New York Herald. Concord, N.H., 1928.

Haselberger, Fritz. *Yanks from the South! (The First Land Campaign of the Civil War: Rich Mountain, West Virginia)*. Baltimore, 1988.

Headley, John T. *The Great Rebellion*. 2 vols. Hartford, Conn., 1866.

Hirshson, Stanley P. *Grenville M. Dodge: Soldier, Politician, Railroad Pioneer*. Bloomington, Ind., 1967.

Holien, Kim. *Battle at Ball's Bluff*. 3d ed. Alexandria, Va., 1995.

Hollandsworth, James G., Jr. *Pretense of Glory: The Life of General Nathaniel P. Banks*. Baton Rouge, 1998.

Hornbeck, Betty. *Upshur Brothers of the Blue and Gray*. Parsons, W.Va., 1995.

Howe, Mark De Wolfe, ed. *Touched with Fire: Civil War Letters and Diary of Oliver Wendell Holmes, Jr., 1861–1864*. Cambridge, Mass., 1947.

Jackson, W. Turrentine. *Wagon Roads West: A Study of Federal Road Surveys and Construction in the Trans-Mississippi West, 1846–1869*. Lincoln, Nebr., 1964.

Kenny, Hamill. *West Virginia Place Names*. Piedmont, W.Va., 1975.

Kepler, William. *History of the Three Months' and Three Years' Service of the Fourth Regiment Ohio Volunteer Infantry in the War for the Union*. 1886. Reprint, Huntington, W.Va., 1992.

Keyes, E[rasmus]. D. *Fifty Years' Observations of Men and Events, Civil and Military*. New York, 1884.

Laas, Virginia J., ed. *Wartime Washington: The Civil War Letters of Elizabeth Blair Lee*. Chicago, 1991.

Lander, David. *History of the Lander Family of Virginia and Kentucky*. Chicago, 1926.

Leech, Margaret. *Reveille in Washington*. 2d ed. New York, 1991.

Leland, Joy, ed. *Frederick West Lander: A Biographical Sketch (1822–1862)*. Reno, Nev., 1993.

Lesser, W. Hunter. *Battle at Corricks Ford: Confederate Disaster and Loss of a Leader*. Parsons, W.Va., 1993.

Lord, Francis A. *They Fought for the Union*. New York, 1960.

"Lovejoy" [Samuel Gillespie]. *A History of Company A, First Ohio Cavalry, 1861–1865: A Memorial Volume Compiled from Personal Records and Living Witnesses*. Washington C.H., Ohio, 1898.

Madsen, Brigham D. *Chief Pocatello: The "White Plume."* Salt Lake City, Utah, 1986.

Markenfield, Addy. *"Old Jack" and His Foot Cavalry, or A Virginia Boy's Progress to Renown*. New York, 1864.

Martin, Kenneth, and Ralph Linwood Snow, eds. *"I Am Now a Soldier!" The Civil War Diaries of Lorenzo Vanderhoef*. Bath, Maine, 1990.

Maxwell, Hu, and H. L. Swisher. *History of Hampshire County, West Virginia, from Its Earliest Settlement to the Present.* 1897. Reprint, Parsons, W.Va., 1972.

McClellan, George B. *McClellan's Own Story.* New York, 1887.

McPherson, James M. *Battle Cry of Freedom.* New York, 1988.

Meade, George. *The Life and Letters of George Gordon Meade, Major General, United States Army.* 2 vols. New York, 1913.

Moore, Frank, ed. *Heroes and Martyrs: Notable Men of the Time.* New York, ca. 1862.

————. *The Rebellion Record: A Diary of American Events.* 12 vols. 1869. Reprint, New York, 1977.

National Cyclopaedia of American Biography. New York, 1943.

Newell, Clayton R. *Lee vs. McClellan: The First Campaign.* Washington, D.C., 1996.

Nicolay, John G. *The Outbreak of Rebellion.* New York, 1881.

Nineteenth Massachusetts History Committee, *History of the Nineteenth Regiment Massachusetts Volunteer Infantry, 1861–1865.* Salem, Mass., 1906.

Nivens, John, ed. *The Salmon P. Chase Papers.* 3 vols. Kent, Ohio, 1993–1996.

Oates, Stephen B. *A Woman of Valor: Clara Barton and the Civil War.* New York, 1994.

O'Brien, Fitz-James. *The Poems and Stories of Fitz-James O'Brien.* New York, 1968.

Perkins, J. R. *Trails, Rails, and War: The Life of General G. M. Dodge.* New York, 1981.

Perley, Sidney. *The History of Salem, Massachusetts.* Salem, Mass., 1926.

Poirer, Robert G. *By the Blood of Our Alumni: Norwich University Citizen-Soldiers in the Army of the Potomac.* Mechanicsburg, Pa., 1999.

Potter, David M. *Lincoln and His Party in the Secession Crisis.* New Haven, Conn., 1942.

Pugh, T. S. *Biographical Sketch of Mrs. F. W. Lander, Formerly Miss Jean M. Davenport, Tragedienne, with Criticisms of the Press on Her Rendition of Elizabeth, Queen of England.* Philadelphia, 1867.

Quaife, Milo M., ed. *From the Cannon's Mouth: The Civil War Letters of General Alpheus S. Williams.* Detroit, Mich., 1959.

Rawling, C. J. *History of the First Regiment Virginia Infantry.* Philadelphia, 1887.

Richards, Kent D. *Isaac I. Stevens: Young Man in a Hurry.* 1979. Reprint, Pullman, Wash., 1993.

Roehrenbeck, William J. *The Regiment that Saved the Capital.* New York, 1961.

Rubinstein, Charlotte Streifer. *American Women Artists: From Early Indian Times to the Present.* New York, 1982.

Sawyer, Franklin. *A Military History of the 8th Regiment Ohio Vol. Inf'y: Its Battles, Marches, and Army Movements.* Cleveland, Ohio, 1881.

Sears, Stephen W. *George B. McClellan: The Young Napoleon.* New York, 1988.

Sears, Stephen W., ed. *The Civil War Papers of George B. McClellan.* New York, 1989.

Se Cheverell, J. Hamp. *Journal History of the Twenty-ninth Ohio Veteran Volunteers, 1861–1865.* Cleveland, Ohio, 1883.

Secretary of the Commonwealth. *Massachusetts Soldiers and Sailors of the Revolutionary War.* Boston, 1902.

Shea, John G. *The American Nation: Illustrated in the Lives of Her Fallen Brave and Living Heroes.* New York, 1862.

Sifakis, Stewart. *Who Was Who in the Civil War.* New York, 1988.

Skidmore, Richard, ed. *The Civil War Journal of Billy Davis.* Greencastle, Ind., 1989.

Smart, James G., ed. *A Radical View: The "Agate" Dispatches of Whitelaw Reid, 1861–1865.* 2 vols. Memphis, Tenn., 1976.

Smith, Barbara A., comp. *The Civil War Letters of Col. Elijah H. C. Cavins, 14th Indiana.* Owensboro, Ky., 1981.

Soman, Jean P., and Frank L. Byrne, eds. *A Jewish Colonel in the Civil War: Marcus M. Spiegel of the Ohio Volunteers.* Lincoln, Nebr., 1995.

Stampp, Kenneth M. *America in 1857: A Nation on the Brink.* New York, 1990.

Stevens, Hazard. *The Life of Isaac Ingalls Stevens.* 2 vols. Boston, 1900.

Summers, Festus P. *The Baltimore and Ohio Railroad in the Civil War.* 1939. Reprint, Gettysburg, Pa., 1992.

Swiger, Elizabeth Davis, ed. *Civil War Letters and Diary of Joshua Winters: A Private in the Union Army Company G, First Western Virginia Volunteer Infantry.* Parsons, W.Va., 1991.

Tapert, Annette, ed. *The Brothers' War: Civil War Letters to Their Loved Ones from the Blue and Gray.* New York, 1988.

Thayer, William R. *The Life of John Hay.* 2 vols. Boston, 1915–1916.

Toney, Marcus B. *Privations of a Private.* Nashville, Tenn., 1905.

Utley, Robert M. *A Life Wild and Perilous: Mountain Men and the Paths to the Pacific.* New York, 1997.

Vance, James E., Jr. *The North American Railroad: Its Origin, Evolution, and Geography.* Baltimore, 1995.

Vandenhoff, Anne. *Edward Dickinson Baker: Western Gentleman, Frontier Lawyer, American Statesman.* Auburn, Calif., 1979.

Warner, Ezra J. *Generals in Blue: Lives of the Union Commanders.* 1964. Reprint, Baton Rouge, 1992.

———. *Generals in Gray: Lives of the Confederate Commanders.* 1959. Reprint, Baton Rouge, 1995.

Western Reserve Historical Society, ed. *The James E. Taylor Sketchbook.* Dayton, Ohio, 1989.

Weymouth, A. B., ed. *A Memorial Sketch of Lieut. Edgar M. Newcomb*. Malden, Mass., 1883.

Wight, Jermy Benton. *Frederick W. Lander and the Lander Trail*. Bedford, Wyoming, 1993.

Wilder, Theodore. *The History of Company C, Seventh Regiment, O. V. I.* Oberlin, Ohio, 1956.

Wilson, Lawrence. *Itinerary of the Seventh Ohio Volunteer Infantry, 1861–1864, With Roster, Portraits, and Biographies*. New York, 1907.

Wills, Mary. *The Confederate Blockade of Washington, D.C., 1861–1862*. Parsons, W.Va., 1975.

Wilson, James G., and John Fiske, eds. *Appleton's Cyclopaedia of American Biography*. 7 vols. New York, 1898–1900.

Wolle, Francis. *Fitz-James O'Brien: A Literary Bohemian of the Eighteen-Fifties*. Boulder, Colo., 1944

Wood, George L. *The Seventh Regiment: A Record*. New York, 1865.

Woodward, C. Vann, ed. *Mary Chesnut's Civil War*. New Haven, Conn., 1981.

Worsham, John H. *One of Jackson's Foot Cavalry*. New York, 1912.

Zinn, Jack. *The Battle of Rich Mountain*. Parsons, W.Va.,1971.

WORLD WIDE WEB SITE

"Governor Dummer Academy." In Education and Career Center. Byfield, Mass., ca. 1997 (January 1, 1998). Available from http://www.petersons.com/

Index

Index

Index

Index

Index